The Jews of Sing Sing

Gotham Gangsters and Gonuvim

RON AR

Fort Lee, New Jersey

Published by Barricade Books Inc.
Fort Lee, NJ 07024

www.barricadebooks.com

Reprint Edition 2016
Copyright © 2008 Ron Arons
All Rights Reserved

Library of Congress Cataloging-in-Publication Data
A copy of this title's Library of Congress Cataloging-in-Publication
Data is available on request from the Library of Congress.

ISBN 978-1-56980-333-2 (Hardcover)
978-1-56980-153-6 (Paperback)

9 8 7 6 5 4 3

Manufactured in the United States of America

CONTENTS

Acknowledgments
Preface
Introduction

In loving memory of my parents,

and to Ike, who got me into this fine mess.

ACKNOWLEDGMENTS

WHEN I CONCEIVED the idea for this book, pretty much on a lark, I had no idea of the enormity of the topic. The process of researching this book has taken more years than I care to state. Without a doubt this project has been a labor of love. The good news is that I have met so many wonderful people along the way who provided help in one way or another. Without such assistance, I probably would have never reached my goal of publishing this work.

To begin with, I must thank the people associated with various archives, libraries, universities, and institutions who helped me find the wonderfully obscure material that distinguishes this work from other nonfiction accounts of Jewish criminality. Included in this list are: Ellen Belcher, Sealy Library, John Jay College of Criminal Justice; Lenora Gidlund, current director, and Ken Cobb, former director of the NYC Municipal Archives; many individuals at the American Jewish Historical Society at the Center for Jewish History in New York; Dr. James Folts and William Gorman at the New York State Archives; Tim Reeves at the Kansas City branch of the National Archives (NARA); many people at the New York branch of NARA; Joseph Sanchez of NARA, San Bruno, California branch; Marion Smith of United States Customs and Immigration Services (USCIS), now part of U.S. Homeland Security; the FBI for responding to numerous Freedom of Information Act (FOIA) requests; David Wachtel and Ellen Kastel of the Jewish Theological Seminary Archives in New York; Roberta Arminio at the Ossining Historical Society; the American Jewish Archives in Cincinnati; the J. Murrey Atkins Library at the University of North Carolina, Charlotte; the Hoover Institution at Stanford

University; the Special Collections Division of the New York Public Library; the Special Collections Division of Columbia University Library; and Shuli Berger, Curator of Special Collections, Yeshiva University, New York.

My heart goes out to those brave souls who shared with me family stories about their relatives who served time in Sing Sing or were otherwise involved in Jewish criminality. Included in this lot are Joan Adler and Bobbie Furst, Marilyn Webb, Benjamin Gitlow, Jr., Geoff Fein, Jeffrey Richman, Joanne Shomberg, Sharon Blumberg, Amy Goldman, Hadassah Lipsius, Marvin Rasnick, and Gerald Kauvar.

Many individuals served as my extended research team: Jordan Auslander, Jan Meisels Allen, Jonina Duker, Pamela Weisberger, Diane Jacobs, Rhoda Miller, Larry Freund, Nancy Biederman, Judy Baston, Renee Steinig, Sidney Zion, and Steve Morse. Others helped by answering various questions I posed on the JewishGen online discussion bulletin board. Yet others, including Yecheved Klausner and Jonathan Grodz, helped translate various documents and articles from Yiddish, Aramaic, and Hebrew. Thanks in particular to Timothy Gilfoyle, professor at Loyola University of Chicago, Professor Mark Haller of Temple University, Professor Alan Block of Penn State University, Ken Blady, and Marly and Neil Koslowe. A very special thanks to Rhonda Moskowitz.

Some of the greatest help I received was simply in the form of moral support. First and foremost on this list is my dear Aunt Madelon, who walked with me every step of the journey. Others who provided similar encouragement include my brother Alan, Soni Bergman, David Lehmann, Mark and Betsy Thompson, Warren and Jane Pearlson, Steve and Nettie Robinson, David Robinson, Fred and Bernice Gillman, Shauna Denkensohn, Ira Levy, Gail Lampert, Hasia Diner of New York University, Robert Oppedisano at Fordham University Press, and members of the Lawrence Hackman Research Residency Award selection committee.

Acknowledgments

I would like to thank current and former employees of the New York State Department of Correction: NYS DOCS Commissioner Brian Fischer (formerly Sing Sing superintendent), Correctional Officer Andre Varin, Deputy Superintendent William Connolly, Correctional Officer Art Wolpinsky, and former Correctional Officer Jeff Sarett.

Many have invited me to speak on the topic of this book or about other Jewish criminals. Giving presentations on the topic of Jewish criminals not only provided me with the confidence that the topic was intriguing to a very large potential audience, but also gave me additional questions to ponder. Thanks go to the following individuals for inviting me to speak to their groups: Beth Bernstein and Robert Friedman, Samberg Program, Center for Jewish History, New York, Dale Rosengarten, College of Charleston, Program Chair of the 2006 AJHS Scholars Conference, Charleston, South Carolina; Amy Ripps, Program Chair, CAJE 31; the selection committee for the 2004 Researching New York Conference, Albany, New York; Zachary Baker, Program Chair for the 2005 American Jewish Libraries Conference, Oakland, California; Elizabeth Stabler and Elka Daitch of Temple Emanu-El of New York City; Gloria Birkenstat Freund of JGSNY; Carole Montello; Diane Freilich, JGS of Michigan; Bob Koltnow, JGS of Broward County; Susan Spector, American Jewish University, Los Angeles; Marty Flam of Temple Adat Elohim, Ventura, California; Miki Raver, Marin JCC; Rabbi Bruce Greenbaum, Congregation Beth Israel, Carmel Valley, California; Judith Krongold and Howard Gannes of Congregation Beth David, Saratoga, California; Jehon Grist of Lehrhaus Judaica, Berkeley, California; Carol Goldman of the Reutlinger Center, Danville, California; and Michael Nathan, Larchmont Temple, Larchmont, New York. I thank all of my audiences who not only have received my presentations so warmly, but also have expanded my knowledge of the subject by sharing their stories and asking truly incisive questions.

Acknowledgments

I would like to thank trailblazers Albert Fried and Jenna Weissman Joselit for their seminal works on Jewish criminality published more than twenty years ago, when it was not so fashionable to air dirty laundry about an ethnic group's problems. Kudos also go to those who followed in their footsteps, including Rich Cohen and Robert Rockaway, whose books further paved the road for me. Thanks to Bill Jordan, who helped with understanding the publishing industry and contract negotiation, to Beth Galleto for her proofing help, and to Ed Hamburg, who provided me statistical software to analyze the mountain of data I collected from thousands of Sing Sing admission records. Finally, many heartfelt thanks go to three special people: Carole Stuart, publisher at Barricade Books, who shared my vision; Adam Bellow of Random House, who first suggested a prosopography as the structure for this book; and Jane Anne Staw, my writing coach, who asked the right questions to clarify my thinking and writing.

PREFACE

THE GODS MUST BE CRAZY and the Internet has made them even crazier. After publishing each of my three books, all of which included some aspect of my great-grandfather the criminal's story, I discovered even more about his remarkable life online. His life story continues to unfold, answering many questions while simultaneously raising even more.

A *Brooklyn Daily Eagle* article dated July 10, 1921 informed me that he passed the civil service exam, which qualified him to work as an auditor for the New York State Income Tax Bureau. This boggles the mind, given he served years in Sing Sing Prison as a convicted felon. More remarkable yet was a *Buffalo Evening News* article just fifteen days later announcing the marriage of a Joseph N. Spier from Brooklyn to a woman named Anna Meredith. Was it possible that my great-grandfather learned nothing from his experience in Sing Sing Prison? Was it possible that he was a serial bigamist?

Truth be known, I found only one man named Joseph N. Spier living in Brooklyn in that timeframe – an unusual name, indeed. So, I ordered the Buffalo marriage certificate and started comparing what was on this document to what I knew about my great-grandfather. Name: Joseph N. Spier. Check. Residence: Brooklyn. Check. Parents' given names: Arthur and Elizabeth – not the true names, but the same names he gave on his marriage certificate to his second wife. Occupation: auditor. Check. Birthplace: Scranton, PA – the location he provided for his World War II draft registration card. A lie but nevertheless, check. With so many documents collected about my great-grandfather I could even examine the consistency of his lies.

Finally, I found my great-grandfather listed in the 1925 New York State Census twice: once with my great-grandmother Ida and a second time with Anna Meredith, his third of four wives.

—*Ron Arons, January 2016*

INTRODUCTION

MORE THAN A dozen years ago I had no idea I would write a book about Jewish criminals who served time in Sing Sing Prison in New York. Such a project could not have been further from my mind. I was simply trying to cope with a deep depression. In a period of eighteen months, both of my parents had died of cancer, I had lost two jobs to general economic woes, and my two-year-long relationship with a special woman had ended. For a period of six months, about the only thing I was capable of doing was watching daytime television soap operas.

When my brother and I met in New York to sell our childhood home, we were forced to deal with the chaos of papers my packrat parents had collected during their lives. (My father had newspapers dating back twenty years.) We packed up my parents' china, which I really could not use for everyday purposes, and shipped it to my house in California. UPS would not transport the dishes and FedEx agreed to ship the boxes only if the items were not insured. In retrospect, this was a free license to mishandle the china, which reached my home in a thousand pieces.

Luckily, or perhaps it was *beshert* (the concept of "meant to be" or fate in Judaism), a couple of items that my brother and I found in our childhood home would significantly alter my path forward. These items, untouched for years and stored in the attic, were a family tree my father had begun and a box of puzzling old postcards. The writing on some of the postcards showed my paternal grandfather's name in English, while others, in either Cyrillic or Yiddish script, made no sense to me. I hoped they might be love letters between my paternal grandparents or would tell me much more about their lives. I was curious to learn about my grandparents, since they had died when my father was just a young man and I never had the opportunity to meet them.

As for the family tree, my father had proudly shared this labor of love with me when I was a junior in college. At that time, I could barely muster any excitement. Truth be known, I thought, "How boring!" Years later, after so much loss, I was ready to embrace my ancestry. I hoped that by exploring my past I might learn more about myself—and the process would be healing. This was simply self-preservation.

I ran with my father's work and at the same time tried to build a family tree on the maternal side of my family. A beginning family researcher usually asks living relatives to provide details concerning the who, when, and where of ancestors, that is, their names, dates, and locations of important events (births, marriages, deaths, and so forth). With neither my parents nor my grandparents to help, I began my search in the next logical place: the U.S. federal census. I quickly found both sets of grandparents listed in the 1920 federal census, which was the most recent census available at the time. In one of these records, I came across a reference to my mother's paternal grandfather, my own great-grandfather. As I collected more items, most notably my grandfather's birth certificate and my mother's paternal grandparents' marriage certificate, I found myself faced with a conundrum. I had a great-grandfather who claimed to have been born in three different locations. This was a feat difficult to replicate even by Harry Houdini, a Jew who performed magic tricks, most notably escaping from handcuffs for inquisitive and fascinated inmates at Sing Sing. Furthermore, my great-grandmother's death certificate listed her surviving husband with a first name that was different from the given name I had been told my great-grandfather had.

I could have, and probably should have, given up my research right then and there. But I couldn't let go of a gnawing question: where was my great-grandfather born? Looking back, I see that

I already suffered from a case of the "genealogy bug," a disease that family researchers have a hard time eliminating from their systems. In fact, most embrace the affliction—we are a compulsive lot, constantly yearning to learn more about our families. We get hooked and few of us ever seek therapy, at least for this condition. At the time, in search of my great-grandfather's birthplace, I investigated all of the records available. None of them provided the information that would have answered my question. But instead of losing hope of ultimately finding the answer, I decided to let the question of my great-grandfather's birth location lie dormant for some time, perhaps to be answered later.

For several years I did nothing. Then the genealogical bug attacked me anew, and I took up the cause of my father's family once again. In 1998, six years after my first foray into investigating my family, I flew to Salt Lake City, ostensibly to photocopy a book containing seven censuses of my father's ancestral town of Smorgon in Belarus, made during the seventeenth and eighteenth centuries. As I was riding on the bus from the Salt Lake City airport to the Latter Day Saints Family History Library downtown, it dawned on me that it could not take all day to photocopy a 250-page book. I decided that once I had completed that task, I would look one more time for an answer to the mystery of my great-grandfather's birthplace.

Fortunately, that year the LDS Library had converted the 1881 British census to an electronic database. All I had to do was type in my great-grandfather's name, and three possible hits flashed onto the computer screen; two did not appear to match the birth year of my great-grandfather. The remaining record led to my Rosetta Stone: a census record that provided the names of my great-great-grandparents and their children, the true birth location of everyone in the family, and the occupation of my great-great-grandfather—a rabbi.

I subsequently wrote a two-hundred page manuscript about my great-grandfather and his father, only to learn that the apple did not fall far from the tree. Father and son had much in common. They both: left their country of birth, married at age twenty, changed their first or last name, and participated in multiple weddings. And both found trouble. My great-grandfather had served time in Sing Sing and made newspaper headlines for other crimes decades later. In the process of researching that manuscript I explored the why of my great-grandfather's life. I wanted to peek inside his head to understand the *reasons* behind his actions. By taking a genealogical approach, collecting documentation about the lives of both my great-grandfather and those who surrounded him, I achieved this goal to some degree. For example, my family lived in Brighton, England, home of the Royal Pavilion. The Pavilion was the Prince of England's summer home, where he invariably took his mistress. I can just imagine my great-grandfather telling himself, "If the Prince of England can have an affair, so can I." I have used the same genealogical approach to explore the childhoods and families of all of the characters in this book, with similar success.

When I submitted the manuscript about my ancestors to publishers and literary agents, the responses I received had a common theme: "We don't need another stinking memoir." Although I felt discouraged at first, one day I had an epiphany—I should write a book about every Jew in Sing Sing. So, I set to work. My early investigation into this larger topic proved fruitful. Both in federal censuses, held once a decade (in years ending with zero), and in New York State censuses (held every decade in years ending in the number five), I found between 100 and 200 Sing Sing inmates whose names sounded Jewish. Furthermore, I knew from the experience of researching my great-grandfather's life that every Sing Sing admission record listed the inmate's stated religion. Spending more than five weeks at the New York State Archives in Albany, I took photographs of thousands of admissions records in which the inmate claimed to be Jewish. (Detailed statistics of the numbers of Jewish Sing Sing inmates, the crimes they committed, and other details are presented in an appendix at the end of the book.)

I was stunned. My parents and Hebrew school teachers had taught me that Jews not only believe in but also abide by a high moral value system. In the Torah, specifically Leviticus 18:26 and 18:28, God directs the Jewish people with the following words: "Ye therefore shall keep My statutes and Mine ordinances, and shall not do any of these abominations; neither the home-born, nor the stranger that sojourneth among you"; "that the land vomit not you out also, when ye defile it, as it vomited out the nation that was before you." In numerous verses in Deuteronomy, God goes so far as to threaten the Jewish people if they do not follow His commandments, summarizing in 28:45: "And all these curses shall come upon thee, and shall pursue thee, and overtake thee, till thou be destroyed; because thou didst not hearken unto the voice of the Lord thy God, to keep His commandments and His statutes which He commanded thee." Judaism also encourages its followers to engage in *tikkun olam* (healing of the world). So with all these prescriptions toward goodness, how could there have been so many Jews incarcerated in Sing Sing?

What my research proved to me was that Jewish criminality was far more pervasive than most Jews have been taught or would want to believe. In the early 1900s New York City authorities criticized the Jews, suggesting that they were responsible for half of the crimes being committed. Publicly, Jewish community leaders complained that this was an exaggeration of the truth. Privately, however, these same *machers* (big shots) established multiple organizations and agencies in New York to deal with the problem. *The Jews of Sing Sing* also explores these organizations and shows that they were, in the main, highly successful in reducing the level of Jewish criminality not only in New York but also across the nation.

In the course of my research I encountered certain misconceptions about the factors that contributed to Jews' involvement in crime. Most people point to *immigrant status* as the root cause of breaking the law. Yes, a portion of almost every immigrant group succumbs to the lure of the fast buck. Most do so as a means of survival and, to a lesser extent, from a lack of knowledge of how the "system" works. But according to the admission records I found for Jewish Sing Sing inmates, those admitted to Sing Sing between 1880 and 1950 were divided almost evenly between inmates who stated they had immigrated and those who claimed to have been born here. It is true that most of these criminals born in America were the children of immigrant parents. Yet, although being an immigrant or the son of immigrants may be a contributing factor, it is neither necessary nor sufficient to explain how or why these Jews became involved with criminal elements.

There were other contributing factors. The overwhelming majority of those profiled in this book spent many of their formative years on New York's Lower East Side, which stretches from Bowery Street on the west, to East Houston on the north, and the East River to the south and east. Today the Lower East Side is experiencing a gentrification, but for more than a hundred years the neighborhood represented the first residence of immigrants of many ethnic groups. During most of the 1800s the Irish dominated the landscape. A smattering of Polish, Dutch, and German Jews arrived in the 1830s and 1840s, as did many more Italians. With the great influx of Eastern European Jews between 1880 and 1920, the Lower East Side transformed into a melting pot of different languages and customs.

Living conditions there were harsh, primarily because of overcrowding and lack of employment. Most immigrants on the Lower East Side lived in dumbbell-shaped tenement buildings that each contained sixteen to twenty-four apartments. In turn, each apartment consisted of a parlor, a living room, and one or two bedrooms. Despite an apartment's typical size of about 500 square feet, it was not uncommon for a family of eight to ten to live together in these cramped quarters. Whereas in 1895 the section of the Lower East Side known as the city's tenth ward had an estimated 536 inhabitants per acre (just a smidgen larger than a plot 200 hundred feet square), by 1900 the population density had increased to more than 700 citizens per acre.

Work was difficult to find. By far the most common profession for the Eastern European Jewish immigrants was that of tailor. Others earned their livelihoods as peddlers, selling a variety of edible and dry goods from pushcarts, and as clerks, laundry workers, and cigar makers. On Thursday and Friday mornings one could find almost anything (with the notable exception of a pig or its by-products) at the *Chazzer-Mark* (pig market) on Hester Street. Vendors peddled ties, suspenders, eyeglasses, buttons, and underwear. In the food department, one could purchase an entire chicken, just a wing or a leg, an egg, or even just the white or yolk of an egg. Haggling was the norm and both peddlers and shoppers alike sharpened their negotiation skills trying to get the most for their goods and money, respectively, in order to survive within the difficult economic climate.

Amid the crowding and poverty, or perhaps because of them, the Lower East Side was active with political discussions, frequently with a Socialist or Communist leaning. Lectures on a variety of subjects, political and other, could be heard on a daily basis at nearby Cooper Union, located at Third Avenue and Sixth through Ninth Streets in the East Village. This is where Benjamin Gitlow listened to speakers and garnered the inspiration to get involved in politics. Gitlow, a New York assemblyman, would serve time behind bars at Sing Sing for his political beliefs.

Given the Lower East Side's overpopulation, rancid living conditions, and limited opportunities for legal forms of employment, it should not come as a surprise that many resorted to crime to survive. What *The Jews of Sing Sing* brings to light is that another factor, namely the home environment, may have significantly increased these men's propensity to fall into trouble and decreased their interest in finding lawful employment.

Most of the well-known gangsters profiled in this book experienced one or more serious setbacks in their early childhood. Some had one or both parents die at an early age. Others found themselves lost within a large pack of multiple siblings or in "blended" families. Some had unkind stepparents. One had an alcoholic parent. Yet another's father left the state to find meaningful employment, abandoning his family. While the siblings in these families managed to live their childhoods without taking the same path as their criminal brothers, such environments increased the probability that these children would eventually get into trouble.

Given the fact that a high percentage of Jewish gangsters lived close to each other on the Lower East Side, it should come as no surprise that they were closely connected: having mentor–student relationships, using the same defense attorneys, appearing before the same judge, or sharing mutual relationships through other individuals or events. One can observe this interconnection among criminals across decades. Monk Eastman, Benny Fein, and Irving Wexler all used the same defense attorney. Fein was a graduate of Eastman's gang, while Wexler was Fein's protégé.

By employing a genealogical approach—analyzing documents related to individuals and events in their lives—we also learn that many of these people knew each other, not only from the street but also from behind bars. Network connections were maintained at Sing Sing and other correctional facilities where these individuals served time, most notably the New York State Reformatory at Elmira, the New York State Correctional Facilities at Dannemora (Clinton Prison) and Auburn, and the Federal Penitentiary in Leavenworth, Kansas. (The charts in the Appendices H and I list various prisons and the dates when the characters in this book served concurrent terms.)

Although these individuals were all criminals and all served time in Sing Sing, of course, their lives outside of prison did not consist solely of criminal activity. *The Jews of Sing Sing* shows that these men's lives were far more complex than most earlier books have suggested. Many of these criminals, if not most, had families. They ate at fine restaurants and enjoyed leisure travel to Europe and elsewhere. They attended sporting events, most notably boxing matches. They played cards or golf. This is to say, they were human beings with multifaceted lives.

My research also demonstrated to me the difference between Jewish criminals and those of other ethnic and national backgrounds. Quantitatively and qualitatively, Jews were different from their Irish and Italian counterparts. In the main, Jewish criminals were less violent than the Irish and the Italians; they committed acts mostly against property. Just three crimes—burglary, grand larceny, and robbery—accounted for more than two-thirds of all crimes committed by Jewish inmates in Sing Sing. In general, Jewish criminals also demonstrated less recidivism than their counterparts of other ethnicities. (More details are provided Appendix B.) Whereas lesser-known criminals typically committed just one type of crime, the more hardened gangsters had more varied careers. There is no accurate stereotype of a Jewish gangster. Each one was different, depending on when he lived and with whom he worked.

Many books about Jewish criminals are not only incomplete but, far worse, woefully inaccurate. Authors before me have relied on oral histories or on other people's work that was not properly checked for accuracy. It takes time to conduct research properly. The following example is a case in point. In September 2005 I sent a letter to the United States Customs and Immigration Services (USCIS), formerly Immigration and Naturalization Services (INS, now a division under the auspices of the Department of Homeland Security), concerning the deportation hearings of Louis Shomberg. As of July 24, 2007, I had moved up in the queue—my inquiry under the Freedom of Information Act (FOIA) was ninety-sixth in line, ahead of more than 77,000 other requests. A week later I had rocketed to thirty-first place in the queue. One week after that the National

Records Center in Lee Summit, Missouri, informed me that I had been moved to another line because the file I had requested was "classified." On August 30, 2007, I received a CD in the mail that included a PDF file containing 5,536 pages of documentation about this criminal. Filled with juicy anecdotes not available in materials found through other government agencies and newspapers, the file was definitely worth the wait. Not surprisingly, then, this book has taken years to produce, in large part because of the challenges of collecting the facts to put together these subjects' lives in a comprehensive manner.

If there were *thousands* of Jewish criminals in Sing Sing, primarily in the years 1880 through 1950, I figured that the most basic of demographic principles would predict that there must be tens to hundreds of thousands of descendants of these *gonuvim* (thieves) alive today. In fact, I have met several of them across the country while giving presentations on the subject of Jewish criminality. Others have contacted me after learning about my project either through newspaper articles or by word of mouth. I feel that my talks have created a warm, nonjudgmental, and safe environment for open and honest discussions of family members or friends who strayed from the law. I hope *The Jews of Sing Sing* will continue to expand this phenomenon. In the past it has been relatively easy to sweep such stories under the carpet. Now, with increasing numbers of tools and databases available for family research, it will be harder to keep these stories a secret.

What, you may ask, is the benefit of not keeping family criminality a secret? Doesn't hiding these truths help avoid embarrassment? I'm not convinced of that; in fact, my experience has been just the reverse. I have been enlightened and empowered. Even though my great grandfather died nearly a decade before I came into this world, exploring his life has helped clarify events of my own childhood. For example I now know why my grandmother once told me never to use the words "Sing Sing" in front of my grandfather because that "would upset him." I also understand why my grandfather howled the name "Minah" to tease my grandmother if she did anything to annoy him. From those who are still living I learned about the various ways in which families dealt with the knowledge that they had a criminal relative. There was no single method used by a majority of families; each family reacted in its own unique way as a function of the circumstances. From my experience and from talking with others, it is my belief that truth is liberating. Instead of protecting a child by covering up the past, such "preventive" measures actually rob the younger set of knowledge about their ancestors, which might help them to understand themselves better.

It may sound trite, but my journey to write this book has been truly *beshert*. Aside from my having an ancestor who himself served time in Sing Sing, other aspects of my life and other incidents along the way have confirmed that this is my "life's work." Take, for example, my name—Ron Arons. Also consider that I was raised as a goodie-two-shoes. I've really never broken the law beyond the four moving violations I received (for doing 40 in 30 MPH zone in Texas on a Sunday morning, for doing a "California roll" through a stop sign a block away from my home, for flashing my bright headlights on a driver ahead of me, and for something else equally miniscule that I have forgotten). Well, to use an SAT test analogy, if the opposite of a goodie-two-shoes is a criminal, then the opposite of spelling my name forwards would be my name spelled backwards, right? Doing so, we wind up with the words "Snora Nor." "Snora" sounds like the Yiddish word *schnorrer* (beggar), while the word "nor" sounds like the Yiddish word *nar* (fool). That's what we're dealing with in this book, beggars and fools. Along the way there have been many, many "coincidences" that have led me to shudder. Having studied engineering in college, for a while I considered myself crazy for believing that a higher power or fate had led me down this path. Now I know I would be crazier to believe otherwise.

The Jews of Sing Sing represents a pioneering effort to quantify Jewish crime in New York City. Further, the book expands knowledge about well-known gangsters and paints a fuller qualitative canvas of the Jewish criminality problem in the city. The book corrects errors, completes prior research, and presents new material, including FBI and USCIS files. It is my hope and prayer that *The Jews of Sing Sing* will encourage others to go on similar journeys to explore their families in depth, regardless of whether or not a black sheep was grazing here or there.

The book is laid out as a set of chapters, each one focusing on a particular criminal. I thank Adam Bellow (Saul Bellow's son and an editor at Random House), who graciously proposed this format at lunch one day. I tried to select criminals, well-known gangsters and lesser-known individuals alike, who represented various time frames and a wide breadth of crimes. Quite frankly, I also selected my subjects on the basis of their ability to add value to what others have contributed in the past. Most notably my choices of most of the subjects were based on the availability of new and exciting sources, particularly FBI files and court transcripts available at John Jay of School of Justice's Sealy Library in New York. These materials provided me with substantial information about their lives beyond just the most serious crimes they committed, material not normally found in true crime books. Only after I had written much of the book did I realize the connection across the characters (see the diagram in Appendix D). One character, Benjamin Gitlow, is somewhat of an anomaly, but his story is so compelling that I could not resist including a chapter about it. Interspersed among these chapters are three chapters about my efforts to learn more about my great-grandfather, why he committed his criminal acts, and what life must have been like for him behind bars in the Big House. Doing this allowed me to tell my ancestor's story against the larger backdrop of Jewish criminality.

Enjoy.

Isaac Spier: Part I

SETTLING MYSELF IN front of one of the more than 50 micro-film readers at the National Archives facility in San Bruno, California, I peered into my family's past. The 1920 federal census taker had recorded that my great-grandfather, Isaac Spier, lived in Brooklyn with his wife Ida and their three children—Sidney (my grandfather), David, and Lillian. The card also showed that Ida, a native Russian, was a naturalized U.S. citizen and that Isaac had been born in New York in 1873. The family lived at 620 Sixth Street, a four-story apartment building in the Park Slope section of Brooklyn.

I found all of this information back in 1994 before census records were available online. I had to search for my relatives the "old-fashioned" way, viewing microfilms containing scans of "soundex" (short for sound index) cards. (The Federal government organizes many of its records, including censuses, passenger ship manifests and naturalization papers, using this phonetically-based indexing system.) The soundex card also provided the Enu-meration District number, which led me to the more comprehensive census sheet containing information beyond names, ages, and birthplaces—occupations, parents' native language, and details about immigration and naturalization.

This was almost the beginning of my journey, but not quite. My excursion began after I lost two jobs, a significant relationship, and both of my parents to cancer in a period of just eighteen months between 1989 and 1991. I was devastated by the cumulative losses and felt a strong urge to learn more about myself and my family. My brother and I converged on our childhood home on Berkshire Road in Rockville Centre, Long Island, to sort through our parents' belongings in an effort to get the house ready for sale. In the attic I discovered, sitting on a bookshelf near the dormer window, a box one-fourth the size of an ordinary shoebox that contained postcards, with illustrations and photos of the "Old Country" on one side and handwritten notes on the other, some in Cyrillic script and others in Yiddish. In addition to the box of postcards, I found another item of interest—a family tree my father had shown me when I was a junior in college. Back then I struggled not to yawn when my dear father presented the product of his laborious efforts to chronicle his family's past. With both a completely new perspective and my brother's approval, I snatched up these links to my ancestors and ran with them. I was on a mission to learn more about myself by exploring the past.

When I returned to California, I enlisted the help of a Russian immigrant family I had "adopted" from Jewish Family and Children's Services in Berkeley. I had made a commitment to spend at least one hour a week for six months teaching the mother, father, and two daughters the basics of English. I wound up spending three years helping this family not only with the English language, but also with job hunting and retooling to be qualified to break into the American workforce. In return, the family gave me the unlimited, unconditional love that I could no longer receive from my parents. I now had a favor to ask of them—to translate the postcards written in Cyrillic. I also hired someone conversant enough in Yiddish to translate the postcards written in that tongue. In both cases, the postcards proved disappointing. I thought they might be love letters between my father's parents, who passed away when my father was a young man and years before I came into this world. Unfortunately, the messages sent from the old country to America and back were simply mundane. One card asked why the other party had not written in some time. In another, the writer claimed to be ill but gave no details. With the postcards leading to a dead end, I once again looked at my father's family tree. He had done a wonderful job documenting his side of the family, but nothing to preserve my mother's family history. That's where I began my research. I knew that my maternal grandfather had been born in the United States, so the U.S. population census seemed the most logical place to start. The rush I felt by finding census records for both sets of grandparents at the National Archives was my initiation to genealogy and those endorphins are what keep millions of family researchers going even after decades of investigating their ancestors.

After I found the 1920 federal census record indicating that my maternal great-grandfather, Isaac Spier, was born in 1874 in New York, I wanted more information about him. It is difficult for me even to remember why; I just did. Perhaps it was the taste of success that spurred me on or the possibility of finding out more deeply who I was and where I came from. Pursuing this information, I traveled to New York City. census records report ages in *years*, but vital records (such as birth, marriage, and death certificates) provide exact *dates*. At the New York City Municipal Archives in Manhattan, I searched for and located the birth certificate of my grandfather, Sidney Spier, which showed his birth date as May 30, 1895. Curiously, this certificate specified the birthplace of his father, Isaac, as Hanley, Staffordshire, England, which matched what my mother had told me years before.

While on vacation in London in 1976, I had paid a visit to the Public Records Office and searched the vital registration (birth) index for the specifics of Isaac's birth in an attempt to fulfill my mother's desire to learn the truth. Unfortunately, my efforts proved unsuccessful. Even to this day I have not found a birth record for Isaac. All I know for certain from my grandfather's birth certificate is that in 1895 my family lived at 664

Fourth Avenue in the Sunset Park section of Brooklyn, just south of the more fashionable Park Slope district. The family's four-story walkup building was just a block away from "Hosch's Corner," which housed Hosch, a leading men's clothing store, and the Anna Feld Cigar Store.

With key facts about Sidney's birth in hand, I was able locate the marriage certificate for his father, Isaac, and Isaac's wife, Ida Tarshis. According to that document, Isaac was born in 1872 or 1873 in London, not in Hanley, as was shown on my grandfather's birth certificate, or in New York, as was listed in the 1920 U.S. census. Both Ida and Isaac listed 267 Twentieth Street as their residence, the same address where her family lived. Only later did I realize the significance of yet one more detail—the date of the wedding—November 18, 1894, just six months before my grandfather's birth. Either my grandfather was a premature baby, or, more likely, my great-grandfather was forced into a shotgun wedding.

Instead of solace, the intended goal of my early family research, I found myself caught in a web of intrigue, which increased my craving for an ever deeper comprehension of the secrets in my past. All the records I discovered relating to my great-grandfather's life through 1933 listed him as Isaac Spier, including the 1933 Brooklyn City Directory, which showed his residence as 1374 East Ninth Street. However the name *Joseph* Spier appeared as her spouse on my great-grandmother Ida's 1934 death certificate. Before she died, she, and presumably her husband, still lived at the East Ninth Street address. The 1935 Brooklyn telephone directory listed a Joseph Spier, but not an Isaac Spier, at 1374 East Ninth Street. From 1941 through 1952, no listings for Isaac Spier appeared in the Brooklyn telephone directories, but the same directories listed Joseph Spier at 1014 Avenue N, just around the corner from 1374 East Ninth Street. Conclusion: Isaac Spier and Joseph Spier simply were one and the same person.

Now I had discovered something really intriguing: I had an ancestor who claimed to have been born in three different locations and who went by two first names. I certainly couldn't stop my search for the truth now! In an effort to find his true birth location, I sought records, including the 1900 federal census. In 1900 the census listed three people named Isaac Spier in New York State. Data for the first two did not come anywhere close to matching any of the information I had; the age of the third Isaac Spier approximated that of my great-grandfather, but the birthplace (Pennsylvania) did not match. Furthermore, Isaac Spier number three resided at the New York State Penitentiary in Ossining, New York, otherwise known as Sing Sing! I drew a deep breath.

Every family has its secrets. More often than not, they are swept under the carpet, if not hidden in a deep grave somewhere. Even in my immediate family, a secret came to light only at the end of both my parents' lives. Just days before my mother passed away, my brother told me that my mother had been married to someone else before she married my father. My brother had accidentally learned this information ten years earlier when he overheard a conversation among some relatives. Not sure what to do with the knowledge, he kept it a secret from me, too. He told me Mom had wed a taxicab driver but then had the marriage annulled shortly thereafter. The news did not shock me, nor did it change the way I felt about my mother. She had always given all of herself to my father, my brother, and me. Why should news of her secret upset me? I suspected she was trying to protect my brother and me from unpleasantness and confusion.

Thinking about the possibility that my great-grandfather was a criminal was a different matter. I had always been told to obey the law. Not only was I taught by my parents and in Hebrew school to do the right thing, I was led to believe that my family was composed entirely of upstanding citizens. My mother's first cousin had been a district attorney in Los Angeles. Furthermore, at age six I was caught trying to lift a toy from a hotel gift shop in Florida while my family was vacationing there. The embarrassment caused by this incident set me firmly on the straight and narrow path.

But suddenly I was confronted with the possibility that my great-grandfather had served time in Sing Sing. Then other questions tumbled into my mind. If my great-grandfather was behind bars in 1900, where was my great-grandmother? Had she lived without him for a period of time? I searched for Ida Spier in New York in the 1900 U.S. census index, but without success. The index did, however, include a divorcée named Ida *Spear*, who lived alone as a boarder with the Thomas family in Yonkers, just north of Manhattan and 22 miles from Sing Sing. The more detailed 1900 census record revealed that Ida *Spear* had previously given birth to one child who did not live with her. Another part of the 1900 census listed my great-grandmother Ida, under her maiden name of Tarshis, living with her parents and siblings elsewhere in Brooklyn. Quite possibly the 1900 census counted Ida Spier twice, if Ida Spear was absent when the Yonkers family gave information about their boarder to the census taker. Regardless, whether the census recorded her once or twice, in 1900 my great-grandmother clearly lived apart from Isaac.

With this information in hand and confusion in my mind, I rushed off to ask my Aunt Madelon what she knew. The possibility that her grandfather had spent time behind bars came as news to her, and she assured me that my mother had no idea about this either. At my urging, she agreed to ask other cousins what they knew about Isaac. A few weeks later word came back that he "found trouble with the IRS." This did not make any sense. Sing Sing and the IRS?

To better understand Isaac, I decided to examine Ida's family in more detail. My Aunt Madelon said that Ida's sister Florence had gained notoriety as a stage actress. Skeptical, I went to the New York Public Library for the Performing Arts at Lincoln

Center, where I discovered a collection of files about successful entertainers. Although Florence was not among them, I did
find a file for her husband, Harry First, an accomplished Yiddish comedic actor. Harry had performed in Montague Glass's
Potash and Perlmutter, a play about the adventures of two bum-
bling storeowners in the *shmatte* (clothing) business. While
most newspaper articles only reviewed his performances across
the country, two *Variety Magazine* articles mentioned Harry's
alleged spousal abuse and acknowledgment of marital infidelity.
This meant that both sisters had married knaves! The magazine
articles provided the first detailed proof of dark secrets hidden
in my family's past.

With four different birthplaces (New York, Hanley, Pennsylvania, and London) and two different first names, along with
the information about Harry, the reality that Isaac served time
in Sing Sing sank in. There was no other logical explanation; the
information about other men listed by the name of Isaac Spier
in the 1900 census just did not match up. At this point I could
have denied the mystery and stopped my research right then
and there; and I believe many genealogists might have done just
that. The thought never crossed my mind, however; something
told me my great-grandfather must have been in Sing Sing and
I had to find out why.

Pondering the mystery of my great-grandfather, I recalled
an incident from my childhood as if it had occurred just yester-
day. Playing at my grandparents' apartment one day, I had said
to my grandmother, "If I am a bad boy today, you are going to
have to send me away to Sing Sing." My grandmother promptly
pulled me aside and, in a very stern voice, said to me, "Do not
use the words Sing Sing in front of your grandfather. That will
upset him." Now, as an adult, I wondered why I would have
said something like that to my grandmother. Had I heard the
words "Sing Sing" mentioned in my grandparents' house, or had
I simply seen an old movie in which a criminal served time "up
the river"?

Remembering this story and with such a set of conflicting facts regarding my great-grandfather, I figured the situation deserved further investigation. The next logical step for me was to contact the prison. When I did, a prison official told me that all prison records were in the New York State Archives in Albany. A spokesperson at the Archives said that Sing Sing admission records dated back to 1842, but the Archives would not research anything for me over the telephone unless I had an exact admission date. I could, however, view the admission records myself if I went to Albany. The spokesperson said that, on average, the prison admitted 200 to 300 people each year, and each page of the admission book listed two individuals. I calculated that I should be capable of finding Isaac's admission record in a single day. After I hung up the phone, I distinctly heard an inner voice urging me to "Go to New York."

A few weeks later I boarded a plane from San Francisco to New York. Because I had called ahead, an archivist in Albany had pulled the original Sing Sing admissions records from the stacks and had them ready. Arriving early in the morning, I was the only visitor. The library's silence, as I thumbed through the faded pages of the 100-year-old Sing Sing registers, gave me a sense of the prison's solitude.

Locating the record of Isaac Spier, alias Herbert Edward Spier, took barely one hour. The record provided a full physical description: 5 feet, 5½ inches tall, 131 pounds, medium (red) hair, blue eyes, hat size 6⅞, and shoe size 7. Distinguishing marks included a "cod scar" on the index finger of his left hand. Isaac listed his occupations as trolley car conductor and entry clerk. He claimed not to smoke, not to drink (temperate), and identified himself as a Protestant! He had been arrested for—of all thigs—bigamy!

At first, a curious mix of shock, amazement, fear, sadness, and thrill swirled inside me. I could not believe my eyes. Goosebumps covered my body and I had to take several deep breaths. It took a few minutes to digest the fact that I had descended from a criminal! This meant that my grandfather was one half criminal. And my mother, whom I adored, was one fourth criminal. By extension, I was one eighth criminal, a concept that certainly shattered my self-image of a shameless goodie-two-shoes, who went pretty much by the rules and could not comprehend the minds of those who did not. At the same time, I felt a vicarious thrill knowing I had descended from someone who had served time.

When I told my brother this news, we both howled with laughter. An attorney, he suggested I contact the King's County Courthouse to get more information. When I called, the person I spoke to was so amused by my story that he too wanted to know where such records were kept and agreed to search for me. A few weeks later he sent me copies of pages from the Kings County Clerk's notebook. He also recommended that I contact the New York City Municipal Archives and ask for the court case file.

On my initial call to the New York City Municipal Archives, the clerk seemed annoyed with my rather unusual request. Most requests at the Muni Archives are for birth, marriage, and death certificates from a multitude of researchers whose relatives once lived in any of the city's five boroughs—Manhattan, Brooklyn, Queens, Bronx, and Staten Island. Instinct, however, insisted that a file regarding Isaac's bigamy case had to exist, so I persevered. After six months of periodic telephone call reminders, the New York City Municipal Archives informed me that they had located the file.

The file contained both the Grand Jury testimony of all parties involved, the marriage certificate to the "other" woman, and a letter sent from the Raymond Street Jail to Ida. The names of the groom and bride on the marriage certificate were Herbert Edward Spier and Minnie Ott. The name Minnie Ott explained other events of my childhood. My parents, brother, and I would frequently visit my grandparents in Brooklyn. Invariably, my grandmother would do or say something that irked my grandfather, at which point he would yell out the words, "Minah, Minah." No one beyond my grandparents seemed to know who Minah was, or what my grandfather meant, but the shtick was hilarious to everyone but my grandmother. Now I figured that Minah was the contraction and bastardization of the name Minnie Ott. My educated guess is that my grandfather was teasing my grandmother that if she did not pull her act together, he would fool around with another woman.

Several New York and Brooklyn newspapers carried articles about my great-grandfather's run-in with the law. The *Brooklyn Citizen* reported that Isaac was the son of a well-known rabbi and that the police thought he might have married as many as four wives. The *New York Herald* described the Keystone Cop-like series of events that led up to Isaac's arrest. Through a friend, Ida learned that Isaac lived with another woman at 108 Havemeyer Street in Brooklyn. On July 27 Ida enlisted the services of police officer James V. Short and went with a warrant and her father and son, probably via trolley car, to the Havemeyer address. After a knock at the door, Isaac answered. Understanding what was happening, he bolted out of the apartment and jumped on the Grand Avenue trolley headed eastbound. After a mile, he realized that Detective Short had climbed aboard the same car, so Isaac jumped off this trolley and ran across the street, where he caught another trolley going in the opposite direction toward the Bedford Avenue police station. Short apprehended Isaac and brought him to the station, where the two fuming wives confronted him.

"What's the trouble?" Minnie asked Isaac, to which he replied, "This woman claims to be my wife, but I never saw her before in my life. I guess it will come out all right." Incredulous, Ida shrieked, "Do you disown me and your children? Do you deny that this is your son [holding my grandfather Sidney up in the air]? You're a brute and this other woman has been deceived by you." Ida's father attempted to strike Isaac but was prevented from doing so by policemen. The newspaper article stated that the two-year-old, my grandfather, was "an exact image of the prisoner," an important detail since the family had no pictures of Isaac.

In the Lee Avenue Police Court, both wives pressed charges against Isaac: abandonment in the case of Ida and bigamy according to Minnie, in what was reported by the *Brooklyn Citizen* as "one of the most dramatic incidents which ever took place in that police station." The court ruled that Isaac be held on $300 bail for the first charge and $1,500 for the latter offense. Isaac pled with Ida to withdraw her charge, but to no avail. With both charges sticking and no money to pay bail, officials carted Isaac to the Raymond Street Jail in Brooklyn.

The next night, Isaac wrote the following letter (found in the case file) from his holding cell:

Dear Ida,

Please call & see me as I wish to talk to you. I am so miserable & you have made me so. Don't forget to come & see me at once as I must see you, as my heart is nearly broke with grief. Please bring something to eat as I cannot live on bread & water. Send my love to Sidney and Lillie & the best to you and yourself. I am sorry that you had me arrested so hastily, as I intended to give you the money I earned. But you have made me lose my job on the cars & now you have to be without money. I was only just working the first week & you should have waited a little longer, as I told you before I went that I would go & look to make a living for you & as soon as I did that I would have a home again. I have been out of work all winter & spring, & I owe more for board than I can pay in a long time. I wish you would come down as soon as possible. Your uncle can get you a pass to see me & also help me if you ask him. Do as I ask you & forgive me if I have done wrong. Yours, I. Spier

My cheeks flushed with embarrassment at these lies. How Isaac's letter found its way into the court case file is unclear. Either the letter was confiscated and never sent to Ida or Ida presented this as evidence at the court proceedings. According to the *New York Times*, on August 5, 1897, the temperature in Manhattan reached a high of a very mild 67 degrees. Inside Brooklyn's Third District Police Court on Lee Avenue, however, many of those waiting for justice, starting with the plaintiffs and defendants, probably simmered.

At the opening of the trial, a bailiff stood at the front of the courtroom, near the judge, and read the charge aloud:

The People of the State of New York versus Isaac Spier, alias Herbert Edward Spier. The Grand Jury of the County of Kings, by this indictment, accuses Isaac Spier, alias Herbert Edward Spier, of the crime of BIGAMY, committed as follows:

The said Isaac Spier, alias Herbert Edward Spier, on the eighteenth day of November 1894, at the City of Brooklyn, in this County, was lawfully married, under the name of Isaac Spier, to one Ida Tarshis, who thereupon became Mrs. Ida Spier, and thereafter did live with the said Isaac Spier as her lawful husband, and she, the said Ida Spier, is still living and is still his lawful wife.

And, the said Isaac Spier, alias Herbert Edward Spier, on the fifth day of August 1896, in the City of New York, in this State, being lawfully married as aforesaid to the said Ida Spier, and then and there knowing the said Ida Spier was still living and was still his lawful wife, feloniously and unlawfully did marry, under the name of Herbert Edward Spier, one Minnie Ott, and thereafter did live with the said Minnie Ott as her husband.

And the said Isaac Spier, alias Herbert Edward Spier, was thereafter, to wit: on the twenty-seventh day of July 1897, arrested in the County of Kings upon said charge, and being arraigned in due form of law before Andrew Lemon, Esquire, a Police Justice of the City of Brooklyn, was by him on said day held to await the action of the Grand Jury of this County.

The bailiff concluded with the Grand Jury's charge against Isaac Spier, alias Herbert Edward Spier: guilty of the crime of *bigamy!*

Assistant District Attorney Caldwell represented The People of the State of New York, while Isaac indicated he "was not represented by counsel." After Ida Spier swore to tell the truth, Mr. Caldwell began his examination.

Q. The question is, do you know him [referring to Isaac]?

A. Yes, certainly.

Q. How long have you known him?

A. Three years.

Q. You were married to him?

A. Certainly.

Q. When?

A. I have here my paper.

Here Ida produced her marriage certificate, which stated that she and Isaac were married on November 18, 1894.

Q. How long did you live with him?

A. I lived with him a year.

Q. Where did you live with him?

A. In Seventeenth Street.

Q. In Brooklyn?

A. Yes, sir.

Q. Did you have any children by him?

A. Certainly. Two children.

Q. When did he leave you?

A. A year ago.

Q. Had you seen him from the time he left you up to the time of his arrest?

A. No. I was looking all over for him and didn't know where he was.

Q. Who married you?

A. Ettinger.

Q. Give him his full title. Was it the Reverend A. Ettinger?

Here Caldwell referred to the marriage certificate proffered by Ida Spier.

A. Yes, sir.

Q. What was he—a Minister?

A. A Jewish Rabbi.

Remember that Isaac claimed to be a Protestant when he entered Sing Sing Prison.

Q. Did you ever have a divorce suit against him?

A. No.

Q. Has any decree ever been entered in any Court, to your knowledge, dissolving the marriage relations between you and this man?

A. No.

Though not on the stand, Isaac interrupted and asked, "Are you willing to get a divorce, if you claim to be my wife?" The Court responded, "That is an improper question. She cannot make any bargains and sales from the witness stand." Twisting Ida's words, Isaac mocked, "She claims that I lived with her one year and she claims that she had two children. I would like to know how a woman could have two children in one year." The Court reprimanded him, "You may ask her any questions you desire, but you must not make a statement at this stage. You will have an opportunity to do that later on."

Next the People called as a witness Minnie Ott. Having sworn to tell the truth, Minnie Ott testified under direct examination by Mr. Caldwell:

Q. Do you know this defendant, Edward Spier?

A. Yes, sir.

Q. When did you first become acquainted with him?

A. A year last March.

Q. Were you ever married to him?

A. Yes, sir.

Q. When?

A. A year ago today.

Q. The fifth of August 1896?

A. Yes, sir.

Q. Who married you?

A. I couldn't exactly say [the name of] the alderman that married me.

Their first anniversary—that very day. Minnie had met Isaac in March 1896 and married him a few months later, not knowing he had already tied the knot. In response to Assistant District Attorney Caldwell's request, Minnie Ott produced a paper certifying marriage between her and Herbert Edward Spier, dated the fifth day of August 1896. The prosecutor admitted the marriage certificate as evidence and marked it "People's Exhibit 1."

The judge asked Minnie Ott:

Q. You were married at the City Hall, New York, were you?

A. Yes, sir.

Q. How long did you live with him?

A. I never lived with him.

Q. Didn't you live together in Brooklyn?

A. We lived together after we were married.

Q. How long did you live with him after you were married?

A. I started housekeeping about the last of September.

Q. Of last year?

A. Yes, sir.

Q. How long were you housekeeping with him?

A. Until the day that he was arrested.

Q. When was that? Do you know?

A. About two weeks ago—two weeks ago Monday.

The judge intervened:

Q. Did he state to you that he had ever been married before?

A. No, sir; he did not.

Q. You had no knowledge of his previous marriage?

A. No, sir; I had not.

Finally, the judge asked Isaac, "Do you wish to ask the witness any questions, Spier?"

"No questions."

After the People rested, Isaac asked, "Can my trial be brought before the Grand Jury before it sits next?"

"No," the court responded. "If you go on the stand and disprove all those circumstances here brought out, I have the power to discharge you. If at the end of your examination there appears to be probable cause to hold you for the Grand Jury, I will hold you; and then the Grand Jury will pass upon your case, and if they indict you it goes before a petit jury for trial."

"I wish to make a statement," insisted Isaac.

The judge warned him again.

Sworn in, Isaac provided both Isaac Spier and Herbert E. Spier as his name and 108 Havemeyer Street [Brooklyn] as his address.

JUDGE: You can make any explanation that you see fit, remembering that it is purely voluntary, as to the circumstances, or in exculpating yourself from the circumstances that have been stated by the previous witnesses.

ISAAC: Minnie Ott claimed that I was married to her a year ago and that she didn't live with me but kept house. Now, I suppose…

JUDGE: Did you go down with Minnie Ott to the City Hall in New York and meet an alderman by the name of Goodman?

ISAAC: I object to answering that question.

JUDGE: Well, any explanation that you have to make, make it.

ISAAC: I wish to say that this...

JUDGE: Do you know the Reverend A. Ettinger?

ISAAC: I have heard of him.

JUDGE: He was a rabbi, wasn't he?

ISAAC: By his title, he is, I suppose.

JUDGE: Did you attend before him with this lady with the red waist over there?

The judge pointed to Ida, Isaac's first wife and mother of his two children.

ISAAC: I can't recollect.

JUDGE: Were you married by him?

ISAAC: I can't recollect.

JUDGE: Any other explanation you wish to make, you may make it now.

ISAAC: I waive examination.

The judge set bail at $2,500 and waited for the action of the Grand Jury. C. S. Findlay, the official stenographer, certified that "the foregoing are true minutes of the testimony taken by me," and Police Justice Andrew Lemon signed off on it. Realizing he was going back to jail, and in a moment of desperate magnanimity, Isaac offered to support both women if they would only forgive him and drop their charges.

More than a month later, on September 23, 1897, Isaac pled guilty to the charge of bigamy. Once again both wives appeared in court to testify against him. According to the *Brooklyn Eagle*, "Two court officers had to hold Spier on either side while he answered the judge's questions as he was in a state of utter collapse. He became hysterical while being led back to the pen and was attended [to] by Dr. George F. LeMont, who was in court."

Four days later the judge sentenced Isaac to serve four years in Sing Sing. Ironically, the date coincided with Yom Kippur, the holiest day of the year for Jews. While four years seems like a burdensome penalty for what is today considered a far lesser crime, it was not an uncommon sentence in those days. At the end of the nineteenth century, bigamy was on the increase, possibly because of the surge in the number of immigrants. By increasing the punishment for those caught and convicted of this crime, officials were trying to reduce its frequency.

I now had uncovered the details of Isaac's sordid affairs, but this information simply whetted my appetite for more. I still did not know where he was born or why he committed this crime. At the time, I did not yet realize that Isaac had found additional trouble years later.

Sing Sing's Beginnings and the
Earliest Jewish Inmates

IN **MARCH 1796**, New York State's legislature approved a bill to build the state's first two correctional facilities: one in Manhattan, the other in Albany. Located in Manhattan, Newgate Prison opened a year later. Auburn Prison, New York's second facility, opened in 1815, in the town of the same name instead of the state capitol. With a capacity of fewer than 450 inmates, Newgate was doomed from the start. A sharp increase in the number of convicted felons meant that the prison, even with the assistance of Auburn, could not satisfy demand. Furthermore, Newgate's poor construction eliminated the possibility of expansion. In 1825 three commissioners—George Tibbets, Stephen Allen, and Samuel Hopkins—were appointed to select a site for a new prison. Understanding that New Hampshire and Massachusetts both generated profits from quarrying, the men decided it would be financially expedient to look for a site that was near a quarry and that also had water access for transportation. Two sites fit the bill: New York City's Marble Hill district and Mount Pleasant in the town of Sing Sing (now Ossining). By the spring of 1825, former Auburn Prison Warden Elam Lynds had selected 100 Auburn inmates, loaded them into a canal boat, and sent them to the Hudson, where they boarded freight steamers for the remainder of the excursion to Sing Sing. Without even a wall to enclose them, the inmates built temporary barracks, a cook house, and carpenter and blacksmith

shops. By the winter of 1826, 60 cells of the proposed 800 had
been constructed. By 1827, 428 cells had been finished and in
October 1828 the entire cell block was completed. In May 1828,
three years after work had begun, all the Newgate inmates were
transferred to Sing Sing and the old prison was sold.

BECAUSE OF THE lack of records from the prison's earliest years,
it is impossible to determine exactly when the first Jew served
time in Sing Sing. We do know, however, that large numbers of
German Jews migrated to the United States in the late 1840s
and early 1850s, after the failed German revolution of 1848 and
the political repression that followed. Housed at the New York
State Archives, admission records beginning in 1865 clearly
show that Jews were represented in the inmate population from
as early as this time period.

Salomon Kohnstamm, from Hamburg, Germany, may not
represent the typical Jewish inmate of the time, but a great deal
of information is available to describe his life. Born around
1812, Kohnstamm arrived sometime around 1840 in New York,
where he worked as a merchant. He is listed in the 1841–1842
Manhattan City Directory as Kohnstamm, S. & H., jewelry,
76 Maiden Lane. The H stands for Heiman, Salomon's distant
cousin, who dissolved the partnership a few years later and went
into business for himself, importing dyes and paints. A highly
successful company, by 1957 H. Kohnstamm was selling products used in soaps, cosmetics, foods, medicines, and plastics. In
1988 the company was sold to Sensient Technologies Corporation, a company that today markets dyes and fragrances to food
and cosmetic companies, specialty chemicals for inkjet inks, and
display imaging systems. (The year 1988 was also the year that
Ralph Nader's Public Citizen group achieved success in forcing

the federal government to ban the use of Red Dye No. 8, Red Dye No. 9, Red Dye No. 19, and Orange Dye No. 17—the very same products sold by H. Kohnstamm Co.—in drugs and cosmetics because of tests showing that they caused cancer in animals.)

Salomon continued his importing of dry goods and shawls, first at 62 Broadway and then at 33 Nassau Street. Presumably he was successful, if we judge from the accolades of both businessmen and other men of high social status when he petitioned for a pardon in 1867. He also resided at 116 West Sixteenth Street, a somewhat more fashionable neighborhood than the Lower East Side.

Although the admission record listing Salomon's religion is not available, we know that he was Jewish. First, the origins of the Kohnstamm family can be traced to Spain in 1650. The family moved first to Holland and then in the 1700s to Germany, where Salomon was born, in Niederwerrn, about 60 miles due east of Frankfurt. Next, a subscription list to *Israels Herold*, a New York-based Jewish newspaper, includes his name. One can find Jewish genealogists in the online JewishGen(ealogy) FamilyFinder researching the Kohnstamm family living in Niederwerrn. Finally, an article in an 1856 issue of *Occidental and American Jewish Advocate*, the first Jewish periodical published in the United States, lists Salomon Kohnstamm as residing at 62 Broadway and being a member of the "Committee" (beyond the officers and directors) that oversaw the operations of the Jews' Hospital in New York.

It appears, then, that Salomon had a fine start in life and that he continued to do well until November 11, 1862, when he was arrested and held on $150,000 bail on charges of presenting false and fraudulent bills to the United States Disbursement Office in Manhattan. The bills were for both food and lodging of Civil War soldiers. Kohnstamm was accused of violating a Congressional act of 1823 that stated that "Any person, who shall present at any office of the Government of the United

States any deed, Power of Attorney or other writing in support of, or in relation to any account, or claim, with intent to defraud the United States *knowing the same to be false,* altered or counterfeit; every such person shall be deemed and adjudged guilty of a felony, and being thereof duly convicted, shall be sentenced to be imprisoned and kept at hard labor for a period of not less than one year, more than ten years; or shall be imprisoned not exceeding five years and fined not exceeding $1,000."

On June 11, 1863, the Federal Grand Jury returned with 41 separate indictments. However, acknowledging that many of the accusations against Salomon Kohnstamm were based on affidavits by individuals who spoke only a foreign language and did not have their statements taken by a sworn court interpreter, the Grand Jury reduced Kohnstamm's bail from $150,000 to $75,000 ($925,000 in 2006 dollars).

The trial began in May 1864 without Kohnstamm's attorney, Mr. Evarts, who had been sent by the U.S. government to Europe and did not return until the third day of testimony, just before the trial ended. Evarts argued that the indictment should be tossed out, since the 1823 Act had been repealed by the Act of 1863. (Congress passed the "False Claims Act" of 1863, also known as "Lincoln Law" and the "Informer's Act," in an attempt to mitigate the widespread instances of military contractor fraud, including illegal price gouging of the Union Army. Whistleblowers were encouraged to come forward by being offered a portion of monies recovered as a reward.) The judge refused to accept the argument, indicating that it should be saved for later for an "arrest of judgment" (appeal).

During the trial, John Bauer, a former employee, provided damaging testimony against Kohnstamm, claiming that another employee, by the name of Bessold, had come to him and asked him to write out a bill for $2,200, representing the cost of housing and feeding 75 men. According to Bauer, Bessold was a "runner," a person who went looking for others who had difficulty in getting paid for their claims. Furthermore, Bauer testified that Bessold went out and found a man named Killian, who signed the bill, and that after the document had the signature on it, Bessold sold the bill to Kohnstamm for $200 or $250. Bauer told the court he believed the bill to be false.

Bauer further told the court that Kohnstamm had ordered him to make out a bill for the amount of $1,668, even though Kohnstamm had paid a man named Schober $200 for the bill. After receiving $200 for the original bill, Bauer contended, Schober signed the newer fraudulent bill for $1,668. Schober then took the stand, reiterating Bauer's story and adding that the Federal Disbursing office had rejected his claim for $203 more than twenty times because it had not been "made out right." Schober claimed that Colonel Egelloffstein, a military recruiter whose office adjoined Kohnstamm's, directed him to visit Kohnstamm to "get your money."

The defense retaliated by placing several business associates on the stand, including Henry Vail, a cashier at the Bank of Commerce; Joseph Stewart, another banker; William J. Quinlan, a fellow importer; Lewis Loder, another dry goods merchant; and Simeon Draper, who had conducted business transactions with Salomon Kohnstamm. All testified to Kohnstamm's upstanding nature. Ex-judge Gilbert Dean argued that the "tables be turned" and that the man who investigated the proceedings should be placed in Kohnstamm's position. With a total of more than $700,000 worth of fraudulent claims at the disbursement office, Dean could not understand why some of the army officers who worked there were not guilty and on trial by court martial. Unfortunately, these measures were for naught; Salomon Kohnstamm was found guilty and sentenced to ten years at Sing Sing.

Kohnstamm's defense team wasted no time filing a motion for arrest of judgment based on three claims. First, as argued before the trial, the Congressional Act of 1863 repealed the Act of 1823. Second, the bill presented in the trial was not Kohnstamm's but instead belonged to a man named Pfiffer. Mr. Evarts

then argued that the bill was made out to Pfiffer and could not
have been assigned over to Kohnstamm, as was claimed by the
prosecution, since it had been neither considered "allowed" nor
signed by two witnesses as required by statute. Finally, Evarts
claimed that there was no evidence that the bill was ever in
Kohnstamm's possession. Despite the collective force of these
arguments, Judge Nelson was not won over and he confirmed
the judgment against Salomon Kohnstamm.

A feverish publicity campaign was launched months later,
led by Salomon's sister Fanny Berger, who left her home in Mu-
nich to help his cause. She obtained letters of recommendation
from numerous former business associates, who wrote to President Andrew Johnson, Attorney Generals James Speed and
Henry Seabury, Secretary of the Treasury, Hugh McCulloch,
and Secretary of State, William H. Seward. Somehow she lined
up support and similar letters of recommendation from numerous politicians, the most important of whom included former Governor of New York Edwin Morgan, current New York
Governor Reuben Fenton, Treasury Secretary McCullough,
and Attorney General Speed.

Kohnstamm's case for a pardon was aided by reports from
physicians who examined him and indicated that incarceration
was proving detrimental to his health. On November 1, 1865,
Dr. Fisher wrote:

> *I am positive that his physical and mental health are being
> materially impaired as a result of imprisonment—his punish-
> ment is more intensely severe than that of almost any convict
> I have known for many years past. I know nothing of the
> merits of his case, but I consider it improbable for him to en-
> dure the full term of his sentence without resulting in perma-
> nent sacrifice of health or mental alienation, which is more
> to be dreaded than death itself. I have long been opposed to
> executive clemency, but I believe it would be a wise, humane,*

and justifiable exercise of executive clemency to pardon Salomon Kohnstamm.

Responding to the attorney general's request for a diagnosis, Sing Sing physician and surgeon Dr. P. Pryne wrote in February 1866: "He has been under medical treatment in the [prison] hospital several times for hepatic and gastric derangement, which appeared as the direct result of mental depression or melancholy. His mental condition remains feeble and impaired and the indications are that protracted confinement will result in confirmed dementia." In December 1866 Dr. Griscom, a member of the New York State Prison Association, wrote directly to President Andrew Johnson, stating, "About the middle of October, I became convinced that his mental powers are failing in such a manner as must eventuate sooner or later in confirmed insanity." A month later Griscom wrote to Attorney General Stanberg reiterating his earlier convictions: "The only hope of his [Kohnstamm's] being saved from complete dementia or insanity lies in his discharge and restoration to his former social relations."

The public relations campaign worked, and on April 30, 1867, President Johnson signed and sealed an executive order giving Salomon Kohnstamm an unconditional pardon. Sometime after his release Kohnstamm returned to his native Germany, where he stayed until his death in Hamburg on January 23, 1876.

SING SING ADMISSIONS records for the 1870s list many Jews, the vast majority of German descent. We know that by the 1870s there were sufficient numbers of Jewish inmates for a minyan, justifying the gathering of Hebrew inmates to celebrate the more important Jewish holidays. In 1875 Alderman Samuel Lewis petitioned the warden, who agreed to allow the Jewish inmates to eat matzah during Passover. In 1877 a chaplain appointed by Rabbis "H. P." and Dr. DeSola Mendez, from the Nineteenth and Forty-fourth Street synagogues, respectively, conducted High Holy Day services for the Jewish inmates.

IN THE LATE 1800s Jews were frequently involved in arson. Many had determined that collecting insurance money after setting fires proved more lucrative than their legal occupation—as a peddler, tailor, grocer, or insurance agent. Some acted alone, but many were part of the arson gangs operating in the early to mid-1890s in both New York and Philadelphia. The most prolific of these groups was the Zuker-Schoenholtz-Krone gang, a.k.a. the "Isaac gang."

Born around 1848, Isaac Zuker immigrated to the United States from Posen, Poland, sometime in the early 1870s. The earliest record of his living in the United States appears in the 1875 New York City Directory: "Isaac Zucker, hardware, h: 102 Allen Street." Within a year Zuker had changed both his work and residential addresses, moving them to 40 Vesey and 87 Orchard Street, respectively. By 1880 Zuker had moved his family to Philadelphia, where he worked as a shoemaker, according to the federal census of that year. But that residence was short-lived. By 1882 he had moved back to Manhattan, where he worked as a tailor at 1 Essex Street. Zuker's nomadic life continued, and by 1891 he had moved a few more times, ultimately setting up his tailoring operations at 264 Division Street and his residence at East Eighty-fifth Street.

Morris Schoenholtz had immigrated to the United States from Poland in 1876 and, because he had poor English skills, worked as a peddler. While walking down Hester Street one day, he was arrested for grand larceny when he sold a stolen piece of cloth but, curiously, was subsequently convicted of carrying burglar's tools. The conviction landed him in Auburn

Prison, where he served six and half years before his release in 1882. In 1884 he married and tried to earn an honest living as a presser in an "east side sweat shop." Quitting this job in 1889, Schoenholtz switched to earning money as an expressman. It was around this time that he renewed a friendship with Max Blum, who grew up in the same Polish town and now resided at 266 Division Street, adjacent to Zuker's operation.

On October 16, 1895, Schoenholtz was convicted of arson. Many fellow firebugs testified against him, and the jury convened for just over an hour before returning its guilty verdict. Since it was his second offense, the Court had no discretion in terms of sentencing. As a result, the judge handed down the mandatory punishment of forty-eight years, effectively a life sentence for the 45 year-old Schoenholtz.

It is likely that Schoenholtz ratted out Zuker and possibly others. On May 30, 1895, Schoenholtz spoke with Fire Marshall Mitchell, who in turn told reporters that "some developments could be expected in a few days." Just four days later the police, working in conjunction with the district attorney's office, arrested several individuals thought to be members of the "largest gang of incendiaries that was ever at work in New York." Among those arrested were Abraham Krone, Morris Schoenholtz, Morris Weiner, who had previously testified against Schoenholtz, and Abraham Zuker, Isaac's brother. Detective Bryan Isaac arrested Zuker at his new abode at 312 Lewis Street in Union Hill, New Jersey, a place where he probably felt he could not be found.

The district attorney's office and the police were certainly correct about the size of the Zuker gang and the magnitude of the harm it caused not only in New York but also in Philadelphia and Newark. In addition to Isaac Zuker, Abraham Zuker, Morris Schoenholtz, Abraham Krone, and Morris Weiner, the gang included Max Blum, Louis Wischer, two men named Steinloff and Rosen, and possibly one of Zuker's daughters. In a matter of years the gang had set fires all across New York City: a few in Brooklyn—one on Columbia Street, one on Grand Street, one on Green Street, and yet another on Fourth Avenue; many in Manhattan—one at 264 Division Street, one on Avenue C, one in Park Row in 1892, one at the firm of Seidler & Harris at Broadway and Fourteenth Street, one on Seventy-third Street, where the Zuker family lived, one at Broadway and Great Jones Street, and one at a store at 556 Tenth Avenue. The *Brooklyn Daily Eagle* reported in 1897 that the Isaac gang still had 26 untried cases pending against it.

While the Isaac gang was arguably the largest arson gang of the time, it was not the only one. Max Grauer, an insurance adjuster who struggled to earn enough money to feed his wife and eleven daughters, led a gang that included Louis Rothman; Sarah Silbermeister; Levi Weinberg, who ran a tailor's shop and clothing store at 178 Canal Street; Simon Rosenbaum; Max's brother Louis, who was an insurance agent; and four men named Gleuckman, Lipschitz, Kruschinsky, and Hirschkopf. Adolph Hirschkopf was a graduate of the Milch gang and ran his own operation before joining ranks with Max Grauer's crowd. He also worked with the gang headed by Lewis Gordon, which included Samuel Milch, another insurance adjuster, and Max Gleuckman, a professional firebug. June 5, the day after police rounded up Isaac Zuker, Abraham Krone, Abraham Zuker, and Schoenholtz, the *New York Times* reported that four arson gangs—headed up by Isaac Zuker, Adolph Hirschkopf, Max Grauer, and Samuel Milch—had collected from $500,000 to $700,000 ($11 million to $16 million in 2006 dollars) in insurance claims.

The trial of Isaac Zuker and his codefendant Max Blum began on December 17, 1896, before Judge Edgar L. Fursman. Zuker must have had a cache of dough, since he hired not one but two attorneys, Abraham Levy (the attorney he had hired to defend and silence Schoenholtz) and William F. Howe. The prosecution comprised District Attorney Vernon M. Davis and Assistant D.A. Henry S. Davis.

The prosecutors lined up several witnesses against Zuker. The first two, Morris Schoenholtz and his wife, provided the most damaging testimony. At the outset, Schoenholtz stated that he had taken the initiative to be a witness rather than responding to a request from the D.A. and that he had absolutely no expectations of any remuneration for his time on the stand. While these words were technically accurate, he probably had other incentives to tell the truth on the stand. In an interview he gave a *Brooklyn Daily Eagle* reporter eighteen months earlier, Schoenholtz indicated that the fire marshal had offered him immunity and "his liberty" in exchange for providing evidence that would lead to the "conviction of the firebugs." Additionally, according to Schoenholtz, the fire marshal promised "a written guarantee that he would not be punished."

After his opening remarks, Schoenholtz told the court that he had known Zuker for many years, having met him for the first time in either 1889 or 1890 at 266 Division Street, "Blum introduced me to his side partner, Zuker, who induced me to live with him in Grand Street, Brooklyn." Schoenholtz told a *Brooklyn Daily Eagle* reporter while sitting in his jail cell in the Tombs in December 1896, "Zuker and Blum were partners in the incendiary organization. They made me a criminal. They took me into their confidence knowing that I was a criminal at the time."

It took years for the insurance company and the authorities to catch the perpetrators, but on May 28, 1895, Detective McCauley arrested Schoenholtz at his residence at 142 Lewis Street. Abraham Levy, whose services were paid by Zuker, defended Schoenfeld. At his own trial Schoenfeld admitted that, on orders from Zuker, he had set three fires "in the tenement districts." The first of these was set in 1889 at a tenement house in Brooklyn in which Zuker had a financial interest. The second and third were both staged in 1891, the former on Eighth Avenue in Manhattan and the latter on Fourth Avenue in Brooklyn. Trying to minimize the magnitude of his criminal acts,

Schoenholtz added that, in order to reduce the risk to nearby families, he refused to ignite a fire after 8:00 or 9:00 P.M.

In September 1891, according to Schoenholtz, Zuker had contemplated torching the Grand Street apartment but nixed the idea because he felt his insurance agent was suspicious. Instead, Zuker ordered Schoenholtz to move clothing from 264 Division Street to the apartment of Louis Wischer, Zuker's uncle, at 387 Eighth Avenue. Schoenholtz spent an additional three days moving furniture and other equipment to 140 Mulberry Street in Newark, and he received five dollars per day for his efforts. About the only equipment left at 264 Division Street after these transfers was a small set of sewing machines. With the desired goods out of harm's way, Zuker and Schoenholtz set fire to Wischer's residence, with Zuker's uncle fully cognizant of the plan.

Schoenholtz testified that he and Zuker next discussed burning down the latter's offices in October 1891. According to Schoenholtz, Zuker said: "I have to burn down this shanty or the health department will condemn it. If I fix it up, it will cost $2,000 [$45,000 in 2006 dollars]. I will give the insurance a chance to fix it up for me."

During his testimony, Schoenholtz mentioned that Zuker left a few sewing machines at 264 Division Street for "insurance purposes." He quoted Zuker as saying: "I left those behind for the purpose when the house shall burn down. The insurance company will have no suspicion that the place was set on fire, because there will be so much goods lying around and it will be such an accident[al] fire. Now I am going to prepare this place to burn it down." Zuker next told Schoenholtz that he would obtain twenty gallons of benzene and place it under the gas meter. When Schoenholtz asked why the fire had to be so large, Zuker replied: "I want the shanty to go down right to the ground. If it will only be damage[d], I will have no benefit at all. If it will go down to the ground or it will be at least 60 percent damage[d], then the insurance company has got to pay the full amount or build it anew."

It appears that Zuker did not trust Schoenholtz to prepare the premises for the fire, since he hired him only to ignite the fire by lighting a candle. After Schoenholtz reiterated his concern that the planned fire would be so large that it might incinerate the entire block and, in the process, take the lives of innocent neighbors, Zuker apparently did not respond.

Before Zuker continued his plans for destroying his offices at 264 Division Street, he burned down the Newark facility. Zuker's insurance agent was suspicious of him and wanted to terminate Zuker's policy. Unfortunately for the insurance company, the agent became ill and the policy remained intact. After Zuker initiated the fire at the Newark plant, he left town with a man named Besser.

Zuker had meticulously planned the 264 Division Street fire with the help of his neighbor Max Blum. According to Schoenholtz, Zuker even hired a carpenter to build a partition to hide all of the fire preparations from anyone who might look through the window. Zuker purchased four five-gallon butter tubs in which the benzene was placed. After the tubs were filled, Zuker instructed Schoenholtz to "sprinkle benzene on the walls" of the building. Zuker then spread the remaining benzene on a curtain and staircase. For lighting the candle, Zuker agreed to pay Schoenholtz $25. Zuker explained to Schoenholtz that he himself could not be the one to set the fire, because he was well known in the neighborhood. Nor could Max Blum, because he had previously been convicted of arson in Philadelphia. Agreeing to the request, Schoenholtz later lit the candle, left the premises, and went to a liquor store at the corner of Montgomery and Division Streets a few blocks away.

Days after the fire, according to Schoenholtz's recollection, he reconvened with Zuker at the scene of the crime only to be told by Zuker: "You are a lousy firemaker. You are a bastard; you didn't make that fire right." Zuker's statement makes no sense, since he had set up the fire himself and relied on Schoenholtz only to light a candle to initiate the blaze. Yet in March, 1892

Zuker hired Schoenholtz again, this time to move items that had burned in the Newark fire to the 264 Division Street location; he instructed Schoenholtz to separate the damaged goods from those that were still intact and bring the latter to an auction house on White Street to be sold.

After Morris Schoenholtz finished with his testimony, his wife, Annie, took the stand. She recounted a conversation she had with Isaac Zuker, who told her: "Whatever shall happen, my name should not be mentioned. I will pay everything," referring both to an attorney to defend her husband and five dollars per week in hush money. Zuker also promised to pay the Schoenholtz's rent during the time that her husband was behind bars in the Tombs.

Other witnesses testified on behalf of the prosecution, including a few from the New York Fire Department. Fireman Frank Moss of Hook and Ladder Company No. 19 later testified that he saw oil on the floors of the 264 Division Street building as well as pieces of cloth on fire. It was his belief that this was an incendiary fire.

The jury returned its guilty verdict and the Judge Fursman sentenced Zuker to 36 years. When he arrived at Sing Sing, he was in good company with other Jewish arsonists: Morris Schoenholtz, Louis Gordon, Louis Rothman, and Max Grauer had all preceded Zuker to the Big House.

Morris Schoenholtz received a most welcome holiday gift on Christmas Day of 1903: a commutation of his prison sentence by New York Governor Benjamin Odell. Very possibly the reduction of his sentence from 48 to 35 years allowed to him to serve a term of just 8 years. Isaac Zuker's fortune was not quite as good. He obviously remained in Sing Sing for at least 14 years, since he is listed as an inmate there in the 1910 federal census. Most likely he died in prison, for he is not found in either the 1915 New York State census or the 1920 federal census.

Edward "Monk" Eastman

IN THE BEGINNING there was Edward "Monk" Eastman. Not the first *Jewish criminal* in New York, but, by most accounts the first true *Jewish gangster* in New York. Eastman's gang not only caused trouble and angst among residents of the Lower East Side, but also served as an incubator for many other notorious villains who followed in his footsteps. Eastman is probably best known for his battles with Paul Kelly, a major character chronicled in Herbert Asbury's *Gangs of New York*. Born Paulo Antonio Vaccarelli in Sicily, Kelly changed his name around the time he began his career as a boxer. Kelly, like Eastman, helped bring in votes for Tammany Hall politician "Big Tim" Sullivan and his cronies. (Tammany Hall was the Democratic Party political machine that ruled New York City much of the time from the 1790s to the 1960s.) A few of Kelly's gunmen, who would later defect to Eastman's gang, were Jewish, including Max "Kid Twist" Zweibach and Johnny Spanish.

Monk's true identity and the details of his formative years are up for debate. Many, including Asbury, have written that Monk's true surname was Osterman, his father operated a restaurant, and the family originally lived in the Williamsburg section of Brooklyn, although documents supporting these claims do not appear to exist. It is plausible that, at some point, the family name was Osterman, since both Eastman and Osterman literally mean "man from the East" and are common surnames in parts of Germany. But contrary to Asbury's claim, the 1860 federal census lists Monk's father, Samuel, a paper hanger living in

Manhattan, with the surname Eastman. A year later, on April 20, 1861, military records show Samuel Eastman joining more than nine hundred others as volunteers for Company E as part of the Eighth Regiment of the New York State Militia. The group trained before heading south to defend Washington, D.C. The volunteers were next attached to General Irvin McDowell's army, which participated in the Advance of Manassas, which led to the Battle of Bull Run on July 21, the first land battle between the Union and the Confederacy. For his service, Samuel Eastman received an honorable discharge on August 2, 1861. His activity in the war effort may have indirectly influenced his son, who later in his life joined the military himself.

In 1870 the family, which still resided in Manhattan and not in Brooklyn, consisted of Samuel, still a paper hanger; his wife, Mary Parks; and two children, William and Lizzie. In 1875 one could still find Samuel Eastman in the Manhattan city directory, living at 68½ Lewis Street, virtually under the Williamsburg Bridge. Five years later, however, the family had apparently broken apart since the census of 1880 shows a vastly different composition for the family living on East 75th Street on Manhattan's Upper East Side: George Parks, Monk's grandfather, as the head of household; Mary Parks Eastman; and her children, Lizzie, Edward (age five), Ida, and Francene. At the time, George Parks operated a dry goods store. Samuel Eastman and his son William are not listed anywhere in the same census. We do know, however, that Samuel Eastman passed away from "phthisis pulmonalis" (tuberculosis) on September 14, 1888. Compounding the family's instability even further, George Parks died on June 6, 1896, leaving Edward Eastman without a true male role model.

Maybe it is not all that surprising, then, that Monk (Edward) had his first run-in with the law in August 1898, when he was arrested, under the alias of William Murray, on charges of larceny. This arrest led to a three-month incarceration at the

New York Penitentiary, a.k.a. Blackwell's Island (now known as Roosevelt Island).

Eastman did not have to choose a life of crime, but could have stayed on the straight-and-narrow path he had embarked upon during his teens, when he started purchasing, breeding, and selling pigeons. During his trial in 1904 he testified that he used the apartment of one of his sisters in the Richmond Hill district of Queens as his bird sanctuary. The 1900 census shows Eastman's mother, his sisters Lizzie and Francene, his brothers-in-law Charles Wouters and Patrick Reynolds, and the Reynolds' three young girls all living on Curtis Avenue near Richmond Hill, near Hillside Avenue. At that time Richmond Hill remained relatively undeveloped, so it was possible to breed birds without upsetting neighbors. The census of the same year lists an Edward Eastman living at 101 East First Street, with his occupation as a "salesman" of birds. Eastman reportedly ran his pet shop on Broome Street, not too far away.

Around this same time and to augment his income, Monk took on the role of "sheriff" (bouncer) at New Irving Hall, a building used for social functions, most notably fundraising dances. It was undoubtedly through this role that he became associated with members of Tammany Hall, who would use his talents to bring in votes during election time in exchange for protection when he ran afoul of the law.

Sometime around the turn of the century Eastman formed his own gang of bandits, referred to alternately as the Jack Eastman Gang, the Cherry Hill Gang, or simply, the Eastsiders, although that last term could have applied to any of a number of gangs at the time. Eastman's gang laid claim to a large swath of land covering a bit more than a square mile—from Bowery Street to the East River and from Monroe Street to Fourteenth Street. To the west, Paul Kelly and his gang controlled another neighborhood, known as the Five Points—hence the name of the gang, the Five Points Social Club, or the Five Pointers. Not surprisingly, the proximity of the two gangs quickly led to conflict; Monk felt that Kelly's territory ended at Pell Street just west of Bowery Street, while Kelly believed his turf extended east of the same thoroughfare.

The Five Pointers didn't offer the only competition to Eastman's gang. Also vying for turf were the "Lollie Meyers" and the "Whyos." The latter group formed in the mid-1880s and took the gang name, which resembled a cry members would use either to "summon help or frighten enemies." In one run-in with a rival gang, many shots were fired, leaving one dead and several wounded. As a result of this mêlée, Monk and many of his followers were arrested and found themselves on trial for disorderly conduct. But either Eastman had pull or there wasn't enough evidence, and the state could not secure a conviction. In another incident, two members of the Lollie Meyer gang were stabbed, and once again Monk and his men evaded the jaws of justice. In both cases it is likely that Eastman's friends in Tammany Hall pulled strings for his release. Policemen conveniently feigned amnesia over critical details, including the identity of the perpetrators and specifics about the weapons brandished, which could have led to convictions.

No stranger to violence, Monk brushed up against death many times. On April 13, 1901, Eastman and an associate, Samuel Frankel, walked into "Silver Dollar" Smith's saloon, located at 64 Essex Street. Shortly after, two brothers, one known as "Peggy" Donovan, entered and—for some unknown reason and without any warning—Peggy pulled out his revolver and started firing. Eastman bolted out of the bar, as Donovan yelled after him, "Stop thief!" As he continued to run to Orchard Street, two men, believing Donovan's words, grabbed Monk. Catching up, Donovan then pressed his revolver into Eastman's abdomen and fired. Monk fell to the sidewalk. He later claimed that once he was on the ground, the other brother fired at him behind his ear, "The only reason I can think of is the Donovans were heard to say they intended to kill the gang which hung out in Silver Dollar's place, as it was made up of stool pigeons."

It remains unclear when the Eastman gang and the Five Pointers initiated their fighting, but by late fall 1902 the problem had intensified so greatly that Second Assembly District leader Thomas Foley felt compelled to intervene and work out a truce. In mid-September the Five Pointers accused Eastman's group of severely beating one of their own. Paul Kelly's gang retaliated, assaulting one of the Jack Eastman gang members, leaving him lying unconscious between trolley car tracks. After these two incidents the two rival groups had three more encounters and, as a result, several members went to jail and both sides paid fines for disorderly conduct. At this point, Foley met with both groups and thought he had successfully negotiated peace. Members of the Five Pointers even celebrated the compact at their clubhouse at 126 White Street. But the settlement would not last long.

Just days later, on October 4, 1902, Kelly and his men appeared at a poolroom on the second floor of 96 Suffolk Street, a regular meeting place for Monk's men. With pistols and clubs in hand, 35 Five Pointers scampered up the stairs, to the surprise of Monk and his men. During the ensuing fight, tables and chairs were turned upside down, the noise waking up the entire neighborhood. Two policemen, Rothbath and Cohen, dashed to the scene, concluded that they were outnumbered, and proceeded to head for the Delancey Street Precinct Station for assistance. Thirty-five officers from Delancey Street rushed to the poolroom, where matters had quieted down after the Five Pointers were tipped that the police were on their way. As a result of the clash, 29 men were taken into custody and charged with disorderly conduct. On the poolroom floor, police found abandoned a dozen fully or half-loaded pistols. In the aftermath, two of Eastman's men suffered injuries. Whether to avoid the police or Kelly's men, Alfred Frein jumped out of a window, fracturing his arm and injuring his head. Samuel Levinson suffered a fractured arm from the fracas. Both men went to Gouveneur Hospital for treatment.

While the Five Pointers represented Monk Eastman's primary foe, the Eastmans also fought against the Yakey Yakes, an Irish gang led by George "Yakey Yake" Brady. The two primary rivals competed for control over the Cherry Hill, Chinatown, and old "red light" districts. Sometimes the fights started over a woman. Once a girlfriend of Yakey Yake, an employee of a paper box company, transferred her affections to a member of the Eastman gang and was summarily killed. Later the Yakey Yakes went further, appearing at a dance at New Irving Hall (Eastman's home turf) and leaving with another woman for whom both gangs shared affections. In another instance, right after Eastman opened a new pool hall on Suffolk Street, the Yakey Yakes appeared, as if from nowhere—they had been hiding in the basement of the building—and started firing while others began shooting from outside.

On rare occasions, when their interests coincided, various gangs actually worked together. On September 26, 1903, the Eastmans, the Five Pointers, and members of the Yakey Yakes flocked to the Essex Market Court to witness the trial of Bridget "the Bride" Colonna. Colonna, a pistol-brandishing fifteen-year-old, was considered by all of these gangs to be a "heroine." Magistrate Olmstead threatened to incarcerate her unless she reformed. "That's a pretty tough deal," she replied. "I'll do my time but I don't want any ticket-o'-leave business… This is one on [Inspector Max] Schmittberger. If he'd got me he'd wanted a medal for sending such a tough girl as me to the 'Ref.'" In the end Magistrate Olmstead ordered Colonna to spend an indeterminate amount of time at the House of Refuge (reformatory).

Inspector Schmittberger was no stranger to Monk Eastman. The previous August the inspector had been ordered by Deputy Police Commissioner Piper to explain why the Police Department had been slow to put a damper on the number of holdups and assaults occurring on the Lower East Side. Immediately following the reprimand, 33 men were rounded up seemingly at random and placed behind bars for two days each, waiting for complaints from citizens for proof that the inmates should be locked up for a longer period. Yet, although Schmittberger claimed that his territory was one of the toughest in the city to control, he asked for the discharge of prisoners after their arraignment with Magistrate Hogan—as proof that it was no easy matter to rid the neighborhood of such characters. While it is possible that witnesses could not be found to testify against and garner convictions against these prisoners, it is more likely that Schmittberger requested their release in exchange for bribes.

On September 15 Schmittberger had a second chance when he and Officer Stephen McDermott received a tip that the Eastmans and the Five Pointers were going to have a duel at First Avenue and First Street. After waiting an hour while the two gangs battled each other, the two police officers charged into the fray with the assistance of many other detectives and patrolmen. In response, Eastman's and Kelly's men joined forces against the police. After a half hour of shooting, the police brought to the precinct house fifteen men representing many different gangs. McDermott was credited with the victory, earning a promotion to captain shortly thereafter. However, Schmittberger, on whose beat the skirmish occurred, received little praise. Perhaps demoralized for not obtaining the promotion himself, Schmittberger found other ways to obtain his just deserts later on, leading to the accusation by the NYPD Internal Affairs Department that he had taken graft.

Although the full nature of Eastman's relationship with Schmittberger is not known, it seems possible that money changed hands between the two. One can only speculate, but it seems likely that Schmittberger had something to do with Monk's success at evading incarceration, since Eastman's territory coincided with Schmittberger's beat and for many years Eastman avoided serious prison time.

In December 1903 the Eastman Gang again eluded the law, when he and nine of his men stood in front of Magistrate Pool at the Yorkville court after Captain McDermott and Detectives Ewan, Wasserman, and Lang of the Fifth Street Station turned them in. The officers found Eastman and his men lying in beds or on the floor smoking opium in a den on the first floor of a tenement at 138 Avenue A. Detective Ewan informed Eastman that he would be "dropped" if he offered any resistance. Bail, set for $500 for each of the ten men, was somehow paid by several Lower East Side real estate owners. Once again, Eastman slipped through the hands of the law.

Along with bringing in votes for Tammany Hall, Eastman operated card parlors, where his patrons played stuss, a Jewish interpretation of the more common game of faro, both games very much like roulette, with players placing wagers on different ranks of cards, ace through king. In both games, one card of every rank is laid out (glued) on a table, in a long, quasi-rectangular formation (due to the odd number of cards). In succession, the dealer draws two cards from a standard 52-card deck: first the "losing" card and then the "winning" card. Normally up to four "punters" (players) place their wagers on the board, either on a particular rank, such as a 7, or in between cards, to spread their bets. Should any of the punters bet on the "losing" rank, the house wins the bet and all other wagers remain on the table. Then the dealer pulls the next card from the deck and anyone betting on the winning rank wins at even odds. Bets could be placed on more than one card at a time in "two-way," "three-way," or "four-way" splits. If any number of a split turns up during the winning hand, the punter wins the bet at even odds.

Stuss and faro differed only slightly; in the former game, the house wins any split bet in which one of the cards was the "losing card." The game was played fast and furiously, with almost two "turns" per minute. To keep track of cards already dealt, players relied either on their memories or a "counter," who used a "case counter," which looked somewhat like an abacus. To help players with this chore, counters sometimes used tablets, called "tabs"—hence the origin of the phrase "keeping tabs."

Perhaps because of his success at running card parlors, Eastman also placed his bets on never getting caught, an attitude that eventually got him into trouble. One of his most publicized adventures involved gambling on an acquaintance, David Lamar, a securities broker commonly known as the "Wolf of Wall Street." Lamar conspired to knock some sense into the head of James McMahon, whom he and his wife had hired to drive their horses to Long Branch, New Jersey. One night, while McMahon chauffeured Mrs. Lamar and her dog, the canine jumped or fell from their carriage. Mrs. Lamar ordered McMahon to turn the carriage around and fetch the pet, to which he replied: "I'm paid for driving horses, not for catching dogs. If you want the dog, get him yourself." When Mrs. Lamar complained to her husband, he fired the servant, who responded with his fists and got the better of Lamar. Furious, Lamar first approached a prizefighter to rough up McMahon, but the pugilist refused. Just a few days later, on July 9, 1903, five men accosted McMahon near the Lamars' Long Branch residence, kicked him, beat him with their fists, and finally stabbed him in his chest, causing severe enough injuries that he sought hospital treatment. Shortly after the beating, Eastman called Lamar to confirm his safe return to New York. "That's very good. No harm will come to you," Lamar responded.

A Monmouth County justice of the peace issued an arrest warrant indicating "atrocious assault with intent to kill at the request of David Lamar." After McMahon identified Eastman and Joseph Brown from a gallery of photos as two of his assailants, authorities remanded the two men and threw them into the Tombs (Manhattan's primary local jail). Eastman, apparently comfortable with the notion that his friends in Tammany would get him out of any and all trouble, did not appear concerned about the pitfalls of admitting his complicity in the affair. At the Tombs police court a few days later, Monk quipped, "I think Lamar is a four-flusher, and if he don't stand by me, he'll get a taste of New Jersey Justice."

New York Lieutenant Governor Higgins, as acting governor, gave the authorization to officials in New Jersey to extradite Eastman and Brown. The process took far longer than expected, partly because of New York State Senator Thomas F. Grady's decision to act as defense counsel. Trying to discredit McMahon, Grady intellectually and emotionally pummeled the ex-driver with questions on the witness stand.

Eastman, Brown, Lamar, and Lamar's brother-in-law, Barnard Smith, stood trial in Freehold, New Jersey on October 12, 1903. Smith was charged with acting as an accessory to the crime. Marie Jayne, whose husband ran a hotel in Oceanic, New Jersey, where Eastman, Brown, Lamar, and Lamar's attorney, Edmund Wilson, met a few nights before the altercation, testified on behalf of the prosecution. She claimed to have seen Lamar give money to Wilson to pay for the party of four's bill. At his turn on the stand, Wilson acknowledged that his client had picked up the tab, but he also added that McMahon worked for other Wall Street men who wanted to "blackmail and ruin Lamar."

When Monk took the stand on October 14, he claimed that he had been drinking at a bar in Bennet's Hotel at Seventh Avenue and Forty-first Street when the hotel manager, a man named Thompson, approached him and told him someone named Lamar was in trouble and needed help. Two days later, in Oceanic, Thompson introduced Eastman, Brown, Harry Lewis, Abraham Klein, and others to Lamar, who hired the men to guard his house, claiming that his residence had been burgled and that chickens and other animals had been stolen. After two nights, Lamar dismissed them, saying he no longer needed their services. Brown and Lamar followed as defense witnesses, basically corroborating every word of Eastman's testimony.

Two days later the jury returned its verdict: all four men were found not guilty. "I knew I had proved my innocence by sending one of my men to warn McMahon against harm" was Lamar's only comment on the decision. When Warden Fitzgerald informed them of the trial's outcome, Eastman and Brown appeared stupefied. "We guess you're joking, now, boss," Eastman reportedly quipped. When the two men finally realized the warden's sincerity, Eastman added, "We don't lose any time getting out of this town."

Although Monk evaded justice time and again, the odds eventually turned against him. His downfall began in the early morning of February 2, 1904, when a drunken youth named Wetmore walked out of Jack's Restaurant on the west side of Sixth Avenue at Forty-second Street and began counting his money. According to newspaper accounts, the young man's father was "prominent in national affairs." Truth be known, C. W. Wetmore was a captain of industry—the former president of LaClede Gas Light Company, which he sold to the North America Company (which would be considered a multinational corporation today). Undoubtedly the windfall from the acquisition placed many dollars into the pocket of Wetmore senior, who must have shared a fair amount with his son, whose delinquent behavior was of concern to his father. In fact, Wetmore was so apprehensive about his son's behavior that he hired two Pinkerton detectives, George S. Bryan and John W. Rogers, to shadow his son's movements.

At the same time that Wetmore Jr. exited Jack's, Eastman, Wallace, and more than a half dozen others walked out of Sig Cohen's Saloon. Not knowing that they were being watched, Eastman and Wallace pushed revolvers into the youth's face and attempted to steal his stash. Pinkerton Detective Bryan intervened, chasing Wallace, even jumping over Eastman's outstretched leg, which was intended to trip up the pursuer. Detective Rogers, at least initially, apparently watched events unfold, preferring to "cut off a chew of tobacco." Meanwhile, like an Olympic hurdler, Bryan cleared Eastman's leg and collared Wallace in front of Lewis & Conger, a crockery and home furnishings store located at 130 West Forty-second Street.

At this point Eastman began firing at Detective Bryan, who held Wallace in front of him as a human shield. Trying to achieve a better shooting angle, Eastman moved alternatively to Bryan's right and left sides. In response, Bryan positioned Wallace between himself and Eastman, even placing his arm under the captive's armpit so that he could return fire at Eastman. "Let him go, you god-damned son-of-a-bitch, or I will kill you," Eastman cried. But despite his distance of less than ten feet from Bryan, Eastman failed to hit his mark, possibly because he was inebriated from the time he had spent both at Sig Cohen's and, earlier, at McDermott's Restaurant farther downtown, near Third Avenue, where he drank several lagers with his meal of roasted pig.

Finally waking up to his responsibilities, Rogers yelled to Bryan that he should "let go" of Wallace, and the latter did so. Still in front of Lewis & Conger's window, Bryan ducked when Eastman threw his pistol, empty of bullets, toward the detective. The revolver crashed through the window of the store, where it lay until police retrieved it as evidence. Later, police confirmed that the gun in question was found with its chambers completely empty. With no ammunition, the two culprits were helpless when they ran into Police Detective J. B. Healey at the corner of Broadway and Forty-second Street. Other policemen, who had been keeping local gambling houses under surveillance and had heard the noise of the shooting, helped apprehend the two villains. During his arraignment in court, Monk provided his address as 2660 Second Avenue and his occupation as a "newspaper speculator." He clarified this statement by telling the court that he was a printer but had not worked as such for many years. After the arraignment, Eastman was held for felonious assault and attempted murder, while the court charged Wallace with attempted larceny.

When they were not fighting other gangs, picking on helpless individuals like McMahon and Wetmore was the modus operandi for the Eastman gang. In 1903, members of the Dave

Bernstein gang testified in court that members of the Eastman gang accepted $300 from the wife of Dr. B. B. Brandeis, a dentist. Separated from her husband, Mrs. Brandeis made an inquiry as to whether two Eastman gang members, Nathan Young and Paul Brenner, could "disfigure or put [Dr. Brandeis] out of the way." Fortunately, two friends of Dr. Brandeis warned him of the plot and, despite Young and Brenner's going to the dentist's office, he remained unharmed. On April 1, 1904, a Mr. Brown of Rosenthal & Brown testified in court that a man he knew had approached members of the Eastman gang to determine their rates for injuring members of the Synagogue Darshetoi Ousheplusk, located at 48 Orchard Street, via the use of brass knuckles and iron bars. The answer was simple—$15 for killing a man and only $10 for a maiming. An agreement was reached, and fifteen members of Monk's gang attacked Samuel Yudabitz and Herman Michaelisky as they exited the synagogue on a Thursday. Michaelisky's head suffered cuts, his body had multiple bruises, and his eye was almost knocked out with an iron bar. The culprits ran away before police could apprehend them, leaving their victims unconscious. Because of their incapacitation, the victims could not identify their assailants. The ability to get away with both of these incidents must have boosted Monk's ego beyond belief.

So, as the Wetmore case went to trial later in April, Eastman remained confident that his Tammany Hall connections, who had previously kept him out of prison, would once again come to his aid. Much to his surprise, this time the situation had a different outcome. Eastman's ties had decided that the benefit of the votes he brought in for elections did not outweigh the trouble any association with such a thug would cause with the public. Enough was enough. Defense attorney George Hurlbut charged that there was no case against his client, since the district attorney had failed to produce the victim in court, much less put him on the stand. D.A. Rand scornfully replied: "Never in my experience have I known of such a scoundrel, burglar, thug and self-confessed perjurer as this Eastman. The reason for not producing the drunken boy is that he would have been useless as a witness, because he did not even know that he was being robbed."

The jury struggled for a consensus. One out of the twelve jurors could not agree to the charge of first degree attempted murder, which would have warranted a prison sentence of 25 years. After two hours the jury settled on a lesser but nevertheless serious verdict: first degree assault. For a moment Eastman was stunned, his face turning white. Newspapers reported that his "jaw dropped" before he regained his normal confidence. Judge Goff concluded the case by sentencing Monk to ten years at Sing Sing. According to the *New York Times*, Monk recovered sufficiently from his shock to demonstrate his bravado when led from the courthouse to the city prison. Hearing the music of an Italian funeral, Eastman removed his derby and cracked, "Thanks gents for this flatterin' serenade. De tune, 'Nearer, My God, to Thee' is almost as 'propriate as if I was goin' to de chair."

Upon admission to Sing Sing, Eastman kept up the pretense of model citizen, claiming his occupations as "tar and tin roofer" (his brother-in-law's profession) and keeper of a bird store. The record indicates that Monk had scars all over his body, including two from when he had been shot in the abdomen years earlier, many more surrounding his head and on his ears. One would have to classify his physique as "robust," weighing in at 167 pounds for his 5 foot, 6 inch frame. Intake officers described his head as "good-sized" and "flat-sided" (Eastman was known around town for intentionally wearing derby hats one or two sizes too small). Three more distinguishing features made Eastman an easy figure to identify: a missing tooth, five front teeth capped with gold, and faded tattoos on both hands between the thumb and index finger.

For years, whether their boss was behind bars or leading them on the streets, Monk's men kept busy. At 2:30 A.M. on April

12, 1905, six of them left a "disorderly house" on West Thirty-first Street and walked east to Tobey's Saloon, located on the same street between Sixth Avenue and Broadway. After 10:00 P.M. on a typical day, Tobey's, which had both a back room and a basement, played host to many "dissolute frequenters of the Tenderloin of both sexes." After heading downstairs, Eastman's men started trouble. Roy Joyce, the bartender, jumped over the bar and tried to stop the commotion. Before he knew what hit him, one of the men stabbed Joyce in the heart, killing him instantly. Two other men, also stabbed, were rushed to New York Hospital for treatment. Although women in the bar screamed with horror loudly enough to attract the attention of the police, the Eastmans were thought to have escaped before they could be arrested.

In November, 1906, William Brown, a.k.a. "Boston Louis," stood in front of the Columbia Hotel on Seventy-first Street. Inebriated from drinking with a group of men, Brown got into an argument with a few of his companions, three of whom walked across the street and talked with a man thought to be a member of the Eastman gang. After one of these men said, "You do it, and do it right," the man in question pulled his revolver and shot at Brown, who fell to the ground before getting up on his feet again. Policeman Meyers heard the shot and ran to the scene from Second Avenue, but by the time he arrived, the assailant and all of Brown's comrades had run away. Dr. Philips of Bellevue Hospital attended to Brown's injury, caused by a bullet grazing his skull behind the left ear.

In early June 1907 Lieutenant O'Farrell saw a man run out of a café on Suffolk Street, after hearing shots fired. The man in question, Harry Stahl, claimed that he was the victim; that Charles Greenwich, who lived at 65 Suffolk Street, had threatened to kill him. O'Farrell arrested both men, who were fined $5 each. Police indicated that Stahl and several other members of Eastman's gang were stirring up trouble as they each vied for leadership of the gang in Monk's absence.

Meanwhile, behind bars, the Monk lived up to one interpretation of his nickname: acting like a saint and causing few difficulties for prison officials. According to George A. Lewis, an ex-judge and a member of the parole board, "Eastman's habits are good and that he will keep his parole is the belief of every member of the committee." Lewis further justified the decision by stating that the "percentage of those who break their parole is extremely small, and those who do fall are usually hard drinkers." After earning these high marks, Monk took advantage of the new state law allowing parole after only half of the original sentence had run its course. Although New York Police Department officials complained bitterly about Monk's release, particularly because they had not been consulted in the matter, on June 19, 1909, Eastman walked out of prison a free man.

It did not take long for Monk to prove his rehabilitation incomplete. On April 10, 1911, a highly-placed official in the NYPD complained to Police Magistrate Corrigan that Monk was operating an opium den at 335 East Fourteenth Street, depicting the place as a haven for "all kinds of dangerous criminals." Furthermore, the man continued, the police had never tried to touch the place. In May 1912 Judge Julius M. Mayer sentenced Monk, using the alias William Delaney, to eight months at Blackwell's Island for manufacturing opium.

At 9:00 A.M. on May 17, 1915, police forces between Manhattan and Albany received warnings to be on the lookout for a seven-passenger vehicle reportedly occupied by suspects in a robbery that had occurred in the state capitol. The vehicle could be identified by its license, 34,242, and by its distinguishing coat of arms on the radiator cap. Authorities expected the thieves to drive the car to New York City, where they could more easily dispose of their loot. By 5:00 P.M. the police had watched 15,000 autos on the road that led into Manhattan, when Police Lieutenant Murphy noticed the car in question. A motorcycle cop then trailed the car, stopped the chauffeur, pulled his revolver, and jumped onto the vehicle's running board. "Hands up," he commanded. After Lieutenant Murphy glanced inside, he reportedly said, "Well, if it isn't Monk Eastman." When the police searched a bag in the car, they found silverware and jewelry worth $10,000. For his involvement in this crime of grand larceny and burglary, Eastman received a sentence of nearly three years at Clinton Penitentiary, also known as Dannemora. After an early release, Monk announced his intention to go straight. In 1917 he signed up to fight in World War I, joining the Army's 27th Division, which fought in France. Maybe he had come to the realization that he wanted to follow in his father's footsteps. Possibly his brother-in-law, a naval officer, convinced him the military could use his talents. Whatever his motives, Monk's efforts in the army won the respect of his fellow soldiers and commanders and he received a rating of "excellent" upon his discharge. Some 150 fellow infantrymen signed a petition to reinstate Eastman's citizenship, which had been lost when he went to prison. His petition for reinstatement included letters of commendation from many army commanders, including Captain Robert S. Clever, Captain Robert Conrow, Colonel Franklin Ware, and New York Supreme Court Justice Joseph Morschauser. The justice wrote, "Eastman came to see me here in Poughkeepsie and I was impressed with his desire to make good, if he had an opportunity. He volunteered his services for his country and made good, offering his life to the end that law and order should prevail in the world." Captain Clever remarked that Eastman had served at Kemmel Hill and the Hindenburg line with the "utmost courage and devotion to duty" and that during his tenure he had "been an excellent soldier and has made a good record." These endorsements led New York Governor Alfred E. Smith to restore Eastman to full U.S. citizen status on May 8, 1919.

Eastman's rehabilitation was short-lived, but this time not because of his criminal activity. On December 25, 1920, between 4:00 and 5:00 A.M., Monk Eastman was enjoying music and drink at the Blue Bird Café, just west of the intersection of Fourteenth Street and Fourth Avenue. One of the more popular watering holes in the city, the Blue Bird was originally owned by Pabst Brewing Company and later taken over by former prizefighter Willie Lewis and some others and run as a cooperative. After leaving the pub, Eastman was repeatedly shot at short range. His body lay where he dropped, just outside of the BMT subway entrance, until Police Officer Joseph P. Malloy of the Sixteenth Precinct called first for an ambulance and then for a taxi, which took the body to St. Vincent's Hospital. After being pronounced dead, the body was moved to the city morgue, where Eastman was initially identified by a label in his pocket that read, "E. Eastman. Oct. 22, 1919. No. 17434 W.B," the latter two initials referring to the tailoring firm that made the suit, Witty Brothers of 50 Eldridge Street.

The autopsy showed that Eastman had been drinking excessively; the report listed "present 3+++" after the words "ethyl alcohol." Shots fired at Monk had hit him in both hands, his arm, and his left chest area, causing massive injuries. The right hand alone suffered three separate entrance and exit wounds near the wrist. A bullet to his left hand broke a bone. A bullet hitting the left forearm caused both an entrance and exit wound. One bullet penetrated and then exited his stomach. The most fatal bullet entered Eastman on the edge of his left nipple, piercing and then leaving his left ventricle. With his heart, stomach, and pancreas all damaged, the Monk had no prayer of living.

If Eastman was ever married, no one ever appeared to claim him as her husband. At least one of Monk's sisters, Ida, was notified that the body was at the morgue, but she failed to appear, sending her husband, Frank Wouters, in her place. Wouters identified the body and told Medical Examiner Charles Norris that Eastman had been an auto mechanic and lived at 801 Driggs Avenue in the Williamsburg section of Brooklyn. For reasons unknown, Wouters did not make any plans for a funeral, leaving the task to others.

Instead, two of Monk's army chums from France, John J. Boland and Platoon Sergeant Hank Miller, planned and executed a military-style funeral, dressing Eastman in an army uniform. They decorated Eastman's left chest with the American Legion's wounded men's button, which included a silver crest in the middle, the left shoulder with the insignia of the Twenty-seventh Division, three service stripes on the left sleeve, and two wound stripes on the right sleeve. They also inscribed Eastman's name on the coffin, along with his dates of birth and death and the words, "Our lost pal. Gone, but not forgotten."

Monk Eastman is buried without a tombstone in the Canon Street Grounds section of Cypress Hills Cemetery in Queens. Ironically, he is buried in a large grassy area, a bit smaller than a New York City block, surrounded by many Chinese sections—a fitting tribute to his days of smoking and manufacturing opium.

Police initially suspected that Eastman and the shooter had previously argued about illicit liquor running and a lack of payment. Another report suggested that the dispute occurred over how much to tip the waiter. A week passed by before Jeremiah W. Bohan, an ex-prohibition agent, admitted to killing Eastman, but he said he did so in self-defense. Bohan claimed that Monk had threatened to kill him and called him a "rat" and other "unpleasant things." Bohan himself, a one-time fugitive from justice after he was acquitted for the killing of Joseph Faulker, a.k.a. "Joe the Bear" in 1911, was not above reproach. Police had arrested him four times for disorderly conduct.

Bohan insisted his troubles with Eastman had begun eight months earlier, with the two getting into a quarrel at the Spatz Café on Havemeyer Street in Brooklyn, which led to Eastman pulling his revolver out of his holster. Bohan teased Monk to "go ahead and shoot," but Eastman returned the gun to its harness. Police investigators could not find any proof that the quarreling between Bohan and Eastman had anything to do with illegal alcohol or drug running. An examination of Eastman's furnished room on Driggs Avenue produced no evidence that he engaged in any type of crime on a wholesale scale that would have led to "large profits." In January 1922 a jury convicted Bohan of manslaughter and Judge Crain threw down a sentence of three to ten years at Sing Sing. After serving just one year, and in return for "good work and good conduct," Bohan received his parole.

Two questions regarding Eastman's life remain difficult to answer. First, did he ever marry? The Edward Eastman listed at 101 East First Street in the 1900 federal census was married to a woman named Margaret. According to the same census, the said Edward Eastman was 25, which is appropriate for Monk. During the David Lamar trial in 1903, Eastman claimed to be married but then denied it during his court case in 1904. Flip-flopping once again, Monk told the admitting correctional officer at Sing Sing that he was married. Frank Wouters told the medical examiner that Eastman had a wife and, accordingly, Monk's death certificate yields the same information. Yet a search of the New York City marriage index offers no information about an Edward Eastman marrying during this time frame. Possibly Edward Eastman wedded under an alias. (Note: Many people by the name of William Delaney married in New York during this era.)

A more challenging and intriguing question pertains to Eastman's religion. Herbert Asbury claims in *Gangs of New York* that Monk's parents were Jewish and that the family name was probably Osterman. Once again, the names Eastman and Osterman could be German Jewish surnames, but not necessarily. George Eastman, who founded Eastman Kodak and the YMCA, was a Presbyterian. Charles Eastman is a Sioux Native American. Both Edward and Samuel are typical but not strictly Jewish first names. From the medical examiner's report we know that Monk had been circumcised. While only about 5 percent of boys born in the mid-1870s were circumcised and, presumably, most Jewish males born in the same time frame had a *bris*, circumcisions were not the exclusive domain of Jews at the time. Monk claimed to be a Protestant upon admission to Sing Sing, but so did many others, including the author's great-grandfather. One of the more compelling reasons to believe he was Jewish was Monk's explanation in his 1904 trial of why he wore a black outfit the day of the assault on Wetmore. Eastman claimed he wore the color in memory of his mother, who had died recently. Jewish custom requires survivors to mourn actively for their loved ones for a year after the death, and in fact Mary Eastman had passed away the day before Thanksgiving—about six months earlier. (Note: Monk's mother's demise provides some additional insight into his life. Her death certificate shows cirrhosis as the cause of death. Assuming Mary Ellen Eastman suffered from alcoholism, we can probably deduce that her problem may have contributed to both her son's delinquency and the loss of her husband. She died in 1903, when Monk's gang reached its zenith of power, and alcoholic cirrhosis normally causes death after only a decade of drinking.)

Yet, other clues point in the opposite direction. Wearing black is not one of the general customs for Jews mourning during the year after their relatives' death. Also, while his surname is sometimes used by Jews of German heritage, Monk's father, Samuel Eastman, was born in New York in 1830, well before the mass emigration of German Jews in the late 1840s through the 1850s. In turn, Samuel Eastman's father was born in New Hampshire, reducing even further the likelihood of the family being Jewish. Parks is hardly a common or obvious Jewish surname and is only rarely assumed by Jews. Samuel Eastman and Mary Parks were married on April 3, 1865, by Reverend William Corbet. While in that time frame, rabbis also used the title of reverend, William Corbet is hardly a Jewish name. The first names of Monk's mother and sisters—Mary, Lizzie (Elizabeth), and Francene—are not Hebrew either. More germane is the fact that George Parks died in a Baptist rest home. Additionally, Monk's sisters Ida and Francene hired Newell Woolsey Wells, a Presbyterian minister based in Brooklyn, to officiate at their weddings. Finally, Frank Wouters, Monk's brother-in-law, told the medical examiner that Eastman was not a "Hebrew."

But regardless of his true religion, Eastman remains the father or godfather of all Jewish gangsters in New York, a leader who trained many to follow in his footsteps, not just as foot soldiers but as leaders themselves. His protégés include Max "Kid Twist" Zweibach, "Big Jack" Zelig, and "Dopey" Benny Fein. Even though Eastman's gang fell apart years before he died, his presence and influence were felt for decades after.

4

"Dopey" Benny Fein

TO LEARN BENNY Fein's date of death and real surname required assistance, because I could not find them in books about Jewish gangsters, newspaper articles, or the Internet. I couldn't even establish consensus about his nickname, "Dopey" or "the Dope." Some researchers argue that he suffered from a medical condition—Bell's palsy, a nerve injury, or syphilis—which resulted in droopy eyes that made him look as if he were practically asleep. But there are other opinions about the origin of the nickname as well. According to Abe Schoenfeld, the chief investigator for the Kehillah's Bureau of Social Morals, "Half of the time he acts dopey, from where he derives his name." As for the Dope's character, much of what I read proved contradictory. To learn the truth about this well-known yet inaccurately portrayed Jewish gangster, I would have to speak to a relative.

To track down such a person, I used a series of research techniques. I first located Benny in the 1920 and 1930 federal censuses, which provided me with the names of his children. Next, by combing the Social Security Death Index, I determined that one of Benny's sons, Paul, died on June 29, 2002. I then located Paul Fein's obituary, which provided the names of his wife and two children.

Now I faced a moral dilemma. Should I contact any one of these individuals? What if the relatives did not know much about Benny? I had been in touch with other relatives of famous gangsters, and from what I could tell, they posed potential problems. One had threatened to sue me if I used graphics

from the website she created to memorialize her "grandfather."
(I believe it was her step-grandfather.) If I contacted Benny's
relatives, how would they react to my project? Would my phone
call rock their world? Or would they be pleased to correct the
false information floating about?

I had my answer when I typed the name of one of the grand-
children, Geoff Fein, into Google, and found a book review he
had placed on *Amazon.com* for one of the leading books about
Jewish gangsters. In the review he had criticized the author for
the book's inaccuracies about certain aspects of the Dope's life.
Not only did the grandchild know about his ancestor's shady
past, but he also knew facts about the gangster's life that presumably had never been published. It appeared that Benny was
an accepted clan member and, while his family was not proud
of him, they discussed his life openly and honestly.

In the years since he had written the book review, no one
before me had contacted Geoff Fein about the truth of Benny's
past. Not the author he had criticized. Not any other writers. I
was the first. Only too happy to cooperate, Geoff provided me
with Benny's original surname and the proper death date. As a
sign of both my sincere interest in and appreciation for this initial information, I sent Geoff the various admissions records for
Dopey's entering both Elmira and Sing Sing. Geoff returned
that favor by mailing me photos of various family tombstones
in a cemetery on Long Island. Nearly all the tombstones dis-
played the individual family members with the surname Fein.
One tombstone, rising above the rest, showed the family name
as Feinschneider.

Sometime before 1884, the year Benny's parents were naturalized, they sailed from Germany to Baltimore, where they
eased into American life. Living at 32 Ensor Street in downtown Baltimore, Jacob Feinschneider eked out a living as a tailor. Between 1886 and 1887, according to Baltimore and New
York city directories for those years, the family moved to 13
Forsyth Street in the heart of New York's Lower East Side and

around the corner from the Eldridge Street Synagogue, which still stands today. Around this time, Benny was born, although the exact date and the whereabouts of his birth are unclear, since I could not find a birth certificate from either city. However, Geoff Fein told me that the Dope was the youngest of five children and had to fight for attention with his older siblings—all girls.

It appears that Jacob Feinschneider struggled to earn a living. According to the 1888 and 1889 Manhattan city directories, he either made or repaired shoes at a shop located at 99 Division Street. Probably either because his children were growing or his business was not going well, Jacob moved his family to 239 Henry Street and then to 294 Cherry Street on the Lower East Side. Instead of residential units, the latter neighborhood consisted mostly of warehouses, mills, and a lumberyard. By 1890 Jacob had new shop at 33 Canal Street, where he returned to his former occupation as a tailor.

Jacob spent time teaching his son the trade—knowledge that would not only help the pair to generate more income for the family in the short term but also prove useful in Benny's future escapades. By 1899, when he was just twelve, Benny worked in a shop at 342 Canal Street selling suspenders. By this time, both father and son had changed their surname to Fein, as indicated by the city directory for that year. Just a year later the pair formed a partnership, selling "trimmings" out of a shop located in a more fashionable neighborhood, at 246 Canal Street, right across the street from the Earles Hotel.

Possibly because he had to contend with four sisters for attention, Benny had resorted to crime by the age of thirteen. On August 4, 1900, he entered the New York House of Refuge, a reformatory on Randall's Island in the East River, after officials convicted him of stealing a coat (petit larceny). His admission record, listing his name as Benjamin Feinstein, indicates that his father could not earn a proper living in New York and, as a result, worked as a tailor in Chicago. Benny served nearly three years before authorities released him to his father's custody.

Upon his release, Benny again worked with his father selling trimmings at both 246 Canal and 102 Walker Streets. By 1904, at age seventeen, Benny lived on his own at 47 Norfolk Street after his parents moved to South Brooklyn. By age eighteen, just one year later, the Dope had started a "school" for boys, teaching them the art of purse-snatching and pocket-picking. He recruited his pupils on Forsyth and Stanton Streets near elementary school P.S. 20. With Pied-Piper–like qualities, Fein lured students away from school, telling them, "Come with me and you won't have to sit around school all day." By October 1905 the police had responded to P.S. 20 Principal H. W. Smith's request for assistance in disassembling Benny's gang. Six members of the gang had already served time in prison, including "Julius the Badger," "Dick the Blond," and "Nick the Dago." From this small beginning, Dopey honed his leadership skills.

Benny's troubles continued during the summer of 1906, when he was convicted of grand larceny and sent to the New York State Reformatory in Elmira. Despite a potential maximum of five years, he received parole after only eighteen months. Only ten months later he paid his first of three visits to Sing Sing. Detective Reamy had arrested him on charges of burglary and in October 1908 Judge Foster handed down a sentence of three years and six months, although Fein hardly served a full term. Upon his release, Fein retook the reins of his gang, now shifting his focus to labor racketeering. He and his men, including "Joe the Greaser" and "Abie" Beckerman, always took the side of the trade unions, leading many to claim that at least Fein "had his principles." He would never have dreamed of switching sides and working for the manufacturers.

In May 1912 NYPD Lieutenant John Glynn and Detective Patrick Slevin arrested John Denny, a driver for the Bricker & Delinsky Box Company; Louis Moskowitz, an employee of

Tutelman Brothers, a clothing manufacturer; and Dopey. According to the court transcript, the prosecution tried to build a case that all three men conspired to commit grand larceny—stealing 200 dresses. Ultimately the prosecution failed to make its case and the charges against Fein were dismissed.

In addition to racketeering and burglary, the Dope and his men used strong-arm tactics to bring in the votes for politicians. In 1912, for example, Bennie was on the payroll of an attorney named Wolfson, who, from his office located on either Stanton or Rivington Street, led the campaign for Bull Moose Party candidate Solomon Suffrin in the race for the Eighth Assembly District seat. Fein, with the help of Charlie Auerbach, conducted a fundraising ball at Webster Hall under the name of the "Hemlock Club."

Benny did not need others to help him perform his dirty work. He was quite capable of using his own physical force to keep foes in line—or at least to scare them. At 9:45 A.M. on April 18, 1913, Dopey walked over to "Little Butch" at the Essex Market Court and punched him in the face numerous times. According to a report by a Kehillah investigator, Butch, an employee of the United Hebrew Trades union and member of a rival gang led by "Pinchey," had previously threatened to kill Benny. (The Kehillah, Hebrew for "community," was an organization founded by the New York Jewish community to handle social issues.) Greenbaum, the Kehillah's attorney, who happened to be standing near the two when the incident occurred, grabbed Dopey and stopped the attack. Benny then ran up Second Avenue yelling that he would "get a gun and kill Young Butch." Greenbaum, wanting to avoid bloodshed, advised Butch of Dopey's intentions. About fifteen minutes later Dopey returned with a gun but could not find Butch, who was hiding in Alderman Max Levine's office.

At the height of his career, Benny and his men kept busy. In July 1913 the raincoat makers of New York City went on strike. To help them with their cause, they hired Dopey and Joe the

Greaser to perform guerrilla work. For however long the strike was to last, Benny and Joe were to be paid a fixed salary of $15 a day each. In late August 1913 New York City's 1,500 sign painters went on strike. Sam Liebowitz of the United Hebrew Trades Union hired Dopey, Joe the Greaser, and Little Archie to beat up scab workers and disrupt paint shops. Once again, for their efforts, Benny and his men were paid $15 per day until the strike ended.

On September 12, 1913, Benny went to Philadelphia with a team of ten guerillas to handle a strike by the cloak and suit workers of the city. Investigator Abe Schoenfeld of the Jewish community's Bureau of Social Morals reported that he learned that Sam Liebowitz of the United Hebrew Trades Union paid Dopey $300 to deal with the situation. At about 5:00 P.M., in a skirmish between Benny's men and the workers, the Dope fired his gun. The bullet hit a policeman in the head. Fein was summarily arrested and charged with felonious assault, attempted homicide, and carrying concealed weapons. Two days later Fein's attorney, Mr. Gray, a well-known underworld lawyer from Philadelphia, bailed him out of jail after paying $1,200.

Although there is ample evidence to support many of Benny's convictions, Geoff Fein heard from his father that Benny claimed he was frequently framed. This appears to be the case at least once. In January 1914, NYPD Officer Sheridan testified that Dopey assaulted him on Forsyth Street. According to Sheridan, a seventeen-year veteran of the NYPD, he had been recently reassigned to the Thirteenth Precinct and worked a shift from 4:00 P.M. until midnight. Sheridan stated that his role as a sergeant was to "enforce discipline, prevent crime, disperse gangs, and investigate complaints." He indicated that he had two "communications" from the police chief, which directed him to investigate Dopey and his gang members.

At approximately 4:30 P.M. on August 9, 1913, standing in front of the jewelry store located at the southwest corner of Forsyth and Grand Streets, he and Officer Dunellan saw both

Benny and Owie Cohen loitering in front of Murray's Haberdashery, diagonally across the intersection. Sheridan signaled for Benny to come over to him. The sergeant then asked Dopey if he was, in fact, Benny Fein. When the Dope responded in the affirmative, Sheridan continued: "There is a lot of complaints about you. I have a number of complaints here with reference to you and a gang that is hanging around the neighborhood here." Officer Sheridan elaborated that police reports indicated Benny and his gang hung around the Forsyth Baths located at 79 and 81 Forsyth Street, on the west side of the street just south of Grand Street. Defiantly, Benny responded, "Can't I stand on the block?" Sheridan replied, "You cannot." Unfazed, the Dope protested: "There's a dirty old whore. She has been lying about me. Suppose I did serve a term. So what? She should keep her mouth shut." Sheridan then ordered, "While I'm on patrol, you keep out of here, and that goes." Benny agreed to stay out of the neighborhood and then walked away but, at least in his mind, just for a while.

Sheridan and Fein ran into each other only a few hours later that day. At 9:55 p.m., the sergeant returned to the neighborhood and had a conversation with Adolph Rosensweig, owner and manager of the Forsyth Baths. It was a "warm night," he recalled, and Sheridan wore his "summer uniform" with a T-shirt underneath. The sergeant testified that Benny hit him on his left ear for no apparent reason. Retaliating in "self-defense," Sheridan first struck a blow at Fein between the eyes and then proceeded to beat him on the top of the head with a nightstick. Benny cried out, "You son of a bitch. I will kill you," and then snatched the nightstick away from Sheridan and tossed it across the street. Sheridan indicated that he next grabbed the Dope by his throat and dragged him to the east side of Forsyth Street. Then Sheridan explained that he *single-handedly* brought Benny over to Gershon's Cigar Store at 270 Grand Street, the northwest corner of the intersection of Forsyth and Grand. For whatever reason, it appears that defense attorney Wahle was

asleep at the wheel. He did not question Sheridan's testimony
beforehand about the location. Murray's Haberdashery was at
that location.

In addition to being contradictory, Sheridan's testimony
tended toward the farcical. Sheridan recalled that, apparently
out of nowhere, Officer Henry Hadlich appeared. The two policemen each wrestled with the "assailant," and, according to
Sheridan, he and his fellow officer "dragged" Benny to the east
side of Forsyth Street to Gershon's Cigar Store, at 270 Grand,
and then to the Mutual Alliance Bank. Sheridan then mirac-
ulously and single-handedly dragged Benny two blocks west
to the intersection of Grand and Bowery Streets and into the
lobby of the National Hotel, and then more officers arrived and
helped subdue the Dope.

In his report to the leaders of the Kehillah, Investigator Abe
Schoenfeld provided quite a different perspective of the same
events. According to Schoenfeld, Benny was indeed sitting on
the stoop across the street from the Forsyth Street Baths, where
Sheridan and Rosensweig conversed. And yes, Sheridan "beck-
oned" Fein to come over to him. However, Schoenfeld wrote
that after Benny crossed the street, "the officer struck him a
terrible blow under his right eye without warning or cause, and
almost threw him down senseless. The Dope thereupon retaliated by punching the Sergeant in the ear. The Sergeant then
pulled out his night-stick and struck the Dope across the head
with it. After doing this the officer called for assistance."

A few minutes later, according to Abe Schoenfeld, two other
officers appeared and took Dopey to the National Hotel. Yet
two more policemen appeared and, rather than take Benny
to Police Headquarters, the five officers "threw their prisoner
through the storm door [of the National Hotel] and, once inside, pounced down upon him with their black-jacks and gave
the prisoner the beating of his life. After reviving him, instead
of proceeding to Police Headquarters with him as was their
original intention, they took him to the Clinton Street Station

where he was charged with felonious assault on an on-duty officer." The following morning at the Magistrate House, Benny was charged with assault and held on $5,000 bail.

The attack, according to Schoenfeld, left Benny with two black eyes and six stitches in his head. Additionally two of his front teeth were knocked out and his nose fractured. In contrast, none of the policemen exhibited a single scratch, despite all the scuffling. At the hearing, Benny's attorney accused the police of framing Benny, to which accusation Judge Murphy responded, "According to what you say, Mr. Counselor, we ought to jail the officers and leave the prisoner scott free." Defense counsel continued, "We have fifteen reputable witnesses here who saw the frame-up." The judge, still incredulous, replied: "Bring them along, but I won't hear fifteen. Three are enough." So much for a fair system of justice.

At the trial in January 1914 several witnesses took the stand on behalf of the prosecution, including Sheridan and Officer Hadlich. Among the many individuals supporting their testimony were Joseph Warshaw and Frank Lemmon, both members of the First Inspection District. Defense Attorney Wahle called ten witnesses to the stand. The first of this lot was none other than Adolph Rosensweig, the owner of the Forsyth Street Baths, who was right at the scene of the altercation. He testified that Sheridan had struck Benny, who responded in self-defense. Ida Meyers, who lived just a few doors down at 67 Forsyth Street, bolstered the defense's position. Gussie and Samuel Brandywine were pushing their baby down Forsyth Street in a stroller when the incident occurred. Gussie went so far as to ask Sheridan: "Why hit him? Why not just arrest him?" By her account, Sheridan replied, "Mind your own business!" Herman Stein, a raincoat salesman for the firm of Salz and Burman, happened to be in the neighborhood visiting a "lady friend." He too indicated that Sheridan started the fracas. Rosie Kaplan witnessed the event after attending a movie at the theater located on Grand Street between Forsyth and Chrystie. So, too, did

Sol Manson, a salesman who worked for Julius Bloomberg, the printer and stationer. All ten defense witnesses' stories refuted the words of the four officers. Yet, despite the overwhelming reasonable doubt, Judge Malone found Benny guilty of assault in the second degree and sentenced him to five years in Sing Sing.

By the time Benny left prison, his career as a gang leader was essentially over. Others had taken his place, among them Louis Buchalter and his cronies. Even before this trial, other gangsters had the Dope in their sights. Abe Schoenfeld wrote in his report dated September 25, 1913, that three other gangs, led by Billy Lustig, Little Rothie, and Pinchey, had formed a "combination." These men were jealous of the monopoly Dopey had on guerilla work on the Lower East Side. Schoenfeld wrote: "Every strike that took place on the eastside, under the auspices of the United Hebrew Trades (union), the Dope was contracted to do the guerilla work...We will patiently await the results of this war."

Just three days after Schoenfeld's report, Pinchey and Little Rothie, along with five of their henchmen, walked up to three of Benny's men—Desperate Little Yuddle, Jack Wolf, and Hymie Rubbernose—on Grand Street between Chrystie and Forsyth Streets. As soon as the three men saw the others coming their way, they attempted to run away. Pinchey began shooting at Benny's men, but the only people hurt were some innocent bystanders.

The police and the Kehillah were also after Fein. Through the grapevine, Schoenfeld learned that Dopey was going to run a fundraising ball on October 31, 1913, at the Progress Assembly Hall, located at 28-30 Avenue A. Benny and Jimmy Britt went around to various storekeepers and tried to extort monies for advertisements in the promotional "journal" for the event. The Kehillah informed the police, which sent a squad from the Third Deputy Police Commissioner's Office to monitor the event. Additionally, a few members of the Inspector's Office, members of the Second Deputy Police Commissioner's Office, and other lieutenants showed up. The police kept fifty well-known thieves from attending the event. Furthermore, they entered the Assembly Hall and ordered Benny to leave. As Schoenfeld wrote in his report, "If he needed a little more to complete his dopiness—he really went dippy that night," referring to Fein's angry response to being removed from his own party. Others at the affair continued "dancing and enjoying themselves."

Despite his loss of stature as a gang leader, Benny continued to commit crimes and spend time in court. In the latter part of 1914 the Dope was arrested on two counts of assault and another for disorderly conduct. The next year he served two months at the New York City Penitentiary for attempting to extort $50 from an agent of Local 509 of the Butcher's Union, threatening to "beat him up" if he did not pay. If he had not "squealed" on four members of his gang, Fein's sentence would have been longer. In 1916 a conviction for felonious assault led to his spending one month in the Paterson, New Jersey, jail. In 1917 a Magistrate's Court discharged Fein after he was arrested for homicide. Also that year Benny served 60 days in the New York Workhouse after yet another conviction for disorderly conduct.

For whatever reason, Fein decided to tell some of the truth about himself during the summer of 1917. Maybe he needed to use his real birth name to hide from his past. On June 28, 1917, at age 30, Benny married Gussie Luosky, a 26-year-old native New Yorker. Benny not only used his full name, Benjamin Feinschneider, but also indicated that he worked as a "head waiter" and that he was born in Russia. Less than a month later, on July 20, the Dope filled out a World War I Draft Registration form. This time he also used Benjamin Feinschneider as his name but indicated that he was "natural born" and that his employment involved working "different auction rooms." The registrar reported on Benny's physical characteristics as tall, slender, and blue-eyed. .

After he married, Benny apparently settled down a bit and spent more time with his family, which now resided at 16 Vernon Street in Brooklyn. However, on July 30, 1931, police arrested him for the first time in thirteen years. The Dope was held without bail, along with Samuel Hirsch of the Bronx and Samuel Rubin of Brooklyn, on suspicion of felonious assault. The three men were thought responsible for showering Mortimer Kahn with acid in front of his neckwear shop at 124 Allen Street.

Another decade passed before Benny made headlines for the last time. A March 13, 1941, *New York Times* article indicated that Benny and Nig Abe Cohen were found guilty for "criminally concealing and withholding" stolen dresses worth $7,500. In the previous years the two men had held up and burgled shops in New York's garment district, obtaining more than $250,000 in merchandise and other loot. As a fourth-time offender, the Dope should have received a sentence of life imprisonment. Fortunately for Fein, Judge Owen Bohan decided that his penitentiary sentence from 1914 was only a misdemeanor and not a felony. As a result, the judge reduced the mandatory sentence of ten to twenty years in Sing Sing to just one year. His final prison admission record provided additional information about the crime: Benny and his accomplice stole a truck containing clothing and rayon.

Benny may have retired from criminal activities upon his release from Sing Sing. One can find little evidence of his activities in later newspapers. On July 23, 1962, just three days after his birthday, Benjamin Feinschneider passed away. A shell of his former tough self, his body surrendered to emphysema. At age 75, Benny died a very old man for someone of his generation. From what information can be collected about his last two decades, he lived a peaceful and crime-free existence. Most likely his earlier years had taken quite a toll.

5

"Gyp," "Lefty," and "Whitey": The Becker/Rosenthal Affair

THE BECKER/ROSENTHAL AFFAIR, as it would be come to be known, was the 1910s equivalent of the O. J. Simpson case. The episode offered something for almost everyone: murder, graft, political corruption, and twists and turns that no one could have expected. Because of the similarity of surnames of those involved (Rosenthal, Rosenberg, and Rosensweig), the case was sometimes called the "War of the Roses." If these names did not make tracking of the case confusing enough, many others who had some connection to the situation all shared the surname Sullivan. In the end, a police lieutenant named Charles Becker and four others died in Sing Sing's electric chair for the murder of gambling casino operator Herman Rosenthal. The electrocutions represent the highest number of death sentences implemented at the prison for any single crime. Of the other four men who died in the chair, three were Jews—Harry "Gyp the Blood" Horowitz, "Lefty" Louis Rosenberg, and Jacob "Whitey Lewis" Seidenschner.

Although the Becker/Rosenthal affair has received quite a bit of attention, most of it centers on the roles of Lieutenant Becker and many others, and very little has been written about the lives of these three Jewish gangsters. Together, Harry Horowitz, Louis Rosenberg, and Jacob Seidenshner formed the nucleus of what was known as the Lenox Avenue gang, a satellite operation of Big Jack Zelig's gang. Zelig was a disciple

of Monk Eastman and took over his gang after Eastman lost
control of his band of *schtarkers* (bouncers) while serving time
in Sing Sing. Constituting approximately twenty members, the
Lenox Avenue boys picked pockets and burgled New Yorkers
on the Upper West Side of Manhattan near 125th Street (and
Lenox Avenue; hence the gang's name) starting sometime in
the very early 1900s.

According to his birth certificate, Harry Horowitz was born
on April 21, 1888, at 419 Third Avenue, the home of Celia
and Joseph P. *Horwitz*, listed in the record as a merchant. Ever
since that initial listing, the spelling of the surname has been
in question. Just a year after Harry's birth, the Manhattan city
directory listed Joseph under the name of *Hurwitz*, living at
the same address and selling clothing at 367 Third Avenue. By
1900, according to the federal census of that year, Joseph was a
tailor and the family had moved to 167 East 106th Street. Now
in a larger family, Harry enjoyed the company of two brothers,
Mortimer and Milton.

Of the three boys, Harry seems to have found himself most
frequently on the wrong side of the law. In his court testimony
during the first trial of Lieutenant Becker, Harry acknowledged
that he had done a three-month stretch in the New York House
of Refuge (state reformatory) after a conviction of burglary in
1906. After breaking parole, he returned to the institution for
additional time. Then in 1908 Harry served six months in the
New York Penitentiary, a.k.a. Blackwell's Island, for petit larceny. Only a year later, he was fined $500 and given another
year's sentence to the penitentiary.

While Harry caused the most trouble in his family, he was
not the only one to attract the attention of the law. On July
28, 1912, the *New York Times* reported that police had arrested
his brother Mortimer for fraudulently endorsing a check for
$1,750, made out to Miller & Company of 29 Broadway. The
article quoted a police report stating that another brother, Milton, had been "recently sent to Elmira Reformatory." Less than

five months later the *New York Times* claimed that yet a third brother, Isidore, had been arrested in Detroit for "peddling cheap jewelry." Although at the time the Motor City did not have an ordinance against selling such items, authorities ordered Isidore out. Whether Harry had a third brother or whether Isidore was simply an alias for either Mortimer or Milton is undetermined. What is clear is that the Hurwitz family and the law were not the best of friends.

Sometimes called "Levy" or "Jones," Harry was more commonly known as "Gyp the Blood," Gyp referring to Harry's dark complexion, which people compared to that of a gypsy. "Blood" has two possible meanings—either slang for someone who killed others, or a dapper dresser. Adding to his debonair looks was Harry's build. At 5 feet, 8¼ inches and 134 pounds, he was taller and thinner than his sidekicks Jacob Seidenshner and Louis Rosenberg. Yet his slender build was no hindrance to Harry, who worked as a bouncer at dance halls in the Bowery. Rumor had it that he boasted about his ability to break a man's spine with his bare hands. Legend suggests more: that he picked on innocent bystanders and "practiced" to maintain his prowess.

On May 9, 1891, the day they brought their son Louis into the world, immigrants Jacob and Anne Weisberg Rosenberg lived at 14 Suffolk Street. Louis was the second oldest of four brothers. At the time, Jacob Rosenberg worked as a grocer, although he would specialize later on, selling meat at 9 Suffolk Street by 1904 and then flour just a couple of years later. By 1907 Jacob Rosenberg had moved the family to 272 East 201st Street in the Bronx, only to resettle at 3078 Perry Street by 1910. The experience of living in the upper part of Manhattan (Horowitz) and the Bronx (Rosenberg) might explain how the two met each other. The knowledge of the local territory must have come in handy for both Harry Horowitz and Louis Rosenberg, who, as members of the Lenox Avenue Gang years later, understood where best to find and assault innocent victims.

While both spent their formative years on the Lower East Side, Harry Horowitz and Louis Rosenberg differed in several ways. Louis Rosenberg was three years younger, an inch shorter, and five pounds heavier. His aliases were "Marks," "Lefty Louie," and "Louis Baker," and his specialties were as a pickpocket and a gun for hire. During his trial in 1912, Lefty claimed to have worked for his father at the Produce Exchange and served summonses for an attorney at 99 Nassau Street. Assistant District Attorney Frank Moss forced Rosenberg to admit that he had been first convicted of picking pockets at age fourteen, just seven years beforehand. His troubles continued with a conviction in 1907 for disorderly conduct in Boston.

The last of the trio, Jacob "Whitey Lewis" Seidenshner, was raised in Lublin (which would now be in eastern Poland and where the surname Zajdensznir was then quite common). Jacob immigrated to the United States with his mother, Chaia Malka (later changed to Mollie), and five siblings—Bessie, Joseph, Morris, Nathan, and Tilley—and the evidence suggests that they followed in the footsteps of the male head of household, Hersh (Harry) Zajdensznir, who arrived in America a year or two earlier. Together they lived in several locations on the Lower East Side including 201-203 East Second Street and 201 Houston Street. Harry worked as a bookbinder or an upholsterer according to different prison records for Jacob's brothers Morris and Nathan. Morris was sent to the New York House of Refuge after he stole a pocketbook containing $8 from a woman on Catherine Street. In 1908 Nathan also served time in the House of Refuge after a conviction for picking pockets. Five years later authorities sent Nathan to the New York State Reformatory at Elmira for attempted grand larceny. Filling up his rap sheet, Nathan, after interfering with police activities, was sent to Blackwell's Island. Jacob's two other brothers fared better. Louis, after serving in the army in Leavenworth, Kansas, worked as a cigar maker and lived at 16 Clinton Street in 1912, the same year he married. Older brother Joseph, who lived on Eldridge Street, worked as a stevedore.

Often going by the name of Frank Muller, Jacob Seidenshner measured 5 feet, 5½ inches and 165 pounds. Reportedly because of his lighter than normal hair color, he was also known as "Whitey" Jack and, more typically, "Whitey Lewis." According to police posters looking for Seidenshner after the Rosenthal murder, Jacob had previously served time in both Elmira Reformatory and Sing Sing. At some point he joined the army and trained at Fort McKinley before he transferred to Southeast Asia to fight in the Philippine–American War, where he found unexpected trouble. When another soldier criticized him for his religion, Seidenshner picked up a knife. Claiming to have been attacked and "forgetting" that he had a sharp instrument in his hand, Seidenschner fought with the other soldier, using his fists. After this incident, Seidenshner left the military in 1911 with a dishonorable discharge.

BEFORE JOINING THE NYPD, in 1893, Charles Becker worked as a bouncer at a German brew pub in lower Manhattan. None other than Monk Eastman was impressed with Becker's physical stature—he stood more than 6 feet tall, weighed approximately 215 pounds, and had established a reputation as a formidable bouncer. Eastman befriended Becker and ultimately introduced him to "Big Tim" Sullivan, Tammany Hall leader and operator of a saloon in the Tenderloin district. Sullivan, too, was moved by Becker's appearance and demeanor and acquainted his new friend with two more people with whom he felt he might share some common interests: Arnold Rothstein and Herman Rosenthal.

It was Big Tim Sullivan who helped Becker secure his position with the NYPD, where the newcomer earned a reputation as a hardworking and effective policeman. His early career was not without controversy, however. After the Lexow Commission, which was investigating political corruption, reported its findings in 1894, concerning corruption among Tammany Hall, the NYPD, and those involved in prostitution, Becker helped chase deadbeats. The commission findings boiled down to the following sentence from the opening pages of its final report:

> *Whereas it has been charged and maintained that the police department of the city of New York is corrupt; that grave abuses exist in said department; that in said city the laws for the suppression of crime and the municipal ordinances and regulations duly enacted for the peace, security, order and the laws of said city are not strictly enforced by said department and by the police force acting thereunder; that said laws and ordinances when enforced are enforced by said department and said police force with partiality and favoritism, and that said partiality and favoritism are the result of corrupt bargains between offenders against said laws or ordinances on the one hand and said department and police force on the other; that money and promise of service to be rendered are given and paid to public officials by the keepers or proprietors of gaming houses, disorderly houses or liquor saloons or others who have offended or are offending against said laws or ordinances, in exchange for promises of immunity from punishment or police interference; and that said department and said police force, by means of threats and otherwise, extort money or other valuable consideration from many persons in said city as the price of such immunity from police interference or punishment for real or supposed violations of said laws and ordinances...Resolved...the committee shall...report...that proper legislation may be enacted to suppress said evil.*

The counsel for the Lexow Commission was Frank Moss, who had previously served as a trustee of Reverend Charles Henry Parkhurst's Society for the Prevention of Crime (SPC).

SPC not only campaigned against police corruption and the excesses of Tammany Hall, but also collected as much evidence as it could to back up Parkhurst's claims. It was Parkhurst's efforts, many believed, that eventually led to the formation of the Lexow Commission itself. Revelations from the committee's work contributed to Tammany Hall's losses in the 1894 election. During the years 1896–1899, Moss worked as counsel for the Mazet Committee, which continued investigation into municipal corruption beyond what the Lexow Commission covered.

Both committees claimed Jews responsible for a significant portion of New York City's crime. Moss, like the Lexow Commission, in general believed that the most brutal thugs in New York were Jewish. Specifically, he did not trust men like Max Hochstim, who, with Alderman Charles "Silver Dollar" Smith (born Solomon), operated the bail-bond company at the Essex Market Courthouse on the Lower East Side and who would later head up the Max Hochstim Association, part of the Independent Benevolent Association. (See chapter 6 for more about Max Hochstim's involvement with prostitution.)

To say that Moss was anti-Semitic would be an understatement. He wrote vivid and vicious diatribes against Jewish immigrants in his 1896 treatise, *American Metropolis*. Referring to the Lower East Side as "the New Israel," he exclaimed: "The ignorance and the dirtiness of New Israel are not its only dark features. It is a distinct center of crime. It is manifested with petty thieves and housebreakers, many of them desperate; and the criminal instincts that are so often found naturally in the Russian and Polish Jews come to the surface here in such ways as to warrant the opinion that these people are the worst element in the entire makeup of New York life."

Max Schmittberger, who would become Becker's supervisor, had helped provide the Lexow Commission with names of policemen on the take. Ironically, Schmittberger himself was indicted for vice, but he received immunity from Counsel John W. Goff in return for his assistance in exposing corruption within the NYPD. In particular, the information Schmittberger provided forced an early retirement for his boss, "Clubber" Williams. Becker, who modeled his strong-arm tactics after those of "The Clubber," particularly in his effective use of a police stick, would naturally become an opponent of Schmittberger.

To make matters worse between the two, at some point Becker learned that Schmittberger collected graft, and he decided that he too wanted a piece of the action. Initially Becker pocketed only a small fraction of what Schmittberger garnered. Regardless of the size of the amount, once Schmittberger got wind of Becker's situation, he called Becker into his office, demanded that the lieutenant turn over 90 percent of what he had collected, and proposed that Becker serve as his official collection agent. While Becker, a wily operator, appeared to concede, over time he not only claimed a larger share of his "earnings" but also gathered enough evidence to lead to a departmental trial against Schmittberger in 1906. After Schmittberger turned state's evidence about other corrupt policemen, charges against him were dropped. Yet, despite his longstanding rivalry with and dislike of Becker, the two agreed that it was in their financial best interest to collaborate. They wanted to ensure that the monies continued to flow into both of their pockets. This relationship demonstrates not only opportunism at its most rampant, but also just how widespread was the corruption throughout much of New York City's government. This explains just how Becker thought he might get away with his shenanigans: it was simply the way business was done for years.

Becker had other enemies beside Schmittberger, one of them the well-known poet and novelist Stephen Crane. Becker had a run-in with Crane during the late summer of 1896, the year after *The Red Badge of Courage* was published. On September 15 Crane and two females attended Broadway Gardens, a music hall on Thirty-second Street near Broadway. When they left the building shortly after midnight, they met up with Dora Clark, a prostitute. After Crane helped one of his two companions onto a streetcar, he turned back to the other two women and saw Charles Becker placing handcuffs on them. The entire group adjourned for the arraignment at the Jefferson Market Police Court, where Crane sided with Dora Clark and complained that the arrest was an "outrage." Crane indicated he was "studying the Tenderloin [district]" for material for magazine studies and that the two women who were accompanying him introduced him to Clark. Magistrate Cornell, believing Crane, acquitted Clark of the charges.

Not satisfied with Clark's acquittal, Crane telegraphed Police Commissioner Theodore Roosevelt and recommended a departmental trial for Becker. Crane's motives for intensifying his complaint against Becker are murky. He might well have been deeply enraged about the unfair treatment of the women, particularly after living in the Bowery in order to observe the poor for his first novel, *Maggie: A Girl of the Streets*. At the trial, which began on October 15, Crane testified that Becker had not even spoken to Dora Clark until he had "accosted" her and had therefore committed a false arrest. On cross-examination, Crane refused to answer questions regarding a possible opium addiction and leeching a living from ladies of the evening. In the end, Charles Becker received only a slight reprimand, after which then New York City Police Commissioner Theodore Roosevelt congratulated him on his solid if somewhat spotty record.

In 1907 Roosevelt's successor, Theodore Bingham, passed up many other policemen for promotion and elevated Becker to sergeant. As number one in his precinct, Becker ruled over collections, and his 10 percent of the take soon grew to twice that amount. For a policeman earning $1,500 a year, his $8,000 windfall was a welcome bonus.

Through the next few years Becker rode high and mighty. In competition with two fellow officers in charge of strong-arm squads, Becker's team, between October 15, 1911 and the following July, posted half of the raids recorded at Police Headquarters on Centre Street, instead of the expected one-third. Although the charges his squad brought against gambling casino operators were dropped, many of these same casino owners lost significant sums because of the inconvenience of the shakedowns. Aside from the monetary cost, though, the operators had little to worry about. Conveniently, Becker's men appeared to forget their evidence when it was time to testify in court and, with little to support convictions, judges frequently had to drop charges against the accused.

By late that year, however, Charles Becker learned that his illicit operation, if not his life, was in jeopardy. A Hearst newspaper reporter warned him that certain other parties wanted to frame him. To say the least, many gambling casino operators, including Herman Rosenthal, had motive to turn him in. Becker's raids on gambling casino operators caused them to lose business at the same time they had to pay graft to policemen. All the while, Becker profited both financially and politically, earning money from the operators while looking good in the eyes of the police commissioner.

THE MURDER OF casino operator Herman "Beansie" Rosenthal, for which our cast of characters went to Sing Sing and eventually the electric chair, occurred on a hot night, July 16, 1912. Just before 2:00 A.M. someone, either Sam Schepps or "Bridgey" Webber, another casino operator, entered the Metropole Hotel on West Forty-third Street, sauntered up to Rosenthal, and requested his presence outside of the building. Possibly drunk at the time, Rosenthal did not appear to question the solicitation. But immediately after he exited the premises, at least five shots rang out, hitting Beansie Rosenthal several times in the neck and head. One bullet hit him on the bridge of his nose, pushing it inward. Another lodged in his forehead. The *New York Times* reported that there was so much blood that "no one could be certain how many shots had hit him." According to some reports, a gray 1909 Packard with four men screeched west along Forty-third Street toward Broadway. Other accounts described a white getaway car. Some write-ups indicated that the auto went eastbound toward Sixth Avenue. Despite all the confusion, a few bystanders had enough time to notice the vehicle's New York license plate number: 41313.

Rosenthal's murder probably came as no surprise to many. He had made his feelings about Lieutenant Becker known, not only privately with District Attorney Charles Seymour Whitman but also more publicly with the press. Just two days before the murder, the *New York World* had published Rosenthal's affidavit that Becker and his men had "disrupted" his gambling operation and that corruption ran rampant throughout the NYPD. And Beansie Rosenthal knew what he was talking about—he and Becker were business partners, with Becker providing Rosenthal protection from police raids of his casino in return for a cut of the gambling profits.

One might think, then, that Becker would be the most likely candidate to have planned, ordered, or executed the murder. He certainly had a checkered past as a member of the NYPD and was the main focus of Rosenthal's diatribe in the *World*. However, many others may have had equal interest in Rosenthal's demise.

"Bald Jack" Rose (born Rosensweig) was Becker's stool pigeon and collector of graft from many gambling casino operators, including Rosenthal, but was also sometimes on Rosenthal's payroll for other services rendered. Rose, just like Becker, had been implicated in Herman Rosenthal's affidavit.

Bridgey Webber, a well-known East Side professional card player, operated his gambling facilities at 117 West Forty-fifth Street in the Tenderloin district before Rosenthal decided to move in on his territory and open a competing facility right across the street at 104 West Forty-fifth Street.

Sam Paul, a graduate of Monk Eastman's gang, ran not only gambling facilities but also his own social club, simply known as the Sam Paul Association. Paul, who also operated the San Souci Hotel on Fourteenth Street (well-known a few years later as one of the top houses of prostitution), complained that he felt "that bum Rosenthal" had provided information to the police regarding various casinos, including theirs, along with names of various dealers. A few months before the murder, Rosenthal had complained to a *New York Sun* reporter that, unlike his place, the San Souci was allowed to reopen after it had been raided by the police. Was it coincidence that less than half a day before Rosenthal's murder, Police Commissioner Waldo ordered a raid to close down the San Souci? Sam Paul had another reason to have a grudge against Rosenthal. Supposedly, Rosenthal had sent "Spanish Louis" to kill Paul months before, according to testimony later given by Jack Rose.

Apart from Sam Paul and before the turn of the century, Rosenthal had originally held a minor controlling interest in the Hesper Club, a social hall located on Second Avenue between Fifth and Sixth Streets. After the majority owners, many by the name of Sullivan, pulled out of the operation, Herman Rosenthal assumed operational control, on a concession basis, of what was now simply a gambling casino and no longer a social hall.

Lastly, by this time Rosenthal had earned a reputation as a cop-hater. No doubt policemen other than Becker shared Becker's sentiment.

Not long after the Rosenthal shooting, tips trickled into police headquarters. One, an anonymous phone call, claimed that "Dago" Frank Cirofici had committed the crime. Other calls provided the license plate of the car seen driving away from the scene of the crime. Within hours the auto was traced to its registered owner, Louis Libby, who operated the Boulevard Taxi Service. Formerly owned by heavyweight boxing champion John L. Sullivan, the auto was the most popular one in Libby's fleet.

When police went to Libby's apartment early in the morning of July 16, he disclosed that the car had been driven by his partner, William Shapiro. Furthermore, Libby noted that Shapiro had taken the car out at 10:00 P.M. and returned it at 2:00 A.M. Libby also acknowledged that the auto had been used in a shooting. Not long after that conversation, both Libby and Shapiro were charged with homicide and locked up in the Tombs.

Despite the arrest of Shapiro and Libby, the list of potential suspects continued to grow. Jack Zelig, who had taken over the reins of Monk Eastman's gang, frequently rented the very Packard driven by Shapiro that evening. Louis William "Bridgey" Webber and Harry Vallon (born Vallinsky) had both been seen near the Metropole at the time of the shooting. Sam Paul and his association convened a social gathering in Northport, Long Island, on Sunday, July 14, the same day Rosenthal's affidavit condemning Becker appeared in the *New York World*. Reports from the affair indicated that Rosenthal's charges were the topic of much discussion. Among those attending the Sam Paul Association event were Bridgey Webber, Bald Jack Rose, Harry Vallon, and Sam Schepps.

In another development, on the advice of his attorney, James Mark Sullivan, Bald Jack Rose turned himself in to the authorities, perhaps to learn what they knew about the shooting, so he could build his defense. Rose told Police Commissioner Waldo that he had leased the Packard the night of Rosenthal's murder but that the car was not near the Metropole when the event occurred. He claimed to have been patronizing the Lafayette Turkish Baths, where he met Harry Vallon and Sam Schepps. The three then teamed up with Charles Plitt, Becker's publicist, and the four walked to the home of Dora Gilbert, Rosenthal's ex-wife, on Twenty-third Street. Rose and the others were determined to learn any dirt they could from Gilbert, to discredit Rosenthal's diatribe, which included charges against Rose as well as Becker.

By July 21 the police had arrested Bridgey Webber, Sam Paul, and Jack Sullivan. Paul, the police learned, had been at Bridgey Webber's poolroom just before the murder occurred. Sam Paul's gambling operation had been raided not only on the day of the murder but also by Becker's men on April 17. Jack Sullivan (no relation to Tim or James Mark Sullivan), born Jacob Reich, a.k.a. Jacob Rich, had visited Webber's pool hall around 1:30 the night of the murder. Harry Vallon, who reportedly was "summoned" by Bridgey Webber to come to police headquarters, tried to talk to detectives on duty, but no one paid attention. Once someone realized his true identity, he too was arrested and thrown behind bars along with his compatriots. Just two days later the police had seven men in custody in the Tombs, all on charges of murder.

Meanwhile politics got ugly between New York City Mayor Gaynor and Police Commissioner Waldo, who conducted their own mud-slinging contest, charging each other with ineptitude. In the process, Gaynor blamed a substantial portion of the city's problems on a group that he called "our Hebrew friends." The mayor pointed out that Jews represented the largest immigrant population in the city at the time and charged:

> *A large number of these are degenerates and criminals. The gambling of the city is almost all in their hands, not to mention other vices and crimes. The published names of everyone connected nearly or remotely with Rosenthal and his murder shows them to be of this same class of lawless foreigners to which he belonged.*

Rabbi Stephen Wise defended the Jewish community, suggesting that Mayor Gaynor was trying to cover up his own shortcomings, if not sins, by "inflaming the public mind against the Jews." Prominent Jewish community leaders, including Jacob Schiff, Felix Warburg, and Cyrus Sulzberger, issued a public statement denouncing crimes where Jews may have been involved but also suggesting that, "practices and vices...have up to very recent years been proverbially unknown among our people." Privately, Jacob Schiff and others set up numerous organizations, not the least of which was the Kehillah's Bureau of Social Morals, to stamp out as much Jewish involvement in crime as possible. Jews as a percentage of Sing Sing's inmate population reached its zenith in the 1910s—a whopping 16 percent. Yet one must keep in mind that the portion of New York City's population that was Jewish was more than 20 percent. (More statistics regarding the numbers of Jews in Sing Sing, their portion of the total prison population and comparative population statistics for New York City can be found in Appendix B.) It is likely that Gaynor's statements were based on anti-Semitism.

By July 29, through his attorney, Rose had arranged for himself, Vallon, and Webber to be transferred from the Tombs to the West Side Jail on West Fifty-third Street. He also ensured that all three would receive immunity in exchange for turning state's evidence. In a five-hour meeting with the district attorney, Rose's attorney, James M. Sullivan; Bridgey Webber and his lawyer, Max Steuer, who was also representing Harry Vallon; and Assistant D.A. Frank Moss, the three accused—Rose, Webber, and Vallon—testified that they had been at the Metropole when the murder occurred, but claimed they had no involvement. In fact, although Rose had originally confessed to the murder, he now stated that he and the other two felt sorry for "poor Herman." Shifting the blame, Rose quoted Becker as saying: "This man [Rosenthal] has to be stopped. Now there's only one way to do it; I'm giving you the chance. If you do it, all right; we can all go along as usual. But if you don't do it, I'll do the job myself; but before I do, I'll send every one of you up [the river] for seven years. I'll frame up something on you—I don't care what it is. I'll drop weapons in your pockets. What good will a 'squeal' do for you? Everybody knows you're gamblers and confidence men—a 'squeal' will get you nothing."

If Rose, Webber, and Vallon used the District Attorney Charles Whitman, the ambitious D.A. used Rose, Webber, and Vallon in return to go after Becker and, he hoped, those higher up in the NYPD. As state's evidence-providing witnesses, Rose, Webber, and Vallon next admitted that they had hired four gunmen through Jack Zelig, having bailed Zelig out of jail for just this purpose. According to the trio's story, they assembled with the four gunmen (Horowitz, Rosenberg, Seidenschner, and "Dago Frank" Cirofici) at Webber's poker room, tracked down Rosenthal's whereabouts, and sent the gunmen to kill him. Furthermore, according to their version of the story, Webber gave $1,000 to Rose, who in turn turned it over to Sam Schepps to pay off the killers after they had completed the task. As a result of this meeting, not only was Sam Paul released, but his homicide charge was dropped. Furthermore, police arrested Charles Becker and charged him with murder.

Rounding up the four "gunmen" took time. Dago Frank turned out to be a misleadingly easy catch. Just under two weeks after the murder an anonymous tip was phoned into Second Deputy Police Commissioner George Dougherty. The caller indicated Frank could be found at a rooming house at 523 West 134th Street. When police arrived, they came upon Dago Frank, Rose, Abraham "Fat Abe" Harris, and a warm opium pipe. Even when he arrived at the Tombs, Frank still appeared to be stoned. William Burns, who ran a private detective agency, was hired to search for the others. Burns's men traveled up and down the eastern seaboard, but to no avail. It was the commissioner's men who found Whitey Lewis Seidenshner on August 1 in Kingston, New York in the Catskills—about to board a train headed for the "West."

With Zelig dead and Frank and Seidenshner behind bars, there remained the two most probable suspects to capture. Harry Horowitz and Louis Rosenberg's ability to stay hidden kept the NYPD and Burns's agents busy throughout August and half of September. Fanning out over the country, agents searched for the "gunmen" in Boston, Tallahassee, Fargo, Denver, and a host of other cities. A team was even dispatched to Panama City after a tip came in to the effect that Horowitz and Rosenberg were enjoying a cruise from New York to California. Police had trailed members of both suspects' families, most notably their wives, who, the police declared, were most elusive. Although police followed the car the two females shared, much to their dismay the women never seemed to drive to the suspects' hangout. Instead they took either the subway or a trolley car to visit their husbands.

Tips trickled in slowly, and although seemingly innocuous, together they provided authorities with enough information to determine the hideaway. Once the two wives, in a conversation they did not know was overheard, commented that Gyp and Lefty Louis were not worried about their living situation since they could watch movies out of their rear apartment window. Another clue indicated that the building in which the two were living housed a laundry business. Between the list of laundry facilities and open air movie theaters, investigators narrowed down the possible locations where the two could be hiding. On the night of September 14 Gyp the Blood and Lefty Louis were found in their underwear, having dinner with their newlywed wives, in a three-room apartment on Ridgewood Avenue in the Glendale area of Queens, just across the border from the Ridgewood section of Brooklyn.

Between Charles Becker and the four other "gunmen," there were three court trials. The first, New York vs. Charles Becker, opened on October 7, 1912. But even before the trial could begin, a dramatic event occurred. Jack Zelig was shot to death by "Red Phil" Davidson while riding a streetcar on Second Avenue. In Zelig's coat pocket, authorities allegedly found several items of interest, including letters from each of the four "gunmen," assuring Zelig that, despite their incarceration in the Tombs, they were in good health. Also in the pocket was a "calling card" of Harry Horowitz's wife and an "advertising contract" demanding both Libby and Shapiro (owner and driver of the getaway car) to pay Zelig $100 a month from their taxi service revenues. It is not clear whether these items were actually found in Zelig's pocket or simply reported or, worse yet, planted. Curiously, as defense counsel would later point out, Davidson had lived right next door to the Sam Paul Association.

Zelig had been the boss of Horowitz, Rosenberg, and Seidenshner. In his testimony to the Grand Jury, Zelig had denied any involvement in the murder of Rosenthal. Furthermore, he had expressed anger, not at Charles Becker, but at Bald Jack Rose. According to Zelig, "I know he [Rose] framed me and I don't believe Becker knew anything about the frame-up of me...It was Jack Rose that had bailed me out...I was scared. If I had been sent to prison as it looked at one time I might be, Rose knew my friends would kill him."

To say the least, the odds were stacked against Becker in the first trial. Completely forgetting what the "facts" might have been in the case, Becker was behind the eight ball because of the personalities of the district attorney, Charles Whitman, the presiding judge (and former counsel to Schmittberger), John Goff, and Becker's defense attorney, John McIntyre. Although Goff and McIntyre were both Irish, the latter's style appeared to irk the former. In just the second day of the trial, Goff warned McIntyre that if defense counsel continued to interrupt the trial with objections, the court would have him arrested and tossed out of the courtroom.

By contrast D.A. Whitman and Judge Goff had much in common. Both were publicity hounds. The judge limited seats in the courtroom to the mass public so that more newspaper reporters could be accommodated. With the 1912 election just around the corner, Whitman was looking for something to get his name out in front of the public. The Becker trial represented just that opportunity.

Some of the most damning information against Gyp, Lefty, Whitey, and Dago came out in the first Becker trial from the mouths of brothers Morris and Jacob Luban, two petit thieves who had been serving jail time in Newark for committing forgery the previous August. Morris Luban claimed that he was at the Lafayette Baths when Becker supposedly told Rose that "Rosenthal needed to be croaked and that if he had to he would do it himself." He further testified that he had been at the Metropole Hotel the night of the murder and could identify "two or three" of the men. After this remark, the judge ordered all the men who had been indicted for the murder to appear in the court. Gyp, Lefty, Whitey, and Dago were brought into the courtroom and placed in a lineup without any other men. Luban, without any hesitation, stepped down from the witness stand and pointed his finger at all of them. Becker's attorney, John McIntyre objected to this clearly biased gesture, but Judge John Goff responded, "I do not wish to hear any further...I have overruled your objections twice before and I hope counsel will interpose no further objections."

Yet on October 27 one New York newspaper published the following:

> *Morris Luban, one of the witnesses in corroboration of Becker's plot against Rosenthal's life, has been abandoned by his family. His brother Alexander Luban of 1450 Forty-sixth Street, Brooklyn, went to the office of the Brooklyn District Attorney yesterday and demanded that the $3,000 security which he put up for Morris when the latter was arrested for forgery last fall, be returned to him. When asked why, the brother said, "Morris is no good. The family is through with him." He testified that he had overheard a conversation between Becker and Jack Rose in the steam room of the Lafayette before the shooting of Rosenthal. "I'm sure he was nowhere near the bath at the time he described. Morris is living like a lord in the Broadway Central Hotel while my property is tied up on his account!"*

Six months after his testimony in the first Becker trial, Morris Luban submitted an affidavit admitting that his testimony was false. This recantation led the Court of Appeals to brand him as a perjurer. Furthermore, Morris Luban and his brother Jake were placed on the public payroll as "attachés" of the district attorney's office. Jake was paid from November 12, 1912, to January 1913, while Morris received similar compensation from November 12, 1912 through December 1914. If that wasn't enough, before he took the witness stand at the trial, Morris Luban was given the opportunity to "conference with Rose, the chief witness for the prosecution, who immediately followed Luban on the stand. Their evidence was entirely harmonious."

Jack Rose testified regarding the "split" between Becker and Rosenthal after the raid on the latter's casino the previous April. He also swore that Becker ordered him to have Rosenthal killed and that the lieutenant promised him that he would see to it that "everybody is taken care of."

In the end, the first trial ended on October 30, 1912, with a conviction against Charles Becker. Through a series of motions, Becker and his attorneys tried to overturn the conviction by both appealing to the Court of Appeals and submitting motions for a new trial. The Court of Appeals agreed, at least initially, that the conviction should be overturned, citing that "without corroborating testimony of the two chauffeurs, no jury could convict."

In the meantime, the trial of Horowitz, Rosenberg, Seidenschner, and Frank began on November 8, 1912, pitting against each other two very different characters, Assistant District Attorney Frank Moss and defense attorney Charles Wahle. Moss could not have chosen a case that matched his interests, biases, and experience more perfectly. Born in 1860 in New York, he had made a career fighting crime, serving as president of the City Vigilance League and New York City's Police Board, succeeding Theodore Roosevelt in the latter position. As was stated earlier, Moss had served on both the Lexow and Mazet committees investigating crime in New York.

With debts of nearly $17,000 and under a cloud of scandal, Magistrate Charles Wahle had filed for bankruptcy and retired from the bench in 1908. Many newspapers campaigned against conditions in the Magistrates' courts and much of the targeting was aimed at Wahle. In at least a few cases, Wahle inexplicably reduced or eliminated the sentences of convicted criminals. Possibly some gangsters had a hold on the judge. Most likely he believed he could earn more money as a defense attorney for the most hideous of all criminals than he could on the bench. His clients in the past had included Monk Eastman and Jack Zelig. In the future he would defend Irving Wexler, a.k.a. Waxey Gordon.

Wahle presumably made a tactical error when he asked the sitting judge for the right to defend the four indicted of killing Rosenthal—Horowitz, Rosenberg, Seidenschner, and Frank—together in one case. No one knows why he made this request, but everyone agrees he was wrong to do so. By defending all four at the same time, he forced the four defendants to share the same story rather than tell stories that might have saved their individual skins. Because it would save taxpayers money and time, the prosecution gleefully accepted this proposal.

With D.A. Whitman as prosecutor and Judge Goff presiding in this case, the outcome was almost guaranteed to be the same as in the first Becker trial. Jack Rose once again was Whitman's key witness. Gyp, Lefty, Whitey, and Dago all denied under oath that they had anything to do with Charles Becker (which may have been true), but Whitman connected the four to the Rosenthal's death anyway. Goff, in his usual way, hurried the case along. The case, in fact, took just one week, and the jury reached its verdict in less than thirty minutes. All four "gunmen" were found guilty of murder in the first degree.

In January 1913 New York Governor William Sulzer held a private meeting in Albany regarding the Becker trial. He would later state: "I intended to commute Becker's sentence if the Court of Appeals sustained the verdict and then to pardon him. I knew some of the things bearing on the case and was convinced of Becker's innocence without considering the affidavits [on his behalf] submitted. I left these affidavits in the executive office when I left Albany, after my removal. Becker never should have been convicted."

After the Court of Appeals overturned Becker's conviction, a second trial began in May 1914. Morris Luban, Sam Schepps, and someone named Margolies were not used as witnesses in the trial, but four new men were recruited by the prosecution to provide basically the same story as in the first trial. Jack Rose also testified, but many of his statements in the second trial contradicted what he had claimed under oath previously. When questioned about these discrepancies, Rose's typical answer would be, "If it isn't in the record, I didn't say it." Bridgey Webber, who followed as the prosecution's next witness, answered questions exactly the same way. In short, Becker's second trial ended with the same result as the first trial—a conviction.

There is much reason to believe that not only were Dago Frank and Jacob Seidenshner not guilty of murder, but also that Harry Vallon should have been found guilty of murder and Rose, Webber, and possibly others guilty of conspiracy. Before he died, Sam Paul was quoted as saying that Harry Vallon had fired the first shot. In the Tombs, Lefty Louis told Deacon Terry, a reporter for William Randolph Heart's *American*, that Vallon had fired the first shot at Rosenthal and that he and Gyp had also fired. He added that he and Gyp had taken drugs at Bridgey Webber's, where they were also supplied guns. While incarcerated in the Tombs with Jack Sullivan, Gyp told Sullivan his contention that Vallon had fired the first shot. Henry Klein, who published his book *Sacrificed* in 1927, claimed that Harford T. Marshall, Bridgey Webber's first attorney, told him that Webber and William Shapiro, the chauffeur, had both relayed the same story—Vallon had shot first. Jimmy Keller, the manager of Jack's Restaurant, told police shortly after the murder that Bridgey Webber had informed him that Vallon was drunk and had fired the first shot.

In a more descriptive version of the story, Gyp told Jack Sullivan that Vallon was drunk and had taunted him, Lefty Louis, and Whitey, quipping: "You call yourself guerillas? Why the best of you fellers can do is to stick up a stuss house or a poker game. If I had a gun, I'd go in there and kill the S.O.B. myself." After this dare, Whitey handed Vallon his gun and added, "Let's see what you will do." Lefty and Gyp both stated that Whitey and Dago Frank did not fire a single shot.

Although Bridgey Webber and Jack Rose had severed relations with Becker a month before the murder, both had their own motives to kill Rosenthal. Bridgey Webber was unhappy not only that Rosenthal had set up a competitive gambling operation across the street from his own, but also that Beansie intended to "squeal" to the district attorney. Such revelations would go public, which might upset Webber's plans to expand his base of operations "uptown" and would also have negative consequences on the gambling business, in general. Webber clearly wanted to be the only game in town in the uptown district. Jack Rose despised Rosenthal, because the latter had thrown him out of his gambling casino and failed to recognize him as a "partner." Rose also tried to pay off Rosenthal so that Beansie would leave town. After Rosenthal turned down $2,500 in cash, author Henry Klein conjectured, Rose and Webber "probably decided that they could better serve their purposes by beating up Rosenthal. If they simply gave him money, Rosenthal would be back in a short time and start all over [demanding more]."

Henry Klein summarized their motivations the most succinctly: "It was primarily to save their own lives that Rose, Webber, and Vallon, with the aid of Schepps, 'framed' Becker, and it was only because of the anxiety of certain politicians to keep their names out of the gambling scandal that the 'frame up' succeeded. Rose and Webber were threatened that if they dragged in others [the politicians], they wouldn't live." As master "double-crossers," Rose and Webber had no qualms about changing stories or switching sides, effectively pitting one ally against another.

Quite possibly Jack Rose did not want things to go so far. His attorney told Henry Klein that "If Rose had his way there would have been no murder." Simply roughing up Rosenthal enough to get him out of town might have sufficed. What Rose did not count on was Vallon's being out of control because of drunkenness and Gyp and Lefty Louis being stoned on opium.

Becker never took the stand in either trial, both to prove his loyalty to Big Tim Sullivan and to save his job, his pension, and most important, his life. Yet in a *New York Times* article dated February 26, 1915, Becker stated: "The man who actually committed murder was Harry Vallon. The immunity contracts of Vallon, Rose, Schepps, and Webber are void, because they lied. The district attorney gave them those life insurance policies on the condition that their testimony should be the truth. I will prove that it was perjury." Several newspapers published articles that Becker offered to "turn up" five higher-ups in the NYPD if his sentence were commuted. Yet in a letter to now New York State *Governor* Charles Whitman, Becker dismissed this idea as nonsense. In his last statement to Father Curry, Becker stated, "I am sacrificed for my friends."

On Saturday evening, April 11, 1914, just days before the executions of Gyp, Lefty, and Whitey, Rabbi Jacob Goldstein conducted a Passover service and holiday meal at Sing Sing with food ordered from Harry Hirschfield, a proprietor of a hotel in Ossining. The menu, based on what "the boys" wanted to eat, included chicken soup, stuffed Hudson River bass, roasted chicken, mashed turnips, matzah, hard-boiled eggs, peaches, and macaroons. Many considered the "feast" to be the last meal the three would have. Those who believed so were almost right.

On April 13, 1914, Dago Frank Cirofici, Jacob Whitey Lewis Seidenshner, Harry Gyp the Blood, and Lefty Louis Rosenberg were successively sent to the electric chair starting at 5:38

A.M. Shortly before Dago's death, Warden Clancy read an oral "confession" from him, "I did not do the shooting. The men who fired the shots were Gyp, Louis, and Vallon. I was five miles away at the time. So far as I know, Becker had nothing to do with this case. It was a gambler's fight." Just before he was seated in the electric chair, Seidenshner struggled to provide his final words: "Gentlemen, I want to make a statement before I go. For the sake of justice, I want to make a statement. Gentlemen, them people who were on the stand who said they see me shoot—they were perjurers. I swear by God I didn't fire a shot at Rosenthal." A few who witnessed the execution thought they saw Seidenshner mouth the word "Vallon" when he "choked," although the *New York Times* reporter claimed not to have "heard" Vallon's name. Rabbi Goldstein quieted down the inmate and then pronounced the *Shema* prayer. The rabbi then led Gyp through a series of prayers, despite Gyp's having been sedated. Lastly, boyish-looking Rosenthal walked to the chair unattended, the only one of the four to do so. Unlike the others, Rosenthal required four applications of current to finish off the electrocution.

In many oral and written statements before his death, Charles Becker maintained his innocence. Yet his time to face the electric chair came on July 30, 1915. Saying goodbye, Becker began enunciating Aspirations: "Into Thy hands, O Lord, I commit my spirit." Just as he uttered the final word, the executioner swung the lever, sending the current into Becker's large body, which "surged up against the thick leather straps."

In the aftermath of the case, the Luban brothers, and Harry Vallon all remained involved in crime in one way or another, while Bridgey went in a completely different direction. Harry Vallon moved to Pittsburgh, where he spent time with family and friends in the underworld. On July 27 Vallon, outed by a local newspaper reporter who knew much about the Becker/Rosenthal affair, felt compelled to identify himself publicly. Asked whether he would provide information that would prove

Becker's innocence, Vallon replied, "Yes, if I get a chance." He continued, "They [the New York police] are hounding me to the nut factory by hanging a perjury charge over me." Vallon also complained that the NYPD had frightened "his girl" away with threats of prosecuting him. On April 24, 1917, New York State Governor Charles Whitman paroled Jacob Luban, commuting his sentence to just thirteen months. Jacob Luban served time in Sing Sing beginning in 1916 after a conviction of forgery in Brooklyn in 1915. But this was not the end of his troubles. In late 1920 Jacob was sentenced to six years in the Atlanta federal penitentiary after a charge of stealing letters from mailboxes.

Adolph Wittner, Jacob Luban's accomplice, turned state's evidence leading to the conviction of Morris Luban, who was held on $20,000 bail. Bridgey Webber went straight, becoming vice president and secretary of the Garfield Paper Box Company in Fair Lawn, New Jersey, before dying of peritonitis in 1936. Many believed Jack Rose would be murdered after Becker and the four "gunmen" died in the electric chair. Yet he appears to have lived a clean life from 1915 until his death from natural causes in 1947. He worked in vaudeville for $1,000 a week and gave many lectures at churches, preaching against gambling and other vices. When World War I started, he provided similar lectures in army training camps. Rose died in 1947 from an intestinal disorder.

6

Isidore Fishbein: Prostitution

WHEN ISIDORE FISHBEIN found himself locked in a Sing Sing cell for violating Section 2460 of the New York State Penal Code—prostitution—his case was not as clear-cut as his conviction. The three primary characters in Fishbein's court case had provided the jury with wildly different perspectives of the same events.

The plaintiff, Anna Ragovin, was just sixteen when she fell into trouble. The daughter of immigrants—Sam, who worked as a cloak operator for the firm of Weinstein and Klipstein, and Frieda—Anna was the fourth of the couple's seven children. She had left school "only recently" and had been earning $5 to $7 per week at the Hebrew Orphan Institute, creating artificial flowers. But sometime before July 1, 1913, the Institute terminated her employment.

According to Anna's testimony, early on the afternoon of July 27, 1913, she went with a friend, Mr. Bernstein, to Coney Island. At about 6:00 P.M., the couple met up with Isidore Fishbein, whom Bernstein asked to "take care of" Anna for "a half hour." After strolling along Surf Avenue, Fishbein invited Anna to "go for a drink." When Anna responded that she did not consume alcohol, Fishbein steered her to a café, where Anna sipped a sarsaparilla. Sometime later Anna agreed to go upstairs to a hotel room, where Fishbein shut the door behind her and asked if she would spend the night with him. After she refused, according to Anna, Fishbein forced her onto the bed, tore her undergarments, and "had his way with her."

Claiming to be a virgin before this transgression, Anna demanded to go home. Fishbein responded by requesting that she visit one of his friends, Hazel Jackson, adding, "We can get married tomorrow." The couple went to Jackson's apartment on the third floor of 320 West Eighteenth Street in Manhattan, where three "fellows" stood next to Jackson, who was dressed in a skirt and a kimono. After Fishbein and Jackson disappeared into the bedroom, where they conversed for a few minutes, Jackson invited Anna to join her in the room and, after showing off her wardrobe, lingerie, and "diamonds," teased, "If you stay here, you are going to have as much as I have." Fishbein quickly jumped on the bandwagon, promising Anna she could have "anything" she wanted—clothes, money, and jewelry—and that she would "be her own boss."

Jackson next undressed Anna and gave her a skirt and kimono. Anna started to cry but, after a minute, one of the three "fellows" entered the bedroom and, with Fishbein, lay down next to her on the bed. With Fishbein holding her down, one of the other men mounted her and raped Anna again.

According to Anna, for the next few days she had sex with four or five men per day, receiving $1 from each of them. As for Fishbein, Anna claimed he came to the apartment every other night. On the stand, Anna also made reference to a man she called "Little Abie." During her internment, Anna reported that she slept in the same bed with Hazel Jackson and her "tall, dark, strapping fellow," Barney Horowitz. When asked why she remained in the apartment for so long, Anna explained that, even though Jackson went out to work as a cashier at the "picture show" during the day, "I was too afraid to try to escape."

During her ten days as a captive, Anna claimed to have left Jackson's apartment only twice: to visit a Dr. Friedman on Henry Street, whom she paid $2 each visit. After the second trip to the doctor, Anna purchased a hat on Sixth Avenue, between Fourteenth and Fifteenth Streets. Asked why she did not say something about her predicament to the doctor, Anna replied, "I felt that if I told anyone, I would be shot."

After ten days Anna's 28 year-old brother Isaac, along with twelve to fifteen other compatriots, went to Jackson's apartment and forced his way inside. When Jackson threatened to shoot him if he dared to move, Isaac knocked the gun out of her hand and demanded she provide Anna clothes to wear. Several days after regaining her freedom, Anna went to the Clinton Street Police Station and reported the crime. Fishbein was arrested and incarcerated in the Tombs. On cross-examination, defense attorney Schloss held up and read from Defense Exhibit A, a purported letter from Anna to Fishbein: "I will only get into trouble for writing you if my father and mother or the D.A. finds out." Schloss entered three more items into evidence but read nothing more to the jury.

After Anna's turn on the stand, prosecutor Ellison called several additional witnesses to bolster his case. The first, Irving Rothenberg, one of the three men who visited Hazel Jackson's apartment the day Anna arrived, confessed that he had sex with Anna in the "disorderly house" and paid her $1. Next Isaac Ragovin took the stand, testifying that when he went to Jackson's apartment to fetch Anna, Hazel pulled a gun on him. According to Isaac, he responded to Jackson's threat, "If my sister should be ruined, I am going to kill you." He then "smashed" Jackson in the face and ripped the gun out of her hand. In response to an inquiry about how he discovered the whereabouts of his sister, Isaac indicated that a boy named "Little Abie" Meyerson had brought him a note, informing him that his sister was in trouble and recommending that he go and retrieve her. Apparently Little Abie heard such gossip by hanging around the corner of Broome and Ludlow Streets, near the County Jail.

Detective John J. Taft from the Eighteenth Precinct took the stand next and told the prosecutor that he arrested Hazel Jackson at her apartment with the help of Detective Bauerschmidt. Taft claimed that at the time of Jackson's arrest there were two

other "girls" in her apartment. He continued that it was Jackson
who told Taft that Fishbein could be found at an apartment
building on Geary Street in Brooklyn and that Fishbein also
used the alias of Issy Redshirt. Additionally, Jackson warned
Taft that Fishbein, who "had many gunmen," could be dangerous. According to Taft, Fishbein was arrested at 9:30 A.M. on
November 12 as he exited 66 Geary Street, the residence of his
sister, Rachel Salow.

Defense Attorney Schloss started his case where the prosecution left off—by calling Rachel Salow to the stand. Salow
testified that Anna had told her the probation officer had offered $350 and expenses if she agreed to testify against Fishbein
and then move to Chicago. Rachel further claimed Anna really
wanted to marry Fishbein "if it would keep him out of trouble."
She argued that the two families had gone "back and forth" as
to whether Anna and Fishbein should marry.

At 5 feet, 10 inches and 142 pounds, Isidore Fishbein was
the next to weigh in at the stand. Under oath, he stated that his
occupation was wood carver and finisher; he made umbrella
handles and canes for the firm of Adelman & Ryan on Kent
Avenue in Brooklyn. He also reported his age as eighteen and
his residence as 81 Bartlett Street in Brooklyn. Unfortunately
the prosecutor did not have at his disposal either Isidore's
birth certificate or the listing of the defendant in the 1900
federal census, the latter of which listed his birth in Chicago
in 1892, some four years earlier than his testimony would suggest. Isidore's parents arrived from Poland around 1890 with
their first of eight children and lived in Wisconsin as well as in
Illinois before moving to Stanton Street in the bowels of the
Lower East Side. As the third eldest child, Isidore probably
received little parental attention.

He acknowledged that he had known Hazel Jackson for three
years and claimed that the two were just friends. Fishbein testified that after he went swimming on July 27 at Coney Island, he
met Anna and a Mr. Bernstein on Surf Avenue just as they were

walking out of a hotel located above a United Cigar Store. Fishbein claimed that Mr. Bernstein asked if he could "mind Anna for five minutes" while he took care of a chore. Fishbein postulated that Anna must have done in the hotel "what a woman would do with a married man." He then explained that Anna told him that Bernstein had "ruined" her and that she had been forced out of her family's home. Furthermore Fishbein attested she was dressed "dirty."

Fishbein offered to take Anna to his friend Jackson's apartment merely as a place to sleep, he claimed. When the two arrived at Jackson's, he gave Anna $4 to pay Jackson for rent. He then left, returning the next morning to find Anna sick, so he gave her $2 to go see a doctor and then did not return for another three days. He also claimed that he gave Anna $2 to purchase a hat.

According to Fishbein, after she left Jackson's apartment, Anna visited *him* several times. The first time, they went bathing at Coney Island. The second time, she asked to be taken to a movie. The next time, Anna inquired about the address of Mr. Bernstein, since she "wanted to get her ring back." After a few more weeks Anna returned, demanding that Fishbein marry her.

Regarding his relationship with Jackson, Fishbein acknowledged that he had known her for three years and that they had met three or four times per week at the Cormitel Restaurant, on the corner of Moore and Leonard Streets in Brooklyn, "kept by Mr. Carneo." During their relationship, Fishbein testified, the couple spent time at the restaurant and nowhere else.

He denied ever forcing Anna to have sex with anyone but admitted he wrote letters to her while he was incarcerated at the Tombs. He stated that he dictated his letters to one of his fellow inmates, Harry Kershberg, who in turn scribed the letters. According to Fishbein, he was introduced to Jackson by a woman named Rosa, on the corner of Lorimer Street and Broadway, a notoriously downtrodden section of Brooklyn. On cross-examination, Fishbein claimed that in one of his letters to Anna he offered to marry her "in reparation" for what he had done. In the same letter Isidore pleaded with Anna to send him money.

The final witness to take the stand, Hazel Jackson, claimed to be 24 and originally from Montreal. After Hazel's parents had died fifteen years earlier, her aunt brought her to the United States. She concurred with Isidore's testimony that they had known each other for three years and that they were introduced to each other by her schoolmate, Rosa. Jackson worked as a cashier at the movie theater at McKibbon and Graham Avenues in Brooklyn, earning $8.50 per week. Previously she had worked as a cigarette packer. She lived at 320 West Eighteenth Street for only three months, having agreed to apartment-sit while the owner, Mrs. Goodman, went on vacation that summer.

Jackson claimed that she worked every day from early afternoon to late in the evening and that when leaving the apartment, she would lock her door. Her arrangement with Anna, Jackson claimed, was that Anna would leave the apartment while she worked at the theater and return after Jackson came home. She further testified that she had recommended that Anna visit a Dr. Friedlander located at either 117 or 127 Henry Street.

In an effort to discredit Isaac Ragovin as a witness, Jackson stated that she was told Anna's brother had spent five years in state prison. According to Hazel, this is one of the reasons that Anna did not want to return to her family's home. To rebut Anna's words, Jackson declared that Anna was "filthy and dirty" when she first appeared at Jackson's apartment.

What happened when Isaac came to retrieve Anna also differed in Jackson's account. Jackson insisted that he hit her with the back of a gun and took $19 from her. According to Jackson, Isaac then slapped Anna in the face and ordered her to dress. By Jackson's count, Isaac arrived with fifteen or twenty others. However, Jackson's credibility came into question on cross-examination, when prosecutor Ellison forced her to admit that she also went by a different name—Sadie Kuperman.

After Jackson's testimony, several of the witnesses were recalled to the stand for rebuttal. Isaac Ragovin denied pointing a gun at Jackson, striking her, or taking $19 from her pocketbook. Anna denied ever leaving Jackson's apartment other than to go to the doctor. She also reiterated her testimony that Jackson never left the apartment during the ten days she was captive there. She corroborated her brother Isaac's testimony that Jackson pointed a gun at *him* and repeated her claim that she, Jackson, and Barney Horowitz all slept in the same bed. Whatever the truth was, the jury found Fishbein guilty and Judge Crain doled out a sentence of three years and three months to six and a half years.

Two documents—Fishbein's admission record to Sing Sing and the 1910 federal census—shed additional light on Isidore's character. For the former, he claimed that his mother was deceased and that he was born in Chicago. However, while the census confirms that he was born in Illinois, the document also lists his birth year as 1892, putting his age at 21 at the time of the crime, not 18, as he stated.

In 1917, after serving less time than his minimum sentence to Sing Sing, Isidore married a woman by the name of Anna Lubin in Brooklyn. This Anna was the same age as Anna Ragovin and there are no listings for such a person in either the Ellis Island database or the federal census. The 1920 federal census does not list Anna Ragovin with her parents and three youngest siblings, who had by then moved from Brooklyn to the Bronx. It seems possible that Isidore's wife was his former accuser.

As the "oldest profession," prostitution has claimed victims everywhere. While vice represented only a small faction of Jewish criminals in Sing Sing, with other crimes such as burglary, grand larceny, and robbery representing a much larger percentage, prostitution caused emotional and physical scars that lasted for years in the Jewish community, coloring the reputation of the community and affecting family life. Because the effects of the profession were so long-lasting, while prostitutes and "johns" did not receive harsh punishment, the pimps did. Such is the case with Isidore Fishbein.

Fishbein's story is not unique. In 1915 Herman Kessler was indicted for procuring Dora Schumovitch for prostitution. Like Isidore Fishbein, Kessler used the promise of marriage as an enticement to befriend the naïve and unquestioning Dora. Knowing Kessler from the old country, she followed his orders to sleep with men "brought up" to the room he rented with his partner, Hyman Wollman. When convicted, Kessler received ten to fifteen years in Sing Sing—an even harsher sentence than Fishbein's.

Jews' involvement with prostitution predates their arrival in New York. In fact, documentation of the trade in the Old Country winds as far back as 150 years. Even before then, the Romans punished Jewish women by forcing them into brothels. By the 1860s Jewish prostitutes could be found in Warsaw, Krakow, Brussels, London, Paris, Hamburg, and Vienna. During the 1870s various censuses attempted to quantify the level of such activity. In 1872, for example, 17 percent of all prostitutes in Warsaw were categorized as Jewish. In 1873 a higher number, 47 percent, was found in Vilna, the supposedly enlightened capital of Eastern European Jewry. Of more concern were Lviv (formerly known as both Lvov and Lemberg) and Krakow, where the percentage of prostitutes who were Jewish fell just one point below the percentage of the respective cities' populations that were Jewish.

One expert on the topic of Jewish prostitution in the Old Country has argued that although poverty was indeed a cause of prostitution, it was not a sufficient cause."[1] There needed to be other forces at work. A love of "finery," that is, material wealth, was considered to be a significant factor encouraging young women to enter the trade. There also seemed to be a strong

---

[1] Edward J. Bristow, *Prostitution and Prejudice: The Jewish Fight Against White Slavery, 1870–1939*

correlation between prostitution and single-parent households. Many girls grew up without fathers, who either were conscripted into the czar's army or worked in trades in which they had to travel frequently. Additionally, one of the few strategies a woman could use to leave the Pale of Settlement—to attend a university, for example—was to register as a prostitute. Unfortunately, some of the women who signed up with ulterior motives fell into the trade. It didn't help that in Warsaw during the 1860s prostitution was actually encouraged by the then Russian governor, General Berg, who schemed to distract the city's population away from politics and make them "merry."

In the 1880s Jewish vice statistics grew like cancer cells. In the 1889 census of prostitution in the Pale of Settlement, Jewesses ran more than 200 of 289 licensed brothels. This number does not even include "clandestine houses," estimated to outnumber the licensed brothels by a factor of four. Odessa, in the Ukraine, was second only to Warsaw in vice. According to the same 1889 census, 30 of 36 licensed brothels in Odessa were managed by Jewish women.

The burgeoning of prostitution among Jews did not go unnoticed. The social-movement-oriented Bundists tried in earnest to reduce Jews' involvement in vice, only to see their efforts backfire. The Okhrana (police) recruited and used prostitutes, pimps, and other criminals as spies who could collect intelligence about the Bundists' activities. The more the Bundists protested, the more their cries fell on deaf ears in high places. If that were not enough, the Cossacks joined the criminals in retaliation against the Bundists.

In Budapest local authorities also used prostitution as a way to keep citizens' minds off politics; they established regulated prostitution in 1842. In 1865 Police Chief Thaiss actually promoted vice as a result of his own love of prostitutes. Close by, in Krakow and the rest of Galicia, vice also flourished. Lviv and Cernauti (formerly known as Chernowitz) were capitals of white slavery procurement. In 1892 procurement reached such a feverish level that a trial was held, leading to the prosecution of 27 traffickers who had recruited women and moved them to Istanbul, Egypt, and India.

Anti-Semites in Austria, already quite vocal, used the Lviv trial as yet another weapon of propaganda against the Jews. Schlesinger, a deputy in the Austrian government, argued that "even liberal deputies would not want their daughters exposed to the filth of such people." Experts on Jewish prostitution have argued that is it not surprising, then, that the visit of eighteen-year-old Hitler to Vienna in 1907 left the future dictator that much more inclined toward prejudice against the Jews. In *Mein Kampf*, Hitler wrote:

> *In no other city of Western Europe could the relationship between Jewry and prostitution and even now the white slave traffic, be studied better than Vienna...An icy shudder ran down my spine when seeing for the first time the Jew as an evil, shameless and calculating manager of this shocking vice, the outcome of the scum of the big city.*

Two additional factors probably played a significant role in Jews' involvement with vice in the Old Country. First, the Russian state's taking control of the sale and distribution of liquor eliminated a major source of income, one of only a few that Jews had previously been allowed. Galicia and Romania were hit particularly hard economically by this policy. With parents working even harder to make a living, children were neglected and open to exploring riskier activities. This situation led to children confronting their parents as they had never done beforehand and not necessarily conforming to their parents' demands or wishes.

What is more, vice did not simply remain a local thorn. It was a problem that knew no boundaries and, indeed, traveled across oceans. Jewish procurers moved their prey around the world to such faraway places as Argentina, Brazil, and South

Africa, most frequently, and to a lesser extent India and China. The Zwi Migdal, an Eastern European Jewish gang, gained notoriety as the chief source of Jewish white slave procurement. New York was one of the key export destinations for Eastern European females, whose presence intensified an already existing prostitution problem in the city. New York City vice was made up of both independent operators and more organized groups. Max Hochstim, a saloon operator who was well connected with Tammany Hall, created the Max Hochstim Association, a fraternal organization of between 200 and 600 members. The association provided insurance, death benefits, and burial plots. More important, it offered networking possibilities across its membership. Thanks to this network, for example, pimps could meet and conduct business with saloon operators. The Max Hochstim Association was, in turn, part of a larger organization euphemistically called the Independent Benevolent Association. The IBA dominated prostitution on the Lower East Side and provided protection fees, bonds, and legal costs for those who ran into trouble with the authorities. In 1911 nearly half of the 66 "establishments" that required a hotel or "excise" license (meaning that no reputable firm would provide them with bonds) were operated by Jewish immigrants. Beyond conducting business in New York, the IBA invested in houses of prostitution in Newark, Philadelphia, Chicago, Los Angeles, and San Francisco.

Hochstim owned and managed the San Souci, a four-story "Raines Law" hotel, located at 100 Third Avenue. The Raines Law included a loophole that permitted hotels to serve liquor at a time when bars could not. The hotel had a music hall on the ground floor where "low-level" vaudeville actors performed. It was so popular with prostitutes they had to place their names on a waiting list in order to work there. Twenty prostitutes conducted business there regularly, including Swedish Dolly, Pretty Francis, Sadie Klein, and Stella White. Hotel guests (johns) were required to register girls as their wives and pay $2 for a room. In addition to their taking johns' money for services rendered, bilking also occurred. It was not uncommon for other workers at the hotel to take a prostitute's clothes away, at least temporarily, as a ploy for the prostitute to abscond with additional monies from johns. (The prostitute would claim that she had never been paid in the first place, as the money hidden in her clothing could not be found.)

New York City landlords were complicit with the purveyors of vice. In the 1880s police who received complaints about brothels and gambling houses forwarded the information to the district attorney. However, residents who might have wanted to complain about prostitutes in their buildings refrained from doing so, since they knew they might be ejected if they caused trouble for their landlords. And in order to prevent prosecution, landlords frequently befriended their local politicians.

Among the most famous of both leasing agents and madams were Jacob and Rosie Hertz, who leased property from a landlord for four to five years at a time for $1,500 to $1,800 annually. In turn, they would sublet the apartments at nearly double their own rent. In addition to leasing, the couple, who had come to New York from Hungary in the 1880s, also owned and managed their own property, most notably the Columbia Hotel, located at 7 East First Street in Manhattan. This five-story building, a former flat house, had forty rooms and a bar downstairs. Also known as "Keene's Stables," the Columbia earned a reputation for having the very best prostitutes, who had to pay $40 per week for the right to work there. Johns were recruited at dance halls, delicatessens, and the Lyceum—a restaurant and café located at 302 Bowery Street. Forty girls worked there on a regular basis, and seven even called it their home. Prostitutes worked in "one-dollar" and "two-dollar" rooms, the girls working the two-dollar rooms receiving one dollar compensation for their services from management.

Rosie "Mother" Hertz, who had learned the trade from her mother, Gittle, arguably the first Jewish madam in New York, typically wore a wig and a white apron, even when she went for a walk down the street. To say the least, the Hertzes were shrewd businesspeople. In addition to the Columbia Hotel, they owned not only horses and a private house in Brooklyn but also a bank account with, reportedly, $250,000. They befriended many important New York figures, including Police Captains Diamond, Church, Hurlihee, Day, and McDermott, Inspectors McNally, Russell, and Cross, and other police officials, such as graft collector Joe Wasserman, who worked for the police captain of the Fifteenth Precinct. In an effort to quash Wasserman's threat to expose the couple, the Hertzes actually paid him $5,000 to resign from the police force. In a related move, the couple donated $1,000 each year to both the Democratic and Republican parties.

It is no wonder that prostitution in New York from the mid-1800s to World War I produced significant profits. A well-run brothel could generate $15,000 per year. During the 1880s houses of ill-repute earned, on average, $40 to $60 a day (close to $14,000 to $21,000 annually), figures that far outweighed what law-abiding citizens earned at the turn of the century. By contrast, the highest-level wage earners only occasionally topped $2,000 per year. Lower-level white-collar workers rarely earned more than $700 annually and, more typically, $300 to $500 per year.

While a select few individuals accumulated substantial wealth through vice, police and other public officials reaped benefits as well. Certain police captains, it was claimed, earned $10,000 annually from their connections. On the Lower East Side even lower-level Tammany Hall officials pocketed anywhere from $20,000 to $30,000 per year.

It was on the Lower East Side that much of New York City's prostitution took place, particularly on Allen, Chrystie, and Forsyth Streets. (In 1910 the Fishbein family lived in the heart of the Lower East Side, so prostitution was a way of life with which Isidore Fishbein was all too familiar.)

The situation was so bad that the *Jewish Daily Forward* warned male residents to avoid walking in these neighborhoods with their wives, daughters, or fiancées. If the Lower East Side was the primary center for New York City prostitution, then Allen Street was ground zero. Martin Engel, another leader of the Independent Benevolent Association and political boss of the Eighth Ward, and his brother Max purchased several houses on the street for $47,000 in the early 1890s. Max and his wife lived at 102 Allen Street, a building that consisted of twenty rooms on five floors. Prostitutes—including Hester Wolf, who was the sister of Delancey Street saloon operator Jake Wolf, and Rose Freeman—operated throughout that building. Along six blocks of Allen Street one could find 26 saloons and at least an equal number of brothels. Hyman's Saloon, at 98 Allen Street, was a popular destination of locals.

Martin Engel was also part owner of the Hotel DuNord, located at the north side of the intersection of Fifteenth Street and Irving Place. This six-story brick building housed a saloon downstairs and 146 rooms. Prostitutes working at the hotel procured their clients at any of three locales—the Alhambra Hotel, Sharkey's Saloon, and Wolfer's Bar—with 120 women using the facility at peak times.

So much illegal activity caused intense reactions against Jews. No more scathing article about Jews' role in New York City prostitution can be found than George Kibbe Turner's treatise, which appeared in *McClure's Magazine* in November 1909. Beyond blaming Max Hochstim, Martin Engel and the Independent Benevolent Association, Turner cast a shadow across the entire Jewish community. He insinuated that a young Jewish woman's future prospect for economic success was limited if she continued to work in a "sweatshop":

> *The odds in life are from birth strongly against the young Jewish-American girl. The chief ambition of the new Jewish family in America is to educate its sons. To do this the girls*

must go to work at the earliest possible date, and from the pop-
ulation of 350,000 Jews east of the Bowery tens of thousands
of young girls go into the shops. There is no more striking sight
in the city than the mass of women that flood east through the
narrow streets in a winter's twilight, returning to their homes
in the East Side tenements. The exploitation of young women
as money-earning machines has reached a development on the
East Side of New York probably not equaled anywhere else in
the world...It is not an entirely healthy development. Thou-
sands of women have sacrificed themselves uselessly to give the
boys of the family an education.

Dance halls were one of the main recruiting grounds, Turner argued, claiming that dancing was the "amusement" of choice of very poor immigrant girls because of its affordability. Whereas a moving picture costing five cents purchased thirty minutes of entertainment, the same nickel could, instead, provide an entire "evening's pleasure" of dancing.

Turner divided dance halls into three categories. "Castle Gardens," most likely named after the New York immigration center used before Ellis Island opened in 1892, had signage "plastered across their front with the weird Oriental hiero-glyphics of Yiddish posters." A two-piece band played music. "Spielers," young men with both a penchant and a talent for dancing, received free admission, and taught the females the appropriate footwork. "These lonely and poverty-stricken girls, ignorant and dazed by the strange conditions and an unknown country, are very easily secured by the promise of marriage, or even partnership," stated Turner.

The second category included dance halls north of Houston Street, catering to Polish and other "Slovak" women waiting for employment as domestic servants. The last category consisted of the "grand civic ball," which took place at several venues, in-cluding Tammany Hall's building on Fourteenth Street, Monk Eastman's Irving Hall in the Russian-Jewish district below

Delancey Street, and Kid Twist's dance hall for Galician Jews on the far (east) Lower East Side.

The term "spieler" was just one of a number of slang words used to describe the New York prostitution world. Disorderly houses were also known as "cathouses, "natches," and "butter factories." Prostitutes were known as "tots," "trotters," "cruisers" (big women), and "broads" (well-built women). Beyond prostitutes, madams, and johns, there were "cadets," also known as "runners" and "macks." Cadets were procurers, most often both handsome and persuasive. After they graduated from an apprenticeship as a "watchboy" or "lighthouse," their job was to convince naïve and unsuspecting young women to enter the trade or simply to lie to them, the promise of marriage being one of their most frequently used scams.

Among the most famous of Jewish pimps was Abe "The Rabbi" Rabbelle, a pioneer cadet who started his career in the 1890s and at one time was the president of the Independent Benevolent Society. Born in Russia in 1858, Rabbelle stood 5 feet, 6 inches tall and was clean-shaven and of medium build. Before his departure from the city in 1901, due to a temporary clampdown on New York's prostitution problem, Rabbelle ran a phony employment agency. After spending several years in Pittsburgh to escape prosecution, he returned to New York and became a partner in Fisher's Restaurant, located at 76 Second Avenue, with the original owner, Mr. Frisch. Rabbelle befriended a server at the restaurant nicknamed "Poor Mary the Slovak" and made her pregnant. After she threatened to turn him in to the authorities if he did not marry her, Rabbelle, with the help of Louis Segal, bought out the restaurant. Almost five years later Rabbelle sold out his share of the venture and purchased Kastner's Restaurant, located down the street at 92 Second Avenue. Among the large cast of characters who hung around the renamed Rabbelle's Café were Sleepy Mike, a stuss (card game) house owner; Kid Rags, a gambler; Cockeye Weiss, an ex-waiter; Annie Moskowitz, a prostitute; Dave Weiner, a burglar; and Charlie Argument, a strike breaker.

Polly Adler became one of the most successful of the madams. Named Pearl at birth in Yanow, Belarus, in 1902, she was forced by her father to leave her homeland. Adler was the first family member to get established in the New World. After being raped by her shirt factory foreman, she was led into the world of prostitution. In 1920 she befriended a gangster, who furnished her with an apartment. Whenever he and his wife were not around, Adler recruited women to entertain his friends and to establish her own enterprise as a madam. Despite her arrest in 1922, Adler opened a lingerie shop and then, after the failure of this business, started a series of extravagant brothels. In her memoir, *A House Is Not a Home*, she would state unequivocally that her goal was to become "the best goddam madam in all America."

Although Rabbelle, the Hertzes, and Polly Adler were the most prolific and successful operators, there were many more, far smaller, independent operators. These independents typically had a half to a full dozen prostitutes and an equal number of cadets working to procure clients. Their facilities were located throughout the city but most highly concentrated below Forty-sixth Street and above 100th Street.

The New York community, and to a lesser degree the federal government, were up in arms about prostitution during the decades before and after the turn of the century. Early in this period, probably no one in New York City protested more against vice than Dr. Charles Henry Parkhurst, pastor of the Madison Square Presbyterian Church. In the 1890s Parkhurst became head of the Society for the Prevention of Crime, an organization founded in 1878 by Presbyterian minister Howard Crosby. In 1892 Parkhurst challenged Tammany Hall, claiming it "manufactured" criminals rather than converted them. His efforts as a crusader against vice paid off: in 1894 the New York State Chamber of Commerce funded an investigation to explore not only the problem of prostitution but also corruption in Tammany Hall, which, Parkhurst and others claimed, provided protection for gamblers and hookers alike. The "Lexow Commission," headed by Republican State Senator Clarence Lexow from Nyack, included reformers John Goff, William Jerome, and Frank Moss, the counsel for Parkhurst's Society for Prevention of Crime. Among the many who testified before the Lexow Commission was Martin Engel, the Tammany Hall leader and brother of Max Engel, the brothel owner. The investigation exposed payoffs to police in exchange for leniency in cracking down on and disciplining the perpetrators of vice. In 1896, as a result of the findings of the Lexow Committee, State Senator John Raines introduced and helped pass legislation that sought to increase state revenues, diminish the Democratic Party's control over saloons, and reduce the level of prostitution. The new law levied excise taxes of $1,200 per year and required an additional $1,800 bond, which would be forfeited for any violation of the law. Despite best intentions, the new law, which gave hotels but not saloons the right to sell liquor on Sundays, backfired and prostitution continued to flourish. As a result, saloon keepers annexed rooms and then applied for liquor licenses, giving rise to even more houses of ill repute.

In 1899 the Mazet Commission (named after the committee's chairman) pursued a similar path and, like its predecessor, the Lexow Commission, found substantiated claims of corruption within the New York City Police Department and a lax policy toward vice. Both the Lexow and Mazet Commissions' reports also concluded that Jews participated in vice and extortion in significant numbers. In 1897 Frank Moss, not only one of the Lexow Commission members but also counsel for both Reverend Parkhurst's Society for the Prevention of Crime and the Mazet Commision, wrote a scathing report, called *American Metropolis*, in which he wrote about Jews' (especially the more recent immigrants') involvement in New York City crime, using the term "New Israel" to differentiate the Eastern European Jewish immigrants from their German counterparts ("Old Israel").

In 1905 the Committee of Fourteen, a private nonsectarian citizens' group, was founded with the aim of abolishing Raines Law hotels. That same year, Abe Schoenfeld, investigator for the Jewish community's Kehillah, reported that in a random sample of 104 prostitutes who used such hotels, nearly 30 percent were Jewish, exceeding the percentage of New Yorkers of the same faith. Furthermore, between 1907 and 1911, of the 181 Raines Laws hotels targeted for closure by the Committee of Fourteen, nearly 45 percent were owned by Jews or Germans. The Federal Immigration Commission in 1907 produced a report implicating the French and the Jews as the worst purveyors of vice:

> There are two nationalities who may be said to control the disorderly house business in New York, namely the French and Jewish...while French houses are said to be worse in their practices, they are not, from the civic side at least, to be so much feared as the Jewish. The French people engaged in this business prefer to run their business as nearly compatible with the rules laid down by the police department as possible...The Jew on the other hand, has been taught early in life the value of morality and decency, and does not take up this business unless he is thoroughly vicious and bad.

Fodder like this would be used years later, in 1911, when the United States Immigration Commission reported that "A large proportion of the pimps living in the United States are foreigners." Furthermore, the commissioners singled out the Jews and the French as the groups most involved in the procurement of prostitutes. Evidence to the contrary—showing that prostitution was as much if not more of a problem with native-born females than with immigrant women—would not appear until 1913, when Katherine Bement Davis provided results of a study she conducted on prostitutes committed to state reformatories.

Davis, the superintendent of the state reformatory at Bedford Hills, reported that American-born females contributed more than their representative share to the overall number of prostitutes. She provided the following opinion for this phenomenon:

> *When we remember that here we have a group in which the fathers and mothers belong to a civilization with speech, tradition and habits different from those of the country in which they are living, the children, native-born Americans with American companions and American schooling, adopt ideals often not of the highest and are very apt, even when quite young, to feel that they know more than their parents.*

In an effort to fend off potential harm to Jews, both physically and emotionally, the Jewish community established numerous organizations and benefited from the efforts of a few strong-willed, civic-minded constituents. In 1893 the National Council of Jewish Women was founded during the Chicago World's Fair, dedicating itself to "service of faith and humanity through education and philanthropy." In 1904 the NCJW responded to a request by the United States government to participate in immigration affairs and the prevention of the exploitation of alien women. The organization sent Yiddish-speaking Mrs. Meirowitz to Ellis Island to record the names of all unaccompanied Jewish females between the ages of twelve and thirty. Meirowitz and other NCJW members distributed leaflets in multiple languages at Ellis Island and other immigration centers warning unsuspecting immigrant women to "beware of those who give you addresses, offer you easy, well-paid work, or even marriage." Meirowitz's salary was paid by yet another Jewish organization, the Baron de Hirsch Fund.

It was also in 1893 that a young nursing student, Lillian Wald, first met Jacob Henry Schiff at the home of his mother-in-law, Mrs. Betty Loeb. Mrs. Loeb, the wife of Solomon Loeb, the co-founder of the investment bank Kuhn, Loeb, & Co., had been supporting a "Sabbath School" on Henry Street on the Lower East Side. Wald, a volunteer teacher at the school, had an idea for establishing a facility to help nurse the poor, even if they could not pay for the services. Schiff provided initial funding to conduct this experiment, which proved enormously successful. With two years' experience in helping 125 families and with additional financial support from Schiff, Wald and Brewster founded the Henry Street Settlement, which continues today, helping an estimated 100,000 per year, according to the organization's website. Wald's reputation knew no bounds, and she earned respect from both Tammany Hall politicians and Republicans. In a 1910 speech she declared that employment agencies were "used as markets for selling girls for prices ranging from $3 to $50 or as procuring places where immoral women and men came and selected their victims." In 1924 Wald rose to such prominence that Eleanor Roosevelt recruited her as an advisor to help with Roosevelt's vision of the New Deal.

Jacob Schiff, a German immigrant and highly successful Wall Street financial mogul, was not above helping his less fortunate co-religionists. By March of 1893 he had already given financially to the struggling Jewish Prisoners' Association and reorganized it into the Society to Aid the Jewish Prisoner. This organization oversaw the selection of rabbis who went into various correctional facilities in the New York area during Jewish holidays and on other special occasions to provide both food and entertainment to the Jewish inmates. In 1914 Schiff donated $5,000 to the "vice fund" of the Jewish community's Kehillah organization. He was joined in this effort by fellow Jewish community leaders Adolph Lewisohn and Felix Warburg, who contributed $5,000 and $2,000 respectively to the cause.

In an effort to confront what they saw as an escalating problem of juvenile delinquency, the Schiffs, the Loebs, and other uptown German Jews founded the first all-Jewish reformatory, the Hawthorne School, in Westchester County in 1907. Located on a 260-acre site overlooking the Hudson River, the facility included a baseball diamond, a football field, and a running track. By 1917 a separate facility, the Cedar Knolls School for Jewish Girls, had been built on the Hawthorne property, allowing girls to be moved from the school's outmoded building in Bronxville.

The Jewish Protectory and Aid Society, which was also established in 1907 and under whose auspices the Hawthorne School fell, kept track of Jewish females who found their way into court because of involvement in prostitution. Annual reports of the organization and later those of the Jewish Board of Guardians, which took control of the JPAS in 1922, tracked women who were arrested for prostitution. Between 1912 and 1921 the portion of those prostitutes who were arraigned hovered somewhere between 14 and 19 percent. The Sisterhood of the Spanish and Portuguese synagogue, Shearith Israel, also logged statistics on this subject and listed them in their annual reports.

Another maverick, Alice David Menken, took direct aim at the Jewish prostitution problem. Born in 1870 and raised in privilege, Menken married Mortimer Morange Menken, a successful attorney. While she could easily have lived the easy life as a country club wife, Menken decided instead to devote her energies to social service. She helped found the Sisterhood of Congregation Shearith Israel in 1896 and served as its president from 1900 to 1929. Furthermore, she recruited other Sisterhood members to join in her crusade against delinquent Jewish women. The Sisterhood's first undertaking was the creation of the Neighborhood House, an institution on the Lower East Side very similar to Lillian Wald's Henry Street Settlement.

Menken's more lasting contribution was her work with delinquent females. In 1908 she helped found the Jewish Board of Guardian's Women's Division and served as its vice-president. Menken also chaired a NCJW committee, working with women paroled from New York State correctional facilities. Not one to rest on her laurels, she helped to launch Jewish Big Sisters in 1911 and served on the Board of Managers of the New York State Reformatory for Women after receiving an appointment from New York Governor Alfred E. Smith. Undoubtedly the Jewish community's most vigorous weapon against vice was its own organization, the Kehillah. Abe Schoenfeld, the agency's chief investigator, followed the comings and goings of numerous Jewish criminals, focusing on prostitutes, pimps, and madams. Schoenfeld spent an inordinate amount of his time from 1911 to 1914 tracking and attempting to foil the activities of Abe Rabbelle. Schoenfeld achieved at least one of his goals, shutting down Rabbelle's Columbia Hotel in late 1914. Although Rabbelle's center of prostitution was closed, however, he never spent any time in jail.

Ironically, Fishbein's and Kessler's downfall was their small-timer mentality. If they had been members of any pimp association or been friendly with the police or politicians, neither one might have laid eyes on the famous prison where they ended up spending a total of ten years.

Israel Dobreniewski:
Abandonment and Bigamy

THE DREARY WEATHER in New York on January 3, 1911, perhaps foreshadowed not only the difficulties Ysrael Dobreniewski would encounter entering America but also the dark and mysterious life that lay ahead of him. That day the weather gods layered the city with a fog not seen in many years, a fog so thick that ships remained anchored offshore for a full 24 hours before their captains could maneuver them into port. Waiting vessels included the Royal Mail liner *Oruba* arriving from Southampton, the *Alliance* from the Isthmus of Panama, the *Afghan Prince*, the Hamburg-American liner *Siberia* from Kingston, and the *Maracaibo* from Venezuela and Puerto Rico—all packed with immigrants eager to go ashore. Ysrael's patience may have been tested even more than that of the other fellow passengers, as he paced the decks of the North German Lloyd liner *Breslau* from Bremen, waiting two days to disembark.

We don't know why Israel (Ysrael's Americanized name) left his home town of Bialystock. It might have been to avoid the harsh economic and political climate and seek prosperity in America. Bialystock, one of the largest Jewish communities in the Pale of Settlement, was founded by a very small number of Jews who settled in the area in 1749. By 1897 the city's population had grown to 42,000, with Jews representing 64 percent of the total. Just after the turn of the century anti-Semitism terrorized Bialystock's Jewish community. Between 1905 and

1906 a strong Jewish labor movement provoked Russian authorities, who tried to quell the unrest. On the first three days of June 1906 the czar's agents shot and murdered 110 Jews and destroyed a large percentage of the Jewish community's property. By the time Israel departed, the Jewish population suffered from pogroms, famines, and lack of economic control over their own destiny. After Israel and his family survived the pogroms, he most certainly felt pressure to earn enough money to support his growing family—as a tinsmith. He went from home to home, refinishing pots and pans and capitalizing on people's fear that the surface below the worn-off copper was toxic. Israel's business usually peaked just before Passover, as families readied their cookware for the festive holiday, but the rest of the year was often very quiet for people of his trade.

It is also possible that Israel simply wanted to leave his family and never see them again. At that time arranged marriages were commonplace in Eastern Europe, often bringing together under one roof two people who had little in common except the animosity that results from irreconcilable differences. According to a few extant documents, Israel had married Zelda, a.k.a. Sadie, in Warsaw in December 1902. However, it is more likely that they were married in Bialystock, since Israel's parents and children all lived in that town. Within nine years the couple had produced five children: Basike (Bessie), born in 1903; Rose (also known as Rachel), born in 1905; Leib (later known as Louis), born in 1906; Abram, born in 1908; and Czerna (Jennie), born in 1911.

Whether because of financial or emotional hardship, Israel left his wife and children and headed for Bremen, where, on December 22, 1910, he boarded the *S.S. Breslau* for direct passage to New York. At the age of 24 Israel was in good company on the *Breslau*, with the likes of Abraham Schulman, a 23-year-old tailor from Minsk; Schmuel Schlossberg, an 18-year-old from Smorgon, and Leib Weinstein, a 22-year-old locksmith from Lvov—all Jews who hoped for a better life in the New

World. These were some of the lucky immigrants who were able to escape the czar's oppression and pass through America's doors while they still remained relatively open and welcoming. The year 1911 would turn out to be near the end of the nearly forty-year "third wave" of Jewish immigration, following earlier migrations of Dutch and German Jews. The Congressional Immigration Act of 1917 enlarged the classes of people who could be excluded from admission to the United States.

According to the ship's manifest, Israel intended to meet his brother-in-law, Wolf Cohen, a plasterer who lived at 84 Madison Street in Manhattan. For Israel, however, obtaining entry to the United States would take longer than normal. On the second floor of Ellis Island's main building, Inspector di Mieli placed an X by Israel's name on the manifest, an indication that his admission would be delayed—if not denied. While most immigrants were detained either because they did not have enough money or their American-based friends or relatives had not yet arrived to receive them, di Mieli marked "420" on the manifest as his reason for holding Israel: a health problem called an "astrophage," or blindness in his left eye.

In 1907 legislation had increased the number of health issues officials could use to prevent entrance to the country. The new law barred immigrants who were suffering from tuberculosis, epilepsy, or physical disabilities. It is likely that immigration agents worried that Israel suffered from trachoma, a highly contagious eye infection, common in Eastern and Southern Europe, which could cause blindness and death; it caused more exclusions at Ellis Island than any other disease.

After his debarkation, officials directed Israel to the Ellis Island hospital for further observation and care before he could receive a discharge to the next stage of the entry inspection. At some point, once he was given a clean bill of health, Israel reached Registry Hall, where he joined other immigrants speaking Polish, German, Italian, Yiddish, and Russian. At one end of the hall Israel responded to 29 questions that verified information already answered on the ship manifest—his name, age, occupation, marital status, and so on. Finally, on January 6, he received the green light to go ashore.

In addition to his in-laws, other relatives had preceded Israel on the great journey to America. Just one month earlier, his brother Motel had arrived from Hamburg on the *S. S. Blucher.* According to the passenger ship manifest, Motel stated that he, too, planned to contact Wolf Cohen upon arrival in New York. Israel's sister Baschke and brother Spurelic arrived in July 1912 and April 1913, respectively. Israel's other brother, Benjamin, had immigrated sometime before Spurelic's arrival. This type of sequential immigration was common and can perhaps be explained by the uncertainty of life in the New World. If families sent different members at different times—and to different locations at well—the odds were that at least someone would succeed and maintain the family legacy in the New World while others could sustain the remaining family in the Old. In addition, families typically sent either the smartest or strongest member, who would be most likely to succeed and eventually pay the passage of the remaining family.

What Israel did between his arrival in this country in January 1911 and the summer of 1912 is unclear. On August 5, 1912, Sadie arrived on the *S. S. Lapland* from Antwerp with sons Leib and Abram in tow. The other three children were temporarily left behind with relatives. Only four years old at the time, the *Lapland* was luxurious compared with the *Breslau.* Built in 1901 and measuring 7,524 tons and 449 feet in length, the *Breslau* had one funnel, two masts, twin screws, and four engines capable of producing a combined total of 3,600 horsepower and a "service" (normal) speed of twelve knots. Operated by a crew of 94 to 120, the ship could accommodate 66 passengers in Second Class and 1,660 in steerage for its twelve day trip across the Atlantic. By contrast, at 605 feet in length and with a gross tonnage of 17,540, the *Lapland* could ferry 450 first-class, 400 second-class, and 1,500 steerage-class passengers at a remarkable seventeen knots.

Normally, mothers and children were detained until their safety could be ensured through the delivery of a telegram, letter, or prepaid ticket from a local relative. Held for three days before being released, Sadie, Leib, and Abram were served three square meals a day and given beds in Ellis Island's Baggage and Dormitory Building. However, Israel was not at Ellis Island when his family arrived because Sadie had not informed him of her plans.

Despite her diminutive 5-foot stature, Sadie was no pushover. She suspected something was not right and did not want to wait for her husband to pay her passage to America. Listed on the manifest as Sadie Alperin, not Dobreniewski, she indicated that she planned to reunite with Hersh Alper, her *husband*, who lived in Manhattan. Hersh, who in the United States went by the name of Harry Alper, was indeed related to Sadie, but he was not her husband. He had married Sadie's late sister Minnie. It is likely that Harry not only had kept in touch with Sadie but also had sent her either a ticket for the ship passage or money to purchase one in Europe. Minnie had died in 1911 and Harry had been forced to send his children to the Brooklyn Hebrew Orphan Asylum. Conceivably, Harry wanted Sadie to parent his children. It is also possible that Harry knew that Israel was not where others expected him to be, and he might have hoped that, in the absence of Israel, Sadie might marry him and pick up where Minnie had left off.

Nobody knows if Israel ever met up with Harry Alper or if he saw Sadie and their two children immediately after their arrival. However, we do know that they were eventually reunited, because records indicate that sometime before April 1913 Israel disappeared from his residence at 151 Thatford Avenue in the Brownsville section of Brooklyn and that Sadie lodged a complaint with the police, who tracked Israel down in Pittsburgh. They then moved him to Wilkes Barre, Pennsylvania, and, after yet another three and a half weeks, transferred him to Brooklyn's Raymond Street Jail to await sentencing. On May 12, 1913, Judge Faucett of the Kings County Court handed Israel, a.k.a. Samuel Dobreniewski, a sentence of one to two years and a fine of $500 for the crime of abandoning his children. One day later, dressed in a zebra-striped uniform, Israel walked into Sing Sing. Upon his imprisonment, prison officials described Israel, a.k.a. Sam, as having a dark complexion, brown eyes, dark brown hair, a "narrow" forehead, a "long, large" nose, a small mouth, medium lips, and missing five teeth. He measured 5 feet, 4 inches, 137 pounds.

Meanwhile the remainder of Israel's family found its way to the New World. On September 16, 1913, Sadie's sister, Ittke Bendnar, escorted daughters Bessie and Rose to New York on the *S.S. Kroonland*, while Jennie, Israel, and Sadie's youngest child, stayed behind in Bialystock with her grandmother. According to the manifest, Ittke planned to rendezvous with her sister Sadie Dobreniewski, living at 238 Thatford Avenue in Brooklyn.

With Israel in Sing Sing and unavailable to support the family, Sadie made the difficult decision to have three of her children endure their own form of institutionalization; Abram, Louis (Leib), and Rose were admitted to the Brooklyn Hebrew Orphan Asylum on October 30, 1913. Sadie may well have been humiliated and embarrassed by the situation, since she told the asylum authorities her name was Jennie Bindler (Bindler or Bendnar was her maiden name). Louis was discharged on May 8, 1914, into the custody of Sadie's sister, Mrs. Eva Peskoff. Rose and Abram remained captive until September 28, 1914, when the orphanage released them into Sadie's waiting arms.

Judging from the growth of the Orphan Asylum, Sadie and her brother-in-law were far from alone in having to relinquish their children for a period of time. Because of spouse desertion and parents giving up their children, the number of Jewish children living away from home climbed steeply. The Hebrew

Benevolent Society established the original New York Hebrew Orphan Asylum in Manhattan in 1860. Located on the north side of Twenty-ninth Street between Eighth and Ninth Avenues, the HOA originally had a capacity for only thirty children. By 1863 it had moved into new facilities on East Seventy-seventh Street between Third and Lexington Avenues and could accommodate 200 boys and girls. Sixteen years later the HOA overflowed with nearly 300 children, exceeding state statutes. Shortly thereafter, the Hebrew Sheltering and Guardian Society (HSGS) assumed operational responsibility for the asylum and moved it to a rented house on Fifty-seventh Street and First Avenue. By August 1884, HSGS had again moved the facility to a new building on Amsterdam Avenue between 136th and 138th Streets, where the facility included classrooms, a dormitory, two infirmary wards, laundry facilities, a bakery, and swimming pools. Over time, many prominent Jewish leaders served as trustees to HSGS, among them the Bloomingdales, Philip and Emanuel Lehman, William Guggenheim, Julius Goldman, Victor H. Rothschild, and Jacob F. Bamberger.

Strangely enough, the HOA and Sing Sing had at least a couple of things in common. Both facilities received funds from movie moguls Jack and Harry Warner to build a gymnasium. Both benefited from the generosity of Adolph Lewisohn, a philanthropist who made his fortune in the mining business. Lewisohn provided funds to build the 6,000-seat Lewisohn Stadium right across the street from the HOA in Manhattan. The Roman-columned amphitheater hosted concerts for fifty years and helped to launch the careers of several artists, including George Gershwin and Ethel Merman. Lewisohn also served as president of the HSGS, the sister organization to BHOA. Beyond tending to the needs of the young and destitute, Adolph Lewisohn was a pioneer in New York State prison reform.

In 1878, because of the increasingly large number of needy children in Manhattan alone, HOA's Board of Directors voted not to accept any children from Brooklyn, which at that time was still operating as a separate city. That same year, New York State granted a charter to open the Brooklyn Hebrew Orphan Asylum to house, educate, and maintain "Hebrew orphans" until they were capable of taking care of themselves. Brooklyn Jews convened and raised enough capital to house sixteen children at 384 McDonough Street, in the Bedford Stuyvesant neighborhood. The Hebrew Benevolent Society provided funds to build a separate facility in Brooklyn, and in 1892 a cornerstone was laid on the block bordered by Ralph, Howard, Dean, and Pacific Streets. The "House on the Hill" took years to build, but eventually its doors opened and the institution housed up to 1,200 children at its peak. The asylum's six-story building combined elements of both Queen Anne and Richardsonian Romanesque architecture styles, with round bays and lots of gables and dormers.

Life in the Brooklyn Hebrew Orphan Asylum was a mixed blessing. One BHOA alumnus wrote, "Being part of a mass gave me a feeling of belonging…For every older fellow ready to beat me up, there was one who patted me on the back and gave me a lift when I needed it." Another alumnus reported that the home had "clean laundry, plenty of heat from the boiler room, clarinet lessons, regular if unsatisfying meals, medical care, and an occasional nickel fare salvaged for other uses by walking instead of riding."

Sometime between 1914 and 1915 Israel Dobreniewski and his institutionalized children all gained their freedom and reunited with Sadie in Brooklyn. According to the 1915 New York State census, the family lived at 157 Thatford Avenue in Brooklyn, and Israel worked as a roofer. Sadie, according to family legend, found employment as a waitress at a restaurant in Queens.

But Israel continued to neglect his family. According to court transcripts, Sadie accused him of committing adultery with "various" women, although she could not cite names or places. She also claimed that between January 1916 and September

1918 Israel had married another woman in Kings County. As it turned out, this accusation held merit: Israel, who lived at 221 South Third Street in Brooklyn, married Sonia Wilehoff on December 29, 1917, at her home at 1347 Forty-fourth Street, Brooklyn. Called before the court, Israel confessed to the charge of bigamy and, on September 3, 1918, Judge Marcus Campbell sentenced Israel, now known as Israel Fox, to four years of hard labor at Sing Sing. The admission record for Israel's second term indicates that his weight had decreased to 130 pounds.

In spending one term in Sing Sing for abandonment and another for bigamy, Israel was rather unique. Most abandoners and bigamists learned their lesson after one term in Sing Sing, deciding upon release either to remain with their wives and families or to leave once and for all. Israel learned his lesson more slowly. After serving his first term, he returned to Sadie, only to quickly resume philandering.

Beyond seeking child support from Israel, Sadie was not yet finished with him. In April 1921 Sadie filed a lawsuit against Israel to obtain an official divorce and in November 1922 the case went to trial. In addition to Israel and Sadie, the trial featured one more witness: Nathan Levitas, a process server for the Jewish community's National Desertion Bureau. Levitas testified that he had first met Israel while "patronizing the couple's restaurant" in 1916. Levitas believed that Israel and Sadie operated the restaurant, but it is more likely that Israel simply hung around the place and collected free meals. Levitas told the court he served Israel with a summons with the words "Action for absolute divorce" at 356 Second Avenue in Manhattan on June 16, 1922. Levitas also testified he saw Israel on January 27, 1918, at 7:00 A.M., on the third floor at 103 Essex Street. Levitas knocked on the door and asked for "Mr. Fox." Someone replied, "Is that Sam?" Levitas replied affirmatively, and Israel, who appeared to have just gotten out of bed and was dressed only in "underclothes," opened the door. The process server then saw a woman jump out of the bed, also in undergarments.

When Israel took the stand, he acknowledged that he had previously been convicted in 1918 for bigamy and that he went by the names of Samuel Dobreniewski, Israel Fox, and Israel Dobreniewski. He also acknowledged that he was the defendant being sued by Sadie. On December 13 the New York Supreme Court Justice ruled in favor of Sadie, saying she was entitled to a provisional divorce.

WHEN ISRAEL WAS sentenced for bigamy, he had plenty of company. Beginning in the 1870s, the number of bigamy cases reported by New York newspapers mushroomed.

Jews were not the only group to commit the crime in the New World, where bigamy cut across most population boundaries, going back to the early part of the nineteenth century. Several conditions created the optimal setting for the high incidence of this crime. First, for nearly two centuries divorce had been difficult to obtain in the state of New York. Until 1966 the state granted divorce only in cases where adultery could be proven. In addition, the price associated with divorce far exceeded the resources of most couples; fees were usually more than $100 per person (the equivalent of $1,800 in 2005). Perhaps most important, because of the high number of common-law marriages in the United States and the absence of *banns* (advertisements of marriage), which had been a mainstay in the Old Country, a spouse's task of proving bigamy was an arduous one.

Furthermore, the way New York State dealt with the crime changed over time. Before 1860 only about 10 percent of convicted bigamists received jail sentences. After the Civil War, however, marriage, pornography, prostitution, and birth control were subjected to increased state regulation and law enforcement. In New York, just as in London and Paris, the state took over from families and clergy the role of enforcing marital contracts. Judges doled out increasingly severe punishment in the hope of stabilizing marriage as an institution. During the next two decades nearly three-quarters of those convicted of bigamy received some sort of prison sentence, often for as many as five years. Bigamy was not unique to the New World either. The "marriage crisis" caused havoc in London and Paris as well, although the problem in America seemed to draw more attention. The freedoms of the New World led to the consideration of marriage as only a transitional relationship. For every man who was convicted of bigamy, there were many more who were not caught. Perhaps husbands had no intention of abandoning their wives when they set out for the New World but, after arriving and seeing the difference between the women of the *shtetl* (small village in the Old Country) and those in the United States, they were tempted. In the New World, long gone were lengthy courtships and *shidduchim* (family-arranged marriages), as was the social custom of remaining married to your family-arranged wife.

The situation in the Old Country regarding divorce differed dramatically from New York. In fact, divorce occurred frequently in Eastern Europe. Under Jewish law, husbands could exercise their prerogative to obtain a divorce, even without their wives' approval, under several circumstances: first, husbands could charge "antenuptual sexual activity"—the disclaimer of a wife who claimed to be a virgin before the marriage. In such cases, if the husband were a member of the priestly class of *cohanim* Jews, not only was divorce permitted, it was also sometimes obligatory. Another cause for divorce was the husband's mere *suspicion* that his wife had committed adultery—no eyewitness or other proof was necessary. The third and most controversial reason was the accusation that the wife was a *moredet*, a "rebellious one." Some rabbinical authorities interpreted this "rebellion" as the wife's refusal to perform "the seven types of household duties" specified by Jewish law, most commonly, sexual relations. A fourth major reason given for divorce was the inability to bear children. More precisely, a man could receive a divorce if his wife did not provide children within the first ten years of the marriage. If a wife miscarried, the term of the marriage was reset to the date of the miscarriage. Unfortunately for women, there were many other miscellaneous reasons a husband could dissolve the marriage.

Women in the Old Country, at least in theory, also had the right to initiate a divorce although in practice this situation occurred much less often and was much more problematic. The first reason women could use for divorce was that the husband became "repugnant" because of a physical ailment or occupation. Specifically, men had to divorce if they suffered from "intolerable odors" from their mouths or noses or if they suffered from leprosy. A woman could even prevent a marriage from taking place if she knew about such a condition beforehand. Second, a wife could initiate a divorce if her husband failed to fulfill his basic marital obligation of earning a living in order to provide food and shelter. If a husband specifically declined to provide such support, the wife was entitled to a divorce because she was suffering as though living "in a basket with a serpent." Another reason for divorce was when the husband refused to have sexual relations with his wife for more than six months. Finally, wives could ask for a divorce when their husbands were impotent.

The roots of wife desertion trace back to the rabbinical interpretation of Deuteronomy 24:1–4, where the initiative for the issuance of a *get* (religious divorce) lies solely with the husband. The Talmud, however, went so far as to rule that a woman who could furnish proof that her husband had died could be declared a widow and, therefore, was free to remarry. Before granting such a request, however, rabbis searched for the missing husband in an effort to persuade him either to reconcile with his wife or to grant her a Jewish divorce.

If a woman could not obtain a *get*, she was considered an *agunah* ("chained wife"). The agunah problem usually fell into one of four categories. The first category was a woman whose husband obtained a divorce in the civil courts but refused to give his wife a *get*, from either malice or greed. Most of the time the husband wanted to avoid both the hassle of getting a divorce and the associated costs, including an obligation to repay the dowry provided for in the *ketubah* (wedding contract). Sometimes, the husband even tried to extort money from his wife as payment for the *get*. A second, malicious situation was the husband's leaving the wife without a trace, so that he was not around to provide the get that the Jewish law required. Third, if a husband died during military service or in a mass explosion, for example, there was no firm evidence that the husband was dead; therefore, neither could he be declared "legally" dead nor could the marriage be dissolved. Fourth, a childless woman could not request a divorce from her husband, even though he had died. Instead, the law required that the wife marry her brother-in-law and name her first-born after her late husband. In order to be free of this "chain," a widow was required to obtain a release from her brother-in-law before she could remarry.

The *agunah* problem was not so formidable while the Jewish community in the Old Country held onto its authority and could enforce its decisions. Unfortunately, because of the frequent uprooting of the communities, migration, and transplantation of individuals, as well as natural disasters such as famines, or massacres, the Jewish community lost its power over these matters and the number of *agunot* increased substantially.

Advertisements, most notably in the Yiddish-speaking newspapers *Hamelitz* and *Hamaggid*, often spoke of women seeking their lost husbands. The following appeared in the July 25, 1893, edition of *Hamelitz*:

> *It has been two years since my husband left me and my child in deprivation and great poverty because, six weeks after our marriage, he deceptively took [our] money, saying that he was going for a few days to the town of Bialystock to purchase instruments for his work; he settled down [in another town], and from then on I do not know where he has gone. My husband's*

*name is Eliezer Zeidman, born in the town of Brisk. He is
twenty-three years old, tall, with black hair, a short black
beard, a long nose, with one crooked and short leg.*

In the Old Country desertion was not unique to Jews; the
Orthodox Church also set a minimum number of years that
had to pass before a divorce was granted on the grounds of
"absence of the spouse for unknown reasons."

BECAUSE DIVORCE WAS so expensive and complicated in New York,
many Jewish men found it more practical simply to leave their
wives. In the first decade of the twentieth century deserted
women increasingly applied for help from the United Hebrew
Charities. In 1900 Max Senior, president of the National Conference of Jewish Charities, cited desertion as one of the major
issues confronting American Jewry. Jewish and gentile men differed substantially in regard to the reasons behind the desertion
of their wives. In a large majority of the cases, the husbands'
infidelity was given as the primary reason behind desertion by
Jewish husbands.[1] The long period of separation of husbands in
America from their families in the Old Country, it was contended, explained the high incidence of extramarital affairs. A
secondary major cause of "immoral behavior" of husbands was
said to be to low wages or unemployment, which resulted in low
self-esteem.

According to a report by a committee established in 1913 to
study the desertion problem, as many as 20 percent of children
housed by municipal institutions came from deserted families.

---

[1] In a study examining 260 desertion cases for the year 1902–1903, Morris
Waldman concluded that 30 percent of Jewish husbands were accused of
adultery, compared with only 11 percent of gentile husbands. The same
study showed that nearly a third of gentile desertions could be attributed
to alcoholism, whereas only 3 percent of Jewish men were classified as
intemperate.

Half of inmates at juvenile reformatories and industrial schools were children from broken homes. By 1905 desertion had become such a generic problem that New York State passed a law classifying abandonment of minor children in "destitute circumstances" as a felony. The Jewish community's response to the problem was swift and hard-hitting. That same year the United Hebrew Charities and the National Conference of Jewish Charities established a "Committee for the Protection of Deserted Wives and Children." This committee wasted no time, placing advertisements in all of the major newspapers, asking deserted wives to provide as much information as possible regarding their deadbeat husbands. The papers, most notably *The Forward*, included the "Gallery of Missing Husbands," with photos and descriptions of these men. In just eight months the committee handled 591 cases.

By 1911 the Jewish community, distressed by the frequency of such claims, established the National Desertion Bureau. Headquartered in New York, this new organization sought to help not only locally but nationwide and on an international scale. Initially supported by private donations and money from charitable organizations, the bureau received financial support from the Federation of Jewish Philanthropies after the latter's founding in 1917.

The bureau's agenda was fourfold: (1) tracking down deserting husbands and fathers, (2) effecting reconciliation of deserters and their families, (3) ensuring that the deserters provided financial support, and (4) if necessary, prosecuting those men who refused to cooperate. Sometimes the bureau served as a collection agency, facilitating financial transactions between husbands and wives. The Bureau would go so far as to seek extradition and prosecution for repeat offenders or continued lack of financial support. In most states the penalty for such irresponsible behavior could be as high as two years' imprisonment and a $1,000 fine. The bureau worked hand-in-hand with the Hebrew Immigrant Aid Society (HIAS) and the Immigrant

Aid Department of the National Council of Jewish Women (NCJW). These two groups referred cases to the bureau when a husband abandoned his family in Europe.

In its first year of operation, the bureau handled 852 cases. By the end of that twelve-month period nearly two-thirds of the deserters had been located and 326 were either back with their families or forced to provide support. By 1919 the number of cases had risen to 1,242, with 70 percent of the husbands found and apprehended. In 1922, 1,596 of 2,108 deserters were located. In total, between 1911 and 1922 the bureau handled 12,413 cases across the country. Nearly half, 6,085 of the cases involved deserters from New York City. The bureau's reputation and success rate provided a model for other, non-Jewish organizations.

With so many immigrants struggling to cope with problems of newcomers, including desertion, the *Jewish Daily Forward*'s Bintel Brief ("a bundle of letters") came to the rescue. Started in 1906, the Bintel Brief provided advice akin to Dear Abby (Pauline Friedman) and Anne Landers (Esther Friedman) and, more recently, Dr. Phil (McGraw). Bintel Brief covered a wide range of immigrants' problems from spiritual dilemmas to family squabbles. The following Bintel Brief details the perspective of *husbands* who were thrown in jail for not supporting their wives and families:

> *Dear Editor,*
>
> *This is the voice of thirty-seven miserable men who are buried but not covered over by earth, tied down but not in chains, silent but not mute, whose hearts beat like humans, yet are not like other human beings.*
>
> *When we look at our striped clothes, at our dirty narrow cots, at our fellow companions in the cells, the beaten, lowest members of society, who long ago lost their human dignity, the blood freezes in our veins. We feel degraded and miserable here. And why are we confined here? For the horrible crime*

of being poor, not being able to satisfy the mad whims of our wives. That's why we pine away here, stamped with the name "convict." That's why we are despised, robbed of our freedom, and treated like dogs.

We ask you, worthy Editor, to publish our letter so your readers, especially the women, will know how we live here. This letter is written not with ink but with our hearts' blood. We are coughing from the polluted air that we breathe in the cells. Our bones ache from lying on the hard cots and we get stomach-aches from the food they give us.

The non-support "plague" is the worst plague of all. For the merest nonsense, a man is caught and committed to the workhouse. He doesn't even get a chance to defend himself. Even during the worst times of the Russian reaction people didn't suffer as the men suffer here in America because of their wives. For a Jewish wife it's as easy here to condemn her husband to imprisonment as it is try on a pair of gloves. In all the world there isn't such legal injustice as here in the alimony courts.

What do they think, these women! If they believe that the imprisoned husbands, after the six months, will become purified and come out good, sweet and loving, they're making a big mistake.

The worst offense is committed by the Jewish charity organizations. They sympathize with the wife when her husband is in jail. They forget, however, that they "manufacture" the grass widows and living orphans when they help the women. As soon as the wife tastes an easy and a free dollar, as soon as she discovers that the "charities" won't let her starve, she doesn't care that her husband is condemned. She lives a gay life, enjoys herself and doesn't think of her husband.

Therefore it is your duty as editor of the Forward, *the newspaper that is read mainly by the working class, the class that furnishes more than all others the candidates for the workhouse and for the grass widowhood, to warn all the Jewish women not to take such revenge on their husbands. They do more harm*

*themselves than to their men. They drive away their husbands
for life that way, and make themselves and their children miserable. The women must learn that sending their husbands to
prison is a poor method of improving them. It is a double-
edged sword that slashes one side as deeply as the other.*

*Finally I appeal to all the women whose husbands are im-
prisoned for non-support in the workhouse at Blackwell's Island Prison, and I write to them as follows: Their husbands
have sworn here that if they, the women, do not have them
released in time for Pesach, they will never again return and
the women will remain grass widows forever.*

We ask you to publish this letter immediately.

Respectfully,
[Signatures of 37 men]

The National Desertion Bureau forced a high percentage of
other deadbeat husbands into continued financial, if not emotional, support of their families. Israel was lucky; Sadie divorced
him, so he was never sentenced to support his family. What
happened to Israel after he left Sing Sing the second time is
unclear. The next time he surfaced was in May of 1923, when,
possibly because of fear of deportation, he filled out a Declara-
tion of Intention, the first step toward obtaining naturalization
papers. We can assume he was not living a life of deprivation,
since by then he had gained some girth, weighing 165 pounds
for his height of 5 feet, 4 inches. At the time he lived at 205
South Second Street in Brooklyn.

Sometime in late 1929 or early 1930 Israel married yet again
under the alias of Israel Fox. His new wife, Fanny, had arrived
from Russia just a few years earlier. The couple lived on Vipe
Avenue in the Bronx, where Israel earned his wages, once again,
as a tinsmith. A Brooklyn City Directory from around that time
lists Sadie as living at 315 East Fifty-fourth Street in Brooklyn, and the widow of Israel. However, far from dead, Israel

lived to age 75, dying in 1964. Today he rests at Mount Hebron Cemetery, the same cemetery where another bigamist—my great-grandfather—is buried. Israel is buried next to his third wife, Fanny.

Benjamin Gitlow: Anarchy

ON JUNE 21, 1919, New York City Magistrate William McAdoo issued search warrants against three Manhattan targets: the Rand School of Social Science, located at 7 East Fifteenth Street; the headquarters of the Industrial Workers of the World (IWW), found at 27 East Fourth Street; and the headquarters of the Left Wing Section of the Socialist Party, at 43 West Twenty-ninth Street. Two days later, at precisely 3:00 P.M., agents executed the warrants. During the investigations, part of what were known as the "Palmer Raids" or the "Red Raids" officials seized large quantities of written materials, considered to be "revolutionary, incendiary, and seditious." No arrests were made that day, but authorities used the information collected to mount a campaign against members of these organizations.

Three months later, on November 8, 1919, the day after the two-year anniversary of the Bolshevik Revolution (responding to a request from the Lusk State Senate Committee), Judge McAdoo issued 71 warrants against the various offices of the Communist Party located throughout the five boroughs. Among those arrested were Benjamin Gitlow, former New York State assemblyman and the business manager for *The Revolutionary Age*; and James Larkin, editor of the same publication. Under New York State's criminal anarchy law, both were charged with attempting to overthrow the government.

In 1891, just a year or two after Benjamin Gitlow was born in Elizabethport, New Jersey, his family moved to Cherry Street in New York, most likely because the big city offered better employment opportunities for his immigrant parents. Both worked in the clothing business, an occupation young Benjamin would embrace, at least for a time, after graduating from Stuyvesant High School. It is easy to imagine that, as a youngster, Benjamin listened to his parents and their friends discuss changes in the Old Country—particularly the increasing power and role of the Russian proletariat—as well as the ideals of Socialism. Benjamin's mother, Katherine, participated as an active member of the Progressive Women of the Bronx (formerly known as the Consumers League), making house calls to interest Jewish women in her anarchist propaganda. The league, founded in 1899 by Florence Kelley and other women of the Hull House social settlement in Chicago, advocated better working conditions and higher wages for women and children.

Beyond his mother's political involvement, young Benjamin had plenty of opportunity to discover Socialism outside of his home. At the time, New York was awash with idealism, and speakers could be heard everywhere. Orators preached at street corners, and lectures abounded, particularly those under the auspices of Charles Sprague Smith and Frederick Howe's People's Institute at Cooper Union, which Gitlow frequently attended. Here he heard the likes of Columbia University Professor Adolph Cohn and John Spargo, who lectured about Socialism and the republic and the spiritual significance of the Socialist movement, respectively. After lectures at Cooper Union, audience members hung around to discuss a variety of topics, from philosophy to astronomy and from anarchy to economics. Elsewhere, at Bohemian Hall on Seventy-sixth Street, Gitlow listened to Mother Jones, who was a leader of miners, and Ben Hanford, a Socialist "agitator."

By 1909, at the age of eighteen, Ben Gitlow had joined the Socialist Party, believing "that Socialism would create a new society free from exploitation, a republic of liberty and justice for all." Gitlow himself would soon become an outspoken proponent of the anarchism and socialism developed by Karl Marx,

Mikhail Bakunin, and others. These doctrines proposed that the proletariat should rise up against the government and collectivize. Coming to the New World, Eastern European Jews hoped to escape the discriminating policies of the czar and to be able to choose whatever occupations they desired to earn a living. Many—if not most—Jewish immigrants accepted the drawbacks of capitalism, such as the lack of guaranteed employment, as the price they paid for the potential to achieve significant wealth based on hard work; yet others held out for a more egalitarian society. A minority of them simply could not assume a passive role in waiting for a new world order and took matters into their own hands, organizing, raising the consciousness of their peers, and hoping to gather enough momentum to effect change in their own time.

Among the more notable anarchists were Alexander Berkman and Emma Goldman. Berkman, the son of a wealthy Jewish businessman in Vilnius, Lithuania, was named Ovsei Osipovich Berkkan at birth. After the death of his parents, Berkman came to the United States, where he became active in the local anarchist movement. At some point he met Emma Goldman, who worked in a clothing factory. After a brief romance, the two remained friends, continuing their involvement in politics. Between 1907 and 1915 Berkman wrote articles for Goldman's publication *Mother Earth*. Their political activities earned them frequent imprisonment, such as in 1918, when the pair drew sentences to federal penitentiaries on convictions of conspiracy to obstruct the draft law.

Beyond the leaders of the anarchist and Socialist movements, large numbers of Jewish immigrants fought hard for increased workers' rights, while keeping in touch with family and friends in the Old Country. Word of the working class's rising up against the czar was welcome news to these new citizens of the Western World, if not a call to action to achieve the same result in their new homeland.

The American Socialist Party boiled over with many hot ideas and activities. Despite many factions within the party, members collectively opposed the United States' going to war in 1914 and hoped Woodrow Wilson would keep his election campaign promise of peace. With sentiments changing and various fronts calling for American intervention in the Western European conflict, at the age of 23, Gitlow ran for public office in the Third Assembly District of the Bronx on an antiwar platform. Despite his youth, Gitlow had already gained experience in politics by serving as head of the Retail Clerks' Union of New York. He won an assembly seat, as did nine other candidates who ran on the Socialist Party ticket throughout New York City. It was the party's best showing ever.

At the time, the overwhelming majority of American Socialist Party members were foreign-born. In the clear minority as American-born, Gitlow made it his goal to "destroy the party" in favor of something better. After all, he thought, why should foreigners decide how to change this country? To that end, Gitlow joined the Left Wing of the American Socialist Party which, unlike the Right Wing, condoned violence if it were necessary to effect change. To push his agenda further, he invited John Reed, a journalist who had won fame both for his reporting of the Russian Revolution and for his Bolshevik politics, to speak in the Bronx on September 13, 1918. (Reed was the main character of the 1991 movie *Reds*, starring Warren Beatty and Diane Keaton, who played the role of Louise Bryant, John Reed's wife.) Reed's speech, held at Hunts Point Palace at 164th Street and Southern Boulevard, was a rousing success, generating the largest demonstration in favor of Bolshevik Russia held in the United States up to that time.

However, the evening had a nearly disastrous start. The boisterous cheering and waving by the crowd initially caused Reed, an inexperienced orator, to hesitate and appear nervous, if he did not actually feel so. Once he started speaking, however, he captivated the audience by speaking about the Russian Revolution and insisting that time could not be wasted in replicating the same action in America. Slipping a few Russian words into his talk, he appealed directly to the crowd, made up mostly of Eastern European immigrants, who screamed with approval. There was no dissent at this gathering.

So the Socialist Party as a whole struggled with factionalism, due to its various constituencies—groups including the Russian Federation, the Jewish Federation, the Ukrainian Federation, and the Polish Federation. The vast majority of the Socialist Party's 70,000 members were foreigners, most of whom considered themselves Right Wingers. Working against Gitlow's desire to create a party composed primarily of American-born members, immigrants constituted the about half of the Left Wing group he joined. Increasing the tension was the foreign members' belief, regardless of their political leanings (Left or Right), that they understood Bolshevism better than did native-born Americans and were, as a consequence, the only ones qualified to follow through with the movement's goals and strategies.

Describing these claims, Gitlow wrote, "Not only did they [the foreigners in the Left Wing] let the American Socialists know that, when it came to Bolshevism, they knew all about it, but they went further and insisted that they alone should be recognized as the leaders of the Left Wing."

In February 1919 the Socialist Party's Left Wing held a convention at Odd Fellows Hall on St. Marks Place in Manhattan. Built in 1890 with Philadelphia brick and terracotta, the five-story structure served as New York headquarters of the German Odd Fellows organization, a local chapter of the International Order of Odd Fellows, a fraternal group formed to help common laboring men congregate for "fellowship and mutual help." The convention led to the formation of two committees: (1) a "National" committee, organized to carry on the planning and high-level decision-making for the party and composed of fifteen individuals, including John Reed, Benjamin Gitlow, and Dr. Julius Hammer (father of industrialist and collector

Armand Hammer), and (2) an "Executive" committee, designed to carry out the day-to-day activities of the party and composed of nine individuals, among them James Larkin and Benjamin Gitlow. Gitlow had carried more than his share of influence in the decision-making, since only he, James Larkin, and Nicholas Hourwich were elected to both committees.

In April 1919 the Left Wing of the Socialist Party established its own newspaper, *The New York Communist*, with John Reed as its editor. Benjamin Gitlow was appointed business manager, a job that entailed finding and securing distribution outlets for the newspaper.

Meanwhile, tensions increased not only within the Left Wing of the Socialist Party but also across the party as a whole. As Gitlow explained, the Left Wing was cleaved by two main factions: the "American elements," represented by James Larkin, John Reed, Benjamin Gitlow, Dr. Julius Hammer, and Gregory Weinstein, who felt that America was their native country and that they knew what was best for their country, and the Russian Federation, led by Louis Fraina. To complicate matters even more, the Right Wing portion of the Socialist Party, led by Morris Hillquit, expelled all Left Wing members on May 21, 1919. As a result, a referendum was called, with Hillquit and the Right Wing losing the vote.

If the Socialist Party did not have enough problems caused by its own internal squabbles, the New York State Legislature voted overwhelmingly to investigate "seditious activities" and authorized police and other agents to break into Socialist Party offices to destroy property and confiscate money and records. Shortly after these raids were conducted, the Left Wing moved into new offices on Twenty-ninth Street, between Broadway and Sixth Avenue, and held its own conference. In attendance were both Charles Rutherford from Cleveland and Isaac Ferguson, who became the first secretary of the National Left Wing portion of the Socialist Party. This group's mission was to wrest control of the entire Socialist Party from the more moderate incumbents and transform it into a Communist Party. During the conference nine individuals, almost all Americans— including Charles Rutherford, Isaac Ferguson, and Benjamin Gitlow—were elected to the Left Wing's National Council. The foreign factions (Federations, as they were officially called), representing immigrants mostly from several Eastern European nations, appeared to go along with the elections.

In early July a new journal, formed by the merger of the Boston-based *Revolutionary Age* and T*he New York Communist*, published its first issue. The lead article was headlined as the "Left Wing Manifesto," which, authorities claimed, called for the overthrow of the government. In essence the manifesto updated Marx and Engel's *Communist Manifesto* published in 1848. While both papers concurred with Marx and Engels in the need for the proletariat to seize control from the bourgeoisie, the new *Revolutionary Age* intended its rhetoric to raise eyebrows, even those of fellow members of the Socialist Party. One particular issue, edited by John Reed and Eadmonn MacAlpine, masqueraded as the Right Wing's paper the *Socialist*. In this satirical issue, Reed and MacAlpine used every trick in the book, with the exception of a minor difference in the type font, to make the mock paper appear authentic. However, the articles completely ridiculed the Right Wing so deftly that readers believed the stories and lodged complaints to their own paper's editorial board. The *Socialist* fired back, charging Gitlow, Reed, and MacAlpine with forgery, but the charge never stuck.

Meanwhile, Gitlow continued to forge ahead with the Left Wing's agenda. When on August 31 the Socialist Party held its national convention in the auditorium on the second floor of Machinists' Hall in Chicago, the Left Wing simultaneously conducted its own caucus on the first floor of the building. But difficulties erupted immediately. Upon their arrival, Gitlow and Reed realized that not only had the national convention organizers required people to register, but they had also limited admission to "accredited delegates," individuals who were not "contested"—excluding such members as Reed and Gitlow. In response, Reed and Gitlow quickly gathered their delegates and ordered them to take seats in the convention hall and, when it was time for the call to order, demanded an election of both a temporary chairman and a credentials committee, to determine who was qualified to attend and vote.

If there wasn't enough chaos across the national party, the Left Wing continued to struggle with its own factionalism. When on September 1 this wing held its own convention, three different factions vied for leadership of the group: (1) the Russian Federation and other Slavic federations, which together held the largest bloc of votes; (2) the Michigan delegation, which was largely irrelevant; and (3) the English-speaking contingent. Far from reaching any compromise, each group expressed the opinion that it should lead the larger group. With no agreement on leadership for the group as a whole, three subgroups were established: (1) The Communist Party of America, basically the Russian Federation, headed by Charles Rutherford and consisting of approximately 24,000 members; (2) the Michigan group, which remained unchanged; and (3) the Communist Labor Party—led by John Reed and Benjamin Gitlow—a 10,000-strong contingent, with the largest number of native-born Americans. In order to solidify its position, the Communist Labor Party sent John Reed to Moscow to get its official blessing. But things did not turn out as party members anticipated. Not only did John Reed fail to obtain the official seal of approval, he was never allowed to return to the United States.

Despite the lack of sponsorship from Moscow, the Communist Labor Party moved into new headquarters at 108 East Twelfth Street, a house initially rented by Dr. Julius Hammer, who later purchased the property for the group. The most radical of all of the factions, this group, according to Gitlow, "openly called for the overthrow of the United States government." The Bolsheviks' recent power takeover in Russia empowered radicals around the world, encouraging them to think they could effect change in the same way. This seemed like the most advantageous time for the Left Wingers to promote change in the United States. The more moderate factions seemed likely to let the opportunity pass by. One of the Communist Labor Party's main targets was the American Federation of Labor, whose members, the faction felt, should use strikes and other mechanisms to change the balance of economic power and the government as a whole.

In an attempt to recruit and rally forces for its cause, the Communist Labor Party tried to organize a meeting on November 7, the anniversary of the Bolshevik Revolution, but the police made sure that any halls hired to host the celebration were closed. The next day Benjamin Gitlow spoke at the Lettish (Latvian) Club in Manhattan. Midway through his talk fifty police and other detectives, on behalf of the State Senate Lusk Committee, arrested dozens among the audience and drove them to police headquarters. Members of the New York State constabulary and nearly 700 members of the NYPD simultaneously entered 71 premises around New York City at 9:00 P.M. and arrested dozens. Gitlow and Larkin were tossed into the Tombs, where they stayed until Dr. Julius Hammer provided $25,000 in Liberty Bonds for each.

Gitlow and Larkin were hardly alone. This was the beginning of a two-year federal search and prosecution program known as the Palmer or Red Raids. United States Attorney General Alexander Mitchell Palmer and his very young legal assistant, J. Edgar Hoover, led the charge to enforce the provisions of the 1917 Espionage Act and the 1918 Sedition Act. The former legislation was passed by Congress to counteract mounting public sentiment against American involvement in World War I and to mitigate the difficulty in finding new military recruitment recruits. The law provided for penalties of up to twenty years imprisonment and fines of up to $10,000 for such interference. In a landmark case, *Schenck v. United States*, the Supreme Court upheld the law allowing the Congress to enact legislation that would normally be unacceptable—if it faced a "clear and present danger." The Sedition Act strengthened and expanded the capabilities of the Espionage Act by allowing the arrest of individuals who publicly criticized the government, including making derogatory comments about the American flag, the Constitution, or the military. Both acts were intended to apply to situations where actions sometimes proved louder than words.

After bombs were detonated in eight cities on June 2, 1919, Palmer intensified his focus on political dissent. By October 1919 J. Edgar Hoover had amassed a database of 150,000 names of suspected dissenters. Starting on June 7, 1919, for a period of two years, federal agents assaulted labor union offices and headquarters of Communist and Socialist organizations, sometimes without search warrants. In December 1919 federal agents arrested 240 radicals and deported them on the *S. S. Buford*, nicknamed the "Red Ark" or the "Soviet Ark." Included on the passenger ship manifest were Emma Goldman and Alexander Berkman, who, upon arriving in Russia, spent the next two years supporting the Bolsheviks in their new government. However, after becoming disillusioned with the new Russian government's development of its own form of repressive leadership, the couple left for Germany.

As a result of their arrests, Gitlow and Larkin went on trial in early February 1920. According to Gitlow, the trial was rigged in a sense, since the prosecutor selected a jury consisting totally of members uniquely from the "silk stocking district"—ultraconservatives who "could be depended upon to bring in the verdict against the Reds, as desired by the prosecutor." Gitlow also asserted that the judge went out of his way to help the prosecutor both select a jury and present his case, while simultaneously thwarting the defense from doing the same. With the verdict all but certain, and most likely over the objection of his attorney, Clarence Darrow, Gitlow decided there was nothing to lose and proceeded to address the jury. Before Gitlow began speaking, however, Judge Giovanitti cautioned him to stick to the facts of the case; "preaching to the jury was not allowed."

Although Gitlow was accustomed to addressing large audiences, the prospect of speaking to a jury that had his life in its hands left him admittedly nervous. He felt that "the room was surcharged with hostility." Without notes, but with an outline in his head of the points he hoped would stick in the jury's minds, he spoke, hoping that they would have patience and understand his arguments. The judge repeatedly interrupted Gitlow's comments.

> **GITLOW:** It [the Left Wing Manifesto] is a document based upon the principles of socialism from their early inception. The only thing that the document does is to broaden those principles in light of modern events... What is capitalism? Capitalism is that system of society in which the means of production and distribution are owned by a few individuals for their own profit... The manifesto maintains that all our institutions are based on labor power of the working man. Without that power society could not exist. Not a wheel could turn...Capitalism, as it stores up its wealth, does not desire its wealth to remain idle. Its wealth must be converted into capital, and the capital applied to the developed areas for the purpose of getting more wealth... [Capitalism is] always looking for markets, for new areas to exploit in order to procure more and additional capital.
>
> **COURT:** I must interrupt you, because you are stating as facts matters which are not facts of this court and which the court has no reason to believe are facts at all.
>
> **GITLOW:** If Your Honor please, the manifest touches on that very clearly.
>
> **COURT:** It touches on it, and you may use the language of the manifesto, but you may not make a speech beyond

the language of the manifesto.

DARROW: Your Honor, he has a right to explain the meaning of it.

COURT: No sir, he has no right to explain the meaning of the manifesto because he is not subject to cross-examination…

GITLOW: The manifesto of the Left Wing Section of the Socialist Party is a statement of the principles of Revolutionary Socialism. These principles maintain that in order to bring about socialism, capitalist governments must be overthrown, and in their place a new form of government must be set up, known as the dictatorship of the proletariat…

COURT (interrupting): The court must interrupt you again. The court has advised the defendant that he cannot make statements of what he claims to be facts… You will refrain from saying what you would do if you could, or what you will do if you can.

GITLOW: I want you to realize that I believe in those principles, that I will support those principles and that I am not going to evade the issue. My whole life has been dedicated to the movement which I am in. No jails will change my opinion in that respect.

After what appears to be an honest if not suicidal presentation, the jury deliberated for just three hours before returning a verdict of guilty on two separate charges of "criminal anarchy," the first that Benjamin Gitlow had advocated the overthrow of the government and the second that he published this directive in the *Revolutionary Age*. The judge handed down the maximum sentence under the law: five to ten years in state prison. Willing to die for his principles, Gitlow took the sentence in stride. And in a sense, he got off easy. Other anarchists were deported to Russia as part of the "Red Scare" period, never to return to the United States.

Just two days later, on February 13, 1920, marshals took Benjamin Gitlow and other prisoners by train to Sing Sing. After the horrible conditions of the Tombs, Sing Sing may have been a step up in accommodations but not by much. Gitlow complained that his prison clothing was made from "rough" material and did not fit all that well. Supper consisted of white bread and corn-starch jelly along with a cup of black coffee. His cell contained an iron cot and a stone floor, with a refuse bucket that he emptied every morning.

Despite the poor conditions, Gitlow made the most of his time at Sing Sing. He quickly befriended a "chain" of well-connected African-American inmates. For 25 cents apiece, they helped him sneak messages in and out of the correctional facility.

In his autobiography, *I Confess*, Gitlow wrote, "I soon discovered that following all of the prison rules got you nowhere." Very often those who most strictly adhered to all of the regulations found themselves in trouble. As part of his survival within Sing Sing, Gitlow learned to manipulate the work assignment system once he realized that various assignments were doled out by neither merit nor fitness for the job but were more often than not based on the amount of money you could pay or the political favor you could generate. Originally Gitlow was assigned to Yard 2, and his first job included washing windows and "manicuring" bricks—piling bricks into a wheel barrel, moving the wheel barrel to another location of the yard, and then assembling another pile with the bricks just moved. His next position, in the knitting shop, was much better, but the assignment landed him in trouble. Working as efficiently as possible rather than at a slower pace, Gitlow would finish his tasks early, only to be caught standing around doing nothing. After learning his lesson, he slowed his pace in order to look busy.

Because of its proximity to New York City, Sing Sing frequently acts as a gateway to the rest of the state penal system. Like many Sing Sing inmates, Gitlow was transferred to other prisons in the New York State Department of Corrections Sys-

tem. Wardens have the right to transfer inmates to other prisons by what is known as the "draft." Through his chain network,
Gitlow normally received heads-up notices of inmates who had
been drafted to other institutions. That is why his transfer—with
no advance notice whatsoever—came as somewhat of a shock.
On June 15, 1920, officials transferred Gitlow to Clinton Prison
in Dannemora, New York, close to the Canadian border.

By September he had a received writ of *habeas corpus* (a paper
contesting wrongful incarceration), allowing him to appeal his
conviction. In order for him to be close to New York City, while
he awaited his day in court, Gitlow was temporarily relocated
back at Sing Sing. It was at this time that he ran into Dr. Julius Hammer in the "Big House." Hammer was officially convicted of abortion, but Gitlow suggested that possibly some of
the doctor's political enemies targeted him and trumped up the
charges. When the court ultimately turned down Gitlow's request for another trial, he received a transfer to Auburn Prison
in upstate New York.

At the time of his imprisonment, Gitlow was single and still
living at home with his parents. His transfer sent his mother,
Katherine Gitlow, into despair. In a letter dated July 20, 1920,
she wrote to someone named Barney (presumably an attorney):

> *I believe it is hypocrisy on my side to beg the one that repre-
> sents the class I am fighting. Believe me Barney, I could never
> think of it. My desire to help Ben and my conception of the
> class struggle conflict with one another. What shall I do? I am
> fighting within myself and can't make up my mind. Maybe
> Ben will never forgive me. Oh how I would be relieved if
> things could be done without me knowing anything.*

Just a few months later, on October 27, Gitlow received a
letter from his mother regarding the death of Jack Reed due to
typhus, in which she tried to comfort her son for the loss:

Ben, I can hardly talk to you about Jack Reed as I know what it means to you to lose a friend and comrade like Jack. Ben, you know better than I do, that great ideals for which Jack fought requires great sacrifices...Jack is the first great American to die in the struggle in Russia for the workers' republic.

Gitlow continued to move frequently within the prison system. His next transfer, sometime in early 1921, found him once again at Sing Sing, this time transferred from Clinton Prison in Dannemora. Despite all his transfers and the poor prison conditions, neither Gitlow's spirits nor his determination to push forward his agenda was dampened, as is evident by a letter he wrote from Sing Sing on May 1 titled "Greetings from Ben Gitlow." He maintained that Communism promoted a society based on a scheme in which all individuals work for the good of all and, by extension, for each individual. By contrast, he argued, capitalism causes people to work under a "lever of class suppressor." Communism, he continued, allows the individual to "enjoy the greatest degree of freedom." At the end of the document, he encouraged all Communists to coerce American labor workers to join the Communist International.

So little was he daunted by life in prison that Gitlow actually tried to run for mayor of New York City, as *New York Times* articles show, on the ticket organized by Communists and other radical groups. These groups hoped to garner enough votes to put a dent in the campaign of the Socialist Party, which they felt was too conservative. It was probably from his success in communicating with people on the outside that Gitlow was able to engineer such an unlikely situation, although prison officials most likely caught wind of some of Gitlow's correspondence; in early September they transferred him once again to Auburn Prison, where communications with his contacts in New York City would be virtually impossible. In the end Gitlow's name was never placed on the ballot, but not through the intervention

of prison officials. The New York Election Board did not deem
him a fit candidate.

In the meantime, Gitlow appealed his conviction to the
New York Appellate Division, but the appellate court upheld
the lower court's decision. On April 22, 1922, he received word
that New York Supreme Court Justice Benjamin Cardozo had
granted a "certificate of reasonable doubt." (This is a document
required in order for one to appeal the denial of a writ of habeas
corpus, today referred to as a "certificate of appealability.")

Gitlow was released from prison to prepare for his various
court appearances. Despite being outside the walls of a prison,
however, Gitlow was not actually free. Suspecting that he would
return to his anarchist ways, the authorities did not leave him
alone. Between December 1922 and March 1923, according to
FBI papers, the agency had several agents track the whereabouts
and activities of both Benjamin and Katherine Gitlow. Katherine was the agency's most active subject, but they were never
able to gather much evidence against her. All that they could
ascertain was that she went to the Worker's Party of America,
located at Fifth Avenue and Eleventh Street, or 110 West For-
tieth Street, "where radical organizations had their offices," and
later returned to her home at 46 Greenwich Street. They had a
bit less luck with Katherine's son, however. Following up on a
tip, the FBI waited for Gitlow to arrive at the New York Public
Library, where, the FBI learned, he hung out on occasion. Such
attempts to catch him failed, since he never appeared at the
library, although during this time he did attend a secret convention of the Communist Party in Bridgeman, Michigan.

Less than ten days after the convention, officials apprehended Gitlow and sent him back to Sing Sing for a violation of
his parole—or so the FBI thought. The good news for Gitlow
was that in the meantime he had received an "adjournment of
surrender," allowing him to apply to the U.S. Supreme Court's
Justice Brandeis for a review of his state court hearings. The
Supreme Court agreed to hear his case, which was argued on

March, 23, 1923.

Around this time Gitlow started working for the Yiddish newspaper *Freiheit* (Yiddish for "freedom" or "liberty"), whose mission went beyond contributing to the local Jewish community; it also wanted to aid cultural development in Russia. First published in 1879, *Freiheit* had earned a solid reputation as a literary journal that attracted not only the most provocative and innovative novelists and poets but also a young audience. Contributing writers met their readers in various forums, including social clubs, dramatic groups, and summer camps. In the winter of 1922–1923, the paper's two editors, Olgin and Shachno Epstein, resigned after their positions had been undermined by Alexander Bittleman, advisor to William Foster, leader of the Communist Labor Party at the time. The Communist Party then designated Ben Gitlow as the new editor and business manager. Unfortunately, Gitlow knew no Yiddish and little about the Jewish community's issues. He was strictly a figurehead. But the paper offered something unique to Gitlow: He met his future wife, Badana Zeitlin there—although the couple did not legally marry until the 1960s, allegedly because marriage was simply too bourgeois for them in the 1920s.

Judging from his correspondence with Badana, we can see that Gitlow was just as passionate about his personal life as his politics. In letter after letter he wrote to her of her eyes, her smile, and her kisses. In the midst of a description of the Hudson blanketed in snow, he proclaimed his deep love for her. In a letter dated January 1, 1925, he penned a letter on stationery from the Twentieth Century Limited train:

> *Badana, my love for you just grows and grows with each day...I look at the snow. But what I see is only the surface and not the true picture of what nature is mothering underneath. The cold snow is but a warm blanket for the earth. Tenderly underneath it life is kept secure and warm. When the spring comes, the snow melts. The barren earth becomes transformed*

*with life, color, and song. Mother earth, with her love for life
presents us with all its glory. And, Badana, we are but part of
this scheme. Badana, listen to me. I am calling you. As I do, I
see you. Come to my arms and let me hold you. And, Badana,
don't, don't let me go. I wish I could sing you a love song simple
yet sweet, the strains of which would come from my heart.
Then I would let each note reach your heart and, there against
its walls, beat each plaintive note of love to you. Badana, such
songs I feel but cannot sing.*

In another letter, written the following day, we see him sharing his dreams with Badana while at the same time expressing
his frustration with the materialistic nature of the West:

*In a few minutes I will be in Chicago...Last night as I sat
in the car recalling many of the pleasant moments you and I
spent together I could not help but hear the conversation of two
American petty bourgeois gentlemen from Westchester County.
I thought, Badana, I was in another world. They spoke about
automobiles, golf, lunches, school boards, and business. One
was such a golf enthusiast that he had so transformed his living room that he could play golf in it in the winter. The other
said that his greatest enjoyment is to walk into one of his three
cars and order the chauffeur to go. They talked quietly in mono-
tones, seldom smiled, showed no emotions and looked bored.*

While romancing Badana, Gitlow was also preparing his
case, which he and his attorneys argued before the Supreme
Court in 1923 and 1925. In Gitlow's defense, counselors Walter H. Pollak and Walter Nelles argued that the Manifesto did
not contravene the state statute and furthermore the state statute was a violation of the due process clause of the Fourteenth
Amendment. Unfortunately for Gitlow, the Court rejected both
of these arguments in 1923.

The results of the June 1925 appearance before the Supreme Court were similarly unfavorable. The Court decided by a vote of 7–2 that, although the Fourteenth Amendment afforded citizens of any state the benefits of the Bill of Rights, New York State's 1902 law making criminal anarchy a felony should be upheld. Justice Edward Sanford, writing the majority opinion, stated: "It [the manifesto] advocates and urges in fervent language mass action which shall progressively foment industrial disturbances and through political mass strikes and revolutionary mass action overthrow and destroy organized parliamentary government. It [the manifesto] concludes with a call to action in these words: 'The proletariat revolution and the Communist reconstruction of society—the struggle for these—is not indispensable. The Communist International calls for the proletariat of the world to the final struggle.'"

Sanford continued, "It was not necessary, within the meaning of the statute, that the defendant should have advocated 'some definite or immediate act or acts' of force, violence or unlawfulness. It was sufficient if such acts were advocated in general terms; and it was not essential that their immediate execution should have been advocated."

Justices Oliver Wendell Holmes and Louis Brandeis, the latter a fellow Jew and the judge who had granted Gitlow the certificate of reasonable doubt to appeal to the U.S. Supreme Court, dissented. Holmes wrote in the minority opinion: "There was no present danger of an attempt to overthrow the government by force on the part of the admittedly small minority who shared the defendant's views. It is said that his manifesto was more than a theory, that it was an incitement. Every idea is an incitement…The only difference between the expression of an opinion and an incitement in the narrower sense is the speaker's enthusiasm for the result…If the publication of this document had been laid as an attempt to induce an uprising against government at once and not at some indefinite time in the future, it would have presented a different question."

Although Gitlow did not win a reversal of lower courts' decisions, *Gitlow v. New York* did serve as a landmark case. The ruling reversed, at least in part, the Court's decision in *Barron v. Baltimore*, which prevented the federal government from interfering with a state to enforce its own law that may restrict rights found in the Bill of Rights, such as freedom of speech. Since the time of the Gitlow case decision, the Court has generally ruled in favor of the Bill of Rights applying to both the federal government and states.

Repeating the roller-coaster pattern of Gitlow's life, the Supreme Court decision quickly became a moot point. In December 1925 New York Governor Alfred Smith granted Benjamin Gitlow a full pardon, even though the governor acknowledged that Gitlow had been properly convicted. "The question for me," he wrote, "is one of whether he has been sufficiently punished or not."

Even before the Supreme Court decision Gitlow had teamedup as vice-presidential running mate with William Foster, another Socialist and one-time competitor of Gitlow, who campaigned for President of the United States on the Workers (Socialist) Party ticket. In September 1924 the FBI followed the two candidates to a meeting at the Labor Lyceum in Pittsburgh and then to the Labor Educational Alliance Hall in Hartford. In neither case did FBI agents consider Gitlow's remarks to be "in violation of any state or federal statute." On Election Day Calvin Coolidge won 54 percent of the popular vote and 72 percent of the electoral votes. The Worker's Party hardly came close to receiving 1 percent of the vote. Undeterred, Foster and Gitlow campaigned again in 1928, with exactly the same outcome. Herbert Hoover won 58 percent of the popular and 83 percent of the electoral vote, with the Worker's Party receiving less than one quarter of one percent of the vote.

Between 1927 and 1929 Gitlow made yearly visits to Moscow to attend the annual executive meeting and plenary sessions of the Communist International (Comintern). Since it was virtually impossible to travel directly from the United States to Russia, he traveled as a Canadian citizen under the alias of James Hay and entered Russia via a circuitous route that entailed landing in a port such as Le Havre or Hamburg, taking a train to Berlin, and then crossing the border into Poland or Latvia.

Gitlow enjoyed his trips to Russia, both politically and esthetically. In awe of Moscow, he wrote extensively to Badana about his travels:

> *Moscow is a very old city. Moscow, in spite of its dilapidated appearance, gives one the impression that great steps have been taken. One thing is certain. Stifled spirit, the oppressive atmosphere that prevails in Poland is entirely missing here. The streets are crowded with people happy, joyful, and contented. Most of them are fairly well-dressed. Street vendors are everywhere. Book stores all over. The stores are full of all kinds of goods imaginable. The people are very interested in window displays and crowd around the windows, showing a keen interest in the goods displayed.*
>
> *Difficulties there are many here. There is a danger a very serious one that England with the other powers will make war against the Soviet Union. Such a war may break out at any moment. It would temporarily arrest the great work that has been done here.*

Several days and letters later, Gitlow continued his expansive writing:

> *The Russians, may be very poor, they may be struggling with great difficulties, they may be dressed shabbily, they may eat very little, but they cling to the poetry and beauty of life. No people admire flowers and treasure them as much as the Russians. All over Moscow, boys, peasants, men and women*

sell violets, lilies of the valley, forget-me-nots, and bunches of
blossoms and flowers of different descriptions.

There is a soul in a people that responds so to the beauty
of flowers and the fragrant call. This attitude of the Russian
masses to flowers is genuine. To sacrifice from one's meager re-
sources, to respond and not forget regardless of all other cir-
cumstances, the delicate colors, the waft of spring they inspire,
the poetry and romance of fields and forests, the wild songs of
birds, and the compassioned kiss they recall proves how deeply
ingrained are these big factors in the lives of the Russian peo-
ple.

Gitlow returned to Moscow two more times, the first in
1928 and the second time in May 1929. By his last trip he was
co-heading, along with Jay Lovestone, the majority faction of
the American Communist Party delegation. The minority faction was led by none other than William Z. Foster. In letters to
Badana, Gitlow noted his disdain for Foster, referring to him as
"Zig-Zag," undoubtedly because of his former running mate's
tendency to change his mind and political leanings as quickly
as the wind.

Both groups, led by Foster and Gladstone/Gitlow, sought
approval and blessing from Stalin and the executive committee
of the Communist International. However, Stalin, very much
dismayed and disappointed with the fighting and petty politics,
lashed out at both groups during the meeting of the American
Commission of the Presidium of the ECCI, on May 6, 1929.
Angry at the Americans for not falling in line with the Russians' agenda, Stalin condemned them to leave the party:

I shall not deal with the political position of the leaders of
the majority and the minority (factions of the American Com-
munist Party). I shall not do so since it has become evident
during the course of the discussion that both groups are guilty
of the fundamental error of exaggerating the specific features

of American capitalism....

What are the main defects in the practice of leaders of the majority and the minority? Firstly, that in their day-to-day work they and, particularly the leaders of the majority, are guided by motives of unprincipled factionalism and place the interests of their faction higher than the interests of the Party.

Secondly, that both groups, and particularly the majority, are so infected with the disease of factionalism that they base their relations with the Comintern, not on the principle of confidence, but on a policy of rotten diplomacy, a policy of diplomatic intrigue.

The majority, under the leadership of Lovestone and Gitlow, again resists this demand and does not find it necessary to carry out the decision of the ECCI.

[After many examples of how both the majority and minority factions behaved, Stalin continued:]

There you have the fruits of the factionalism of the majority and the minority. But Comrades, the Comintern is not the stock market. The Comintern is the holy of holies of the working class. The Comintern, therefore, must not be confused with a stock market. Either we are Leninists, and our relations one with another, as well as the relations of the sections with the Comintern, and vice versa, must be built on mutual confidence, must be as clean and pure as crystal—in which case, there should be no room in our ranks for rotten diplomatic intrigue; or we are not Leninists—in which case rotten diplomacy and unprincipled factional struggle will have full scope in our relations. One or the other. We must choose, comrades.

Stalin's "solution" to this mess consisted of several points, collectively boiling down to the eradication of factionalism between the American majority and minority group, condemning the leaders of the majority group (i.e., Lovestone and Gitlow).

In response to Stalin, Gitlow charged, regarding the stock market analogy, that Stalin was guilty of the very thing he charged the Americans with. "But that was precisely how Stalin was running the Comintern—buying, selling and ruling its leaders. It is the holy of holies; therefore, those who control it, namely Stalin, do all manner of things by divine right. Their rule is holy. They can make no mistakes. That racket is as old as the hills."

Despite his express anger at Stalin's behavior, Gitlow wrote to Badana on May 8 as if nothing had happened:

> *We are fighting a fundamental principled fight. We will not accept anything that is handed out to us. We have firm convictions and we will fight regardless for our convictions. Thinking politic will not work. We will not spit in our own faces. And while Hari Kari may be heroic and a good method for old generals, we are yet young and on general principles do not believe in suicide. This is as plain as I can make it now.*

For many more days Gitlow and Lovestone fought their battle with Stalin and the Communist International, but the net result was the same. Lovestone and Gitlow, effectively if not officially, had been ousted from the Comintern.

After returning to the United States, Gitlow continued his involvement with Socialist Party politics. And although their views diverged, he kept in touch with Jay Lovestone, telling Lovestone that he held Stalin responsible for the declining economic and political environment in the Soviet Union and that he resigned from Lovestone's group. Despite their differences, Lovestone and Gitlow were viewed by Moscow as enough alike to expel both of them from the Communist party a year later.

In late 1929 Gitlow also returned to publishing the *Revolutionary Age*, although Postmaster General John J. Kiely banned distribution of six issues. With the aid of American Civil Liberties Union attorney Arthur Garfield Hays, Gitlow filed suit in United States District Court in New York. In his complaint,

Gitlow charged that the publication intended to provide "free and untrammeled discussion of public questions, especially those concerning the labor class." Despite this setback and his poor treatment by Stalin, Gitlow continued his support for the Communist movement and lobbied for the rights of the working class. Over the next few years he founded several organizations, including the Workers Communists League, the Organization Committee for a Revolutionary Workers Party, and the Labor Party Association.

In 1933 he traveled to Europe to attend a conference on Socialist Party politics but was kept out, probably because of his expulsion from the Communist International. In a letter to his friend Max Eastman, Gitlow explained, "It was primarily a Brandler–Lovestone affair," referring to his old comrade and Otto Brandler, who had been expelled from the German Communist Party. Gitlow continued, "The United Front must be established against Hitler on the realization of a struggle for proletarian dictatorship."

Most likely because of his protracted tensions with the Communist Party, by the late 1930s Gitlow experienced a profound a change of heart and turned anti-Communist. When and how he achieved this metamorphosis is not exactly known. However, it's possible that the switch came after the death of Nikolai Bukharin, one of the leading proponents for a proletarian revolution around the globe. After Lenin's death, in what was most likely a savvy move, Bukharin changed his political views to support Stalin's view that revolution just could not succeed in capitalistic nations of the West. In about 1928 Bukharin had proposed agricultural collectivization. However, Stalin not only criticized these plans, but demanded that Bukharin denounce them. In 1929 Bukharin joined the ranks of Gitlow and Lovestone as ex-officials of the Comintern. In 1937 Bukharin was arrested for attempting to overthrow the Soviet state. After a trial in 1938, the NKVD (Russia's department of internal affairs) executed Bukharin in 1939.

During this time, Gitlow apparently did not hold a paying job but instead worked for political causes. Finally, depleted of any wealth and desperate just to survive and support his family, he took a job making electrical appliances, for which he received $20 per week. In whatever spare time he had available, he penned his experiences, which led to the publication in 1939 of his first autobiography, entitled *I Confess*. Upon receiving a copy, Gitlow's old friend Max Eastman wrote Gitlow in January 1940, saying: "Thank you sincerely for the graciously inscribed copy of your book. I read excellent reviews of it and hope the sales are going well, too."

Not all the reviews were so positive, however. The review of the book in the *New York Times* concluded: "Mr. Gitlow lacks a sense of proportion…A reader may wonder, after pursuing the long record of trickery, bigotry and betrayal, why Mr. Gitlow's eyes were not opened fifteen years ago. That, however, is Mr. Gitlow's secret."

The review in *The Nation* was even more condescending: "Six hundred pages of it is plain overindulgence…The Moscow comrades confessed the sins they had committed or said they had committed against the Communist Party. For the most part, Gitlow confesses the sins which the party committed against him [individually]."

The whole time, Gitlow continued his attack on American Communists, and in 1940 he appeared before the House Committee on Un-American Activities (HCUA) and, according to an FBI document, made a most thorough and complete exposé of the Communist movement, of its tactics, and illegal practices in the United States. By this time Gitlow had completed a full role reversal and was intent on destroying anyone associated with the Communist Party, which had treated him so poorly.

Over the next three years the reformed Gitlow filled some of his time with two activities about which he was passionate. The first was a correspondence with former President Herbert Hoover about how to keep the United States out of war while, simultaneously avoiding the "abandonment of civilization." The second more time-consuming activity was working with the FBI to weed out Communism in America. In the course of this work Gitlow turned over 2,700 pages of documentation regarding policies and practices of the American Communist Party and spent hours dictating his analysis and interpretation of these documents to a stenographer. For this job he received $75 per week.

Despite the negative reviews, Gitlow appeared to enjoy writing, and during the latter part of the decade he wrote a second book, *The Whole of Their Lives*, concerning the lives of Jack Reed, Big Bill Haywood, and others with whom he had interacted during his involvement with the Socialist and Communist Parties. This book received a better review from the *New York Times* than *I Confess*, although the reviewer criticized it for not providing sources for various claims and leaving the reader to make multiple leaps of faith as to the accuracy of Gitlow's accounts.

Meanwhile, in the United States, anti-Communist sentiment was rising. In the fall of 1947 Rabbi Benjamin Schultz of Temple Emanu-El in Yonkers wrote three articles for the *New York World Telegram* in which he labeled religious Protestant, Catholic, and Jewish leaders as "either Communists, Communist dupes, or Communist sympathizers." In response to these allegations, the congregation of Temple Emanu-El demanded Schultz's resignation. A spokesperson for the synagogue stated, "We are not interested in [the] anti-Red campaign." In a related move, the New York Board of Rabbis adopted a resolution condemning Schultz for his actions.

Although he lacked any Jewish education and was a secular rather than an observant Jew, in 1948 Benjamin Gitlow cofounded the American Jewish League Against Communism (AJLAC). One should not be surprised as to who served as executive director of the organization at its inception: none other than Rabbi Benjamin Schultz. The organization, which operated for more than a decade, had several goals: "(1) to uncover the anti-religious plans and conduct of the Communists, (2) to act as a clearinghouse in the fight against Communism, and (3) to print, publish, and disseminate literature, hold public forums and discussions, and use every available means of informing the American public about the menace of Communism to our national security, freedom, democratic institutions and to civilization everywhere."

With his connection to the AJLAC, Gitlow established a reputation as an earnest if not reliable whistleblower and source of information regarding Americans who still participated in the Communist movement. In 1949 the Illinois Seditions Commission hired him to assist in an investigation into Communist infiltration of the University of Chicago and Roosevelt College. That same year the Hoover Institution at Stanford sent him on a mission to Europe to collect materials on political and subversive movements. In the course of five months he traveled to France, Belgium, Holland, Sweden, Denmark, Germany, Switzerland, Italy, and Israel.

Such work must have empowered Gitlow to go on a rampage against American Communists. In 1950 the FBI received information regarding an organization known as "Theatre for Freedom," which was active in fighting Communism on the stage. In a *New York Times* article dated October 10, 1950, the "Duke," a.k.a. John Wayne, announced the formation of the organization, which urged members of the entertainment business to "use their talents for an all-out offensive against Communism." Other members of the organization's national board included Kirk Douglas, Douglas Fairbanks, and Dick Powell, with Benjamin Gitlow as executive director.

In January 1951 the *New York Journal American* reported that the Theatre for Freedom would air a radio program over the NBC radio network, defending anti-Communist legislation, and the group called for vigilance against Communists. This program came as a response to Nevada Senator McCarran's call for time to respond to attacks on his anti-subversive control bill made by Jewish actor John Garfield (born Jacob Julius Garfinkle).

As passionate as ever, nothing seemed to stop Gitlow. In July 1953 he followed in the footsteps of Rabbi Benjamin Schultz and testified before the House Committee on Un-American Activities (HCUA) regarding Communist infiltration of churches and other religious institutions. In particular, he identified two prominent, yet deceased, rabbis as Communists: Stephen Wise, a key figure in the American Zionist movement, and Judah Magnes, former rabbi at Temple Emanu-El of New York. Supporting Gitlow in his statements was Rabbi Schultz, who claimed, "A powerful minority of the clergy has too much influence—on the pro-Communist side." However, Dr. Israel Davidson, president of the American Jewish Congress and former Jewish chaplain at Sing Sing, denounced Gitlow for his statements. Additionally, Brooklyn Democratic Representative Emanuel Celler urged the HCUA to reply on behalf of the deceased rabbis, who obviously could not defend themselves.

By this time in his life, Benjamin Gitlow was hurting financially. A New York journalist wrote in his column that Gitlow was "broke and wasting his time on unavailing little errands while his knowledge and authority also go to waste." Gitlow and the FBI toyed with the idea of working with each other, but these negotiations fell through. Wanting to rehabilitate his reputation, Gitlow wrote to J. Edgar Hoover requesting reinstatement to full American citizenship, to get around President Truman's executive order of 1947 banning ex-Communists from employment with the federal government. However, Hoover turned down the requests for both reinstatement and a simple letter of recommendation, and six months later he told the FBI's New York City branch that Gitlow should no longer be treated as a "confidential" source since he was "widely known as an anti-Communist." The FBI, it appears, used Gitlow to obtain a brain dump of his knowledge of Communist Party activities in America and then left him out in the cold. No thanks. No return of citizenship. н и ч е в о (*neechevo*; Russian for "nothing").

At some point the FBI wanted to rehire Gitlow, but the tables had turned. He complained that, while he worked for the Immigration and Naturalization Service, he had been terminated with just thirty minutes' notice. Furthermore, he asserted that the Department of Justice and the attorney general had afforded ex-Communists shabby treatment.

It was also in the mid-50s that Roy Cohn, former counsel to Senator Joseph McCarthy in the House Committee on Un-American Activities hearings, was named chairman of the executive committee of the American Jewish League against Communism. The AJLAC changed numerous times, although Roy Cohn remained involved for at least a decade. By 1960 Cohn was vice-president and treasurer, while Gitlow continued to serve as a member of the board of directors. In April 1960 Irving Schwartz, the current president of the AJLAC, wrote to Cohn complaining about the lack of support and cooperation from others, and as a result, stating his intention to resign as leader of the organization. By 1962 Roy Cohn had taken control as president of the AJLAC. He drafted a recruitment (fundraising) letter stating that the majority of American Jews are vigorously opposed to Communism in "all of its manifestations, both at home and abroad."

Just as Gitlow absorbed Communist talk at home, his son was steeped in anti-Communist propaganda. In researching this book, I called Gitlow's son on three occasions. The first time I simply introduced myself. In response, he asked me, "What are your political leanings?" I told him that, while not affiliated with any political party, I tended to vote for Democrats. To this he bellowed, "Well, that just does not leave me with warm feelings." In a subsequent discussion he confessed that he too was officially an independent voter but was more conservative in his political views. He is not the least bit religious but instead believes that "man created God." To my amusement, he informed me that he had worked as a process engineer for several defense-related companies, including Sikorsky Aircraft and Pratt & Whitney. For a period of time he worked for Combustion Engineering, a company involved with the building of nuclear submarines. Not too far from his father's goal of keeping the Russians in check.

In 1964 Benjamin Gitlow died of a heart attack at his home in Crompond, New York, a Socialist commune where he had resided with his wife and son for years. Despite his death, his fame continued to grow. In 1986 he was listed in the Biographical Dictionary of the American Left. Just a year later the Dictionary of American Conservatism included Gitlow's name. He was one passionate man whose views spanned the political gamut.

9

Isaac Spier: Part II

ONE DAY AT the New York Public Library, I stumbled across the *New York Times Personal Name Index,* a list of everybody ever mentioned in the newspaper. My great-grandfather Isaac appeared in the index for 1925 under the alias of Joseph Spier. Accused of extortion, Isaac had made the newspaper on June 28 and 29, 1925, the latter article appearing next to one about the famous Scopes Trial. (In the Scopes trial, attorney Clarence Darrow defended the right of 24-year-old Tennessee school-teacher John Scopes to educate his students on the theory of evolution.) I hoped this item would confirm my cousin Gloria's memory about Isaac's trouble with the Internal Revenue Service. I immediately contacted the New York City Municipal Archives to obtain the court case file. While perusing the file I found a police report for yet another crime he committed—forgery in 1916.

An article in the *Brooklyn Eagle* reported Isaac's arrest on a charge of larceny (not forgery) while working as a cashier for Gretsch, Inc., a manufacturer of musical instruments. Despite my great-grandfather's shenanigans, Gretsch remains a success-ful business concern today, boasting Elvis Presley and George Harrison among its customers on the company's website. In 1916 the company accused Isaac of taking $400 in cash and finagling the company's financial records to the tune of $5,000, roughly one-third the salary of New York City's mayor at the time. According to the article, detectives attributed Isaac's trouble to "his love of automobiles and the white lights of Broadway [in Brooklyn]."

In addition to the police report of Isaac's arrest for forgery in 1916, the extortion case file contained more than a hundred pages of testimony and correspondence among the various local, state, and federal government agencies. While working as an investigating officer in 1925 for the New York State Income Tax Bureau's Personal Tax Division, instead of concentrating on reviewing personal income tax returns, Isaac audited the books of Garant Art Lamp & Novelty Company. Harry Drucker, an officer of Garant, lodged a complaint against Isaac, leading to a Grand Jury hearing.

On July 7, 1925, Drucker provided testimony to the Grand Jury. After being sworn in, he explained that Garant, located at 14 Powers Street in Brooklyn, manufactured and sold lamps. Drucker acknowledged knowing Louis Leffler, whom Garant had hired five years earlier as its accountant. He indicated that, at his office, he met a man named Joseph N. Spier on Friday, June 19. Drucker asserted that, after Spier flashed his badge proving he was an agent from the State Tax Department, he demanded to audit the company's books for the years 1920–1923. Drucker obliged, giving Isaac a place to sit down and any financial records he requested, including vouchers, checks, and bills.

Isaac Spier returned to Garant's office almost two weeks later on Monday, July 19, at which point he asked about the company's former accountant:

> **Q.** What did he ask you about?
> **A.** His first question was: How can you give me any information on your stock [inventory]? I says, "Yes, sir." He said, "Why do you have your stock so small at the end of the year?" I explained to him this is a novelty [company]; we work four months, everything we sell out before Christmas. He said, "Who was your last

accountant?" I says, "What difference does that make, anyway? For your information, I will give it to you. In case you want more, I will call my new accountant back." He demanded the name of the old accountant; so I told him his name was Leffler. He said, "Can you put me in touch with him?" So I called up; picked up the receiver and I located him by telephone.

Drucker testified that when he called Louis Leffler on the telephone, Leffler asked to speak with Isaac Spier. The two agreed to meet the following Monday at Garant's office. The following Monday Isaac appeared at Garant's office and asked if Leffler had shown up. Drucker replied, "No sir. Leffler cannot come for certain reasons." Isaac Spier then asked for the cash book and the general ledger. When he reached the year 1924 in the general ledger, Isaac marked crosses for entries he felt indicated fraud. Alarmed, Drucker asked Isaac for clarification. Spier responded with a threat to return a few days later with "several men to audit the books." However, instead of arriving on Thursday, he arrived on Wednesday and in the company of Louis Leffler.

In the next part of his testimony, Drucker discussed how Isaac Spier and Louis Leffler demanded that Garant pay both of them $300.

Q. Who came with him [Spier], anybody?
A. Leffler came with him. Leffler came in at 1:30; Spier came in at 2:30. Leffler came in before and demanded $300.
Q. Who did he ask?
A. Asked me and asked the boss of the corporation.
Q. How many people were in the place when Leffler came there?
A. There was five members of the corporation. I think my wife was back that afternoon. Also Mr. Joseph

Schleifman, Morris Levine, Max Fox, and Gabriel Gross.

Q. What did Leffler say about the $300?

A. He wanted $300.

Q. What for?

A. He asked for—we didn't know what that money was for. I asked him, What do you want the money for? He said the money is coming to him.

Q. Did Leffler ask for that money before Spier came in?

A. Before Spier came in.

Q. Was there any conversation had between this Leffler and Spier that afternoon?

A. Yes.

Q. State what it was.

A. Well, Spier came in and we were talking to Mr. Leffler inside of the shop; he was still insisting upon getting his $300. If he didn't get $300, he didn't intend to give Spier any information. Finally Spier came in right to the office; my wife came out and told me that a gentleman wants to see me; I knew it was Spier, because I saw him come in; I told Leffler, Spier came in, you better go in and see what you can tell him; finally he did go in with me; the moment we come, he looked at Spier; he said, Spier, I don't think I will be able to give you any information; these people owe me money; if I get my money I will give you information. So Spier says, I am not interested whether you get it or not. I am going to audit the books just the same. He asked for and opened the cash book and started; he says, started to talk about it, while he was making a check in the book; Mr. Leffler asked him; he says, Spier, have you any blank [forms] of a certain report? Spier opened his brief case; he looked in, he said, no, sir, I ain't got it; we only get two blanks at a time; the Department does not give me any unnecessary blanks; he started to check up certain business concerns; they stood around for about an hour and a half, then Leffler says to me; he winked at me, I should go out; I went out.

Drucker then testified that he left his office, leaving Louis Leffler and Isaac Spier alone. But before he left, he had a conversation with both Spier and Leffler.

Q. What conversation did you then have with Spier and Leffler?

A. When I went into the office, Leffler says, Spier you are out of your way; you will have to come down; Spier laughed to himself; I says, what is all about it? Spier says, I want $750. I says, $750? I says, we haven't got 750 pennies in the bank today. Well, he [Isaac] says, I will tell you; he opened the cash book and he looked in it. [Spier said,] "Here is, I can see there is five or six thousand dollars fraud in the books; it will cost you— the Government—State Tax Department so much, the Federal so much, then a fine, will be imposed upon you. You will have jail or, if you get off it will cost you $2,200 in cash. I think $750 is worth it, well worth it."

Just before Leffler left Garant's office, he advised Drucker that "It is a bad case. He [Spier] said it is fraud. There is jail for that, if that case goes to court." Drucker complained to Leffler that $750 was "too much." Sometime later, both Spier and Drucker called back and asked to meet with him.

Q. Tell us what the conversation was between Leffler, Spier and yourself.

A. When I came in the room again, Leffler say to Spier, "You are out of your way; you want too much money." When I heard that I said, "What is all about it?" He [Leffler] said, "Mr. Spier says, well, I want $750. So I kind of felt funny in a little moment." I says, "We have not got any $750 in the bank right now; we had just paid a note for $5,000. You can look through the cashbook and see it." Well, he [Spier] opened the cashbook and he began to write, line up some little items there. He [Spier] says, "This is a case of fraud. You will have to pay to the State Tax Department so much to the Federal authorities, and then it will be double; then a fine attached to it, and I think it will cost you about $2,200. He says, "You can go to jail yet; I think $750 is reasonable."

Q. Did you [ask what the money was for]?

A. Then I asked him, what is the $750 for? He said, "Well, if you give me that money we will give you a clean bill of health. You can go to work and destroy all your books, your records, all the records, you can destroy them, in case the Federal authorities come around; you can tell them we have no room for any junk, to keep a set of books; the State Tax Department examined everything; we destroyed them."

According to Drucker's testimony, Louis Leffler assured Drucker that everything would be okay and instructed him to take his accounting books home if he did not want to destroy them. The officers of Garant sat down with Leffler and Spier and told the latter two men that they did not have any cash for any sort of payoff. Isaac responded that he would have to turn in his report by Friday. The meeting concluded without resolution; "The whole thing was left in the air."

Drucker explained that he saw Spier and Leffler at his office the next day and the latter reiterated that Garant's accounting records were in bad shape and that Drucker had to "fix things up." Leffler once again demanded payment of $300, but Drucker instructed Leffler to settle the matter with Spier. Isaac Spier called twice the next day and demanded to know what

Drucker was going to do. Drucker replied, "What can I do? I ain't got any money." The two men agreed to meet in the center of the platform at the DeKalb subway station in Brooklyn at 5:30 P. M. Isaac Spier appeared with his wife (Ida), whom he introduced to Drucker. After Ida left the group, Drucker and Spier went to the St. Regis Restaurant on Fulton Street, just opposite the Woolworth's Five and Ten Cent store. Isaac lowered his demand for payment to $250 for himself and $300 for Leffler, and he threatened to turn in his report the next day if Drucker did not comply. The two men agreed to meet the next day, Saturday.

The next morning Drucker met with his accountant, Mr. Bobick, at the latter's office at 1133 Broadway. From Bobick's office the two men went first to police headquarters, where they met with the chief of police and Drucker lodged a complaint against Leffler and Spier. Mr. Schleifman, one of Drucker's co-workers, brought $400, which a detective marked for a planned sting operation. Mr. Loughman, deputy commissioner of the New York State Tax Bureau in charge of the Metropolitan District (Manhattan, the Bronx, and Richmond), recorded the numbers of the four $100 bills.

Drucker then proceeded to go to Leffler's office in the company of Schleifman, Detective O'Brien, and Loughman, where they met with Spier and Leffler. Drucker told Isaac Spier that he "got the money." Isaac replied, "Everything is alright; we will fix that up."

Drucker, Spier, and Leffler then went into Leffler's private office.

Q. What, if anything, did Leffler or Spier say at the time you went to Leffler's office?
A. When I came in we all sat down and I said, why I got the money. Mr. Leffler says, everything will be fixed up nicely in the Garant's report, State tax report. They brought in the report. Mr. Leffler had it in his hand, was

looking through, he looked at me; he said, this way—so I knew what he meant, the money. I put my hand in my pocket, took out $400 in $100 bills. Four bills, $100 each. I gave $200 to Mr. Spier and $200 to Leffler.

At this point Leffler complained that Drucker should have brought $550. Drucker replied that he could deliver only $400 at the time; he had no more. Drucker handed Leffler a blank check signed by an employee of Garant, which Leffler filled out for the remaining $150. Leffler then rang a bell alerting a switchboard boy to come into the room. Drucker instructed the boy to go to the bank, break the $100 bill he was handed, and bring back two $50 bills. The boy dutifully followed these orders, a signal to Detective O'Brien, who waited outside of Leffler's office, that the sting operation was proceeding as planned.

After the boy returned with two $50 bills, Drucker handed them over to Leffler, who stuffed one bill in his pocket and gave the other to Spier. Isaac Spier then opened his briefcase, retrieved yellow blank forms, and began filling them out. Leffler shared a state income tax report guidebook with Spier, and the two men discussed exactly how the form should be completed. Leffler left the room and Drucker followed, introducing him to "Mr." O'Brien, who had remained inconspicuous up until that point. Detective O'Brien then grabbed Leffler. Drucker, Leffler, and O'Brien entered Leffler's office, where Isaac Spier was still filling out the yellow forms. Drucker informed Spier that "They got the money," to which Isaac Spier replied, "Give me the money." O'Brien took out his gun and said, "Stay still," and ordered Drucker to telephone Mr. Sachs at the police station and tell him to appear at Leffler's office. Unfortunately for Drucker and the police, the sting operation did not go exactly as planned. The bills were not in Isaac Spier's possession but instead on the floor by his chair.

Many were called to testify before the Grand Jury, including some of those previously mentioned in Drucker's testimony:

Joseph Schleifman, another Garant Lamp employee; Samuel Rosensweig, a member of the firm of Leffler, Neidle & Frank; Michael Loughman; Detective John O'Brien; Sidney Bobick; James Donovan, chief of the New York State Tax Department field bureau in which Isaac Spier worked and Spier's supervisor. Their testimonies corroborated Harry Drucker's statements. The Grand Jury indicted both Isaac and Louis Leffler and remanded each with a fine of $2,500.

In his defense, Louis Leffler signed an affidavit with a somewhat different account of what transpired. Leffler argued that Garant owed him $258.34 for previously rendered services and an additional $50 for answering a request from Drucker to come into Garant's office to review the company's accounting books. Isaac Spier signed a similar affidavit, which dovetails with Leffler's statement that no wrongdoing occurred.

The trial began in March 1926, and ended two weeks later with a hung jury. At the request of the U. S. attorney for the Eastern District of New York, the Federal Grand Jury indicted Louis Leffler for preparing a false income tax return form, but dismissed the extortion charges. Leffler endured a subsequent trial in federal court but once again won an acquittal.

Isaac also won the acquittal, and documents in the case file explain why. One reason, according to the notes the assistant district attorney's wrote in preparation for his closing statement, that the attorney for Louis Leffler claimed that his client tried to frame Isaac. Even if Leffler had framed Isaac, Isaac was guilty of failing to follow procedure. Isaac should have reported any income tax deficiency to his superior at the New York State Tax Bureau. In a memorandum, Tax Commissioner Merrill wrote that if Isaac had performed his job properly, he would have been "in the midst of making the amended returns" at the time of his arrest. In court, trial witnesses gave conflicting testimony regarding who extorted whom; most of the witnesses chose Leffler as the true instigator.

Lastly, only one witness said he actually saw Isaac take the two marked $100 bills and the $50 bill in the sting operation. Most other witnesses were not involved in the sting operation; they only saw bills lying on the floor next to Isaac during the operation and did not hear Isaac make any propositions. The New York State Tax Bureau did not accept the trial verdict for Isaac. In fact, the bureau questioned Isaac again. In a letter to the Commissioner of the New York State Tax Bureau, dated June 29, 1925, Isaac's supervisor, James Donovan, wrote:

> *Auditor Spier has been suspected for some time past. It is my opinion that he is the author of anonymous letters sent to the department complaining about various employees. I have not been able to prove this nor could I discover any irregularities in his actions. Apparently he was a hard worker. His record for completed audits and the amount of additional taxes collected is good. He is queer in many ways and very stubborn in his dealings with taxpayers, but investigation of complaints against him never seemed to warrant any action more drastic than a reprimand.*
>
> *I was surprised to learn of his part in the present case, particularly as he was at the time practically suspended and awaiting the action of Commissioner Lynch on charges against him on Tuesday in another case.*
>
> *He was taken from the field on June 23 and notified to remain in the office until further notice. He was in the office Saturday morning until about 11:50 and must have gone directly from the New York office to the office of the accountant with whom he was apparently in league.*
>
> *I take it you are as familiar with this latest case as I am, still would like to discuss it with you.*

Donovan's description of Isaac Spier as "queer" may have derived from Isaac's speech patterns and appearance. Cousins told me that Isaac talked in a hurried manner and either stuttered or stammered. He also blinked uncontrollably, possibly because of a nervous tic.

The other case that James Donovan obliquely referred to in his letter above involved the London Button Company, at 5 Union Square West. Isaac had audited the company even though he had no directive to do so. Since Isaac was not a member of the Corporate Audit Division of the New York State Income Tax Bureau and had no authorization to do so, he could not audit a company. The fact that Charles Frost, the London Button Company's outside accountant, and Louis Leffler, Garant Art Lamp & Novelty's former accountant, both worked at 292 Madison Avenue suggests that Isaac probably met the latter during his audit of the London Button Company.

During the period 1926 through 1929 the Internal Revenue Service, the New York district attorney's office, and the Department of Justice continued to pursue Isaac Spier and Louis Leffler. The Internal Revenue Service was concerned about Leffler's application to practice accounting for the Treasury Department in tax matters. The Treasury Department wanted to know whether it should afford Leffler this right.

In 1928 Leffler once again faced the same charges in a new trial, but this time he was the sole defendant. The jury acquitted him by a vote of nine to three, and Judge Campbell felt another trial would only end in the same result. In 1929, four years after Louis Leffler's and Isaac Spier's arrest, the district attorney's office finally capitulated: "The People have no additional evidence to support the indictments. I am of the opinion that, if this case were tried again, it would result in another disagreement or acquittal, and I believe that a jury would be justified in having, and would have, a reasonable doubt of the defendants' guilt. I therefore recommend that the bail of both defendants be discharged."

I had now reached another point where I easily could have stopped my research. But I still suffered from a nagging feeling. I knew so much about his life, more than that of any other ancestor or anyone else in my life, yet I could not find where he had been born. I searched all of the records that were available at the time—the New York City birth index, the United Kingdom civil registrations index, the 1880 United States federal census, and the 1881 British census (only for London; other counties were not available at the time)—to no avail. The answer to the mystery of my Isaac's birthplace would remain unsolved for many years.

Dopey Benny Fein entering the New York State Reformatory at Elmira. (Elmira Biographical Registers and Receiving Blotters, New York State Archives, Albany)

Benny Fein with wife Gertrude and sons Paul and Morton. (Geoff Fein)

Monk Eastman.

Sing Sing Prison mug shot of Harry Horowitz, alias "Gyp the Blood," 1914. (Lewis Lawes Papers, Special Collections, Lloyd Sealy Library, John Jay College of Criminal Justice)

Harry Horowitz, "WANTED" poster, 1908.

Louis Rosenberg (left) and Harry Horowitz.

Sing Sing Prison mug shot of Louis Rosenberg, alias "Lefty Louie," 1914. (Lewis Lawes Papers, Special Collections, Lloyd Sealy Library, John Jay College of Criminal Justice)

Louis "Lepke" Buchalter, seated behind table. (Library of Congress)

NYPD identification photo of Louis "Lepke" Buchalter, 1933. (Burton Turkus Papers, Special Collections, Lloyd Sealy Library, John Jay College of Criminal Justice)

Louis "Lepke" Buchalter. (Library of Congress)

Above: Irving Wexler entering New York State Reformatory at Elmira.
(Elmira Biographical Registers and Receiving Blotters, New York State
Archives, Albany)

Below: Irving Wexler entering Leavenworth Federal Penitentiary,
Leavenworth, Kansas. (FBI file)

ary, Leavenworth, Kansas, or his authorized representative, to open all mail mat-
ddress, and to sign my name as endorsement on all checks, money orders, or
as long as I am a prisoner in said institution.

Signature *Irving Wexler*

Louis Shomberg entering New York State Reformatory at Elmira. (Elmira Biographical Registers and Receiving Blotters, New York State Archives, Albany)

Benjamin Gitlow. (Library of Congress)

Fiftieth wedding anniversary party for Louis Shomberg's parents. Back row (left to right): brother Dave, sister Esther Laug, Louis Shomberg, sister Rose, brother Isaac. Front row: brother Dave, mother Rebecca, father Abraham, sister Ray Rothenberg. (Joanne Shomberg)

Sing Sing Prison mug shots of inmates Jacob Seidenshner, alias "Whitey Lewis" (1914), and Charles Becker (1915). (Lewis Lawes Papers, Special Collections, Lloyd Sealy Library, John Jay College of Criminal Justice)

NYPD identification photo of (from left to right) Louis Kravitz, Jacob "Gurrah" Shapiro, Phillip Kovolick, and Hyman Holtz. (Burton Turkus Papers, Special Collections, Lloyd Sealy Library, John Jay College of Criminal Justice)

NYPD identification photo of Jacob "Gurrah" Shapiro (left) and Albert Tannenbaum. (Burton Turkus Papers, Special Collections, Lloyd Sealy Library, John Jay College of Criminal Justice)

NYPD identification photo of (from left to right) Joseph Rosen, Benjamin Siegelbaum (alias "Bugsy Siegel"), Harry Teitelbaum, Harry Greenberg, and Louis Buckhouse (upper part of Siegel's image removed in 1932).(Burton Turkus Papers, Special Collections, Lloyd Sealy Library, John Jay College of Criminal Justice)

View of the Old Cell Block, overlooking the Hudson River. (Author's photo)

View from inside the Old Cell Block. (Author's photo)

Jewish chapel, Sing Sing prison. (Author's photo)

Piyut (religious poem) written in Aramaic by inmate Moses Rosengarten with help from Rabbi/Chaplain Israel Davidson, 1902. (Courtesy of the Library of the Jewish Theological Seminary of America, New York)

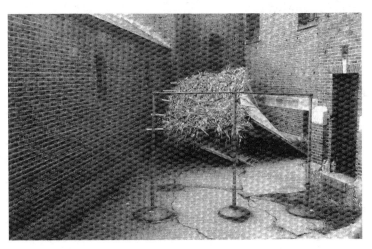

Sukkah built by Jewish inmates, blown over by wind. (Author's photo)

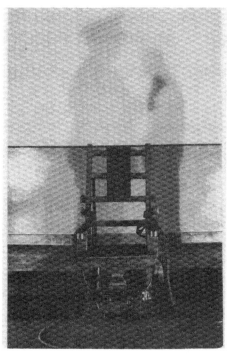

Publicity photo of Sing Sing's electric chair taken for Warden Lewis Lawes' book 10,000 Years in Sing Sing. *(Lewis Lawes Papers, Special Collections, Lloyd Sealy Library, John Jay College of Criminal Justice)*

The "Death House," where electrocutions occurred. (Author's photo)

Sing Sing perimeter wall and guard tower. (Author's photo)

Looking out a window of the Old Cell Block. (Author's photo)

Cell Block A today. (Author's photo)

Gymnasium built by Warner Brothers and originally used as a movie production set. The Warner Bros. were Jewish. (Author's photo)

10

Louis "Lepke" Buchalter

BY THE END of his career, Louis "Lepke" (a Yiddish diminutive of Louis) Buchalter had compiled almost as many aliases and nicknames as arrests and convictions: Louis Buckhouse, Louis Buckholtz, Louis Kauver, Louis Kawer, Louis Cohen, Lou Brodsky, Judge Brodsky, Judge Lewis, The Judge, Judge Louis, Judge Louie, Murphy, Louis Saffer, Sefky, Lefky, Lepky, Lepke, The Leopard, The Rockefeller of Rackets. One name, "Schnozzle," referred to what the FBI described as a "nose large, rather straight and blunt," which fit with his "prominent" ears and "alert and shifting" eyes. The Feds also reported that Louis Buchalter habitually wore snap-brim felt hats with the brim intentionally turned down to "offset the length of his nose."

Lepke represents the worst of the worst in Jewish criminality. Highly successful despite his numerous convictions and prison terms, Buchalter ultimately rose to achieve the position of "Public Enemy Number One" in New York. Lepke served time in more big houses than any other criminal in American history, with the possible exception of Irving Wexler. The Feds even considered transferring Lepke from Leavenworth to Alcatraz, a move that would have catapulted him onto the very short list (a list of one—Irving Wexler) of those who served time in Sing Sing, Leavenworth, and "The Rock." In the end, the Alcatraz Warden decided against this move, fearing that, "He might become a leader among the more dangerous and disreputable elements of the inmate population here." Unlike

Wexler, however, Buchalter did not die in prison of natural causes. He died in the electric chair.

BARNETT BUCHALTER, LOUIS'S father, who had been married twice before, brought four children to the marriage with his last wife, Rose DeWaltoff. She also contributed four children to the party, from her late husband, Solomon Kauvar. If eight children were not enough, the couple conceived three more in the late 1890s. Louis, born on February 12, 1897, at 88 Essex Street (now home to the Henry Street Settlement), was the second youngest in the family. With a band of eleven children, Barnett, who had sold lumber in Russia, struggled to earn a living managing a hardware store on Essex Street, frequently moving his minions to new residences on Madison and Henry Streets, possibly because he earned too little to both put food on the table and pay rent. For a time the family lived at 217 Henry Street, a two-family, five-room "old style" brick house, in a slum littered by factories, poolrooms, and saloons. Records indicate, however, that family life was upright; according to FBI reports, Barnett and Rose regularly attended an Orthodox synagogue and, less surprisingly, spoke Yiddish at home. Legend also says that Louis attended Hebrew school.

The eldest children left the nest early on in Lepke's childhood. First to depart was Charles Kauvar, a rabbi who trained at the Jewish Theological Seminary and taught Hebrew at Temple Emanu-El of New York before moving to Colorado in 1902. Heavily recruited, he took over the pulpit at Denver's Congregation Beit Medrash Hagodol, where he served for 69 years, a tenure matched by few if any other American rabbis. Half-sisters Sophie, Minnie, and Sarah Kauvar all married. Brother Jacob Buchalter did not marry until 1926, but he too felt compelled to break out on his own. According to the federal census, of April 1910, that left the parents with just Philip,

Leah, Emanuel, Louis, and Isidore, a more manageable number of mouths to feed. Unfortunately, Barnett died in November 1910 of a diabetic coma, putting the family once again in jeopardy. Without the resources provided by her late husband, Rose struggled to keep her family housed and fed. Some criminologists believe that mother Rose moved to Denver in 1912 to stay with her rabbi son, leaving Lepke alone in New York and opening the door for trouble. More accurately, although Rose may have frequented Denver or left New York for a short period of time, possibly to tend to Charles's two newborn sons. There is no evidence that she moved west permanently. In 1920 she is listed in the federal census as living in Brooklyn. Whether or not her next-to-youngest son, in his teens at the time, was abandoned by his mother or frequently left to fend for himself while she traveled west, the net effect was certainly the same. Lepke did not get the attention necessary to divert his thinking toward more law-abiding activities. As early as 1909 he had developed a penchant for stealing oranges and bananas from pushcarts. And in 1912 he received his initiation to law enforcement, when police brought him into children's court for participation in a gang fight.

Lepke's earlier history foreshadowed a much more law-abiding direction. He attended P.S. 76 through the sixth grade and then P.S. 62. After Barnett's passing, the family, supported by one of Lepke's half-sisters, moved to Brooklyn, where he continued schooling at P.S. 94, at Fifty-fourth Street and Sixth Avenue, and he graduated on June 28, 1912. After school, Lepke found work as a delivery boy to supplement the family's paltry income. (Rose earned income working in a home for elderly widowers, serving kosher food sent by the rabbi of a local synagogue.) In school Louis received good grades not only for his studies and attendance but also for his behavior. If we consider his report cards, nothing then points to his future in crime.

In fact, Lepke could have gone to college if he wanted. He had the necessary grades. But Louis turned down his half-brother Charles's offer to finance the education. Rather than choosing academics, he worked briefly as an errand boy and then as a salesman for a firm that sold theatrical goods, including spangles, tights, and costumes, as well as imported Austrian chandeliers. From the looks of an FBI report, it seems that having a job and earning his own money caused Buchalter's attitude and conduct to change. Increasingly independent, he exerted little effort to find new employment after he lost his job, preferring to spend time with companions in his old neighborhood on the Lower East Side, where he snatched purses and stole packages.

Somewhere between 1913 and 1915, assuming an FBI report is correct, Lepke rented a furnished apartment on the Lower East Side and led a "delinquent existence." It was probably around this time that he teamed up with Jacob "Gurrah" Shapiro, who lived in the neighborhood, on Rutgers Street. Shapiro, like Lepke, came from a large family—four sisters and four brothers—which might explain again why he failed to remain occupied with more legitimate activities. Like Meyer Lansky and Bugsy Siegel, two other notorious gangsters who grew up near each other, on Cannon and Columbia Streets on the Lower East Side, Lepke and Jacob "Gurrah" would remain friends and partners throughout their lives. As comrades, the two frequently crossed the Williamsburg Bridge, which took them to the Brownsville section of Brooklyn, where they tormented pushcart peddlers. Lepke's mischief continued, leading to two arrests for burglary, in September 1915 and January 1916. Fortunately for him, the charges were dismissed on both occasions. However, his luck ran out in May 1916, when he was caught carrying away two suitcases of clothing left in front of a retail store by a sales representative. This arrest led to a one-year sentence to the Cheshire, Connecticut, reformatory, which he entered under the alias of Kauvar—his half-siblings' surname.

Upon release, Louis wasted no time finding trouble. He was arrested, along with Philip Kaplowitz and Rubin Weiss, on

September 28, 1917, for stealing a package containing women's apparel worth approximately $130. Kaplowitz was stock clerk and messenger at a clothing manufacturer, where one day he was given the package to deliver to an express office. Instead he gave it to Lepke and Rubin, who managed to run into a policeman. For this infraction, Buchalter went to Sing Sing for a year. But he had company; in April, after a conviction for attempted grand larceny, Jacob Shapiro joined him at the correctional facility. Prison did not have much of a redeeming effect on Lepke. In fact, it seemed to up the ante. In June 1920, just eighteen months after his release, Lepke and others attempted to steal a quantity of women's apparel valued at $25,000 from the Deluxe Dress Company at 129 West Twenty-second Street. For this crime, Buchalter returned to prison for another two years.

Eventually Lepke became involved in larger and more organized crime. There are several explanations given for this shift. One story is that Arnold "Big Bankroll" Rothstein offered Lepke the opportunity to take a piece of the rackets and Buchalter jumped at the opportunity. Another legend suggests that Lepke and Shapiro joined Nathan "Kid Dropper" Kaplan's gang. While either one of these scenarios is possible, it is more plausible that Lepke and Shapiro learned their trade with the help of Jacob "Little Augie" Orgen, whom they knew from the neighborhood.

Diminutive in size, Orgen lived in the same building as Buchalter, at 88 Essex Street, and was a lieutenant in the gang led by Hyman "Curley" Holtz. Probably better known to the public than Holtz, Orgen had established a reputation as the leader of a strong-arm force in labor disputes, playing both sides, sometimes working for manufacturers and at other times for unions, wherever the money was best. Orgen's mob competed for business with Nathan Kaplan's thugs, and at times both gangs were hired on either side of a strike. On a personal level Kaplan and Orgen were on far from good terms. Kaplan, who had inherited

Dopey Benny Fein's gang, had slashed Orgen's face with a knife, a favor Orgen returned by firing at Kaplan.

But Kaplan wasn't a man to give up. On August 1, 1923, Jacob Shapiro was standing on the sidewalk in front of 75 Essex Street when a car drove by unloading shots. Shapiro took a few hits but survived the attack, and later he identified one of the men in the car as Kaplan. A few days later Shapiro sought revenge and took a few shots at Kaplan, but failed at his mission. Days passed before Kaplan fired back, killing Louis Schartzman, an ex-pugilist who not only had defected from the Dropper's gang but also had stolen Kaplan's girlfriend (even though Kaplan was married). The police arrested Kaplan, a.k.a. The Dropper, for this murder on August 28, but just as he was about to be arraigned in court, Shapiro recanted his previous statements, now saying that he could not recognize Kaplan as the shooter. Shapiro's change in testimony was just a ploy to let Kaplan free so that he could be killed and done away with once and for all rather than be incarcerated by authorities.

Lepke and Shapiro then hired Louis Kerzner, a.k.a. Louis Cohen, to pull the curtains on Kaplan. Toward this end, Cohen waited outside of the Essex Market Courthouse, where Kaplan was being arraigned for assaulting Shapiro. When Magistrate Stanley Renaud gave police the order to take Kaplan into custody to a different court across town to face charges of violating the New York State Sullivan Law for purchasing a handgun without a permit, he was actually signing a death warrant. Escorted by Sergeant Jesse Joseph, Captain Cornelius, and Captain Willemse, Kaplan left the courthouse, where he encountered his wife, Veronica. Before kissing him, she gleefully exclaimed, "Jack, you've beaten all other cases and you'll beat this one uptown." Willemse ordered Mrs. Kaplan out of the way as The Dropper entered the taxi that would escort him to his next court appearance. Suddenly, out of the crowd bounded Louis Cohen, who, as a result of his short stature, had to walk on tiptoes to see his intended target. After pulling a revolver from his pocket, Cohen fired three shots through the cab's rear window. The first shot hit Kaplan square in the back of his head. The second hit the cab driver's ear, and the last shot hit Captain Willemse's straw hat. Mrs. Kaplan ran to the back of the cab when Cohen fired the third shot and screamed, "Don't shoot him!" Cohen pushed her aside and fired another shot through Kaplan's head.

Without its leader, Kaplan's gang lost its prominence in the strong-arm business, and Augie Orgen's gang was the beneficiary. Furthermore, mayor-to-be James J. Walker appeared as counsel for Cohen and Orgen, against whom there was not a shred of evidence. With Lepke pulling the strings behind the scenes, a deal was struck that allowed Cohen to spend a very short term in prison before returning to the streets to create more havoc. Meanwhile, Lepke managed to keep himself in the shadows. Early in his career he had bumped plenty of heads himself, but now that he had come to power he let others do the dirty work for him.

With enough money to diversify their activities, Buchalter and Shapiro founded their own small clothing business, separate from Little Augie's gang, by the latter part of the 1920s. After working together for several years, the two had begun to differ with Orgen on how to run gang operations. Lepke and Shapiro viewed Little Augie as always out for the quick dollar rather than planning a long-term strategy that could result in more sustained revenues and probably less risk. In Lepke and Shapiro's view, prolonged strikes increased the potential profits for everyone, with higher workers' wages leading to increased extortion fees.

A veteran racketeer, Lepke understood the value of his services. While he worked with Little Augie Orgen, he had performed all of the dirty work and yet he was handing over all the profit to Orgen. All that Lepke, Shapiro, Waxey Gordon, the Diamond Brothers, and Lucky Luciano received from Orgen for their efforts was $7.50 a day. Separate from Orgen's tutelage,

Lepke had taken the initiative to extort from the leather workers' union, which at the time, had 20,000 members. In 1922
Lepke double-dipped and took 25 cents per week from every
union member *and* 10 cents per week from employers for each
of their employees. By 1926 Lepke felt confident enough that
he raised the employers' weekly fee for each union employee
to $1, as well as instituting a semiannual fee of $25. The gross
revenues for Buchalter's efforts amounted to more than $2 mil-
lion annually.

Since they had largely taken control over both the garment
manufacturers and the trade unions, Lepke and Shapiro no
longer needed Orgen. Their diverging modus operandi became
quite evident when Orgen received $50,000 from the Building
Trades Employers Association (BTEA) to protect strikebreak-
ers and beat up protestors during the painters' union strike in
1927, while at the same time the painters had already hired
Buchalter and Shapiro's men to protect them during picket-
ing. Curly Holtz told Orgen to walk away from the BTEA
offer, but Augie refused and instead brought in Jack "Legs" Diamond and his brother, Eddie Diamond. On October 15, 1927,
Orgen and his two co-workers met at the corner of Norfolk
and Delancey Streets at 8:30 P.M. Lepke and Shapiro were to
meet with the triad, ostensibly to participate in Orgen's plans.
However, as their car pulled up to the corner, Shapiro and two
others jumped out and started firing. In little time Augie Orgen
was no more and Legs was wounded, though not mortally. On
October 25 Lepke and Shapiro walked into the Clinton Street
Police Station and explained that they heard they were suspects
in the killing, at which point both were booked and charged
with the murder. A few days later the pair was released from
the Police Headquarters building on Mulberry Street, because
of lack of evidence. Apparently out of fear of retaliation, Legs
Diamond refused to name the men who had wounded him and
killed Augie. This meant that, with Orgen out of the way, Lepke

and Shapiro, by default, became the leading racketeers in New York City, with Curly Holtz working for them.

With their costs escalating, thanks to Lepke's increased demands, many manufacturers were forced to move to Bridgeport, Connecticut, and to Pennsylvania to survive. In the meantime Lepke expanded his operations into the fur-dressing industry, charging each shop $50,000 for the right to continue operations without interruption. Many did not care for or could not afford Lepke's tactics: Samuel Nissenbaum, for example, who operated the Acme Fur Tanning Company and refused to pay the requisite fees, suffered from a bomb explosion in his factory, which resulted in $3,000 in damages.

Lepke, the ultimate schemer, realized that since he could not stop manufacturers from moving out of town to avoid paying their "dues," he needed to devise a method to maintain his control over them. At that time, clothing manufacturing was not an integrated business but rather a piecemeal operation. One company would create one portion of a clothing item and then have it shipped to the next company in the process. Realizing that this arrangement required transportation, Lepke seized power over trucking operations, putting him back in control: Manufacturers that did not continue the payoffs would not get piece goods with which to work and would effectively be out of business.

Toward the end of the 1920s the criminal underworld experienced a changing of the guard. In November 1928 the king of the underworld, Arnold Rothstein, was murdered. It took five months, but in May 1929 Frank Costello called a meeting to divvy up the "hidden assets" of Rothstein's empire. The garment business remained with Lepke Buchalter. Lucky Luciano and Lepke took over narcotics. New Orleans went to Kastel and Meyer Lansky. Control of Florida was transferred to William Moretti. Bugsy Siegel was to oversee Las Vegas and Southern California mob operations. All criminal activity in New Jersey belonged to "Longie" Zwillman.

Not satisfied with simple extortion in the garment industry and narcotics, Lepke seized the opportunity to capitalize on his power and position in the underworld. In 1929 he gained control of the flour trucking and baking industries by muscling in and placing his own men in high positions in these organizations. They in turn would extort monies as demanded by Buchalter. The process was not always a smooth one, however.

On April 24, 1933, *Women's Wear (Daily)* reported that the American Federation of Labor had agreed to become involved in a dispute between the Associated Fur Coat and Trimming Manufacturers' Association and the fur workers who were members of the Industrial Union. Just before 10:00 A.M. that day a woman appeared in the offices of the Fur Division of the Industrial Union, at 131 West Twenty-eighth Street, and asked for a "working card" as an employee of the shop of Fox & Weissman. The request generated suspicion, since furriers never asked their workers for cards from the Industrial Union when they obtained jobs. Furthermore, the firm of Fox & Weissman had no connection to the Industrial Union; it was controlled by the Joint Council, another labor organization. The woman's appearance struck the workers as odd, also as if she were staking out the offices, ready to give a signal to others to pounce.

Just moments later, fifteen members of Lepke's mob, presumably representing the manufacturers' association, stormed the building armed with revolvers, knives, and lead pipes and began firing at workers in the building. Shirley Kravitz, an astute switchboard operator, called upstairs to alert union officials to the crisis. When she refused to tell one of the mobsters the location of a particular supervisor, he cut many of the switchboard cables. After his departure, she plugged in one of the remaining working wires and alerted the police. Word of the situation traveled quickly, not only through the building but around the entire neighborhood. Hundreds if not thousands of workers left their posts and joined the fracas. In less than fifteen minutes the entire rampage ended. Two gangsters were dead and the bodies of another six lay strewn in front of the building. The remaining hoodlums ran for their lives. After this incident Lepke and Shapiro and his henchmen kept their distance from the fur-dressing industry and focused their efforts elsewhere.

One of Lepke's many other rackets involved members of Local 138 of the Flour, Furniture, Grocery, and Bakers Supply Drivers union. In 1931 Buchalter installed his own men, Danny Richter and William Snyder, in the bakery industry, from which they collected monies for every barrel of flour transported. The racket worked well until two brothers, Aaron and Isidore Held, brazenly refused to pay their "fees." Aaron Held filed charges in the Bronx County Court against Buchalter, Richter, and Snyder. Snyder and Richter received indictments, stood trial, and were ultimately acquitted. Even though Richter won an acquittal, Buchalter replaced him with another operative, Max Silverman. Snyder posed more of a threat, since he did not tow the line with Lepke's game plan.

On the night of September 13, 1934, Snyder attended a meeting at Garfein's Restaurant at 10 Avenue A in Manhattan. As far as Snyder knew, the meeting had been called to discuss a strike threatened by union officials. The chair reserved for Snyder was conveniently positioned so that its back faced a doorway a few feet away. During the meeting Morris Goldis, one of the other meeting attendees, got up from the table, then returned a few minutes later to shoot Snyder in the back. Shortly after the murder, William Goldis, Morris's brother, took over the reins as president of Union Local 138. In a similar fashion as with the garment industry, members of the Flour Truckman's Association were charged weekly fees of $75 to $100 in addition to their regular dues. These monies were to be divided among William Goldis, Buchalter, and a handful of other union officials.

Around this time, with his business operations running like a well-tuned racecar, Buchalter turned his attention to his personal life. In 1931 he married Betty Wasserman, a divorcée and mother of a son, Harold. Lepke undoubtedly met her at one of many different clubs where she worked as a hostess. The two were so passionate about each other that Lepke went through the official adoption process, treating Harold as if he were his own son. As newlyweds, the couple took two cruises to Europe, in 1931 and 1933, and two more with Harold in tow in 1935 and 1936.

During this time Lepke turned more of his attention to the business of narcotics inherited from Rothstein. At the time, smuggling narcotics into the country was a simple matter—especially since a few Customs officials cooperated after receiving graft. Not only did Customs officers look the other way, but they also provided the appropriate stamps to place on cargo to mark them as legitimate. Even though Customs used different colored stamps every day, Lepke's men had sufficient supplies to handle any situation.

Lepke's lead narcotics agents included his old boss Curly Holtz and Romanian-born Jacob "Yasha" Katzenberg, who had dabbled in liquor distribution during Prohibition. Buchalter had given Holtz and Katzenberg the assignment of locating drugs in Europe, but the latter also went to Asia toward the end of the decade for the same purpose. Passenger ship manifests show both returning from Europe half a dozen times, and Katzenberg's arrival in San Francisco in 1937 on a boat from Manila. In 1938 Yasha returned home from Pireaus, Greece, where he most likely met with George and Elias Eliopoulos, who claimed to be honest businessmen and owners of bauxite and gold mines in Greece. U.S. federal officials held another viewpoint in 1942—the Eliopoulos brothers were "not only the largest narcotic dealers in the United States, but in the entire world." The Feds arraigned the two men for bringing many kilos of heroin and other narcotics into the country.

Like the Eliopoulos brothers, Katzenberg and Holtz saw their careers come to an end during this period. At one point, instead of purchasing the intended contraband with monies Lepke had given him, Curly Holtz used some of it for gambling and other personal expenses. Returning to the United States and sensing that he might be caught by Customs officials or knowing that he had purchased "inferior stuff" with whatever money remained, he disposed of the drugs. Buchalter fumed when he caught wind of this mishap, and shortly thereafter Curly Holtz disappeared forever. Many speculated that Holtz was thrown into the East River with his feet fixed in a block of cement. Katzenberg, whom the League of Nations labeled "a menace" for smuggling opium and morphine into the United States from China, was handed a ten-year sentence for trafficking, after the State Department received Greece's help to extradite him back home. In an effort to cover his tracks, Katzenberg eliminated his own chief of staff, Sammy Lee. Probably on Buchalter's orders, three of Katzenberg's lieutenants were murdered over a five-year period. In one instance someone set off an explosion at the home of Pietro Quintos, at 2919 Seymore Avenue in Brooklyn, where federal narcotics agents found 1,100 ounces of morphine with a street value of $117,000. In the end, however, Katzenberg's efforts were not sufficient to allow him to stick around the neighborhood. After leaving prison, he seems to have disappeared without a trace.

Meanwhile Buchalter appeared to be living a life of leisure. On September 3, 1935, he arrived home in New York with his wife and son on the *S.S. Berengaria*, which had sailed from Southampton and Le Havre in late August, a crossing that might have looked like a vacation for Buchalter. However, passenger ship records indicate Le Havre and Cherbourg were the ports from which Holtz and Katzenberg most often left Europe after conducting their narcotics operations.

In late 1935 the NYPD assigned a number of detectives to track Lepke's comings and goings. Police recorded sightings (or lack thereof) not only at the suspect's residence, 25 Central Park West, and his primary business headquarters, the Raleigh Clothing Company, located on the eleventh floor of 200 Fifth

Avenue (and Twenty-third Street), but also at numerous restaurants known to be frequent haunts of the suspect, sporting
events at Madison Square Garden and Yankee Stadium, and
other locations in the garment and "upper Broadway" districts.

The earliest NYPD "yellow sheets" reported sightings of
Lepke at 10 West Twentieth Street, home to the Perfection
Coat Front Company, a firm that manufactured "fronts," pieces
of fabric that appeared in the front of men's coats. Though Louis was supposedly winding down his connections as a partner of
the concern, throughout November and December 1935 detectives spotted him entering and leaving this building and having
numerous conversations with other men.

By this time Buchalter controlled rackets beyond those of the
garment and fur-dressing industries. They included the Empire
Motion Picture Operators Union, the Leather Goods Workers'
Union, the Bakery and Pastry Workers' Union, the Newspaper Drivers and Helpers' Union, the Laundry Drivers' Union,
the Wholesale Tobacco Drivers and Clerks' Union, retail stores
selling ladies and men's apparel, the Shoe Salesmen's Union,
and the Ladies Millinery Union. Chances were, if you worked
for a union in New York, you paid graft to Lepke. Lepke's am-
bitions kept him busy.

On December 3, 1935, police watched Buchalter as he left
his residence of 25 Central Park West at 9:20 A.M. and caught
a taxi to 1440 Broadway, where he remained for fifteen minutes before proceeding to Perfection's offices. At 11:30 he left
the building and walked to Twenty-second Street and Fifth
Avenue, where he hopped a cab going north. At 12:35 Lepke
and Jacob Shapiro both entered Perfection's offices, where they
stayed for about an hour before leaving with an unidentified
man and walking to and entering 159 Fifth Avenue. Later in
the evening detectives noticed Lepke once again leaving 10
West Twentieth Street and strolling with the same unknown
man to 1440 Broadway, the two entering the building together.
What the police did not know was that, according to an FBI

file written much later, 37 kilos of heroin arrived in New York's harbor that day.

Detectives continued to indicate in their filings from December 21 through December 23 that they had sighted and spoken with the suspect, even though it is unlikely he was even in town, since on December 21, when the *S.S. Georgic* sailed for the West Indies, on board were Lepke, his wife, and son Harold. Of course, it's possible that Lepke and his family flew to the West Indies and simply took the cruise ship home, since the family is listed on the manifest of the passenger ship only on its return to New York on January 2. It's more likely, however, that the police filed bogus reports.

On January 20, 1936, Lepke failed to appear at the Federal Court House for a hearing. As a result, the prosecutor asked for a delay of his case until such time as he could ensure the appearance in court of all the defendants. On February 5 Lepke was not seen at his residence or at the Raleigh Coat Manufacturing Company location. That same day, 100 kilos of heroin arrived in New York City. On April 1 another 120 kilos arrived in the port of New York.

With the narcotics trade booming, Lepke celebrated his success. On April 12, 1936, police tracked him as he left the side entrance of his residence and enjoyed the movie *The Great Ziegfeld*, which played at the Astor Theatre. Less than a week later "family man" Buchalter and his wife joined Mr. and Mrs. Benjamin Levine, their daughter, and twenty others at the Paradise Restaurant, located at Forty-ninth and Broadway, to celebrate the girl's birthday. The party no doubt enjoyed the entertainment of headliners Milton Berle and mimic Jack Gilford, who were appearing in the club's revue.

Daily police reports continued in May 1936. Lepke often entered 200 Fifth Avenue through various stores located in the lobby of the building, including Loft's Candy Store. Lepke's favorite hangout besides his office, however, was Frank's Barber Shop, at 157 Fifth Avenue and Twenty-second Street. On May

19, a day Lepke told police detectives he was headed over to
Frank's, yet another 100 kilos of heroin arrived in New York. In
a period of less than a year Lepke and his gang imported, according to the FBI, "enough narcotics to supply approximately
one-fifth of the entire illicit narcotics market in the country."

Lepke knew he was being followed. To confuse investigators, he altered not only the timing of his daily routine, but also
which doors he used to enter and leave various buildings. With
very few exceptions Lepke usually won the daily cat-and-mouse
game with the police. On September 12, for example, detectives witnessed Buchalter entering 200 Fifth Avenue through
the Twenty-third Street entrance at 12:05 P.M. A bit later they
went to Raleigh's offices on the eleventh floor to find that their
suspect had skipped out. They could only conclude that Lepke
had left the building through the basement exit, which led into
the subway.

The case against Lepke, based on charges of racketeering in
the fur-dressing industry, opened on October 26, 1936, when
the jury was selected. Special State Prosecutor Thomas Dewey,
who had successfully convicted Waxey Gordon for income tax
evasion, charged that Lepke and Shapiro had each grossed more
than $1 million per year. Opening the proceedings, John Har-
land Amen, special assistant to the attorney general, claimed
that the two held responsibility for beatings and violence during
1932 and 1933, when members of the Protective Fur Dressers
Corporation, a trade organization, worked with somewhere between 20 and 30 million rabbit skins, with an estimated worth
of about $14 million. The Protective had sent proposals to both
the Needle Trade Industrial Workers Union and the Lamb and
Rabbit Workers union offering a 100 percent increase in wages
as well as an unemployment fund. In return, the unions had to
agree to unionize all dressers' shops in New York and New Jersey.
Nonmembers were to be "kept in line" by harsh means. Among
the tactics used to bring others around were stench bombs and
stabbings. Firms and individuals who did not comply were also

subjected to explosives. Morris Langer, the New Jersey manager of the union, died after a bomb went off in his car. Julius Litwack of the Waverly Fur Dressing Company in Newark testified that his company joined the Protective after his factory had been bombed and acid had been thrown in his face.

Others testified to intimidation by Lepke, Shapiro, and their lieutenants. Irving Potash, the assistant manager of the joint council of the International Fur Workers Union, claimed that Samuel Mittleman, president of the Protective, tried to bring him into the fold. When Potash told Mittleman that he would have "nothing to do with Mr. Shapiro," Mittleman responded, "You will have to deal with Mr. Gurrah [Shapiro], because Mr. Gurrah is the protective." At one point Ben Gold, the national secretary of the left-wing (Socialist) union, joined the conversation, which had switched to the bombing murder of Langer. Mittleman warned, "You union officers should be practical and avoid things like that in the future. You know that in back of this association are Gurrah and Lepke and they're not playing with toys." Another witness, Julius Bernfield, a partner of Brickner & Bernfield, alleged that he had been attacked three times, which led to the loss of his left eye. "The first time was in my car with my little daughter present. Someone threw acid into the car. It went all over me and some of it went on my daughter's clothing."

The prosecution next tried to connect Harry "Big Greeny" Greenberg and his activities with Lepke and Shapiro. Albert Law, special assistant to the attorney general, tried to show that Greenberg had gone to the Arlington Hotel, at 18-20 West Twenty-fifth Street, and had set up an account under the alias of "Solomon" for visits by "strange men." Law argued that the account had been "very active" in the days leading up to a raid on the Needle Trades Workers Industrial Union on April 24, 1933. Specifically, one of the witnesses had attended a meeting at the hotel, where Greenberg handed out iron pipes to eight or ten men to be used to break up a meeting at union headquarters. Max Engler, the manager of the Arlington Hotel, claimed that he could not recall any trouble in the first police district on the date of the raid. Then again, Engler testified, the hotel's telephone record sheet for the day of the raid was missing and he was unable to find it after a "long search." Mr. Law also showed an item of "Shapiro and party" on February 4, 1933, in the "Solomon Account."

On November 4 Federal Judge Knox reserved his decision, in response to a motion by J. Arthur Adler, Lepke's attorney, to dismiss the case because of lack of evidence. Knox acknowledged that he felt the prosecution needed to provide more evidence or else he would be forced to dismiss the charges. "You haven't a thing in this case connecting Lepke with the conspiracy except the statement of Mittleman that telephone calls were made to telephones with which he had access," Knox warned the prosecution.

With boosted confidence, Maxwell Mattuck, Lepke's chief defense counsel, decided to rest without calling a single witness. He told Judge Knox that none of the more than thirty witnesses for the prosecution had "connected either of the defendants with a single act of violence testified to." Despite his lack of confidence in the prosecution's case, Knox refused to dismiss the indictments against Buchalter or Shapiro and instead handed the case over to the jury.

After two weeks of testimony, the jury toiled to reach a verdict. Judge Knox ordered the jury locked up in the Commodore Hotel until such time as it reached a unanimous decision. After a total of 33 hours, the group concluded its deliberations: Both Lepke and Shapiro were found guilty on all four counts of violating the Sherman Anti-Trust laws. According to the *New York Times*: "The court made no effort to conceal its pleasure at the verdict. Smiling and rubbing his face with his hand, the judge said, 'I am glad you have reached a verdict. It would have been unfortunate if twelve men could not. You have rendered the public a great service.'"

Knox then handed down the sentences for the two defendants: two years and a fine of $10,000 each, the maximum allowable under the law. While the Judge was not impressed with the prosecution's case, that fact did not stop him from wanting to serve justice to these rogues. After he pronounced the sentence, Knox remarked that it was a "mere slap on the wrist." He continued, "I certainly hope that Congress will deal with cases commonly denominated as rackets, when they cross the path of interstate commerce, in much the same manner as is done in kidnapping cases, and provide punishment that will fit the crime, because this trade piracy cannot be permitted to continue in a free government." Furthermore, he refused to hear motions to set aside the verdict, ordered U.S. marshalls to take Lepke and Shapiro into custody, and denied motions to release the two on bail.

In December, just four months later, Buchalter's luck returned when the U.S. Circuit Court overturned his conviction, even though the court upheld the determination for Shapiro. Judges Martin Manton, Harris B. Chase, and Augustus Hand claimed that the prosecution had not provided sufficient evidence against Lepke. As a result, both he and Shapiro were freed in March, 1937 on $10,000 bail each. In his autobiography, Thomas Dewey claimed that Manton had taken a $25,000 bribe before he rendered this decision. While these allegations never led to any sanctioning of Manton, they fit in with a pattern of behavior that caused Manton to resign from the bench just two years later, when the U.S. attorney put him on trial for taking a $10,000 bribe.

On June 21, 1937, when Lepke and Gurrah failed to appear in court for a hearing regarding their trial, scheduled for July and involving antitrust allegations, warants were issued for their arrest. The two were not to be found, at least not in New York. In November an embarrassed sheriff in Clark, South Dakota, admitted that he had held them on charges of soliciting without a license. Out of jail on bond and pending a hearing,

Buchalter and Shapiro, under the aliases of Harry Miller and Sam Bedrick, simply skipped town. The two continued to hide from authorities, with Raleigh Manufacturing sending checks to Lepke for expenses. On April 14, 1938, after a year on the run, Shapiro turned himself in, admitting his exhaustion from evading the authorities.

Lepke, on the other hand, was both determined and a survivor. It took longer for him to come in from the cold. Both New York and federal officials stepped up their efforts and pressure to force the issue. The Feds offered a reward of $10,000 for information leading to Buchalter's arrest, while New York put up $25,000. In August 1939 Thomas Dewey, now federal district attorney, warned bond companies not to assist gangsters unless the latter paid in cash. Furthermore, Dewey warned physicians not to assist Lepke, who had a known kidney ailment. If this were not sufficient, the New York Police Department printed one million wanted posters and plastered them across the nation—in every police station, railroad station, steamship line, airport, bus terminal, and even at the World's Fair. The poster included both a mug shot and another photo of Buchalter dressed in suit, tie, and top hat. The police described him as 5 feet, 5½ inches, 170 pounds, large nose with a blunt end, prominent ears, black hair, dark complexion, and a large slight dimple on his left cheek.

Whether Lepke was afraid is unclear, but others in the underworld questioned the sense of continued association with New York's public enemy number one. Many felt their fate was safer, if not brighter, if they distanced themselves from Louis. Between 1936 and 1939 Lepke conducted a house cleaning, eliminating anyone in his operation or elsewhere he felt might provide information to the authorities. Eat or be eaten, he seemed to feel. On September 5, 1936, Emanuel Weiss, Allie Tannenbaum, and Abraham "Pretty" Levine murdered onetime Lepke slugger Irving Ashkenas in Fallsburg, New York. Ashkenas allegedly was on the New York City district attorney's payroll to serve as an informant against Buchalter. On January 10, 1939, Irving "Knaddles" Nitzberg and Allie Tannenbaum drove to East Ninety-fourth Street and Avenue A, where Nitzberg shot and killed Albert "Plug" Schuman, a known stool pigeon suspected of providing the police with dirt on Lepke. Eighteen days later, at the intersection of Lewis and Grand Streets, Lepke associates Louis Cohen, Murray "Sheppy" Shapiro, and Jacob "Cuppy" Migden shot and killed Daniel Friedman, a.k.a. Danny Fields, a go-between for Lepke and the Amalgamated Workers Union whom Lepke considered a possible source of intelligence to the New York City district attorney. Louis Cohen, who killed Nathan "Kid Dropper," got caught in the crossfire during the Fields murder and died the same day.

Not yet finished with his dirty work, on April 25, 1939, Lepke gave an order to Mendy Weiss to drop Abraham "Whitey" Friedman in order to prevent him from giving information to the district attorney. Harry Strauss, who used a double-barreled shotgun, successfully carried out this operation, assisted by Mikey Sycoff, Allie Tannenbaum, and Seymour Magoon. Then on May 25 Morris "Mersh" Diamond fell to the ground at Sixty-eighth Street and Fifteenth Avenue as he left his home. This time Jack Parise pulled the trigger and Julie Catalano provided the getaway chauffeur services. Lepke felt that Diamond might divulge his knowledge of Buchalter's bakery and flour extortion activities. Irving Penn, an innocent music industry worker, lost his life on July 23, 1939, when he left his home at 178th Street in the Bronx and ran into Jack Parise, Seymour Magoon, and Jacob Migden, who mistook him for Philip Orlovsky, whom Lepke considered a risk to spill the goods to the D.A.

By early August 1939 five gangsters—Morris Goldis, William Goldis, Max Silverman, Abe Cohen, and "Big Harry" Schoenhaus—stepped up to the plate to help Dewey with his search for Lepke. Whether it was the understanding that his own lieutenants had turned against him, ill health, or sheer mental and physical exhaustion is unclear, but on August 24,

1939, Lepke turned himself in, ending a worldwide manhunt that stretched to Cuba, England, France, Puerto Rico, Carlsbad, and Costa Rica. Ironically, all of the efforts to locate Lepke were in vain; most of the time he had been hiding right in Brooklyn, thanks to the help of Abe "Kid Twist" Reles.

The feds had kept his entire family under surveillance and had handed down indictments against the Raleigh Manufacturing Company, thereby eliminating the $250 payments Lepke received for subsistence while in hiding. Acting simply as a messenger, radio announcer Walter Winchell promised Buchalter he would be handed over to the Feds and not to New York State officials, whom he feared more. The Feds simply wanted Buchalter for federal narcotics law violations, while New York wanted to prosecute for several murders. What Lepke did not immediately understand was that he had been duped by an associate who encouraged him to cooperate with Winchell in order to obtain a fair deal. The Feds would ultimately turn him over to New York for prosecution, but not before a political battle.

While awaiting his trial for violating federal narcotics laws, Lepke spent time at the Federal Detention Facility on West Street in Manhattan. Here he wielded enough influence to have a radio in his cell, unlike his peers, and also the freedom to leave his cell and talk to other inmates when he so desired. Donald Wetzel, a conscientious objector in World War II and fellow inmate, wrote in his memoir, *Pacifist*, about the incongruity of his incarceration with Lepke. One simply objected to killing another soul, while the other made a living at the same.

Elsewhere in the Buchalter family times were tough. Louis's half-brother Jacob and his wife Zilpah committed suicide. Consolidated Edison Company employees received a phone call from other tenants in the couple's apartment building complaining that they smelled gas. When the ConEd workers entered the apartment, they found the two lying on a mattress on the kitchen floor, along with three notes detailing the couple's poor health and financial woes. One note, addressed to Zilpah's mother, Emma Smith, explained that the couple had accrued debts of $200 and instructed that these liabilities be paid out of insurance proceeds. Even if he had wanted to help his family, Lepke was behind bars.

The Feds punished Buchalter first by indicting him on several counts of narcotics trafficking. In January 1940 the Feds got what they wanted: a conviction of Buchalter on ten counts of conspiracy charges for involvement in a $10 million narcotics ring. Federal Court Judge Knox delivered the sentence: fourteen years, ten years probation, and a ludicrous $2,500 fine. The worst news for Lepke: Attorney General Frank Murphy agreed to turn him over to District Attorney Thomas Dewey to stand trial on racketeering charges in New York.

One charge in particular would represent the final nail in Lepke's coffin. Indictments rained down in early 1941 on Buchalter, Harry "Pittsburgh Phil" Strauss, Emanuel "Mendy" Weiss, James Fraco, Philip "Little Farvel" Cohen, and Louis Capone for the murder of candy store proprietor Joseph Rosen, a former trucker and potential witness against Lepke. Brooklyn District Attorney William O'Dwyer worked with federal authorities to transfer Buchalter from Leavenworth to Brooklyn to stand trial, and by April 1941 the move had been completed.

Through all this, Betty stuck by her man. Letters she wrote to Lepke in the penitentiary indicate that she either believed in his innocence or loved him beyond his failings. One letter, received at Leavenworth on May 9, 1941, is typical:

Hello Darling,

Sweetheart, I'll stop at nothing and do everything within my power to help you. So will Mannie [brother Emanuel Buchalter] and Phil [half-brother Phil Kauvar]...With all this darn aggravation darling, my only great worry is how you feel. Please keep your chin up and try not to lower your sense of reasoning...All my love and, believe me, dearest, you're every-

thing in the world to me. So buck up, chin up and keep well.
Lovingly,
Betty
xxxxxxxxoooooooo

The trial against Buchalter for murder in New York opened
in August 1941, although the *voir dire* (jury selection) took
months—a Brooklyn court record—to select a jury of twelve
men and two alternates. Nearly 150 out of 250 prospective jurors were excused. Very few wanted to put their lives at stake by
potentially ruling against these hoodlums. Undoubtedly, to al-
lay potential jurors' fears as well as to protect them from retaliation, Judge Franklyn Taylor ordered all jurors to remain at the
Knights of Columbus clubhouse for the duration of the trial.

Max Rubin served as the prosecution's key witness, declar-
ing that he overheard Lepke threaten that he would prevent
Joseph Rosen from testifying against him. Doing this, Rubin
instantly transformed himself into a target; he was shot in the
head after his time on the stand. Fortunately the wound was
not fatal and he was able to continue answering the prosecutor's
questions, informing the court that he had overheard a conversation between Buchalter and Emanuel Weiss in which the two
discussed killing Rosen.

In 1932 Buchalter had told Rubin that he wanted a work
stoppage of all trucks transporting cloth out of New York City.
All trucking companies adhered to the request except for three,
including one owned and managed by Joseph Rosen, who
threatened to complain to the authorities. Ultimately Lepke
disrupted Rosen's operations and forced him out of business;
Rosen then managed a candy store in Brooklyn, an occupation
that barely provided subsistence.

The prosecution bolstered its case by calling two other witnesses: Sholem Bernstein acknowledged that he drove one of
the cars to Rosen's candy store, helped some of the gunmen
leave the scene of the crime, and then ditched the stolen get-

away car. Paul Berger, an innocent bystander, identified the defendants as individuals he saw in the neighborhood the night before the slaying.

Beyond the trial at hand, Lepke tried to limit his exposure to witnesses in other court cases. Abe Reles, who had helped Buchalter while he hid in Brooklyn, was scheduled to testify in the trial against Knaddles Nitzberg for the murder of Plug Schuman. Held by some of New York's "finest" in protective custody at the Half Moon Hotel in Coney Island, Reles was found dead on November 12. The reports suggested that he fell while trying to climb out of the sixth floor window via two knotted bed sheets. More likely, he was shoved out the window. As a stool pigeon, he earned a reputation as the "bird that could not fly."

On November 29, 1941, after just four and a half hours of deliberation, the jury returned verdicts for the three defendants—Buchalter, Capone, and Weiss—all guilty of murder in the first degree. Lepke, determined as ever, fought hard to save his life. He and his attorneys appealed to the New York Court of Appeals, which, on October 30, 1942, upheld the lower court's ruling. Then, as a final last-ditch effort Lepke appealed all the way to the Supreme Court, which on June 1, 1943, also upheld the original decision.

Lepke's life was temporarily extended because of politics between New York State Governor Dewey, federal authorities, and President Roosevelt. Dewey complained via the media in November 1943 that Buchalter was "protected from punishment by the failure of the President of the United States to grant the customary conditional pardon," which would have legally allowed federal authorities to turn Lepke over to New York. A week later Attorney General Francis Biddle sniped back, accusing Dewey of "choosing to communicate" with Roosevelt and Biddle through newspapers rather than in person. Biddle assured Dewey publicly that if he directly asked for Lepke to be transferred to New York, the attorney general would take up the matter with the President.

By late January 1944 the Feds turned Lepke over to New York, where he landed on Sing Sing's death row. Buchalter complained that he was a "martyr to politics." At least several members of Buchalter's family tried to console, if not help him. Possibly the few still interested in helping Louis felt guilty about the suicide of their other brother, Jacob. During his last two months Buchalter received visits from relatives on a regular basis; Betty and Harold saw Lepke every couple of days, but also Emanuel Buchalter, a pharmacist, and Philip Kauvar, a trucker, appeared when they could get away from work.

Short of a last-minute pardon from now Governor Dewey, Lepke, Weiss, and Capone had run out of options. Dewey's refusal was both expected and ironic, however. Years before, when rival gangster Dutch Schultz called on Lepke for the elimination of then D.A. Dewey, Lepke turned down the idea. By trying to keep the focus of the police's light off his operations, Lepke had effectively saved Dewey's life. Dewey did not reciprocate in kind.

Lepke spent three years trying to beat the system, but between 11:01 and 11:17 P.M. on March 4, 1944, the authorities strapped Capone, Weiss, and Buchalter in the electric chair. Once the appropriate lever was pulled, the chair sent between ten and eleven amps through each of their bodies, ten times the amount of current that would normally kill a human.

The *New York Times* reported that Lepke was "a beaten, frightened little man. Gone was his calm disdain, his cocksureness that amounted to impudence. When he entered the death chamber he was subdued." But perhaps appearances deceived. Betty gave the press a final note from Lepke, who remained defiant:

> *I am anxious to have it clearly understood that I did not offer to talk and give information in exchange for any promise of commutation of my death sentence. I did not ask for that. I insist that I am not guilty of the Rosen murder, that the witnesses against me lied and that I did not receive a fair trial.*

*Four out of the seven judges of the Court of Appeals thought
Weiss, Capone, and I were not guilty. Judge Rippey said we
were not given a remote outside chance of any fair consideration of our defense by the jury and that the evidence wasn't
even enough to submit to the jury. The one and only thing I
have asked for is to have a commission appointed to examine
the facts in the Rosen case. If that examination does not show
that I am not guilty, I am willing to go to the chair regardless
of what information I have given or can give.*

Lepke, it appears, was a fighter to the end.

Irving "Waxey Gordon" Wexler

IRVING (**WAXEY GORDON**) Wexler's life is one of the most under-reported and underappreciated American true-crime stories. The less than complete accounting of his life stems, at least in part, from the difficulty in tracking down Waxey's records. Although I had read many books regarding Jewish mobsters and gangsters, no book that discussed Wexler ever provided him the same coverage given to Meyer Lansky, Bugsy Siegel, and Arnold Rothstein, about whom multiple biographies have been written. But after I had copied and transcribed more than 7,000 Sing Sing admissions records for Jewish criminals into a computer database, Wexler piqued my interest. Exploring the level of recidivism among the Jewish inmates, I matched up admissions records of those inmates whose records indicated they served multiple sentences in the prison; and Wexler, with two terms, turned out to be one of them. In fact, once I accounted for his wildly different aliases, Wexler's records indicated he spent time in more big-name prisons than anyone else in United States history!

Already flush with nearly 2,400 FBI documents each about Bugsy Siegel and Meyer Lansky, I investigated the availability of additional information about Wexler at the agency. But Wexler's name, unlike Lansky's and Siegel's, was not posted on the FBI's website. So I filled out the federal government's Form G-639 and applied for all files about him, under the Freedom of Information Act (FOIA). Ten days later a response from the FBI arrived.

Although the agency once maintained four different files on Wexler, the letter explained that the FBI can no longer share a single file today. "Pursuant to Title 44, United States Code, Section 3301 and Title 36, Code of Federal Regulations, Chapter 12, Sub-chapter B, Part 1228, issued by the National Archives and Records Administration," the letter officially mumbled. Once I translated the bureaucratese, I understood that the agency had destroyed two files, in March 1990 and October 2003. A third file, stored on microfilm, cannot be viewed because the agency's equipment is "inoperable." Even if the machinery worked, the FBI continued, the documents would be "almost totally illegible." As for the fourth and last file, the agency admitted it could not be found. "We were advised the records were not in their expected location and could not be located. Following a reasonable waiting period, another attempt was made to obtain this material. This also met with unsuccessful results. Therefore, we are closing your request administrative."

I was disappointed with this news, but my instincts told me other materials about Wexler had to exist elsewhere. My next step was to contact the San Bruno, California, branch of the National Archives (NARA), which houses the case files for the former Alcatraz prisoners. There too I found cooperative personnel but no relevant materials. The specialist at NARA could not locate the inmate file for Wexler, since his name did not appear on the archive's list of more than 1,500 criminals who served time on "The Rock." In fact, the specialist insisted that "If his name is not on the list of Alcatraz inmates, he did not spend any time at the facility." But the archivist's words did not jibe with two documents I had found previously—a *New York Times* article and a California state death certificate. Both indicated Wexler died in Alcatraz in June 1952, when the Bureau of Prisons still used the facility as a federal penitentiary.

Another *New York Times* article provided me with information that further heightened Wexler's uniqueness in my eyes. In 1940 the Feds released Wexler from Leavenworth—along with

Sing Sing and Alcatraz, one of the nation's "big three" prisons known for housing the most notorious criminals. I could not find another criminal who had served time in all three of these institutions.

I next contacted Tim Rives, an archivist at the National Archives facility in Kansas City, who in a previous conversation had provided me with statistics regarding Jewish inmates at Leavenworth. This time I asked whether he had the Leavenworth file for Wexler. He didn't have the file, but he directed me to the "Notorious Offender" collection at the National Archives in the Washington, D.C. area. Sure enough, after contacting NARA in College Park, Maryland, I received an envelope with nearly 400 pages covering Wexler's admissions and other prison records, newspaper articles, and correspondence with relatives and associates. The stamped date and other markings on each page indicated that I was most likely the first person outside the government to view the file after its declassification.

With the combination of Sing Sing admissions registers, newspaper articles, snippets of information from books about gangsters, and the 400-page Notorious Offender file from the National Archives, I was cooking. Additionally, I knew that the New York State Archives in Albany held records for New York correctional facilities beyond Sing Sing, where Wexler served time. Separately, a reference to him in Alan Block's seminal book on New York criminality, *East Side, West Side*, pointed to specific records of the New York Jewish community agency, the Kehillah—an organization that fought crime and helped immigrants transition into society—stored at the Central Archives for the History of the Jewish People in Jerusalem. By combining all of these primary and secondary sources, I was able to assemble a composite picture of Wexler's life.

Wexler's first Sing Sing admission record served as a good base from which to begin piecing together his elusive and convoluted story. According to this document, the prison received Wexler under the alias of Harry Brown on August 12, 1915.

Just three days earlier Judge Malone of the Grand Sessions court had handed him a sentence of two years on a conviction of grand larceny in the second degree as a *first-time offender*. So it appears that the district attorney did not have all of his facts straight: Wexler had already served time in other institutions, and for numerous violations including grand larceny, according to the rap sheet section of his admission record.

As for the events leading up to his arrest and conviction, a *New York Times* article provided details. On February 20, 1915, Wexler and three accomplices raided the merchant's exchange and wholesale store of Joseph Slotopolsky at 383 Grand Street in Manhattan, taking $460 in cash and jewelry worth hundreds more. Although not immediately apprehended, he did not evade the law for long. Months later Detective Sergeant Patrick Sheridan located Wexler at a swimming pool at "North Beach," on East Ninety-sixth Street. Demonstrating exceptional bravado, Sheridan jumped into the pool, introduced himself by saying, "Hello, Waxey," and arrested the subject.

Although he was not slippery enough to avoid capture, Wexler's admission record to Sing Sing demonstrates that assuming aliases—among them Benjamin Lustig, Waxey Gordon, and Louis Wechsler (his father's name)—was one of his escape routines. Some said it was Gordon's gift for picking pockets that led to his nickname Waxey. His skills were considered so advanced that he earned a reputation of being able to pluck objects from his victims as if their pockets were "lined with wax." Others offer a much simpler explanation, suggesting that Wexler's name simply morphed from Wexler to Wexie to Waxey.

If Waxey used his father's name as one of his aliases, he did not do so because they were close. Louis and Beila Wechsler, born in Lemberg (now called Lvov) and Berlin, respectively, immigrated to America in the late 1880s. Louis, an Orthodox Jew and "expressman" (trucker), and his wife raised Irving and their three younger children, Rachel, Lena, and Nathan, on Forsyth and Chrystie Streets on Manhattan's Lower East Side in the heart of the Jewish district. The family home was just a few blocks north of the pushcart merchants on Hester Street and west of Allen Street and its streetwalkers.

It was on Forsyth Street that on April 1, 1898, when Irving was about ten years old, Beila collapsed and died of heart failure. Shortly thereafter Irving dropped out of school and joined the workforce, running errands and subsequently becoming a bellhop, according to his FBI file. By 1900 Irving's father had remarried a Romanian woman named Bertha, who, according to Gordon, was "mean" to him. Louis and Bertha would create their own family of four, starting with the birth of their first child, Gertrude, in 1902.

In October 1905 Gordon was convicted of grand larceny truly for the first time, and the judge sentenced him to serve up to a maximum of five years at the New York State Reformatory at Elmira. When he was admitted to Elmira, Wexler contended several things that do not hold up to scrutiny. First he gave his name as Benjamin Lustig, which prison officials quickly dismissed, recording his real moniker as Isidore Wexler. He furthermore indicated that he lived down the street from his family in the home of his employer, at 140 Forsyth Street. The 1905 New York State census disputes these facts and even suggests that Wexler's first name was not even Isidore or Irving. According to this census, he still resided with his family at 101 Forsyth Street and worked as a cap maker. The census also indicates that his family called him Ike. The 1900 federal census also lists his name as Isaac, so this is likely his true name.

Opened in 1876, Elmira redefined the term "reform." Instead of preaching and attempting religious conversion, as did all other prisons at that time, this new institution concentrated on education, ultimately teaching 34 different trades to its inmates, among them telegraphy, clothing cutting, and plumbing. Located on a 280-acre site, the facility received only first-time offenders between the ages of sixteen and thirty, as mandated by the state. These were the "hopefuls," young men the authorities believed could be rehabilitated and returned to society. Elmira garnered so much notoriety, largely from the publicity generated by the facility's founder, Zebulon Reed Brockway, that judges sent convicts to the facility faster than existing inmates could be paroled. As a result, the number of cells grew from the original 504 to 1,296 in 1892, and by the late 1890s the number of inmates had swelled to nearly 1,500.

Upon his entrance to Elmira, Waxey weighed 110 pounds— lean and muscular for a scrapper only 5 feet, 1¼ inches tall. Possibly because of his diminutive size, officials also assessed his mental capacity as "little." This would not be the first time Irving's "talents" were underestimated. Judging from his subsequent successes in crime, we shall see that Gordon may have been using some of his wiles to outwit the authorities. Whatever he may have lacked in mental faculties, he more than compensated for with a combination of brawn, quickness, and determination.

Although he received his parole almost a year to the day after his admission to Elmira, he quickly returned to his old habits. Just a few months later, in January 1907, Judge Rosalsky of the General Sessions Court convicted Wexler, now under the alias of Benjamin Lester, of grand larceny and ordered him back to Elmira, where he spent three months. Upon his second release from the reformatory, Wexler loitered in Boston and Philadelphia, two cities that convicted him of picking pockets under the alias of Harry Middleton. In Philadelphia authorities arrested him for snatching $3.72 from a woman's purse during the height of the Christmas shopping season and sentenced him to nineteen months in the county prison in Holmsburg, Pennsylvania.

No one knows why he did not return to New York directly after his second release from Elmira, but two plausible explanations present themselves. First, he may have felt he was too well known by New York authorities to continue plying his trade.

Second, some have conjectured, he may have wanted to learn the ins and outs of the criminal world in other metropolises. Philadelphia *would* serve his needs down the road.

After violating parole, Irving again returned to Elmira in 1912. Then, after serving his last term at the reformatory, he returned to New York City and married Leah Goldman, the daughter of a tailor, in mid-December 1913. Waxey and his wife received two marriage certificates: the first from December 9, for a civil service at City Hall, and the other dated December 12, on which Dopey Benny Fein is listed as a witness. On both certificates Waxey listed his first name as Isidore. Over the next few years the couple led, by all appearances, a law-abiding life, creating a family with three children: Theodore, Beatrice, and Paul.

But the appearance was not the reality. Sometime before he married, Wexler had joined Dopey Fein's gang of hoodlums. It is likely that the two met each other at Elmira between 1905 and 1910, since "The Dope" had also served multiple terms in the reformatory. Benjamin Fein, known as the first true American racketeer, and his followers were involved with aiding union labor in their strikes against clothing manufacturers. On the other side of these struggles, the rival Italian Jack Sirocco gang sided with the companies.

While the two gangs frequently knocked heads, temperatures did not rise to a dangerous level until November 29, 1913, when the groups took opposite sides in a strike involving the Handle and Umbrella Makers' Union. A fight in front of S. Feldman's Hat Frame Factory at 168 Greene Street led to the murder of "Little Maxey" Greenwalt, one of Dopey's men. Benny's gang held a memorial ball for Maxey at the Frankford Social Club, and advertisements for the event alluded to the potential for "pistol skirmishes."

In response, on January 9, 1914, the Harry Lenny and Tommy Dyke Association, composed largely of members of the Sirocco gang, rented Arlington Hall, at 19-23 St. Mark's Place (between Second and Third Avenues), for their own ball. Originally built in 1833 as a German music center, Arlington Hall became a dance and social club used by families for weddings and bar mitzvahs. The Lenny and Dyke Association advertised their ball with placards that listed names of famous gangsters. The Sirocco gang no doubt intended to antagonize Benny Fein's group even further by holding their affair in what was considered Jewish territory.

The night of the event, several of Dopey Fein's men, including Benny, "Little Abie" Beckerman, Rubin Kaplan, and Wexler, took stakeout positions near the entrance to Arlington Hall and waited for their opportunity to retaliate. Their intended target was Charles Piazza, who Fein gang members believed had killed Greenwalt. As Piazza walked up the stairs to Arlington Hall carrying a box of badges for the event, Fein's men opened fire. Not a single shot hit Piazza, but one misfired bullet mortally wounded City Court Clerk Frederick Strauss, an innocent bystander.

Samuel Lipsig, who was walking with his son to hear a lecture at Cooper Union, overheard one of the gunmen say to Edward Morris, the bouncer at Arlington Hall, "Fat Bull, hide me!" Lipsig quickly located Patrolman Sullivan and convinced him to take Morris to the Fifth Street Police Station. Eventually, Benny Fein and a few of his men were apprehended and held without bail. Unfortunately for Waxey, Lipsig identified him as the gunman who asked for Morris's assistance after the shooting. Under tough and exhausting questioning by Second Deputy Commissioner Dougherty and Inspector Faurot, Morris finally admitted that Wexler had spoken to him. But this time luck was on Waxey's side; Assistant District Attorney Deacon Murphy had no corroborating evidence and was forced to free Benny, Little Abie, Rubin, and Wexler. In an ironic twist of events, Police Captain John F. Sweeney, who was managing the Fifth Street Police Station on the night of the Strauss murder, was put on trial for not taking precautions to prevent such violence from occurring. Neither Waxey nor Benny went to prison for this incident, but the latter had an altercation with Officer Sheridan just a few days later, winding up in a conviction that sent Benny back to Sing Sing for two years. The fall of Fein's gang forced Wexler to look for new opportunities. For some time until his admission to Sing Sing in 1915, he worked as a strong arm for Arnold Rothstein. Waxey served seven months in the Big House before receiving a transfer to Auburn Prison in upstate New York. On March 16, 1917, 53 weeks later, he received his next parole.

It took little time for Waxey's name to get the attention of Abe Schoenfeld, chief investigator for the Bureau of Social Morals, part of the New York Jewish community's Kehillah organization. In mid-1917 Schoenfeld, in a report to his superiors, wrote about Wexler:

> *A gangster and a tough man...His notorious deeds would fill many pages...He worked with Dopey Benny and was mixed up with everything the Dope was interested in. He broke many a poor Jew's head and was always a bully in the mob.*

Around the same time, Schoenfeld reported to his superiors in the Kehillah that each month Jewish dealers imported $100,000 worth of cocaine from Canada. By contrast, Italians shipped their goods primarily from Italy. Drugs were also obtained from the West Indies and South America. Schoenfeld identified 263 separate dealers, of whom nearly a third were Jewish. The group also consisted of twenty-three Italians, eight Irish, five blacks, and three Greeks. Nearly half of the dealers worked in groups called "combinations."

Waxey belonged to several combinations simultaneously. In the first, he teamed with Hymie Fishel, a pimp; with a man named Mahlo, who frequented subways to steal from women's pocketbooks; and with Little Nadie, a pickpocket and burglar. In what arguably was the best-connected group, Waxey worked with Jonsey and Al Lampre. Jonsey, alias Jonsey the Wop, had experience selling "opium toys" in his cigar store at 129 East Fourteenth Street. Lampre, alias Cockeye Al, was an independent wholesaler who sold narcotics to at least ten dealers in the city. This group frequented Odd Fellows Hall, located at 98 Forsyth Street, just across the street from where Gordon used to live. A third combination, which focused its sales on Harlem, was composed of Waxey, Nigger Snyder, and Waxey's brother, Nathan, who used the alias of Harry Irving. Waxey also participated in a Philadelphia-based combination that included Irving "Jew Murphy" Cohen and Jack Pipes. Jew Murphy, a former member of Benny Fein's gang, broke up strikers and had served time in the Tombs for burglary. Schoenfeld referred to Pipes as a "lammister," because he had skipped a bail bond in Brooklyn. Finally, Waxey worked with Little Simon and Hershel Chalamudnick, meeting at a tearoom on Grant Street.

Although Wexler worked in multiple combinations simultaneously, he set ground rules for others in his groups—they could not switch from one of his groups to another. However, that rule did not stop individuals from joining other combinations, those that did not include Waxey, in order to increase their chances of getting a larger piece of the action. Waxey's various partnerships made him one of the leading forces in the narcotics trade. Without a doubt, this position prepared him for the next phase of his criminal career.

Waxey became one of the leading bootleggers in the New York metropolitan area, but he did not accomplish this on his own. Instead he received experience and financing from other sources. One of his helpers was Big "Maxie" Greenberg, a former member of the Egan's Rats, a gang formed in 1907 in St. Louis and named after its founder, Fifth Ward Democratic Committeeman Thomas Egan. The gang focused its efforts on burglary, robbery, and theft from railroad boxcars, and it would become one of the leading illicit trafficking forces during prohibition. After Egan died of natural causes in 1919, his brother

William took over the reins. Once in the driver's seat, Willie
pulled numerous political strings to reduce Big Maxey Greenberg's five-year prison sentence for interstate theft to just six
months. Showing barely a smidgen of gratitude for Egan's assistance, Greenberg joined the rival Hogan Gang after his release and shortly thereafter moved to Detroit, where he learned
the business of smuggling liquor from Canada.

Now knowledgeable about the business and interested in
carving a niche for himself, Greenberg contacted Wexler, who
had experience on a par with Greenberg's. In addition, Greenberg hoped Wexler would put him in contact with Arnold
Rothstein, who had bankrolled a number of other big-name
gangsters. A former Rothstein employee, Wexler obliged. Apparently this was a good move, because Rothstein ultimately
accepted the proposal from Maxey Greenberg and Waxey Gordon to invest the $175,000 required to buy boats, ammunition,
and bootleggers and start the operation.

According to legend, Rothstein initially met Greenberg and
Gordon in Central Park and listened to the former's plan to
smuggle whiskey across the Canadian border. The timing was
right—the Volstead Act had gone into effect just a few months
beforehand and bootlegging offered an inexhaustible potential
for generating riches. The day after the Central Park meeting, Arnold Rothstein reportedly agreed to the financing but
changed the source of the goods: the liquor would be imported
from Great Britain, not Canada. Rothstein wanted to use existing overseas connections and also believed the best whiskey
came from Scotland.

As compensation for making the connection, Wexler asked
for a cut of the action. What Wexler may not have known was
that Rothstein had or would cut similar deals with others who
showed promise, namely Bugsy Siegel, Meyer Lansky, Lucky
Luciano, Arthur "Dutch Schultz" Flegenheimer, and Longie
Zwillman. Nearly all of these men, unlike Wexler, did not have
prior histories of criminal activity. Instead Rothstein took them

under his wing as protégés and for the most part planned for each to run his own territory: Zwillman in New Jersey, Dutch in the Bronx, Meyer and Bugsy in Manhattan. The states of New York, New Jersey, and Pennsylvania alone provided enough potential business to support many operators.

Ready to retire, Rothstein dissolved the partnership with Wexler only a year later but supposedly continued in the background as a financier. It was probably around this time that Wexler changed his modus operandi and started importing whiskey from Canada and the Bahamas instead of directly from England or Scotland. By this time, he had a fleet of "rum runner" boats which often carried other cargo as camouflage. Upon arrival in the New York area, the boats would anchor along "Rum Row," just beyond the three-mile offshore limit. After the alcohol was brought on land, it would be cut, stored, and delivered to restaurants, nightclubs, and other bootleggers. Favorite customers typically received uncut liquor.

Not satisfied with only one product to market, Waxey resorted to his old routine of trafficking drugs—in this case opium. And it was this diversification that eventually got him into trouble. In March 1924 he was arrested on charges of shipping two truckloads of drugs from New York to Duluth. Fortunately for him, this time he was acquitted. However, this skirmish with the law put Waxey on the police's radar map and he found more trouble by acting illegally shortly thereafter.

Sailing from Nova Scotia in April 1925, the *S.S. Nantisco* sailed past a prohibition blockade of Coast Guard cruisers. Traveling under the guise of a ship carrying lumber and laths to fulfill the needs of substantial housing construction in Queens, the three-masted schooner was seized in Astoria. Customs officials took hours to search the ship before they located the cache of 500 cases of whiskey. Officials held the boat and its contents as evidence for future proceedings.

In September, with warrants for fourteen men, the federal and local agents raided the Knickerbocker and Longacre Buildings, located at Broadway and Forty-second Street, from which Gordon ran his operation. In total, 27 men were rounded up and charged with violation of the prohibition law. Nowhere to be found was Waxey. Apparently tipped off, he had sailed to Europe with his wife just a week earlier in one of the most luxurious suites on the White Star steamship *Majestic*.

Besides luxury travel abroad, Waxey and his family indulged themselves in a comfortable home, living in a spacious West End Avenue apartment that had ten rooms and four baths. Beyond the yearly rent of $6,000, Gordon splurged $2,200 for an interior decorator to build a combination bar/bookcase in the library. The bookcase held classics in "magnificent bindings." Wexler also owned a fleet of cars including multiple Lincolns, Pierce-Arrows, and Cadillacs.

Agents did not find much liquor in the Knickerbocker and Longacre buildings. In fact, they found only 27 pints of whiskey. However, they located customer and merchandise price lists, which they hoped would substantiate conspiracy charges. While the agents were gathering the documents, the telephone rang and a restaurateur named Joseph Delponto tried to order "a case of claret immediately." The Department of Justice agent replied, "Alright, come over and get it." Agents arrested Delponto when he arrived just minutes later.

The "star" witness for the prosecution was Hans Fuhrman, the skipper of the *Nantisco*. The prosecution team held him and his wife in protective custody, fearing reprisals for his turning over state's evidence. The real informant, however, was Furhman's wife, who complained to officials that her husband returned home from his trips not only intoxicated but also "broke." The prosecution's hopes for Furhman's testimony against Wexler evaporated when the skipper's body was found in the Hotel Ariso, on Sixth Avenue and Forty-fourth Street, with a bullet in the left temple. Medical Examiner Louis Wolfe declared the death a suicide, but Mrs. Furhman violently disagreed. She claimed that her husband must have been drugged and then taken to the hotel, because he had no reason to go there on his own. Furthermore, she argued, she would make a "wholesale exposure of prohibition graft" if officials did not investigate his death more thoroughly. Regardless, with its key witness dead, the prosecution watched its case implode, eliminating any chance of nailing Waxey.

Another crisis occurred in 1927, when Wexler and his gang had a run-in with Bugsy Siegel and Meyer Lansky's gang. In one of his biographies, *Meyer Lansky: Mogul of the Mob*, Lansky told the story of how he and Bugsy stopped a shipment of whiskey. At the time, neither one knew that the intended recipient of the cargo was Joe Masseria, who planned to turn it over to Waxey. With the help of Lucky Luciano's men, Bugsy and Meyer set up a trap near Atlantic City and waited for four truckloads of alcohol. When the convoy approached, the Bugsy and Meyer gang opened fire, killing three of the men guarding the goods and seriously wounding five others. Not content with just the apprehension of goods, Lansky's men continued to bruise the remaining men who had surrendered. This overexposure allowed one of the men to identify Lansky as a perpetrator.

Waxey fumed when he learned what happened. Beyond the loss of the shipment and the expected profits, Wexler worried that Rothstein would learn of his arrangement with Masseria, whom Rothstein detested. Waxey and Lansky openly accused each other of being liars and double-crossers. At one point Luciano interrupted both and tried to defuse the matter. After all, fighting among "brothers" was not good for business. The excited Lansky calmed down to his normally cool and collected self and waited for an opportune time to seek revenge. Separately, Arnold Rothstein was shot in the abdomen in November 1928 and never recovered. Waxey no longer had to worry about the Big Bankroll (Rothstein's nickname).

As a result of increased turf wars over whiskey and the amplified surveillance by government agents, by 1930 Wexler had switched from importing hard liquor to brewing and distilling.

This switch came quickly and easily. He did not simply purchase a brewery or build one from scratch. It is possible that he shot his way into two New Jersey plants. Between November 1929 and March 1930 Frankie Dunn and James "Bugs" Donovan, two former partners of the Union City Brewery, were murdered. The two had quarreled before their partnership dissolved and some detectives held to the theory that Dunn's killing was revenge for the murder of Donovan. Others suspected Waxey, since shortly after these murders he walked into both the Union City Brewery and Eureka Cereal Beverage Company in Patterson, New Jersey and announced that he was in charge.

Under Prohibition, breweries were permitted by law to manufacture and distribute "near beer," which had measured .05 percent or less alcohol. However, in order to create the legal beverage, the brewery first had to brew the contraband. Through elaborate schemes, Waxey's breweries tried to throw off the authorities. Trucks left the plant with near beer while the hardcore alcohol was sent underground, via an elaborate network of pipes, to a machinery shop located next to the brewery. From there, the pipes led to a truck foreman's house, from which a detachable hose led to the main sewer in Paterson, New Jersey. In turn, the detachable hose connected to a line in the sewer pipe, which ultimately led to a garage located several blocks away. There the beer was pumped into freshly washed barrels and carted away.

Prosecutor Thomas Dewey claimed that you "had to be thirsty to drink Waxey Gordon's stuff." Waxey didn't seem concerned with his clients or the quality of his product, obsessed as he was with cutting costs and maximizing profits. Normally, decent-tasting beer took six days to brew before maturing in vats for eight to twelve weeks. Gordon's plant held beer in vats for no more than two days before moving it through the sewer.

If the physical activities of the brewery were complicated, they paled in comparison to the shell games performed on the operation's finances. Waxey and his chief financial officer, Sam

Gurock, established accounts at numerous banks in New Jersey under different aliases. Waxey reportedly maintained a special notebook to remind himself where each was located. Such complicated money arrangements inevitably left Waxey susceptible to even the slightest mistake. It was just such an error, in fact, that would lead to his downfall.

By 1931, just months before the Volstead Act was revoked and Prohibition ended, a young Thomas Dewey was handed the task of shutting Wexler down. A former Wall Street executive and graduate of Columbia Law School, Dewey would prove himself a match for the elusive Gordon. During the two-and-a-half-year process, Dewey and his team examined 1,000 witnesses, 200 bank accounts, and "toll slips" of more than 100,000 telephone calls. The indictment was not for violation of the Prohibition Act but, rather, for income tax invasion. Waxey claimed that he had earned only $8,125 in 1930 and $35,000 in 1931, for which he paid taxes of $10.76 and $2,605, respectively. By contrast, the government calculated that Waxey owed $325,306.37 and $244,846.30 for the same years.

Although he failed to pay income taxes, Gordon spent a substantial sum of money for insurance. Records indicated that he insured the furnishings in his lavishly appointed apartment at 590 West End Avenue for $100,000. He also took out policies for general liability for $30,000, for auto liability in the amount of $100,000, and against burglary for $5,000. Curiously, Waxey insured himself for $30,000 against the unlikely event of an accident while golfing. For the year preceding the verdict, Wexler and his family lived at 55 Central Park West, an even more exclusive residence than the West End Avenue apartment. He would later brag to prison officials that he lived next'door to prominent individuals. How he could earn only a measly income and still support such extravagant residences must have amused the prosecution team.

Despite substantial physical evidence, the prosecution's case was hindered by the loss of witnesses, who seemed to have a knack for dying at inopportune times. Maxey Greenberg, Waxey's original partner in the alcohol trade, and Max Hassel were gunned down at the Elizabeth-Carteret Hotel in Elizabeth, New Jersey, in April 1933, after the former had testified before the federal grand jury. Waxey had been at the same hotel the night of the murder but was nowhere to be found afterwards. Two plausible theories have been offered about these murders. The first is that Wexler felt Greenberg and Hassel knew too much about his business and had become more liabilities than assets as partners. Others claim that Dutch Schultz's men pulled the triggers in a turf battle. The latter theory is bolstered by the fact that in May, only a month later, and just a week after Wexler was put behind bars, many of Schultz's men were targeted in a drive-by shooting at Broadway and Eighty-first Street in Manhattan. William Oppenheim, who the prosecution claimed played an integral role in running Wexler's business, was killed a day before he was to testify. Abe Durst, Wexler's chauffeur and the man who disclosed where Waxey went after skipping town, met the same fate. With the "squealer's" information, agents eventually tracked Gordon down at a summer cottage at White Lake in the Catskills. Though armed with a loaded gun hidden under his pillow, Gordon offered little resistance. Murray Marks, Gordon's bodyguard, was also gunned down. These murders discouraged others from testifying. As just one example, Dr. Abraham Hoffspiegel, a real estate operator from New Jersey, received a five-month sentence for contempt of court when he provided only evasive answers to the Grand Jury regarding the use of a garage at 600 Main Street in Paterson.

The prosecution faced other challenges. It appeared that Wexler cooked the financial records and paid off bank workers to hide his true records. At one Paterson bank every deposit slip from one Gordon account magically disappeared just before Dewey's men arrived. Other times, federal agents walked into banks only to be told to sit and wait. In the meantime Wexler's men would appear from nowhere, close all of his bank accounts, and walk away with any evidence that Waxey ever conducted business there. Checks from beer accounts were traced to the books of the Hotel Piccadilly, for which Wexler provided part of if not all of the construction funding. Yet before the hotel's books could be examined by officials, they had been rewritten.

Breaks in the case came from several sources, not the least of which was handwriting expert Scott Leslie, who for months analyzed signatures on a variety of documents. Wexler had slipped—he had signed either his own name or that of someone else on the back of checks from several dummy accounts. Leslie ultimately tied the checks and the accounts to Waxey. This evidence, combined with phone call records, linked Wexler and his cronies to the breweries, garages, offices, and hotel suites.

Of equal if not greater importance was the assistance Meyer Lansky provided the prosecution—if the story holds true. According to the same Lansky biography, Meyer and Lucky Luciano devised a plan: Meyer's brother Jacob would go to Philadelphia to deliver secrets of Waxey's operation to intrigued and appreciative Internal Revenue agents.

On December 2, 1933, the jury convened for a grand total of 51 minutes to reach the verdict of guilty on all four counts of tax evasion. In reading the verdict, Federal Judge Coleman added his two cents: "The defendant has had as fair a trial as is possible for any man to have. The government attorneys and witnesses at least as far as the government agents and lawyers are concerned, have been scrupulous in their treatment of this defendant. The defendant has been represented by two able attorneys who have had years and years of experience. The jury has given strict attention throughout this long trial and has evidenced every disposition to be fair and dispassionate. The evidence has been overwhelming. I am in accord with the verdict." Apparently Gordon took the news well. After clearing the courtroom, he calmly lit a cigar before U.S. marshalls escorted him to the Federal House of Detention.

If the verdict did not faze Waxey, the saddest day of his life was right ahead of him. After the decision, Nathan Wexler called Theodore Wexler, then a pre-med student at the University of North Carolina, and told his nephew to drive north and testify on behalf of his father to reduce the sentence. Near Chester, Pennsylvania, Theodore encountered dense fog, lost his way, and crashed into a fence. Leah Wexler collapsed when she received the news of her son's death, which also left Waxey in despair. "That boy was my one hope," he told the judge. "I counted on him. Everything I did centered around him."

Two days later funeral services were held at the West End Chapel at Ninety-first Street and Amsterdam Avenue. Federal marshals escorted Waxey first to the service and then to Mount Hebron Cemetery in Queens. Accompanied by his wife and two younger children, he recited the traditional burial *Kaddish*. According to the *New York Times*, Waxey "muttered" the words "like a man in a dream" while tears rolled down his cheeks.

A few days later Waxey began serving his sentence for tax evasion at the U.S. Federal Penitentiary in Lewisburg, Pennsylvania. The bureau of Prisons sent him there because it was reserved for convicts from New England and Mid-Atlantic states. The Bureau also felt that Lewisburg should be used for those convicts whom they felt could be rehabilitated. From almost the very beginning of his tenure at Lewisburg, Wexler antagonized the correctional officers with repeated violations of the prison code. Once he assaulted another inmate. On June 27, 1934, Lieutenant A. W. Trankle found contraband food in his cell, which landed Wexler in the isolation chamber on a restricted diet for three days. Apparently Wexler had befriended the inmate chef in the hospital mess hall, as well as others who would smuggle sandwiches to him in his cell. Additionally, he allegedly used other contacts to get mail through the system without officials' logging or review of the contents.

Probably tired of his misdemeanors, the U.S. Bureau of Prisons transferred Wexler to the U.S. Federal Penitentiary in

Atlanta, an older prison reserved for more hardened criminals. Here his antics continued. On June 24, 1936, Waxey assaulted Grover Cleveland Etheridge, another inmate. In his own defense, Wexler claimed that prison officials concocted a scheme to incite him. Documents written by two other inmates corroborated this claim and indicated that Waxey was most likely framed. Jimmy Clark, a recently released inmate and a witness to the event, wrote in a letter to someone named Max Wexler (presumably Waxey's brother Nathan) that Etheridge had called Wexler a "Jew bastard" and had been planted in the cell right next to Waxey's. A similar letter from inmate Herman Rappoport, corresponding with Nate Wexler, indicated that the authorities wanted to move Wexler to Alcatraz and schemed to obtain solid evidence against him. Rappoport, who was secretary to the penitentiary's rabbi, claimed "prejudice and an anti-Semitic attitude toward every Jewish inmate in the facility." He stated that he intended to correct the situation by contacting B'nai B'rith in Cincinnati, where he lived after his release. Rabbi Marks, the chaplain Rappoport assisted at the Atlanta penitentiary, would claim no such anti-Semitism.

Largely because of Wexler's "conniving" activities, the Bureau of Prisons decided to transfer him to Leavenworth in July 1936. The BOP director had harsh words for the staff of the Atlanta penitentiary, saying, "You and your institution are just as much in the dark as to whether there was such conniving, and if so, how it was brought about, as you were before the incident of June 24." He continued: "I do not want you to think that we are overrating the importance of our investigation into the possible framing of this inmate nor to feel that we are not appreciative of your efforts to prevent the development of any situation whereby 'big shots' can be preferred. But there is a right way and a wrong way to handle these things and you must see to it that your guard forces are properly advised, and understand that we will not tolerate any attempt of this sort in the future."

While at Leavenworth, Waxey filled out the appropriate forms for parole. However, prosecutor Dewey filed his opposition to any such move, saying: "The prisoner is a habitual criminal who, so far as we are able to ascertain, has engaged in criminal enterprises for the past thirty years; that he has given no indication at any time in his entire career that his liberty is anything but a menace to society; that he was a leader for many years of an organized gang of criminals to whom a large number of murders and assaults were attributed over a period of time; that his associates were men of the worst criminal type and that he should be incarcerated for the longest period of time as a protection to the public. He is commonly known as New York's public enemy number one." Despite this strong statement against him, Wexler appealed all the way to the U.S. Supreme Court, which on January 13, 1936, refused a review of his conviction.

Between 1937 and 1938 a few individuals wrote a rash of letters to the Department of Justice, the Bureau of Prisons, Leavenworth's warden, and various congressmen requesting a transfer for Waxey from Leavenworth to some facility closer to New York. Wife Leah complained of ill health and even persuaded her doctor to write a note on her behalf. A year later, though, the doctor wrote another note indicating that Leah successfully survived a hysterectomy and that a breast tumor had turned out to be benign.

In 1939 the Justice Department, following up on a request by the Internal Revenue Service, filed suits against Wexler both in the Southern Federal District of New York and in Kansas, so that he could be served papers in prison. The government claimed that he still owed back taxes amounting to $1,862,402. Wexler agreed to repay the government, but only at the rate of $6 per month. At this pace it would have taken him more than 25,000 years to eliminate his debt. With all this evidence and sentiment against him, it's difficult to believe that in late 1940 he received a conditional release. Once again, it was not much later that he found trouble around the country.

On November 11, 1941, Waxey was arrested for vagrancy in Los Angeles. Less than two weeks later he received the same treatment in New York. By October 1942 the federal government charged Waxey with creating a black market, in violation of the nation's sugar rationing laws. Wexler, Simon Hirshberg, and Oscar Hausner had pooled their resources to accumulate fifty rationing tickets, each good for 10,000 pounds of sugar. Using just three coupons, the contingent obtained 30,000 pounds of sugar, a key ingredient of bootleg alcohol. The three men defended their actions, claiming that they worked in the soft drink business, making a beverage named Vita Cola, and that the sugar went into the syrup that constituted the drink. On October 20, after Magistrate Andrews heard that Wexler worked as a $60 per week salesman for a wrapping paper company, he freed the former beer baron on $5,000 bail.

Just ten days later Mayor Fiorello LaGuardia wrote to the U.S. Attorney General Francis Biddle, complaining that Wexler was a "nuisance." He continued: "We are short of police and it takes too much of our police manpower to watch this bum and criminal. In as much as he is a parolee of your department, I would greatly appreciate it if you would get him out of this city. He has violated his parole." The attorney general replied meekly ten days later, saying: "We can't do anything. There would be no legal authority by which the [Federal] Parole Board could revoke his release and assume custody of him." However, in January 1943 the federal government ordered Waxey back to the penitentiary in Atlanta to serve one year.

Just two months later Gordon was already resorting to his old tricks. Correctional officers found him in possession of cigars and other commissary items apparently obtained while in quarantine. Because of his behavior, officials denied visits by either his wife or brother. Around this time, Waxey tried to communicate with Nathan regarding the sale and disposal of "certain machinery." The way he described it, the two machines, weighing 700 pounds and costing $2,100 each, manufactured wrappers for banks. He explained that the machines wrapped coins of a similar kind (pennies, nickels, dimes, quarters, and half dollars) and could crank out 25,000 rolls an hour. We can only conjecture as to what equipment he was really referring or its intended purpose. (He really was working for a wrapper company, so it might have been legitimate.)

Wexler's name appeared in the newspaper next in September 1944, when he was the subject of a federal investigation into black-market activities involving military surplus. Even Mayor Fiorello LaGuardia inserted himself into the investigation. New York City was unable to find the heavy tires used by the city's garbage trucks, at least not "through regular business channels," and it was assumed that Waxey had cornered the market. LaGuardia testified in Chicago that all such tires were in the possession of "one of these outfits formed to buy up and control military surpluses." He further complained that when he was given an address of where to find such tires, he would first "Check with the police department and the FBI" instead of checking the company in the Dun & Bradstreet Directory of businesses. Albert Fayhe, president of Consolidated Industries (the firm from which Wexler reportedly purchased the surplus equipment), took the stand and testified that he had engaged Waxey with the hope of using the former bootlegger's experience to attain a contract for supplying boxes for the transport of beer and soda. Fayhe further stated that he told Wexler that morning that "no amount of business was worth the annoyance" that was brought upon Consolidated by its relationship with Wexler. According to Fayhe, Waxey understood and agreed. The charges apparently were dropped, since Gordon never served any time for this activity.

Yet the Feds and the NYPD were not done with Waxey. Together they set up an elaborate sting operation to catch and convict him. To do this, the authorities enlisted the help of Morris

"Kayo" Lipsius. After stints at both Sing Sing and Comstock Correctional Facilities, Lipsius attempted to live a clean life. He even wrote a commercially successful book in 1950 with fellow former inmate Frank O'Leary, titled *Dictionary of American Underworld Lingo*. However, in the latter part of that year the Feds charged Lipsius with bootlegging. Faced with the option of going back to prison or taking advantage of the "opportunity" to help pinch Wexler, the choice was clear.

Lipsius spent seven months befriending Wexler. He would appear at bars where Waxey hung out and at restaurants on lower Second Avenue, treating Waxey with money provided by the authorities. Fortunately for Lipsius, many people in the neighborhood knew him, so his presence did not cause any suspicion. On July 14, 1951, the Feds indicated that they wanted Lipsius to make his first buy of "H" (heroin) from Waxey. The two met at a bar on Second Avenue and, at first Waxey refused, saying, "I don't touch the stuff." But after Lipsius headed for the door, Wexler agreed, as long as he could pocket a profit of $500. The two consummated the deal and Lipsius walked off with the heroin.

The Feds and the NYPD were in no hurry to arrest Wexler. In fact, they intentionally continued the ruse, hoping to net a few more big fish. The third and final purchase occurred on the night of August 2, 1951. Using an elaborate system of signals and marked money, the authorities followed Lipsius and Wexler around Manhattan, borrowing a taxi from a cab company and substituting one of their own officers as the driver. Incredibly, Waxey followed Lipsius's instruction to hail a cab—the very cab driven by NYPD Officer Fitzgerald. The cab deposited Waxey and Lipsius at a location where Sam Kass was to supply Waxey with the heroin. The police caught Wexler purchasing 18 ounces from Kass.

Waxey had had enough of prison and, after the authorities apprehended him, he complained: "I am an old man and I'm through. Let me run and then shoot me!" Rather than spend another day in jail, he preferred to die. Knowing this, his associate Sam Kass tried to get Wexler off the hook. Kass pulled two diamond rings worth $8,000 and $2,500 in cash out of his pockets and told NYPD Detective Johnny Cottone: "Take this. You can have anything I got. Just let Pop go." After receiving no response from Cottone, Kass upped the ante to $25,000, but the NYPD and the Feds were not going to stop what was considered to be the largest dope break in recent memory.

Officials believed Wexler headed a drug network whose tentacles spanned the nation. Scheduled to testify in a court case with ten of his West Coast cronies, authorities transferred him to California on May 21, 1952, and locked him up in the San Francisco city jail. Probably because of a combination of security issues and his ill health, he was then transferred to Alcatraz Island, which had an infirmary.

On May 28, 1952, just two days after his incarceration on Alcatraz Island, Dr. Milton Meltzer gave Wexler a physical examination and wrote on his chart: "Obese, blood pressure: 250/150, pulse: 80, slight degree of cardiac enlargement and moderate peripheral arteriosclerosis." Less than a month later, on June 24, Wexler passed away of a massive heart attack.

Louis Shomberg: Behind the Scenes

LOUIS SHOMBERG ASSOCIATED with the best of them—Meyer Lansky, Bugsy Siegel, Frank Costello, Louis Buchalter, Abner "Longie" Zwillman, Willie Sutton, Owney Madden, and Waxey Gordon. His activities, including picking pockets, bootlegging, manslaughter, gambling, jewelry fencing, sales of gas ration coupons, investments in hotels and nightclubs, and stock fraud, created a crime portfolio matched by few, if any, of his peers. Yet the entire life story of this man, who made New York newspaper headlines as "the most powerful man in the country if not in the world," has not yet been told. Depending upon whom you ask, opinions about Shomberg differ.

Within his family, he was a loving patriarch. When Joanne Shomberg reminisces about her grandfather's brother, she sees a lavish family man. "My father tended to embellish his stories, and the whole family truly downplayed the brutality piece of Uncle Lou's personality. He was larger-than-life through the family folklore—but the stories, in a sick sort of way, were glamorized by those who told them. We all listened intently, often mesmerized, largely in part due to the fact that the Uncle Lou of my childhood and the Papa Louie/Dutch Goldberg [Louis's nickname] could not possibly be the same person. I saw him wear suits to special occasions, like my brother's bar mitzvah, but more often remember him with a cigar and a silk robe, sitting in a chair in his luxurious apartment. He used to buy dresses for me as presents."

Others had quite a different impression. A column in the November 16, 1937, edition of the *New York Herald Tribune* called him "one of the biggest if lesser-known racketeers." In 1940 Craig Thompson and Allen Raymond published the book *Gang Rule in New York*, in which they describe Shomberg as "a silent and seldom mentioned fellow who was more widely known as Dutch Goldberg. He has been owner of hotels, in the rum business, and emerged in the eventual monopoly as the 'impartial arbiter' of the crime industry." In the 1950s, in the *New York Journal American* and other newspapers across the country, nationally syndicated columnist Westbrook Pegler quoted Barney Ruditsky, a criminal who had testified before the Kefauver (Senate) Commission investigating organized crime a few years earlier. He regaled his readers with stories about Bugsy Siegel, Meyer Lansky, and a collection of lower-level operatives, but Ruditsky singled out Shomberg, "There's a fellow named Louis Shomberg, known as Papa Louis. In my opinion, this is the man that is the [underworld] boss throughout America." On August 13, 1953, Lee Mortimer, substituting for syndicated columnist Walter Winchell, wrote that Shomberg was the "most powerful man in the country if not in the world." In 1954 an FBI memo quoted an informant as saying that "Goldberg is one of the last remaining Jewish hoodlums, who still maintains power control in the underworld." And in 1975, shortly after Shomberg died, journalist Sidney Zion wrote:

> *Dutch, whose name was Louis Shomberg, was a.k.a. Poppa Louie, after his role as arbitrator in the twenties and thirties for disputes between the Irish, Italian, and Jewish mobs of New York and the nation. No bigger honcho lived in that time, not ["Lucky"] Luciano, not anyone, and if I sound perversely chauvinistic, let it ride that way. I am indeed annoyed at the myth that Jews were mere lobbyguys, executioners, and financiers for the Italians. It was the reverse in the halcyon days of Dutch Goldberg and if it is at all true now it is only because*

the Jews ran out of a bench once they left the slums [implying Jewish criminals were more ruthless and violent than previously characterized].

Officially named Elya Yershombek, Louis Shomberg was born in the Whitechapel section of London to Abraham, a tailor, and Rebecca Seigel (no relation to Bugsy Siegel), both immigrants from the Lomza Gubernia (region) of northeast Poland, where the surname Jarzombek was common. Louis fell close to the middle of seven children, including David, born in Poland; Isaac, born in 1883 in London; Harry, a native-born American; and three sisters: Ray, Esther, and Rose. Family legend suggests that Abraham was a kind and gentle soul. According to Joanne Shomberg, however, Rebecca "ruled with an iron fist. She probably was the only person in the world Louis feared." Looking at a photo of Rebecca, even at what anyone would expect to be one of her happiest of moments, surrounded by her family, one would worry that she sits, straight-backed, almost expressionless. If eyes could kill, Louis would not have been the only murderer in the family.

For reasons unknown, Abraham and Rebecca decided to move the family from England to America around 1903. By 1910 most of the family resided at either 114 or 149 Stanton Street on the Lower East Side, just a few blocks to the west of the neighborhood where the families of Meyer Lansky and Bugsy Siegel lived on Columbia and Canon Streets, close to the Williamsburg Bridge and about the equivalent distance to the northeast of the area where Benny Fein and Irving Wexler played as kids on Forsyth and Christie Streets. Just about four blocks south and another two to the west stood the Essex Market Court and County Jail, where many a criminal came and left (or not) morning, noon, and night.

Abraham, according to Louis's testimony decades later, left the family to find employment in Colorado. Without a strong male role model, it's probably not surprising that one of the boys in the family fell into so much mischief. Shomberg also claimed later that as a child he worked for the Weingart Brothers Company, located in the Marbridge Building at Thirty-fourth Street and Sixth Avenue, helping the firm's sales representative, D. Klein, *schlep* (carry) clothing samples. Obviously this work provided too little excitement for the teenager.

December 12, 1912, marked the first time authorities took official action against Louis, under the alias of Harry Goldberg—in this instance for attempting to grab $16 (about $337 in 2007 dollars) from the handbag of Agnes Weidig, 32-year-old housewife who lived on Fulton Street in Brooklyn. During his deportation hearings decades later, Shomberg testified that he changed his name to Goldberg to avoid the consequences should his mother find out. It appears that he was so intimidated by his mother that he somehow managed to solicit the services of a woman who testified under oath as his mother "Minnie." Whoever she was, she performed admirably in the witness chair, crying before the jury and claiming that her son could do no wrong.

Continuing the charade, Shomberg first pled "not guilty." Fortunately for him, when the case went to trial a month later, the jury struggled to come to a consensus. And two weeks later, on February 5, 1913, Shomberg pled guilty to larceny in the second degree and received a suspended sentence. The reason: he had already spent more than two months in the City Jail awaiting prosecution. Just three months later Shomberg perjured himself, claiming to have been employed as a messenger by the Standard Hat Company. After investigators verified that his employment claim was untrue, the judge revoked the suspended sentence. Finally, on May 8, 1913, a year after his first offense, Louis Shomberg entered the New York State Reformatory at Elmira, carrying a sentence of up to five years.

Released in June 1914 well before his maximum sentence time, Shomberg continued to fall into trouble, and on March 12, 1915, he and George Snyder found themselves on the Manhattan Docket, arrested for possession of a blackjack. This was a device similar to a billy club but shorter (for easier concealment) and made partially of lead in order to inflict greater damage than a wooden club. Judge Joseph F. Mulqueen dismissed the case on the motion of the district attorney, who pointed out that Shomberg was over 16, yet less than 21 years of age, and was currently confined to the City Jail on another indictment—hence his absence in court at the time. This blackjack case was small potatoes in the mind of the district attorney, who preferred to focus his efforts on the more serious indictment. Whatever the other crime, which remains unknown, the D. A. failed to serve justice on Shomberg, who gained his freedom once again but only for a couple of months.

On May 11, 1915, Police Officer Healy arrested Shomberg and partner Izzy Presser, and both were charged with the murder of Maurice Rubenstein, shot in front of 185 Allen Street that same day. Shomberg, Presser, Rubenstein, Barney Ginsburg, and a man named Joseph Berger all belonged to the "same crowd." To be sure, Rubenstein was no saint. Two months earlier he had approached Joseph Berger from behind and slashed his face with a knife. The attack was likely retaliation for Berger's purchase of goods that Presser and Sam Ripstein had stolen, including jewelry that presumably belonged to Rubenstein. This wasn't the first run-in between Berger and Rubenstein. The two had also fought each other five or six weeks earlier at Mack Grosser's barber shop at 167 Stanton Street. After the knifing, Berger informed Izzy Presser of his run-in with Rubenstein, whom Presser called a "rat" and a "squealer" and urged that he should be "treated accordingly." Presser had reason to call Rubenstein names: according to Berger, Rubenstein had "made a play for Izzy's woman."

Even though Rubenstein was of a strong build, he was no match for Shomberg and Presser, who both fired their pistols at him. Shomberg fired first, his bullet hitting Rubenstein in the torso, causing him to fall to the ground. Rubenstein struggled to get to his knees, pleading, "Izzy, please do not kill me." When Shomberg's gun jammed, Presser finished the deed, firing one bullet into Rubenstein's neck and rupturing his carotid artery and another one into his head slightly above and in front of his left ear, smashing his head and causing a large hemorrhage. The coroner testified that any one of the wounds would have been fatal.

The trial commenced on August 5, with Joseph Berger as a key witness. In his testimony, Berger quoted Presser as saying: "There goes that cock-sucking rat now. I've got to kill him." Berger continued that both Presser and Shomberg developed alibis for their whereabouts during the incident. Presser coerced a woman named Mrs. Gordon to say that he had been playing dominos at the time. Shomberg chose a different strategy: He had met "two girls on Houston Street" and had told them that if he were picked up, they should say that they were with him at the Houston Street Hippodrome (movie theater) at the time of the murder. In a further attempt to confuse the police, Presser and Shomberg swapped overcoats.

Despite Shomberg and Presser's sleights of hand, the prosecution was able to round up additional witnesses to bolster their case. Rosa Kuttler testified that, although at the time of the murder she was inside a drugstore, she could nevertheless hear Rubenstein begging for Presser's mercy. She also was a roommate of a Mrs. Herschkowitz, whom Kuttler had seen take a gun out of the icebox and give it to Presser two weeks before the murder. Barnett Patlin rounded out the People's case. He claimed to be a member of a group, which included Barney Ginsburg, Shomberg, and Presser, that met the morning of the shooting and had breakfast at Ratner's Restaurant, then located on Houston Street between Eldridge and Forsyth Streets. (Ratner's would shortly after this incident move to its longer-standing location of 138 Delancey Street, a frequent hangout for the likes of Meyer Lansky, Bugsy Siegel, Al Jolson, and Groucho Marx. The delicatessen, known for its surly waiters who would serve whatever they felt their customer should have rather than what they necessarily wanted, typically served approximately 1,200 customers on a Sunday morning). Patlin explained that he had been in the Tombs, the local city jail, with both Shomberg and Presser while all three awaited trial, and that the two gunmen tried to get him to testify on their behalf, urging him to state that he had seen Joseph Berger shoot Rubenstein. When questioned by the authorities, Patlin repeatedly nodded his head, giving them the impression that he agreed with everything they said and that he was present at the murder. Under oath at the trial, he recanted his earlier "statement" and claimed that he was not at the scene of the crime. Most damning of all, Patlin stated that in conversations he had had with Shomberg in the Tombs about the murder, Shomberg admitted he had fired the first shot. Furthermore, according to Patlin, Shomberg and Presser were "manufacturing witnesses."

In very little time the jury returned a verdict of guilty of manslaughter in the first degree, and the judge handed down a sentence of up to twelve years in Sing Sing. Shomberg was admitted to Sing Sing on August 10, 1915, at which time he met two other notable Jewish criminals—Irving Wexler and Louis Buchalter—although the budding friendships were put on hold because the warden transferred him to Auburn Prison the following March. Back then, and to this day, wardens in New York State prisons have exercised their prerogative of transferring any inmate at any time for virtually any reason. Most commonly this was done to prevent the prisoner from establishing a strong foothold and creating his own empire, which could endanger other inmates' health, allow messages to reach criminals outside the prison, and toughen the job of correctional officers in maintaining control of the facility.

The wardens certainly took advantage of this prerogative with respect to Shomberg. On April 13, 1917, the Auburn warden transferred Shomberg back to Sing Sing. Less than two months later, on June 5, 1917, Shomberg filled out the World

War I Draft Registration card and claimed "painter" as his occupation. A year and half later, on December 5, 1918, the warden once again transferred Louis, this time to Clinton Prison,
where he undoubtedly spent some time with Jacob "Gurrah"
Shapiro (Louis Lepke Buchalter's right-hand man), but was
bounced back to Sing Sing the following July. During his last
stretch at the Big House, Shomberg saved the life of fellow
inmate Ben Marden when other prisoners tried to kill him
after an argument. This incident gave sufficient reason for the
Sing Sing warden to bump Shomberg back upstate for a second
stretch at Clinton. Shomberg must have felt like a ping-pong
ball. By November 1920 Louis was in Great Meadow Correctional Facility, where he stayed until October 9, 1922, when he
was paroled to L. S. Reingold, who worked for the Jewish Board
of Guardians (a New York City–based social services agency).

During the late 1920s Shomberg moved in new directions.
On the one hand, probably in an attempt to achieve stability or
respectability, he married Becky Mae Fox, a stunningly beautiful 21-year-old clothing model from upper Manhattan. They
married on May 17, 1926, just two months after he got out of
Sing Sing, where he had served a short stint for violating parole.
On the other hand, this was the time when he teamed up with
notable thugs of the Lower East Side, including Bugsy Siegel, Meyer Lansky, Frank Costello, Joe Adonis, Abner "Longie"
Zwillman, Johnnie Torrio (the "abdicated king of the Capone
syndicate"), and Charles "Lucky" Luciano. Most of the gang's
activities involved bootlegging. What is not clear is who led
the pack. The FBI files for both Benjamin Siegel and Louis
Shomberg suggest it was the latter who, along with Charlie
Cramer and "Bill Heisman" (most likely William Weisman),
hired Siegel and Lansky as convoy guards to protect "Alky
Trucks" running liquor between Chicago and New York. Cramer, Weismann, Bugsy Siegel, Meyer Lansky, Nick Delmore,
Jeff Newman, and Shomberg all supposedly had an interest in
the Rising Sun Brewery in New Jersey.

Testimony from Shomberg deportation hearings that were conducted decades later provides a somewhat similar yet different tale. At the hearings the prosecuting attorney, Miss Clara Binder, quoted from a report that in the 1928–1929 time frame, "Among the overlords or top-notch gangsters prominent at the time were Joe Adonis, Frank Costello, "Bugs" Siegel, Meyer Lansky...Charles Lucky Luciano...Dutch Goldberg, Moe "Dimples" Wolensky...and so forth and so on..." This combination began buying liquor from Sam Bloom at a rate of almost six cars a week, each car totaling about 870 cases. In all, about 100 cars of this merchandise came into New York and New Jersey from the South. Out of this amount the Adonis group got about 60 cars, the Dutch Goldberg (group) got about 35, and the balance went to Louis "the Chinaman" and Abe Rosenberg, both of Detroit. (In total defiance, Louis replied to this charge, "My name is Shomberg, not Goldberg.")

In 1930, life was good for Louis and Mae Shomberg. Louis made pretenses to the census taker that he was a "proprietor" in a different kind of work—the "oil business." Around the same time, Shomberg gave the Knickerbocker Oil Company, located at 535 Fifth Avenue (Rockefeller Center), as one of several references when he rented his apartment at 114 West Eighty-sixth Street. Mae vacationed in Cuba in February 1931, returning from Havana to New York on the *S.S. Morro Castle*.

By 1932 the major gangs in New York, New Jersey, and New England involved in bootlegging joined forces in what was to be known as the "Big Seven." After a meeting at the Belle Clare Hotel on Broadway and Seventy-second Street, all of the leaders agreed to join and pay "tribute on each case received in New York." Among the leaders were Moe "Dimples" Wolensky, Joe Adonis, Bugs(y) Siegel, and "Dutch" Goldberg (Shomberg). Bugsy Siegel led one subgroup, which also dealt in dope, whose members included Charlie Lucky Luciano, Joe Adonis, Sam "Red" Levine, Meyer Lansky, and Jake Lansky. This group was in charge of kidnapping and "muscling in at

offices of individuals." Members of Shomberg's subgroup included Murray "Red" Richter, Dimples Wolensky, Mooney
"Baldy" Levy, and Bill Cuddy. The Newark group was headed
by Longie Zwillman. In the agreement, each group was allowed to bring in only a certain amount of liquor at a time,
depending on their "previous business." If one group sold
its allotment, it could not bring in any more until the other
groups had disposed of theirs. If one group did not abide by
these guidelines, the others would enforce the rule by violent
means. The combination of these groups lasted for about a
year before it dissolved. The agreement fell apart because of
"chiseling" among the various members. Then, in December
1933, the Prohibition Act was repealed, changing the rules for
criminal and law-abiding alike.

On January 24, 1934, Louis Shomberg threw a lavish golden
wedding anniversary party for his parents, Abraham and Rebecca (who did not appear any friendlier here than at any other
point in her life—see photo), at the Broadway Central Hotel,
at Broadway and Third Street, at one time the largest hotel in
New York City. The guest list included not only 37 members of
the Shomberg family but also some of the "deadliest killers in
Manhattan." (Also in attendance were prominent businessmen
and politicians, most notably Jimmy Hines.) Before being admitted to the party, all guests, including family members, were
frisked to make sure they parted with any concealed weapons.
In fact, a separate room was set up for the temporary storage
of firearms. Once relieved of their weapons and admitted, the
guests enjoyed two separate orchestras playing dance music and
a stage show performed by the Cotton Club Revue, which had
ventured downtown from Harlem for the affair. In Shomberg's
A(lien)-File from the United States Customs and Immigration
Services (USCIS, formerly Immigration and Naturalization
Services [INS]), it was alleged that he was the "real owner" of
the Cotton Club and that Herman Stark was simply the front
man from 1932 to 1941. Other documents in the same A-File

suggest that Shomberg and Irving Wexler co-owned Connie's Seafood Restaurant, located at 505 West Twenty-third Street, and that the former also had a financial interest in Connie's Inn in Harlem.

It's very possible that the motivation for the party went beyond celebrating the elderly couple's long romance. Shomberg's FBI file indicates that 1934 was the year he shared with Bugsy Siegel, Frank Costello, Joe Adonis, Dimples Wolensky, Longie Zwillman, Meyer Lansky, and others the profits from a $1 million shipment representing 650,000 gallons of "tax unpaid liquor from Belgium." Whether this shipment occurred before or after the party is immaterial. At the time of the party Louis Shomberg knew that he had buckets of money either in his pocket or arriving soon.

It's possible that the wedding anniversary celebration also served as a going-away party for Shomberg himself. Whether to reinvent himself or to hide from an investigation into the murder of a prohibition agent at the Rising Sun Brewery in 1930, Shomberg became a fugitive in 1934. By 1935 he had moved to Los Angeles, where he established his base of operations for new ventures on the West Coast. Sometime that year Louis spent two months at the Murrieta Hot Springs Hotel in Southern California, registering as Louis Solomon. We know from the records of the Los Angeles Biltmore that he checked into that hotel in early December 1935 under the name of Louis Schomberg. Just ten days later, Mae Shomberg left the couple's New York residence at the Lombardy Hotel on East Fifty-sixth Street to join her husband at the Beverly Wilshire Hotel in Los Angeles (according to an interview with her found in the FBI's file for Lepke Buchalter's right-hand man, Jacob Shapiro). Unfortunately for Mae, Louis did not spend much time with her on the West Coast. Instead he went on a trip to Cuba, returning to Los Angeles in March 1936, on the *S.S. Virginia*. It was shortly after this excursion that Meyer Lansky began showing interest in Cuban politics; he had discussions with General

Fulgencio Batista in 1938. There is no documentation demonstrating a connection among Shomberg, Lansky, and Batista, but the former two probably discussed America's neighbor in the Caribbean at some point.

Sometime in 1937 Shomberg and several other parties negotiated to purchase the Dunes Hotel in Palm Springs, California from Al Wertheimer and his wife, Thelma Ryan, the latter a relative of Al Capone; the deal fell through, however. Shomberg's FBI file also states that in July 1937 Shomberg checked into a room at the Riverside Hotel in Reno just adjacent to the room occupied by former Lieutenant Governor George Hatfield of California. When the FBI interviewed Hatfield, he admitted that a mutual friend had introduced him to Shomberg and that the friend had connections to others, including Bugsy Siegel, who had previously been involved in bootlegging in New York. More specifically, some of these contacts were the sole distributors of White Horse Scotch in the United States. It was also in this time frame that, according to his testimony at his deportation hearings, Shomberg suffered a nervous breakdown, forcing him to spend numerous summers at a friend's house in Wisconsin.

With Shomberg spending so much time out of Mae's presence, it may not come as a surprise that she felt neglected. After an argument with Louis, she left him and returned to New York, where she moved into the Grosvenor Hotel, at Fifth Avenue and Tenth Street. She remained there for a few months. Probably wanting to stick her husband with an even higher rent bill, she subsequently moved into the Beverly Hotel (now the Benjamin Hotel) at 125 East Fiftieth Street. This too was temporary housing until April 1937, when she settled in yet a different residence, the Elysee Hotel at 60 East Fifty-fourth Street. Louis and Mae reconnected after he invited her to join him somewhere in New York State (the exact location is redacted in Shapiro's FBI file), where they lived together for five or six months. The couple subsequently took a train to Miami

Beach in 1938, only to quarrel yet again, leading Mae to return to New York, where she checked into the Windemere Hotel.

In 1933, while apparently still living with Louis, Mae invited Betty Buchalter (Louis Lepke's wife) and Pearl "Polly" Adler, a notorious Russian-born madam, to her apartment for dinner. After the trio had finished eating, a knock was heard at the front door. Frankie Carbo (the man who most reports suggest killed Harry "Big Greenie" Greenberg after Bugsy Siegel gave the order) and a handful of his cronies barged in, broke furniture, and assaulted all of the women. Mae would learn through Adler's friend "Dutch" Schultz (a.k.a. Arthur Flegenheimer, another Jewish criminal) that Louis Shomberg had learned of the women's rendezvous and had ordered the "affray" to send a message to Mae that she should not cavort with a "call-house madam." Adler, in her testimony to investigators, called Shomberg a "loudmouth who likes to throw his weight around."

Not successful with his initial business deals on the West Coast, Louis Shomberg continued to seek new opportunities. He tried to inch his way into Hollywood, with disappointing results. On July 22, 1938, Norman Taurog, motion picture director for MGM Studios, told FBI investigators that he knew Shomberg as Lou Solomon and had first met him in Murrieta Hot Springs. After that, Taurog reported, Louis had called him on several occasions, "just to say 'Hello.'" The next year Sidney Kent, president of the board of directors of Twentieth Century Fox Film Corporation, informed FBI investigators that Shomberg, Bugsy Siegel, and Longie Zwillman had come to Twentieth Century Fox Studios on three or four occasions, expressing their interest in getting into the movie business while simultaneously suggesting that Kent pay for protection services. Kent refused the latter offer but told the FBI that the three visitors had expressed an interest in getting out of the rackets business and into more legitimate businesses, even if the process of entering those businesses was not "always legal or without force."

While busy trying to launch new enterprises in California, Shomberg simultaneously tended to various matters on the East Coast. With partner William Weismann, he invested in the Riviera night club, based in Fort Lee, New Jersey. The club was operated by Ben Marden, whose life Shomberg had saved in Sing Sing. Weismann had a criminal record that included killing two federal officers at a brewery in Elizabeth, New Jersey. He also owned a dog race track in Puerto Rico, the Los Monjas Kennel Club, supposedly financed by Buchalter.

By late 1938, with Shomberg's hand in so many pies, it wasn't difficult for the FBI to position him high on the bureau's list of notorious underworld figures. To begin zeroing in on their target, the agency interviewed numerous well-known gangsters and other individuals it believed could broaden its understanding of Shomberg's activities. Abner "Longie" Zwillman admitted that he had known Shomberg for ten years, ever since the two had "dealings in the liquor business," when the latter "was considered one of the biggest liquor operators in the East." Another informant told the FBI that Shomberg and Louis Buchalter had dabbled in narcotics in the Twin Cities, operating out of Minneapolis. An inmate at Riker's Island stated that his uncle, Louis Shomberg, was living on the West Coast and that he was hanging around with Lepke Buchalter. Yet another informant claimed that Shomberg called him from San Diego regarding the publication of some poetry Shomberg had penned about prison life. Meyer Lansky relayed to the Feds that he knew Shomberg, originally in New York and for a decade, but had not seen him for the past five years. Bugsy Siegel told the FBI that William Weismann, Shomberg's partner in Ben Marden's Riviera nightclub, had introduced him to Shomberg but that he had not seen Shomberg for at least three years. Siegel told authorities of Shomberg's "interest in gambling and night clubs" and that the latter owned the Flying Trapeze nightclub in New York. At the end of the interview,

Bugsy mused that Shomberg was not well liked, because he was "argumentative and usually abusive."

Apparently Shomberg's wife Mae agreed, using virtually the same words to describe him. By May 1940 she had filed for divorce, grousing about his "extremely abusive" and "obstinate" nature and his "continuous desertion." Just before this measure, Mae may have also begun to comprehend the scope and magnitude of her husband's shadier activities. Somehow she was tipped off that authorities wanted to question her at her apartment on February 16, 1940. Before they could arrive, she had vanished. Louis Shomberg did not contest the divorce and Florida granted the couple's request. For most individuals, a divorce during this era might have caused at least a modicum of embarrassment, but in Louis's case, given his track record—manslaughter and time behind bars at Sing Sing, Auburn, and Clinton Correctional Facilities—the separation probably generated minimal shame. Moreover, he was not the first in his family to terminate a marriage. His sister Esther had already married twice by this time, and his brother Isaac would ultimately marry three times.

For all of his efforts, Shomberg's ventures on the West Coast did not pan out as he had hoped. By 1941 he had moved back to the East Coast, splitting his time between New York and Florida. He filled out his World War II draft registration card, listing his address as 159 B 133rd Street in Belle Harbor, Queens but with a business at 2304 Collins Avenue in Miami Beach. Like his associate Meyer Lansky, who formed the Lansky Food Company as a front (according to his FBI file), Shomberg claimed he operated the World Fruit Company in Florida. On January 31, 1941, the Miami Police Department arrested Shomberg for providing misleading information on his draft registration card and for picking pockets but released him on February 12. In January 1942 he filed the Social Security Administration's SS-5 form, on which he claimed to live at 700

Euclid Avenue and work for Quality Fruit Shippers, Inc., also at 2304 Collins Avenue in Miami Beach.

For a couple of reasons, Shomberg moved back to New York in the 1940s. First of all, his time in Florida was apparently no more productive than that in California. He also moved back to the Big Apple to tend to his sister Rae, now a divorcée, and their father, who suffered from ill health. Shomberg moved with his family into apartment 11-G at 205 West Eighty-ninth Street for yet another motive. For years he had visited Harry Stolper, a friend and optician, and his wife Gertie in apartment 3-H in that building. Interviewed by authorities involved in Shomberg's deportation hearings, the building's assistant superintendent, Gus Franz, repeated a rumor that had spread though the building to the effect that Gertie was Shomberg's girlfriend.

In addition to apparently having an affair with his friend's wife under the same roof where his family lived, he took care of his libido elsewhere. According to testimony in 1954 by Irving Kalish, a room clerk at the Hotel Bretton Hall at Eightieth Street and Broadway, Shomberg rented out a double room once or twice a month. Kalish also recalled that a blond woman typically joined him in the room just an hour after he booked it. A decade earlier, Shomberg apparently chased after a harem of younger women. According to New York columnist Lee Mortimer's article written in 1953, Shomberg "practically adopted the entire chorus of the Ziegfeld Follies. None of the cuties knew his background. They thought he was merely an eccentric millionaire. They referred to him as 'That nice old geezer.' That was in 1936, but such is ancient 40 to young 18, even if she's a sophisticated Follies girl."

On the business front, Shomberg explored completely new opportunities. By January 1943 he had tried to purchase a sizable amount of gas ration coupons burglarized from the Office of Price Administration (OPA), set up by President Roosevelt just after the outbreak of World War II to stabilize prices of various consumer goods. Shomberg reportedly was willing to pay $35,000 for the coupons. At the same time, he opened a bank account under the business name of the Miss Gertie Dress Company. According to the New York County Clerk's Office, the company was located at 113 University Place, and Shomberg's partner in the venture was his brother Harry. Despite his return to New York and new businesses, Shomberg maintained ties to Florida, according to his FBI file, continuing as operational head of the Quality Fruit Company. He was also believed to have had a financial interest, along with Frank Costello, Meyer and Jacob Lansky, and a man named Erickson, in the Colonial Inn, located near the Gulf Stream Park Race Track in Miami. In 1945 the Colonial generated $7 million in revenues.

With all his different ventures, it appears that during the mid-1940s Louis Shomberg achieved most success at the time as a fence for stolen goods, especially jewelry. An FBI informant posited that Shomberg would "go to any part of the United States when a large robbery or burglary took place and endeavor to make a contact to purchase the loot." The money was supplied by Frank Costello and Owney Madden, the latter an Irish ex-bootlegger and onetime leader of the Gopher Gang in lower Manhattan who managed hotels and brothels and owned a portion of a large jewelry store in Hot Springs, Arkansas. Shomberg would take his goods to Owney Madden in Hot Springs, where Madden would cut the jewelry into less identifiable pieces. When Madden wasn't available, Shomberg patronized anyone he could find as a buyer in New York. Also sometime in the 1940s Shomberg was reportedly on "very good terms" with notorious bank robber Willie Sutton.

According to Sidney Zion, a journalist for both the *New York Daily News* and the *New York Post*, Shomberg was instrumental in providing oil and financing for the *S.S. Altadena*, the ship used by the Irgun, the Zionist movement group that operated in Palestine between 1931 and 1948 and helped with the for-

mation of Israel. The Irgun used the *Altadena* to ship arma-
ments there to aid its fight for an independent nation, until
David Ben Gurion decided to sink the ship in Tel Aviv's harbor.
This action caused Irgun's leader, Menachem Begin, to become
irate. The Irgun was an offshoot of the Haganah, the original
Jewish resistance group formed to defend against Arab attacks
against Jewish settlers in Palestine. While the Haganah took a
defensive approach—responding only to Palestinian attacks—
the Irgun preferred to go on the offense, committing preemp-
tive strikes against Arab militants, even if there were no provo-
cations. While Shomberg assisted the Irgun, Meyer Lansky and
Abe Zwillman apparently helped provide supplies and money
to the Irgun's rival, the Haganah.

Beyond memorializing Shomberg for his efforts to help with
the formation of Israel, after his death in 1975 Sidney Zion cast
Louie as a central figure in his 1990 novel *Markers*. While the
front inside cover of the book states, "This book is a work of
fiction. Names, characters, places, and incidents are either products of the author's imagination or are used fictitiously," much
of the writing about Shomberg matches information found in
publicly available documents. In his book, Zion represents to
the reader that it was Louis Shomberg who made the decision
to have Bugsy Siegel murdered. According to the novel's story,
Meyer Lansky went to Las Vegas to warn Bugsy to stop stealing money in the process of building the Flamingo Hotel. Apparently Lansky left the meeting unconvinced that Siegel had
"gotten" the message and subsequently told Shomberg to "take
care of" the situation. When Shomberg confronted Bugsy, the
latter threatened to expose the fact that he and Shomberg were
both skimming monies from the construction of the Flamingo.
It's possible that with nowhere else to go, Shomberg went one
step further with the mandate than Lansky intended: He arranged the murder of Siegel without approval from anyone.

This story is as plausible as any of the many other explanations for Bugsy's murder. Many have suggested differ-

ent motives, including Chick Hill's anger at the cruel way Ben Siegel treated his sister Virginia Hill; the power lust of Moe Sedway and Gus Greenbaum, Siegel's associates, who marched into the Flamingo Hotel after the murder and claimed they were in control; and the anxiety of other Las Vegas casino operators, who may have felt threatened by the potential success of the Flamingo. Sidney Zion claims he did not fabricate his story but insists that it was relayed to him by someone who he felt "should be in the know." Zion continues in *Markers*, "When Lansky heard about the killing, he was furious that Shomberg proceeded without consulting him and the other members of the Syndicate. It was from this time that Louis lost his power as shot caller of the underworld."

While the mystery behind Bugsy Siegel's death in June 1947 has never been conclusively solved, reports from mutual acquaintances of both Siegel and Shomberg, as well as other facts, suggest that Sidney Zion's scenario may be the true one. We know, for example, that Morris Rosen was a close associate of both Bugsy Siegel and Louis Shomberg. After the murder of Bugsy, Rosen tried on behalf of the Syndicate to wrest control of the hotel from Sanford Adler, another former associate of Siegel, who also claimed he was in charge. According to testimony at the 1950 Kefauver Senate hearings, Rosen, who had been a close associate of Shomberg since Prohibition days, demanded that Adler provide him with stock certificates—effectively giving Rosen and his associates control of the Flamingo. On about April 5, 1948, Rosen and Adler quarreled on the patio of the hotel, after which Adler ran inside calling for help. Whatever Rosen said, Adler apparently feared for his life and turned over his interest in the Flamingo to Rosen and his associates.

There were other strong connections between Bugsy Siegel and Louis Shomberg and additional reasons why the latter might have had motivation to terminate the former. The two had been linked through the alcohol trade ever since the 1920s. Both were members of the Masonic Habonim Lodge #1024, according to membership lists seized by the authorities. Normally, Masonic lodges do not allow criminals as members, yet somehow Bugsy and Shomberg joined. Sol Wurter, a founder of Twentieth Century Fox, informed investigators that he accompanied Bugsy Siegel to a New Year's Eve party at Shomberg's residence. Papers in Bugsy's FBI file include articles of incorporation for the Nevada Projects Corporation (the owner of the forthcoming Flamingo Hotel) that listed five partners: Billy Wilkerson, the man with the original concept for the Flamingo; Bugsy; Moe Sedway; N. Joseph Ross, a Hollywood attorney; and someone named G. Harry Rothberg, who, the FBI claimed, was the president of American Distillers Corporation. FBI documents show that Morris Rosen was an official of the American Distillers Corporation as well. Other documents in Shomberg's FBI file indicate not only that Shomberg and Rosen had been close associates since Prohibition days, but also that the pair, along with Sidney Kessler, were associates in the American Spirits Company, which handled such specialized liquor products as Gold Cup and Old Orchard. Very possibly G. Harry Rothberg, one of the five partners in the Flamingo Hotel, was simply yet another alias for Louis "Harry Goldberg" Shomberg. If all this wasn't enough, Shomberg had another reason to be angry with Bugsy. Authorities believed Siegel was linked to the murder of Bill Weisman, Louis's partner in the Riviera Nightclub in New Jersey.

In 1948, shortly after Bugsy Siegel's death, Shomberg apparently tried to go legitimate, buying into a dying clothing manufacturer, Madison Apparel Company in Wilkes Barre, Pennsylvania. With the help of Irving Rothman, a friend and accountant, Shomberg analyzed the accounting records of the firm, which had amassed $20,000 in debt. The two owners of the company, Mr. Augenblick and Mr. Ricker, were so desperate to absolve themselves of the firm's liabilities for which they were personally responsible, that they virtually gave the company to Shomberg so long as the latter agreed to assume the obligations. By 1955 Shomberg had turned the company around, with the firm's assets totaling $108,624 (surpassing liabilities by $32,511).

Bugsy's death might be yet one more reason why Shomberg felt pressure to obtain United States citizenship: He wanted to avoid another black spot on his record, which he feared would prevent the citizenship coming through. Shomberg was correct; by the early 1950s the federal government had him in its sights once again, this time conducting hearings with the goal of deporting him. In a desperate attempt to cut off the Feds in their tracks, Shomberg filed a Petition for Naturalization on December 22, 1952, just two days before the effective date of the Immigration and Naturalization Act of 1952, a.k.a. the McCarran-Walter Act, forged by Senators Pat McCarran (D-Nevada) and Francis Walter (D-Pennsylvania). Overall, the act grew out of the rise of anti-Communist sentiment in the United States during the Cold War era. The legislation included provisions for fighting "subversion," which allowed the government to exclude or deport any alien who had engaged in activities "prejudicial to the public interest or subversive to national security." Although Shomberg never obtained naturalization papers, at least one of his siblings, Isaac, achieved citizenship in about 1950.[1]

The portion of the new law that pertained to Shomberg subjected aliens to deportation if they had been found guilty of "two crimes involving moral turpitude." Shomberg, who had been convicted and sent to prison in 1913 and 1915, was a perfect target for the government. He and his attorney tried virtually every trick available to avoid expulsion from America.

---

1 In 1990, Congress repealed most of the ideological grounds for deportation, but some of the McCarran-Walter Act's provisions have been used as recently as 2002, in cases against two Palestinian student activists who distributed magazines and raised funds for an organization the government would later characterize as terrorist in nature. Furthermore, the practice of exclusion based on ideology was resurrected in provisions of the USA Patriot Act of 2001.

This included applying for a "suspension of deportation" in July 1953 and appealing to the Federal District Court. As a result, Shomberg's Petition for Naturalization led to a hearing at the Southern (Federal) District Court of New York in August 1953, with Shomberg and his attorneys pleading that the new immigration law was not retroactive and that the process for his naturalization should go forward before the deportation proceedings could continue. They claimed that the federal government had started the deportation hearings against Shomberg after the new law went into effect. At a strategic level, the federal government argued that the new act had two different sections (318 and 405) in conflict with each other. Their interpretation of the new law, at a more tactical level, was that, in their favor, provisions in the new immigration act cancelled out corresponding law in previous acts, if only for the reason that a semicolon had been inserted in one section of the act instead of another form of punctuation. District Judge E. J. Dimock rejected all of Shomberg's arguments and allowed deportation proceedings to continue. After losing, Shomberg went to the Court of Appeals, which upheld the District Court's decision. But Shomberg wouldn't take no for an answer, and he continued his appeals until he won a *writ of certiorari*, the right to be heard by the U.S. Supreme Court.

While waiting for his appeal to reach the nation's highest court, Shomberg was held temporarily without bail at Ellis Island. His hope for an overruling was not helped any by the FBI, which throughout 1953, in an attempt to build a case against him, interviewed many underworld figures. One informant, considered to be the last member of Waxey Gordon's gang, claimed in March 1953 that Shomberg had been considered at one time as the arbitrator for the underworld, solving disputes among its various factions. On June 24, 1953, the *New York Daily News* ran an article written by Joseph Martin, stating that Shomberg was "a notorious mobster who used to choose victims for Lepke Buchalter's Murder Incorporated killers." The article also noted his involvement in bootlegging and gambling in the 1930s and his participation in a party at the 1932 Democratic convention in Chicago that included known gangsters Frank Costello and Charles "Lucky" Luciano as well as Jimmy Hines, the Tammany Hall district leader who faced jail time for protecting the gang of another Jewish criminal, Dutch Schultz. In November 1953 another informant told the FBI that Shomberg was the boss of the numbers rackets, horse betting, and dice games in the Brownsville section of Brooklyn. By early 1954 Shomberg was under virtual house arrest in New York and needed permission from the government to take a vacation—a respite that would be under surveillance by the FBI.

The Supreme Court heard the case on March 1, 1955, because it too wanted to "determine the relationship between sections 318 and 405 of the McCarran-Walter Act." Section 318, the "priority provision," stated that "no petition for naturalization shall be finally heard…if there is pending against the petitioner a deportation proceeding." Yet Shomberg and his attorneys argued that the language of section 405(a)—"unless otherwise specifically contained in the new act, unless otherwise specifically provided therein, shall be construed to affect…any status, condition, right in process of acquisition…done or existing, at the time this act shall take effect"—maintained his right to pursue naturalization without impediments. The Supreme Court rejected this main argument and all variations on the theme, even while suggesting that the writers of the act could have "been more exact with their language," referring to the placement of the questionable semicolon. The court bolstered its decision by stating that Congress's intent must have been to continue the use of section 318, which had been taken almost entirely from the Subversive Activities Control Act of 1950.[2]

---

2 Before his August 2007 conviction of conspiracy against the United States, enemy combatant Jose Padilla cited the Shomberg case in his *writ of certiorari* with the hope that the Supreme Court would overturn lower court rulings against him, thus releasing him from his detention cell.

Between 1957 and 1963 Louis Shomberg went to work as an employee for a couple of legitimate businesses. He worked as a sales representative for Teddy's House of Seafood, selling fish to various restaurants throughout New York City. He also worked as a salesman for Progressive Color Lithographers and then for Portone Lithographs, two catalog printing firms.

Deportation hearings began in 1962 and investigators tried to interview anyone who might have had a connection to Shomberg during his lifetime. In an attempt to draw the hearings to a halt before they gained any momentum, Shomberg filed a *coram nobis* application, claiming that he failed to receive a fair trial way back in 1912. If he could erase one of the two convictions against him, he most likely calculated, he would expunge the government's case, which relied on the new immigration law's feature that he could be deported for having two felonies on his rap sheet.

Shomberg's new argument was that when he was arrested in 1912, he initially pled not guilty, with the approval of his first attorney, Louis Halle. He further claimed that the presiding judge, Judge Swann, dismissed Halle and replaced him with a public defender, who convinced Shomberg that it would be in his best interest if he pled guilty. The decision regarding this *coram nobis* application was in favor of the government. Shomberg's attorney advised him that he would have to appeal once again.

To build his case this time, Shomberg relied on reference letters from all walks of life. One letter came from Rabbi Wolf Rosenberg of the Congregation Lomza Vegatch at 23 Hester Street, who claimed he had known the defendant and his father for years and that he was a witness to "observe the fine care and treatment of as well as parental respect shown Mr. Abraham Shomberg by his son Louis." He continued, "From my observation of the home life of Mr. Abraham Shomberg, I am of the belief that Mr. Louis Shomberg is a person of good moral character." In another letter, Nat Boriskin, president and executive director of the United Popular Dress Manufacturers Association, claimed to have known Shomberg for twelve years and had also "observed him in his family relationship with his late father. His reputation for fatherly devotion was well known amongst his friends." Yet another recommendation came from Murray Bernstein, who, with his brother Sam, operated a delicatessen at 2413 Broadway. Bernstein stated: "My residence is just two blocks away from where Mr. Shomberg lives. His reputation in the neighborhood is of the highest among those in our community who know Mr. Shomberg. I am able to state that he is a peaceful, law-abiding and well-respected member of this community."

While fighting deportation, Louis Shomberg went back to the other side of the tracks. Whereas in the past he had dealt with gas ration coupons, this time he scammed the public with bogus corporate stock certificates. Indictments filed on July 14, 1964, charged Shomberg, twelve other men, and three securities firms, collectively, with conspiracy and 21 counts of selling corporate stock not registered with the Securities and Exchange Commission and trying to defraud the public in the amount of $1 million. Individually Shomberg was charged with conspiracy, eight counts of selling unregistered stock, and three counts of fraud in the sale of securities.

The district attorney charged the defendants with making the following false statements about Belmont Oil:

- Belmont had fine earnings.
- Belmont had been in the oil business for many years.
- Belmont stock was a safe investment.
- Monies collected from the sale of Belmont stock would be used to develop the company's oil properties.
- Belmont Oil was operating at a profit.
- Belmont was in production and making money.
- There was absolutely no risk of loss in the purchase of Belmont stock shares.
- Purchasers were guaranteed to make a profit after buy-

ing Belmont stock.

- The price of Belmont stock would go from $3 per share to $4 per share in four months.
- The price of Belmont stock would go from $4 per share to $5 per share in another six months.
- The price of Belmont stock would reach $10 per share within a year.
- Belmont stock was listed on the New York Stock Exchange.
- Firms H. G. Stolle and Peerless were members of the New York Stock Exchange.
- H. G. Stolle was one of the oldest brokerage firms on Wall Street.
- Carleton Securities was about to become a member of the New York Stock Exchange.
- Carleton Securities was an old reliable firm.
- Peerless was selling Belmont stock at $.25 below market price.

Federal prosecutor Robert Morgenthau brought the case to trial in 1967. By most measures, it appeared that it would be easy to convict nearly all of the defendants. First, the prosecution demonstrated that Belmont Oil was a shell company. One of the first exhibits shown to the jury was a letter dated September 15, 1958, typed on company letterhead, listing the company's address as a post office box in Wichita Falls, Texas, and telling shareholders that the company had recently acquired 10,000 drilling leases. Another letter, dated February 18, 1959, listed the company's headquarters at 9350 Wilshire Boulevard in Beverly Hills. Another piece of evidence entered by the prosecution was a marketing brochure created by H. G. Stolle & Company stating the following "facts" about Belmont Oil:

- The company had five or more "active" leases.
- One of the active leases was the Whitaker Lease in Wise County, Texas.

- The company had 160 acres, 100 of them in "production."
- The Whitaker Lease was generating approximately 1.3 million barrels of oil per year.
- Belmont's share of the Whitaker Lease was 65,200 barrels per year.
- Belmont was operating in Young, Wise, and Archer Counties in Texas and Okmulgee, Texas, and Tulsa Counties in Oklahoma.

The truth about Belmont Oil differed substantially from what the defendants told their prospective clients. A Mr. James Boren had been the largest stockholder in the company, owning 40 percent of the outstanding shares. He had sold all of his 3.6 million shares to some of the defendants for the sum of $1,000 in cash and $39,000 in notes, which were never paid. From February 1 to November 14, 1958, the prosecution argued, the company earned income of just $6,600 in oil lease payments and had generated $14,500 in expenses. The company consisted of a single employee, Joel Fox, who operated out of a one-room office.

The prosecution won its case against many of the defendants, gaining convictions against Vincent Schwenoha, a known criminal from Chicago, and Nathan Seuss. Gaining a conviction against Louis Shomberg proved more problematic, however. The prosecution's case against Shomberg centered on a conversation held in a room at the Hotel Novarro, among Shomberg, Nathan Seuss, and two men who operated the Carlton Securities firm, Stanley Younger and Murray Taylor. At the meeting Seuss talked to Younger and Taylor about selling them 100,000 shares of Belmont Oil at a dollar a share. Whether Shomberg participated in the conversation or was simply a witness was in question. Taylor testified that he, Younger, and Seuss did all of the talking and that Shomberg was simply a witness to the conversation, interjecting from time to time statements of no

material value to the prospective sale. Taylor further testified
that he spent time with Shomberg at the Turkish baths a few
days later and that Shomberg simply asked, "How is the sale
going?" At the baths, Shomberg told Taylor that Seuss owed
him money and that selling Belmont stock was the way Seuss
could garner enough money to pay his debt.

Fortunately, Shomberg was smart enough to hire one of the
most experienced defense attorneys—Nathan Kestnbaum. Kestnbaum had previously represented Harold "Kayo" Konigsberg,
the subject of nephew Eric Konigsberg's book *Blood Relation*,
as well as three Jews—Calman Cooper, Nathan Wissner, and
Harry Stein—who were electrocuted in Sing-Sing's electric
chair for the murder of a *Reader's Digest* deliveryman in 1952.
On cross-examination Kestnbaum won the case for Shomberg
when he got Taylor to admit he never heard Shomberg say a
word during the conversation at the Hotel Novarro. Additionally, Taylor admitted that Shomberg never owned a share of
Belmont stock, never "controlled" a share of Belmont stock, nor
could he even get hold of a share of Belmont stock.

Despite all the testimony in Shomberg's favor, the judge did
not believe Shomberg's defense and gave the jury other options
to consider for finding him guilty: "It is not necessary that the
defendant himself mailed any stock certificates. If one or more
members of the company [Schwenoha, Shomberg, or Seuss]
was then a member of that conspiracy and the acts which constituted those offenses were done in furtherance of a portion
of that conspiracy...and that defendant might reasonably have
foreseen that those acts would be done, then you may find that
the defendant is guilty of the offenses alleged in the subsequent
counts in which he is named even though he did not otherwise personally participate in the acts constituting those offenses or did not have knowledge of them." Despite the fact that
Shomberg had introduced Seuss to Younger and Taylor at the
Barbizon Plaza Hotel before the meeting at the Hotel Novarro,
the jury remained split as to whether he had truly participated

in the conversation at the latter location. In the end the prosecution was happy to convict many of the defendants and simply accepted their loss in their case against Shomberg. Assistant U.S. Attorney Edward Shaw summed up the prosecution's loss philosophically: "Defendant Shomberg is seventy-one years old and the government does not think that a successful prosecution is possible. The government, therefore, believes that no purpose would be served by a retrial of Shomberg." Louis Shomberg did not need to use any of his "markers" with politicians, law enforcement officials, or other criminals. A simple jury of his peers had let him off the hook.

Despite what might have happened earlier in his life, Louis Shomberg won the upper hand in the end. Beyond winning a hung jury in the stock fraud case, other federal officials threw up their hand in despair and decided not to prosecute him any further. According to an internal memo written in March 1968 by those involved with Shomberg's deportation hearings, the INS faced only two possible alternatives: (1) to continue deportation hearings "in the hope and expectation that either the respondent's application for Suspension of Deportation can be defeated," or (2) "keep the case in its present inactive status." Whoever wrote the memo (the name was redacted) recommended the latter approach, adding: "I doubt seriously we could successfully complete deportation in the subject's lifetime…On the other hand, if we progress for a conclusion of the case, he could conceivably obtain adjustment of status and proceed to United States citizenship."

The government really had no reason to worry, because Louis's health was in a state of deterioration. Already a diabetic, he suffered the first of several heart attacks in October 1970. A year later his cardiologist, Argyrios Golfinos, wrote in a generic letter "To whom it may concern" that his patient "is under my care, treated for recurrent acute myocardial infarction. He is totally disabled and in need of continuous medical supervision."

In October 1973 Shomberg was back in the hospital, having suffered yet another heart attack.

During the last few years of his life, maybe because of his health, Louis Shomberg exhibited behavior that contrasted with his criminal activities. He became ever more the consummate family man. He lived in a luxurious apartment with a fireplace at the Hotel Delmonico, at Fifty-ninth Street and Park Avenue, home to other luminaries including Lucille Ball and Ed Sullivan. Even the Beatles stayed at the Delmonico when Sullivan introduced the band to America in 1965. His brother's daughter, Joanne Shomberg, remembers Papa Louis giving her "three of the most beautiful dresses I ever owned." She also recalls receiving "big hugs and lots of love emanating from his larger than-life persona. He always wore a smoking jacket and often completed his effect with a cigar." Joanne saw Papa Louie about once a year and at special family occasions such as weddings and bar mitzvahs.

While he remained alive and even after his death, the family recounted stories about Louis Shomberg "quite freely around the Thanksgiving table or at a dinner party with extended family on a Friday or Saturday night." Joanne Shomberg's mother used to "cringe regularly" when her husband, Murray, "felt compelled to tell his stories." Given this reaction from his wife, Murray used to have "special Sunday outings" with Joanne. "He used to take me to see Uncle Lou. We always kept this a secret from my mom. When I was younger we saw him often—two to three times a year. By that time he was an old, kind man."

The reality is that Shomberg was a family man his entire life. Although he divorced Mae, he continued to provide for her throughout her life and did not object to her living at the Delmonico while he remained a tenant in the same building. Earlier he had provided jobs for both his nephew and brothers Harry and Isaac, although he fired the latter after Isaac "went about his business abusing and berating all who had the misfortune of working for him." Thanks to Papa Louie, Murray drove a truck for the Empire Liquor Company, headquartered in the Bronx. "Family" to Louis Shomberg extended beyond bloodlines. He was close enough to Louis Buchalter to count on Lepke literally to baby-sit for Shomberg's nephew Murray.

In 1975 Louis Shomberg died of cardiac arrest. The only fellow Jewish gangster of his generation and ilk to outlast him was Meyer Lansky, who passed away eight years later. Both men, despite keeping low profiles and managing to serve minimal prison sentences (considering how much they broke the law), exercised considerable power in the underworld. Both were almost deported by the federal government but, possibly because of their longevity, held on to live out their senior years as free men in America.

The passing of these two brought a virtual end to the notion of the American Jewish gangster. In the 1950s organized crime continued, but Jews had for the most part left the business. Jews, in the main, desired to assimilate and lead safer, more law-abiding lives for their children. As graduate and professional school quotas against Jews were lifted, Jews prospered as doctors, attorneys, captains of industry, and other more legitimate occupations. By contrast, Italian criminals continued their activities as family businesses. Some claim that the Jews didn't leave willingly but that the Italians forced them out of the crime world. Whatever the truth, the numbers of Jewish criminals involved in the most heinous of crimes has dropped dramatically since the heady days of the first half of the twentieth century.

Isaac Spier: Part III

IN 1998, AFTER a several-year respite, I decided once again to research my family. I had learned that Jews in the Old Country used patronymic names up until the early nineteenth century, when they were required under the law to take on surnames as we use them today. A patronymic name uses the first name of the father as the basis for the last name. If I were living in the old country 200 years ago, given that my father's name was Isaiah, I would have been called Ron Isaiovitch or something similar.

Years earlier I had traveled to the Latter Day Saints Family History Library in Salt Lake City to examine a book that contained seven censuses of my father's ancestral town of Smorgon, Belarus, during the seventeenth and eighteenth centuries. Unfortunately, I had copied only those pages on which the "surnames" were Aronowitch, Gilman, or one of the other names on my father's side. Realizing that I had made a huge mistake copying only those pages where the patronymic names matched my ancestral surnames, I decided to return to Salt Lake City and photocopy the entire book so I could more carefully search for possible ancestors.

On the bus that shuttled me from the Salt Lake City Airport to the downtown area, it occurred to me that it could not take the whole day to copy the entire book. In the time remaining before I had to catch the bus back to the airport, I would try one last time to find my great-grandfather's birth location. This time I was in luck.

Just that year the Family History Library had transcribed all of the 1881 British census into an electronic database. All I had to do was type in the name of my great-grandfather to determine whether he was listed in the census. When I did so, summary details of three records appeared, although only one record seemed to match what I knew about Isaac.

The summary details pointed me to the more complete census record on microfilm. When I viewed the record, I realized that I had finally tracked down my Rosetta Stone; the record showed Isaac and his entire family living in Brighton, England:

Address: 11 Devonshire Street, Brighton, U.K.				
Name	*Relation*	*Age*	*Occupation*	*Born*
Abraham Spiers	Head	30	Secretary Minister at a Jewish Synagogue	Poland
Betsey Spiers	Wife	30		Poland
Rebecca Spiers	Daughter	10	Scholar (student)	Poland
Isaac Spiers	Son	7	Scholar (student)	London
Julia Spiers	Daughter	5	Scholar (student)	London
Hyam Spiers	Son	3		Hanley
Eva Spiers	Daughter	3 mos.		Brighton

Isaac's parents and older sister were all born in Poland. Isaac's brother Hyam (and not Isaac) was born in Hanley, Staffordshire, the birth location Isaac provided on my grandfather Sidney's birth certificate. Isaac was born in London. I had finally solved the mystery! Yet with so much new information, I had many new questions to pose and avenues to take. One of the first topics I researched next was the history and environment of Brighton.

I guessed that Abraham had good reasons to leave London for Hanley and Brighton, including better living conditions and a good job. London's East End overflowed with immigrants from Eastern Europe. Surveys conducted by Charles Booth, a wealthy Victorian businessman, showed 523 people per acre in this section of town in the 1880s. Today Seoul, the world's most densely populated city, has only 97 people per acre. Tokyo and New York trail far behind, with 29 and 8 people per acre, respectively. Beyond cramped living conditions, the East End was unsanitary. In addition to the impetus to leave London, there was a positive attraction to Brighton, whose Jewish community probably needed trained religious leaders to help with its growth and to run its new synagogue, built in 1876.

Like San Francisco, Brighton is located near a large body of water. Both places have been havens for the exploration of new ideas. In the case of Brighton, sea bathing and "bathing machines" bolstered the town's reputation for unconventional thinking. In the mid-1700s, Dr. Richard Russell introduced the concept of sea bathing, claiming it helped treat "diseases of the glands." Notables came from near and far to Brighton to cure their ills. Dr. F. A. Struve of Dresden moved to Brighton and opened the "German Spa," where patrons could sample mineral waters found at famous resorts such as Carlsbad, Marienbad, Kesselbrunnen, Kissingen, and Selzer. Dr. Struve avoided overstating the benefits of his establishment yet promised better health if one spent time in his spa. Spa water was sold in bottles, not only at the German Spa, but also in London. Famous patrons of the spa included King William IV, Queen Adelaide, the Duchess of Kent, and other members of the royal family.

Another health entrepreneur, Sake Deen Mahomed, a native of India, opened the Vapour Bath and Shampooing. Via a process of "stewing alive by steam," customers were treated with warm wraps until the "substances of your joints are made as pliable as the ligaments of boiled calves' feet, your whole system relaxed and unnerved, and your trembling legs as useless in supporting your body as a pair of boots would be without the usual quantity of flesh and bone within them." Mahomed claimed his baths cured rheumatism.

Introduced about 1735, bathing machines looked like "Noah's arks on wheels." Bathers used these vehicles as mobile dressing rooms; after a bather entered one on the beach, horses would pull the conveyance into the desired depth of water. The bathers would then slip off their clothing and exit into the ocean. Peeping Toms invariably inspected female bathers from afar with the aid of telescopes. Men did not wear bathing costumes until about 1863; men and women commonly bathed naked in the sea. To avoid exposure, people placed "modesty hoods" over the steps used to enter the bathing machines.

But it was more than its health benefits that attracted tourists to Brighton. By the late nineteenth century the town had a reputation for bawdiness and lascivious pursuits. Two contemporary English travel guides attributed the term "dirty weekend" to Brighton, because the city attracted Londoners in search of a getaway for trysts. Even those members of the highest strata of society took advantage of the atmosphere in Brighton. The Prince Regent, later King George IV, commissioned architect Harry Holland to design a summer villa in Brighton not only to be close to the town's seawater, which, he was told would help with his gout, but also to spend time with his mistress, Maria Fitzherbert. After objecting to the prince's philandering, Queen Victoria appointed architect John Nash to upgrade the venue to exude more grandeur, though it remained as a trysting spot for her son and Fitzherbert. By 1822 the Royal Pavilion, with its cupolas, looked more like the Taj Mahal than Buckingham Palace.

Reading about Brighton's reputation for extramarital affairs, I thought of my great-grandfather and wondered if he had learned some of his bad behavior from the Prince of England himself. If it were condoned for the Regent to bring his mistress to Brighton, perhaps it was okay for Isaac to have relations with more than one woman.

Although my research had been encouraging and I was inspired anew to work on my family genealogy, the trail suddenly went cold again: 1895 was the last year in which the *Jewish Yearbook* listed Abraham Spier as working for the Brighton Synagogue on Middle Street. Not willing to be deterred so quickly, I decided to track the family down by finding where Isaac's siblings married. This proved to be the right decision when I came across the marriage certificate for Isaac's sister Rebecca, who married in Plymouth in 1893. With this information, I found the family listed in the 1891 British census—with two new members, Solomon and Edward (curiously, the middle name that Isaac used when he married Minnie Ott). Isaac is not listed as living with the family, although this omission could simply mean that he was playing with a friend elsewhere at the time the census was taken.

My good fortune continued. In an attempt to learn more about Plymouth, I discovered a book written by the late Rabbi Bernard Susser, *The Jews of Southwest England*. Much to my surprise the book mentioned my great-great-grandfather, Abraham Spier, several times. Between 1885 and 1893 Abraham served as a *shochet* (kosher butcher) for the Jewish community. For this he earned "a mere 40 shillings [equivalent to £2] a week, although the cantor/*shochet* in the neighboring town of Penzance earned half that amount." Also working as the Jewish community's "general factotum," Abraham received free room and board for his family, living in the "synagogue house" behind the synagogue on Catherine Street. (Both structures survive today.) Susser's book also explains that Abraham ran afoul of the local Jewish custom of waiting a full day before burying a child, when he put a child into the ground the day he died. This event caused so much commotion that, in response to a complaint in the *Jewish Chronicle* (published in London), Rabbi Herman Adler, the chief rabbi for all of England, reprimanded Abraham with a stern letter:

> *Ap 13 1890 to Rev. Spier Plymouth*
> *A Mr. Hy Worms wrote to JC* [Jewish Chronicle] *on the*
> *4th inst. re yr Kehilla, a child was buried shortly after death*
> *"highly necessary to prevent repetition of proceeding (event)*
> *which may lead to grave scandal and danger."*

In an attempt to appease the chief rabbi, Rabbi Abraham
Spier on at least two occasions sent Adler pots of "clotted
cream," a delicacy enjoyed in southwest England. In response to
this gesture, Rabbi Adler sent the following letters of thanks:

> *May 27 1890*
> *2580 [To] Rev. A. N. Spier Plym. Thanks for pot of*
> *cream.*

> *Oct 27 1890 [To] Rev. A. N. Spier Plymouth*
> *Wife and I thank you for tin of such delicious cream. I am*
> *glad that the statement about J. C.* [Jewish Chronicle] *is in-*
> *correct.*

Presumably, the chief rabbi assumed that the complaint published in the *Jewish Chronicle* about premature burials did not
specifically pertain to Abraham Spier.

It was also about this time that Abraham Spier must have
taken up a time-consuming and difficult penance—construct-
ing his own *Sefer Torah*. By creating a Torah, one of the Torah's
613 commandments to perform *mitzvot* (commandments), a
sofer (scribe) demonstrates that he is thoroughly familiar with
the contents of the Five Books of Moses, reveres the traditions
of the Jewish religion, and desires to sanctify the world by making the words of God available to the community to read, learn,
and enjoy. Typically a *sofer* spends a year to a year and a half
inking all 304,805 Hebrew characters on specially prepared

parchment. If a *sofer* makes a mistake, the entire section has to be discarded. If a *sofer* incorrectly writes the Divine's name, he cannot simply erase the error, an act considered to be a serious transgression; he must cut out that portion and bury it in a special holding place known as a *geniza*, usually a special room in a synagogue's basement.

I learned about Abraham's *Sefer Torah* from the following *Jewish Chronicle* article:

> *April 8, 1892: On Saturday last the portion of the week was read from a* Sefer Torah *written by the Rev. A. N. Spier, of this Congregation. The Torah is of an extraordinarily small size, and measures five and a half inches in height. The columns are three and a half inches long by one and a quarter wide. Notwithstanding its diminutive size and the extreme smallness of the letters, it is so written that it can be read without the slightest difficulty. The weight of the* Sefer *is one pound six ounces. Mr. Spier is to be congratulated on his work, which must have entailed a large amount of trouble.*

By 1893, the year of Rebecca Spier's wedding, Abraham had lost his position as leader of the Plymouth Jewish community. He nevertheless officiated at his daughter's wedding, listing "gentleman" for his occupation on the marriage certificate. From here the trail went cold once again.

In his book Rabbi Susser provided another potential clue to Isaac Spier's thoughts about how women could be treated and the acceptability of having children before marriage. In the eighty years preceding my family's arrival in Plymouth, the town's Jewish community experienced a high incidence of children born out of wedlock along with frequent marriage infidelity. Susser suggested that these activities were "influenced" by or simply "reflected" the fact that many Jews sold "bad books" of a "most obscene and mischievous kind." Quite possibly, Isaac learned of these books, if he did not read them directly, and the town's reputation for sexual activities that crossed the lines of legal norms.

I looked for marriages of Isaac's siblings to pick up the scent once again, this time in Sheffield, England, where Abraham's second daughter, Julia, married in 1896. In Sheffield Rabbi Abraham Spier shared rabbinical responsibilities with Rabbi Alexander at the synagogue on North Church Street, and he alternated as the official at more than thirty weddings over the span of a few years.

Most of Sheffield's Jewish congregants chose to work on the Sabbath rather than attend services. Another rabbi, Reverend Chaikin, started a new congregation in West Bar in competition with the North Church Street congregation. One day he preached to all attending congregants the importance of keeping the Sabbath. By organizing a society called the Workers of Righteousness and Sabbath Observance, Chaikin brought many back into the religious fold, especially tailors and their employees who abstained from working on the Sabbath.

At the same time that Rabbi Chaikin criticized the community for its poor attendance at religious services, the community came under fire to improve its Jewish education. Although London's Chief Rabbi Adler wanted to become involved in this movement in the "provinces," many community members felt he overextended his purview. Sheffield parents preferred to send their children to private *melamdim* (teachers), despite their "various foreign methods in jargon," rather than to the more official Jewish school. In July 1898 the Jewish school headmaster died and the community named Abraham as a temporary teacher.

In the end, Abraham's position was indeed temporary, for four months later the Committee of the Sheffield Hebrew School advertised for a permanent teacher. "A letter was read from the Chief Rabbi Adler urging the Committee to appoint a teacher who would be able to translate the prayers into the vernacular." In December 1898 Isaac Aarons (no relation to the author) from Manchester accepted the position. Although I found Abraham Spier listed in the 1900 edition of the Shef-field Red Book, the 1901 book had no such listing. The family had moved once again.

By examining marriage and death records for other members of the family, I determined that most of the clan had moved to Manchester. When Abraham first arrived in Manchester, he owned a drapery shop. Once he made connections in the Jewish community, he took on other assignments—as a *chaz-zan* (cantor) and as secretary and investigating officer for the Manchester Shechita Board, which oversaw the licensing and activities of the Jewish butchers in town who, it was hoped, would follow the rules of *kashrut* (Judaic dietary laws). In fact, Abraham responded to the following job posting, listed in the December 28, 1900 edition of the *Jewish Chronicle*:

> *MANCHESTER SHECHITA BOARD*
> *WANTED, a SECRETARY and General Supervisor for this Board. Candidates must have a fair English education, be accustomed to Secretarial work, and be conversant with Yid-dish, and some knowledge of Shechita. Applications must be in writing, and should be accompanied with full particulars of qualifications, references and salary required.*
> *Address to President, Isaac Goodman, Esq.*
> *21 Elizabeth Street, Cheetham, Manchester*

According to the Shechita Board minutes and as part of his 1901 agreement with the Board, Abraham agreed to "improve his knowledge of the English language to the satisfaction of the Executive (committee)." Though Abraham may have spoken English well enough, he nevertheless encountered organiza-tional and communal politics. Between 1904 and 1907 four ko-sher butchers sued the Shechita Board for libel and complained that the board's licensing fees were exorbitant. Simply following the Jewish laws of *kashrut* did not suffice; one had to purchase a permit from the local Shechita Board to be officially licensed as a kosher butcher in Manchester. The board used collected funds for operational expenses and charitable causes, such as free burials for families who could not afford them. Additionally, the plaintiffs complained that the Shechita Board sold too many licenses, generating excessive competition. The Shechita Board defended itself by insisting that the four plaintiffs were not following rules set by either the local Shechita Board or the chief rabbi in London. Despite the best efforts of the Shechita Board to settle the dispute informally, the plaintiffs pressed for a court trial. To the butchers' dismay, in late July 1907 a jury ruled in favor of the Shechita Board.

In April 1907, before this matter ever reached a judge, Abraham apparently insulted the chairman of the Shechita Board. A series of discussions followed, which culminated in the board's calling Abraham incompetent and ending his contract. Why and how did Abraham insult the chairman? Perhaps the chairman made disparaging remarks about or to Abraham. If Abraham spoke "broken" English, possibly the board concluded he was incompetent, but if so, why did the board not fire Abraham years before? More plausibly, the board may have used Abraham as a scapegoat for the trouble the four butchers caused.

The board wasted little time seeking a replacement for Abraham, placing an advertisement in the May 24, 1907, issue of the *Jewish Chronicle*:

MANCHESTER SHECHITA BOARD
WANTED, SECRETARY, the same also to act as Investigating Officer, one who is thoroughly competent and conversant in English and Hebrew, and must have a knowledge of "Shechita" and able to freely converse in Yiddish. State age and salary required and previous experience. Applications with copies of testimonials to J. Susman, Hon. Sec., 97, Cheetham Hill Road, Manchester.

A new secretary and investigating officer, Mr. E. Trotzky, was hired in July 1907 and quickly tried to endear himself to both the Shechita Board and the Jewish community as a whole. In a public notice dated July 28, 1907, less than two weeks after the trial concluded, Trotzky played the role of "enforcer":

> *We have already issued our warning several times that no butcher should go on the Sabbath to the market to buy meat or to transact any other business. Regrettably, our warning until now has been unsuccessful. Woe that ears should hear that Jewish butchers who are entrusted with Kashrut should publicly profane the Sabbath! Therefore we come once more to issue a strong warning that from this day on, no butcher should dare to go to the market on the Sabbath to buy meat or to publicly profane the Sabbath. And whoever should ignore this warning, in accordance with the Law, his shop will be immediately placed under prohibition by us, the Beth Din of Manchester, and this prohibition together with the reasons will be publicized in the streets...*
>
> *Any negligence on the part of a butcher in the fulfillment of this pledge, as well as any other contravention of the laws of* Kashrut, *will lead to the suspension of his license by the Board, who are determined to adopt this course in all such cases in the future.*
>
> *By Order, E. Trotzky, Secretary*

After the Shechita Board's decisive victory, the butchers appear not to have resisted Trotzky's admonitions. Two years later, in 1909, the Shechita Board gave Mr. Trotzky a purse of gold to commend the "zeal and efficiency, which characterized his work." Reading about this in the *Jewish Chronicle* might well have depressed Abraham further—especially because even the press categorized the Shechita Board as overly zealous and heavy-handed.

Abraham died in Prestwich (near Manchester) in 1910. His daughter Eva and son Solomon died in Manchester as well. When I obtained the death certificate for Abraham Spier, much to my surprise it listed "suicide by hanging" as the cause of death. Although it was clear that Abraham had led a somewhat tarnished life, I was surprised at the mention of suicide, and I e-mailed a professional Jewish genealogist in Manchester to inquire whether she could track down any articles regarding Abraham's death. Within 24 hours she delivered the goods—a newspaper article describing in gory detail how Abraham suffered from what we would probably today call a periodontal abscess—an infection which, left untreated, would have been excruciatingly painful. My dentist suggested that Abraham would not have had any alternative but to take his own life since antibiotics were not available at the time. So it was pain and not questionable behavior that led Abraham to take his life.

Some family researchers might have stopped here. Yet once again my thirst for more knowledge grew by leaps and bounds. And once again I focused on my great-grandfather, who had started me off on this journey in the first place. If Isaac's siblings had stayed in England, I realized, I must have some relatives living there today. If so, maybe I could learn more about Isaac. Frank Felsenstein, a friend and a native of England, and former professor of Judaic Studies at the University of Leeds and Yeshiva University in New York, suggested that I place the story of my research journey in the *Manchester Jewish Telegraph*. As Frank put it, "They would love such an article," since the newspaper had recently started a "Roots" section featuring stories like mine.

The *Manchester Jewish Telegraph* gave me top billing the week of November 19, 1999, with the headline "Abraham's Journey." Just ten days later I received an e-mail from a woman named Sharyn, who felt awkward contacting me. She too was descended from Abraham Spier. Sharyn also said that an American cousin—an attorney named Harvey—had called her twenty years earlier. I needed only a few hours to locate Harvey in New York. When I called, Harvey expressed amazement that I had tracked him down. We immediately patched into the phone call his brother Jerry (a professor of pathology in Southern California) who had been researching their family for more than thirty years.

Harvey and his brother Jerry, it turned out, were descendents of Abraham's brother Nahum (Nathan). They informed me that the family came from Suwalki, in northeast Poland. Furthermore, they said the family had changed its surname from Szeszupski (pronounced Sheh-shoop-ski, and possibly derived from the Szeszupa River, which flows through the Suwalki region).

With this new information I was able to piece together Abraham's life in much the same way I had done for my great-grandfather. Summarizing their stories side by side, I now had a much stronger understanding of Isaac. Both Isaac and Abraham had grown up in families with many siblings. Both married at age twenty. Both left their country of birth. Both had changed either their first or last name. Both lived either in or near a prison (Abraham and his remaining family lived on Waterloo Street, just down the block from Strangeways Prison). Both participated in multiple marriages (Abraham as an official, Isaac as a groom three times; after my great-grandmother Ida died, Isaac married a woman named Rose). Both had found trouble (Isaac had committed bigamy, abandonment, either forgery or larceny, and attempted extortion; Abraham had buried a child too soon after its death and gotten stuck in the politics of the Manchester Shechita Board). More and more, this appeared to be a case of like father, like son.

14

My Tour of the Prison

IHAD WANTED TO visit Sing Sing ever since I learned of my
great-grandfather's imprisonment there, but you cannot just
walk into Sing Sing and request a tour. Unlike Alcatraz, which
no longer holds inmates and is part of the National Parks System, Sing Sing is a fully-functional, maximum-security prison
housing 1,700 inmates convicted of everything from substance
possession to murder. So even though I provided ample evidence that one of my ancestors had served time within the
prison's walls, my first request for a tour of the facility was
turned down.

A few months after that request had been turned down, I
sent a second letter requesting a tour of the prison, this time
explaining my intention to write a book that not only discussed
Jews in the prison over time but also included the memoirs of
the late Irving Koslowe, the rabbi/chaplain who between 1950
and 2000 visited the prison and dealt with the needs of Jewish
inmates, including Julius and Ethel Rosenberg. An acquaintance of mine had introduced me to one of Koslowe's sons, who
told me he was trying to publish his father's memoirs. The son
and I had talked about the possibility of joining forces and, for
a time, had an oral agreement to do so. It was Koslowe's name
that caught the prison superintendent's attention. The way the
prison officials talked about Koslowe, you would have to believe
he walked on water. They had that much respect for the man. In
addition to working ferociously as an advocate for Jewish and

non-Jewish prisoners alike, Koslowe also knew how to work with the administration.

Finally granted permission to tour Sing Sing, I arrived in Ossining an hour before my 10:30 A.M. appointment. I certainly did not want to be late! After getting my bearings in town, I drove to the Ossining Community Center, which houses a small exhibit about the prison's history as well as two mock cells and a replica of "Ole Sparky," the electric chair. A wall mirror cleverly placed to the right of the rightmost cell fooled me into believing there were actually four cells making up the block. Each of these cells was of 1929 vintage—longer than those originally available when the prison opened in the 1820s, each containing a sink, a toilet, and a bulb for lighting. Plaques on the wall of the community center exhibit described the various punishments used with those prisoners who got out of line, including the "iron cage," which was worn around the head and probably used to deprive inmates of sleep; the more familiar "ball and chain"; the "gag," a metal device placed in the mouths of those who would not remain silent; and the "shower-bath," which gave the inmate the impression he was about to drown.

When I finished viewing the community center's prison exhibit, I drove a few blocks to a park sandwiched between the Ossining train station and the north side of the penitentiary, where visitors can walk up to an old guard tower and approach the prison fence. Oddly enough, a children's playground, equipped with swings and plastic slides, stands just yards away from the ten-foot chain-link fence, fronting the prison's vehicle maintenance building and the motor pool parking lot. A friend of mine, Rhonda Moskowitz, had warned me that I should not take photographs of the prison, at least not *before* my official visit, as the guards might confiscate my camera and jeopardize my scheduled tour.

Intrigued by the contrast between the stunning fall foliage colors across the Hudson and the austere nature of the prison, I quickly snapped a few quick shots of both. I then returned to my rental car and drove about a mile to the southern end of Hunter Street—the entrance to the "Big House."

Approaching the prison, I saw the four-level parking structure designated for the prison's thousand-strong staff. Just to the left of the structure, I followed a winding road uphill, driving along the northern 70-foot security wall, until I saw a turn-off to the left and a gravel visitor's parking lot. Once parked, I stashed my wallet, house keys, belt, and small change in the glove compartment and prayed that no one would break into the car during my visit. Wearing a red shirt, a color that Rhonda had told me would distinguish me from inmates' garb, and with my California driver's license, my rental car keys, and my digital camera as my sole possessions in hand, I nervously walked down the road, past the parking structure, and toward the main entrance of the facility.

A banner marking the prison's 175th anniversary in 2000 welcomed all visitors to the three-story tan-brick administration building and entrance to the facility. At the same time, a clear-glass booth warned any visitor to comply with its "Deposit Your Weapons in the Arsenal before Entering the Institution" sign. Brass bars surrounded the entrance doors, the bars climbing two stories and covering two sets of windows.

After I pressed the doorbell, a door lock released with a click and I entered the lobby. "Are you Mr. Arons?" a guard asked immediately.

"Yes. I am," I replied, my words echoing across the lobby.

To the left was the reception desk. Straight ahead of me I saw an information board, indicating which of the prison's staff were working that day. To the right stood a full-body metal detector, the kind normally used at airports. I showed my driver's license and subjected both my body and camera to searches. A guard removed the flash memory card from the digital camera, examined it, and then replaced it in its slot. Having left most of my metallic possessions in the car, I easily cleared inspection.

After I completed this ritual, the receiving guard introduced me to my tour guide, Correctional Officer Andre Varin. Almost instantly he put me at ease. Probably 6 feet, 2 inches, and about 250 pounds, he had worked at Sing Sing for years. He was like a gentle giant: strong enough, physically and mentally, to handle tough situations, yet soft-spoken. I would feel safe in his hands. He welcomed me and informed me that he had known and worked with the late Rabbi Irving Koslowe. Varin looked amused when I informed him that my great-grandfather had done a "stretch" in Sing Sing.

He immediately took me upstairs to the administrative offices and briefly introduced me to Superintendent Brian Fischer and William Connolly, Deputy Superintendent of Security. After these exchanges, we descended the stairs, where we were to start the official tour. Before setting out, Varin announced the administration's photography regulation: I could take a photo of *anything*, as long as no *individuals* were included.

We first entered the visitation room, which contained a miniature three-dimensional model of the entire facility. The model gives a modern-day view of both the old section, which lies closer to the Hudson, and the newer portion, up the hill. The Metro North Railroad and Amtrak train tracks, which run north and south through the facility, separate the old from the new.

Varin proceeded to take me outside, where we walked past many of the newer buildings, including the three-story red-brick medical facility. I had my first view of the older section of the prison, where my great-grandfather had spent his time. In the background spread the Hudson and the tree-filled cliffs on the west bank of the river. Green guard towers with 360-degree views were visible everywhere.

Soon we entered E Block, one of the newer cellblocks, where some of the more privileged inmates were housed. With only about 100 prisoners, E Block is a self-contained, open environment. Taking more time to examine the space in detail, I saw its three levels with about fifteen individual cells on either side of a 30-foot-high atrium. In the middle of the ground floor were two high-school-cafeteria-style tables with bench seats. At the table closest to me, a few men played chess at one end while at the other end a group competed at checkers. I told Varin I wanted to take a picture. "Sure," Varin responded. Then, "Get out of the way. This gentleman wants to take a photo of the room," he yelled, announcing my intentions.

Without much hesitation, the inmates interrupted their games and cleared my range of view, enabling me to take my first photo of the living quarters. As we turned around to leave the room, Varin pointed out to me the 42-inch RCA big-screen TV bolted to the railing on the second level. I did not even have a 30-inch television in my own home! "This is not your great-grandfather's Sing Sing," I thought to myself, before I snapped a photo of the television set, so I could prove later, even to myself, that it actually existed.

This was so different from the impression I had gleaned from reading accounts of Sing Sing, past and present, which led me to believe that inmates were confined to their cells to read books, perform isometric exercises, repent, or concoct devious schemes to escape—but not much else. In 1904 inmate #1500 wrote the following about the conditions he endured:

> [My cell] was precisely like twelve hundred other cells arranged in rows of one hundred each, back to back, on six tiers, and was built of solid, fairly well-dressed stone. The gallery was an iron frame with board floor, and the entrance to the cell was through an iron door, which had grating in the upper half, while the lower part was of welded sheet-iron. Through these bars, cutting a space twenty-four by eighteen inches, is admitted the only light and air that enters.
>
> These walls are built of stone and are forty-two inches thick. The cells are seven feet by three feet and six inches, and six feet high. My own contained, when I entered it, an iron-water kit, a wash basin, an iron bed-frame hooked on the wall, with

a dirty, lumpy straw mattress, a filthy straw pillow and two shabby coarse blankets which had never been aired and which were so dirty and stench-pervaded that only fire could have purified them. During the night the prison was still, so that the silence was oppressive.

Books are exchanged weekly, each man being provided with one book, which would be an entirely inadequate supply for a voracious reader; but as no objection is made to the prisoners exchanging with one another, no one is really limited in his supply so long as he can borrow from his neighbor.

We marched to the dining room, a great, low-ceilinged apartment with narrow tables and stools for twelve hundred men. The dinner was already on the table in portions served out in tin basins. It was a stew made of mutton, potatoes, onions and carrots, thickened with flour and steaming hot.

After Superintendent Collins inaugurated his reforms ... the food grew scantier, the soups and stews more watery, and meat rations less and less, until they neared the vanishing point. The bread, however, was abundant and was made of good, white flour and was always sweet.

Conditions certainly have improved dramatically from what they were a century ago. Cellblocks are heated now, and cells have jacks to listen to two radio stations. And here in this room, everyone appeared occupied with some leisure activity—and relaxed!

Meandering down a few more hallways, Varin and I arrived at A Block, with its three levels of cells extending 175 yards, the walkways of the top two layers secured by a floor-to-ceiling chain-link fence. "This is the longest cellblock found anywhere in the country," Varin boasted. Near where I was standing in the center of the block, inmates queued in line to place calls at a bank of ten pay phones.

Ordering all inmates out of my line of sight, Varin provided me with the opportunity to look into one inmate's cell, where

I saw its single bed, toilet, sink, plastic water bottle, soda cans, a roll of toilet paper on the floor, a calendar pasted on the wall, a stack of books at the end of the bed, clothing hanging from makeshift clotheslines, and foodstuffs, including a box of cereal and a partial loaf of bread. Not that bad a stash, I thought.

Our tour continued in the mess hall and kitchen, its metal tables bolted to the floor, each table offering individual round aluminum seats. In the kitchen Varin proudly pointed to five 50-gallon steam kettles and a dozen or more Southbend convection ovens. A storage room off to the side of the kitchen contained crates of Kellogg's Rice Krispies, Corn Flakes, Dakota Growers' Rotini, and Medium Egg Noodles. It was the penal equivalent of Costco.

We once again went outside, where more guard towers overlooked the outdoor gym, equipped with barbells, dumbbells, and a variety of workout benches. Continuing down the road toward the older section of the prison, we stopped at one of the entrances, and Varin showed me the pit in the ground where correctional officers stand to inspect the underbellies of vehicles for both incoming contraband and potential escapees.

Next on Varin's tour was the building that houses the religious observance rooms. The three separate chapels I walked through averaged about 200 seats in capacity and all contained beautiful stained-glass windows. The final stop in this portion of the tour was the Jewish chapel, officially named "The Chapel of Peace and Hope," which was dedicated on December 1, 1959, to Rabbi Koslowe. When Varin tried to open the door, he found it locked. We proceeded to walk back upstairs to ground level, where Varin asked another correctional officer if she could open the chapel door for us. "No! I don't have the key," the guard snarled back. "Can't you see I'm eating my lunch?" Varin and I decided to tour other parts of the prison facility and return to the chapel sometime later.

In the meantime, Varin showed me the Jewish chaplain's office and library just across the hallway. The library's collection included Irving Howe's *World of Our Fathers*, a book about the Jewish immigrant experience; Samuel Drix's *Witness to Annihilation, Surviving the Holocaust: A Memoir*; Victor Ostrovsky's book about Israel's Mossad, *By Way of Deception*; and Gil Mann's *How to Get More Out of Being Jewish*.

Varin then directed me toward a building that houses various classrooms as well as the law library. Inmates with appropriate privileges can conduct their own research using a myriad of WestLaw and other publishers' law books. After Varin initiated a conversation with the one inmate who was in the library at the time, I briefly introduced myself and wished him well with his research. At the time, this inmate interaction was the only one I thought I would have all day. During most of the tour, I tried my best not to engage in conversation with any of the inmates or look into their eyes, fearing that I might stir a commotion. Several inmates had indeed tempted me with, "Take my picture. Take my picture," but I remembered Varin's instructions.

Down the hill, in the old section of the prison, stand the outer marble walls of the original cellblock built in the 1820s. Six stories high and about 100 yards long, the structure is a lasting tribute not only to the original prisoners but also to the inmates from Auburn Prison who built this prison on top of a quarry. The etymology of Sing Sing is Native American, literally meaning "stone upon stone." Although the old cellblock lost its rooftop in 1985 in a fire, it still remains an imposing structure with the wind swirling through the cellblock windows. I wondered if the whispers contained some late inmates' stories.

A red brick building resembling an old-style bowling alley—long and with a convex roof—stood right next door to the old cellblock. Originally built as a set by Warner Brothers in the 1930s, the structure found a new purpose when Harry M. and Lewis J. Warner dedicated it in 1934 as a gymnasium. Is it any wonder that old connections die hard? Varin pointed out the various paint marks on the concrete where actors took their places for screenshots. *Analyze That*, starring Robert DeNiro as a Sing Sing parolee and Billy Crystal as his psychotherapist, was shot on location at Sing Sing. Who released the film? Warner Brothers, which, curiously, also released the cartoon *Big House Bunny* in 1948, starring Bugs Bunny as Inmate #3 ½, who confronts Correctional Officer Sam Schultz, played by Yosemite Sam, at *Sing Song* Prison.

With just a few steps, we transported ourselves from a movie set to the real Death Row, the building formerly known as "The Death House." Inside, I came face to face with the room in which the electric chair had terminated the lives of 614 inmates. Varin pointed to the "last mile," the stretch of hallway through which inmates walked from their holding cells to the electric chair chamber. After this, we walked upstairs to see the cells used by these inmates during their remaining days. The roof of the death chamber has windows that could be opened to allow the smoke from the electrocution to escape. In a closet, Varin told me, in a hushed voice, "This is the wood table Ethel Rosenberg used to write her final letters to her children."

After leaving the Death House we again walked to the Jewish chapel. This time Correctional Officer Varin and I found ourselves interrupting a Sukkot service, the Jewish celebration of the fall harvest, run by five inmates. Once a storage room, the chapel has limited space, with a seating capacity for about twenty. In the front of the room stands not only a bima (lectern), but also a spectacular dark wooden ark, approximately seven feet in height and six feet wide, which shelters the prison's Torah scroll. In front of the ark's doors hangs a banner proclaiming "In Memory of Rabbi Jacob Katz, 1952." From what I have heard about Rabbi Koslowe, who took over the chaplaincy in 1950, the banner must have been his idea.

Entering the sanctuary, I immediately recognized two of the men: Sam and the short Hispanic-looking inmate named Juan. (Their names have been changed for privacy reasons.) I had first "encountered" Sam two days earlier, when I spent time in Boston viewing video footage shot by Rhonda Moskowitz, a documentarian filming Jewish inmates currently incarcerated at Sing Sing and other correctional facilities. She showed me a five-minute portion of the more than twenty hours of a video she had filmed in the prison. Sam, she informed me, had made his way to Sing Sing as a result of repeated sex offenses.

Tall, gaunt, with a salt-and-pepper beard and mustache, Sam appeared to be the leader of this less-than-*minyan* (quorum)-sized group of seemingly serious congregants. He clutched the ceremonial etrog, a Mediterranean citrus fruit resembling a lemon and symbolizing a *tzadik*, a righteous person educated in the Torah; and a *lulav*, a date palm branch, representing a person who has knowledge but does not perform good deeds, and he began reciting the Hebrew Prayer of the Four Kinds: *Baruch ata Adonai, Elohaynu melech ha-olam, ashair kidishanu b'mitzvotav vetsivanu al netilat lulav.* [Praised be You, Lord our God, Ruler of the universe, who makes us holy with *mitzvot* and commands us to wave the *lulav*.]

When he saw me, Sam invited me to participate in the service. How could I refuse? After all, it was a *mitzvah* to do so. So I stepped into the circle of inmates and listened to Sam's instructions. First he indicated which Hebrew prayer I should recite from the prayer book. Next he demonstrated how I should hold the *etrog* and *lulav* in my hands and then extend my arms out and draw them back in three times, all the while facing east. He instructed me to repeat this procedure five more times—once for each of the other major directions, once upward, and once downward. The ritual is highly symbolic, with the directions representing the divine rule of God and the wavings signifying, "Thanks to God for the harvest."

It had been years since I had seen a *lulav* and an *etrog*—not since my childhood—and I had never been fortunate enough to shake them myself. That role had always been reserved for the rabbi. But now I felt both a need to prove my Jewish identity to the inmates and to connect with my great-great-grandfather, who had been a rabbi in England. I stepped in front of the *bima* and, after reciting the prayer, shook the festival items north, south, east, west, up, and down before handing them back to Sam. I am not sure whether my body shook more from moving the *lulav* and *etrog* in different directions or from nervousness at performing in front of convicted criminals. When I finished, to my embarrassment, the inmates all said, *Mazel Tov*, congratulating me on my performance. I thanked them and then explained to them that my great-grandfather had served time in Sing Sing and that I was visiting the prison to experience for myself what he might have endured.

The prison remained eerily quiet during my visit. The inmates had all behaved, following Varin's orders to move out of the way whenever I asked to take a photograph. And I had managed not to cause any disruptions. However, I had lived in "tornado alley" in Texas, an experience that taught me to be wary of such calm, which always precedes the storm. In the prison world you just never know when something will break the silence.

In fact, just four months after my tour, newspapers reported a "lock-down" of the facility following tips regarding contraband entering the prison, threats against staff, and a foiled escape by two inmates. This was Nicholas Zimmerman and Steven Finley's third attempt to bust out of the prison. This time Zimmerman enlisted the help of two girlfriends, one of them, Quangtrice Wilson, a correctional officer at the prison, and four men from Brooklyn, including one who tried to smuggle in fake uniforms, badges, ID tags, and pepper spray. Tony Dubose, one of the inmates' outside helpers, tried to enter the prison posing as a correctional officer and claimed he was transferred from the Fishkill Correctional Facility. Unfortunately for Dubose, an alert Sing Sing prison guard noticed that he sported a fake badge. Realizing his cover was blown, Dubose left his badge behind. Despite his Jewish-sounding name, Zimmerman is an African-American rap artist and not Jewish. He is serving a fifteen-year sentence for a weapons conviction. Finley, convicted of attempted murder, is in Sing Sing for up to twenty years.

Both now have several more felonies added to their rap sheets including first-degree attempted escape and third-degree bribery. Former Correctional Officer Wilson faces up to three years in prison for her role in the attempted escape.

Many months after my tour of the prison, I reflected on the significance of my participation in the service. The Prayer of Four Kinds usually incorporates two other items: *hadas*—the leaves of the aromatic myrtle tree, symbolizing people who perform good deeds but are not educated—and *aravah*, the leaves of a willow tree, which have neither taste nor fragrance and represent the person who neither has an education nor does good deeds. By one's saying the Prayer of Four Kinds and wrapping all four items together, it is believed the good qualities of one will make up for the shortcomings of the others.

During Sukkot, Jews not only celebrate the fall harvest, but also read from Ecclesiastes, King Solomon's commentary on life, which is largely pessimistic. Although the holiday is meant to celebrate the fall harvest, it's also a time for introspection, encouraging people to review what it is that makes them happy. The lesson to be learned from the holiday is that physical objects, that is, material goods, do not make us happy. Instead, the success of our relationships with others, with the Divine, and with ourselves is supposed to sustain us. During Sukkot, people are commanded to take themselves out of their normal comfortable surroundings and sleep in a *sukkah*, an austere hut made with wood, branches, and leaves from the fall harvest. The sukkah is a symbol of peace and openness—to the elements of nature and, more important, to guests from near and afar.

My meeting the inmates during Sukkot was fitting; it seemed to me I was a law-abiding soul mixing with several criminals. Just maybe I could inspire the inmates, if only for a short while. More personally, it felt appropriate to be *the* member of my family to say the prayers inside the prison. I doubt that my great-grandfather had ever done the same. In fact, it is quite possible he came to America to escape the strict religiousness of his household, run by his father, the rabbi. My true journey began when my great-grandfather's stormy history disrupted the otherwise calm process of performing family research. With my visit to the prison, events had come full circle, making me part of the story.

APPENDIX A

Very Short Stories

THERE ARE SOME Jewish criminals about whom one cannot find enough material in *New York Times* articles and other collections of documents to warrant an entire chapter. Yet their stories round out the portrait of Jewish criminality in New York. The following stories involve humor, the unexpected, and the unbelievable.

THE BOLOGNA BANDITS

THESE WERE SEVEN men who would routinely order bologna sandwiches in delicatessens or butcher shops before conducting a stickup operation. During a five-week period in 1938, the group conducted more than twenty robberies. In addition to taking money from the cashiers, the robbers often took jewelry from customers patronizing these establishments. The police caught up with the gang as it tried to take money from a Chinese restaurant in Brooklyn. Among the perpetrators was Paul Salinsky, age 21.

THE PANTS GANG

THIS GROUP OF bandits earned its name by ordering their victims to take their pants down so that their victims could not chase after them while they fled the scene of the crime. Four of the group's members, all Jewish, murdered Patrolman William E. Kelly while in the process of holding up Stoller's Drug Store at Crown Street and Nostrand Avenue in Brooklyn. Samuel Krassner, who drove the getaway car, turned state's evidence against the other three men: Israel Fischer, Isidore Helfant, and Harry Dreitzer, all of Brooklyn. Fischer, Helfant, and Dreitzer died in the electric chair on January 24, 1929. Two other Jewish gang members, Bernard Balkman and Hyman Brecker, received a sentence of twenty-five and twenty years respectively in Sing Sing.

THE BEFUDDLED BANDITS

IN MARCH 1954, three young men, Jerry Feller, William Filner, and Murray Schuster, walked into Hearns Department Store at Third Avenue and 149th Street in the Bronx and stole $11,452. Unfortunately, for reasons unknown, these hapless souls could not find their way out of the store. Eighty store executives, six store detectives, and some of the "bolder salesgirls" located the three in the men's fitting room in the store basement. Filner, afraid of one of the detectives who had drawn his pistol, held out the Hearns paper shopping bag that held the stolen money and pleaded, "Play safe, officer; don't shoot." After this statement Filner and Feller turned over the toy pistols they had in their possession. Schuster, the apparent "mastermind" of the operation, and Feller, both Jewish, received sentences of two and a half to five years at Sing Sing.

JEWISH MEMBERS OF THE "BLACK SHEEP" FOOTBALL SQUAD

ON SUNDAY, OCTOBER 22, 1933, the Kingston Yellow Jackets scrimmaged against the Black Sheep football team, composed of Sing Sing inmates. The roster for the Black Sheep included six players whose names seem Jewish: #40, "Pickles" Liebman, 160 pounds, center; #43, "Lucky" Eiseman, 180 pounds, Captain and tackle; #49, "Blink" Weisberg, 175 lbs., guard; #54, Bernstein, 160 lbs., quarterback; #58, "Wink" Winkler, 150 pounds, quarterback; #68, Kessler (first name unknown), 185 pounds, tackle. Which team won the game is unclear.

DRESSED TO THE NINES

IN 1937, JUDGE Koenig handed Harry Pincus of the Bronx a sentence of thirty to sixty years for holding up Evelyn Dean, a night club dancer, at her room at the Mayflower Hotel on Central Park West. Police suspected that Pincus was part of a gang that dressed up in "evening clothes" and followed theater patrons and performers back to their homes, where they would be robbed.

CONSPIRACY TO BOMB NIXON'S FORMER LAW FIRM

THREE MEN AND three women of the radical "Weathermen" group pled guilty to charges of conspiracy to set fire to several buildings, including one that housed the offices of Richard Nixon's law firm in 1971. Among the six was Martin Lewis, who served time in Sing Sing.

JERRY "THE JEW" ROSENBERG: ATTICA RIOTS MASTERMIND

IN JULY 1972 Jerome Rosenberg won a civil suit in which he claimed that his civil rights were violated by the justice system after his conviction for killing two detectives in May 1962. Representing himself after studying law through a correspondence course, Jerry "The Jew" received a judgment of $7,500, far lower than the $2.5 million he originally requested as retribution. Rosenberg was considered the mastermind behind the riots at Attica Prison in 1971.

MOSES ROSENGARTEN: COUNTERFEITER, GANG LEADER, AND POET

MOSES ROSENGARTEN LED a band of nearly 100 men in a counterfeiting operation based in Astoria, Queens. Police found hidden in the basement of Morris Weitzman's home, 56 Welling Street, "a complete outfit for making twenty-five and ten-cent pieces," including a press, unstamped coins, rolled silver, and unrolled silver ingots. One needed to pull the lever on the press only once to generate the "desired impression" on silver. In a period of just three months, band members had produced about $800 to $1,000 in dimes and quarters (roughly $1,600 to $2,000 in 2006 dollars).

Rosengarten had previously served time at the Eastern Penitentiary in Philadelphia on similar charges. Able enough to lead such a large group of men and devise a scheme to create phony currency, Rosengarten clearly had impressive mental faculties. With the help of Israel Davidson, the Sing Sing Jewish chaplain at the time, Rosengarten penned a poem in both Aramaic and Hebrew (primarily the former, more archaic language) that used the Akdamut as a model.

The Akdamut, a *piyut* (religious poem), was written during the Crusades, a time when Jews participated, most often against their will, in debates with Christians about their respective religions. The debates, which had juries composed of church officials, were rigged against the Jews. Rabbi Meir son of Rabbi Yitzchak, the *chazzan* (cantor and religious scholar), refused to participate in these debates and instead wrote the Akdamut which defends Judaism. In effect, Rabbi Meir debated the Christians in a very private and secretive manner. The Akdamut is sung during the Jewish holiday of Shavuot.

Rosengarten's prose, like the Akdamut, is an acrostic. The beginning Aramaic character spells out the names of Rosengarten and his father. The first letters of subsequent lines spell out the Hebrew prayer *Hazak Ve'ematz* (be strong and courageous). At the end of the poem, one line contains the name Israel ben David, most certainly a reference to Rabbi Israel Davidson.

In the beginning of the words of song and blessing
I will state that I too am counted
Among the Jews that were sent to suffer.
In the prison of "Songs of the Song"
We found workers of justice and mercy
People acting with charity and doing good
Who are working with us: our brothers from the city
That is called "York, the New Big City." [1]
These Jewish men of praise
Take care of our needs faithfully
And come to our aid on weekdays and on Shabbat;
They are called The Society for the aid[2] of the prisoners.
They and their wives merit the glory –
The splendor of their charity and good deeds shines in its holiness.
They love us, the unfortunate prisoners,[3]
We see here the people of action:
Our children and our wives they sustain with compassion,
They are good to them like a father to his offspring,
They pay for them the rent of the apartment.
They distribute their charity wisely
As they saw it written in the Torah
That charity, as we are taught, is the most important of the
    Commandments:
To give to the poor secretly and with humility.
Therefore may You prolong their lives through Your goodness,
By the King of the Universe may they be blessed with joy,
From their business may they achieve strength and wealth,
Great light may prevail upon their ways and in their homes.
Their wives and their offspring shall rejoice with pride.

---

1 The word "new" is translated, not transliterated.
2 Literally, "salvation."
3 Literally, "prisoners of poverty."

They provide us[4] with the "bread of affliction"
Which is the meal of the Jews on the "Holiday of Freedom"[5]
And with meat of fine taste
On the eve of Pesach and the eve of the Day of Atonement.
May the Gates open to our prayers
On Pesach, Shavuot, Sukkoth and Shemini Atzeret,
On the Fast of Kippur and on Rosh Hashanah,
The prayer of Yitzhak on the day of Shabbat,
And our reading of the Torah on the days of the week.
An illustrious Rabbi was sent to us:
Rabbi "Son of David," the chosen of the nation.
The utterances coming from his lips are pleasant words,
He is of perfect virtue and many good qualities,
His name "Israel" is becoming him.
A distinguished scholar in the Houses of Learning,
His keen intelligence earned him the title Doctor.
His wise teachings and sermons are dear to us all,
Day and night we shall bless his name.
He is entirely devoted to his great work for us,
We call him "Father" lovingly,
With his wisdom he gives good advice to all of us.
Erudite in the knowledge of all sciences,
His wise comforting makes our hearts rejoice.
His sermons revive body and soul
And his teaching enters our ears pleasingly,
Carefully he explains the laws and customs.
He puts in writing our requests and pleas,
He is always available and goes to any trouble to handle our
    needs.
He keeps his promises to us in time
And does not fail even in the slightest detail.
We await his arrival with hope and eagerness,
He enchants our hearts with amusing words,

---

4 Literally, "support our hearts."
5 Passover.

His words are fresh and heal our souls.
14 Marheshvan, "The good heart of Israel son of David" by
  the abbreviated era[6]
Sing Sing Prison[7]

—M. I. Rosengarten
(Translation by Yocheved Klausner)

JACK THE RIPPER:
A JEWISH INMATE AT SING SING?

FOR NEARLY A century many have wondered about the true identity of Jack the Ripper, the alias for the serial killer who cut the throats of prostitutes in the Whitechapel section of London and then mutilated them. Some have speculated that Jack the Ripper was a Polish Jew by the name of Martin Kosminski, although this has never been verified. In his recent book *The Fox and The Flies*, Charles van Onselen, a South African historian and professor, believes he has solved the mystery. Van Onselen contends that Jack the Ripper was a Jew by the name of Joseph Silver, who also spent time in Johannesburg and New York. According to Professor van Onselen, while living in New York, Silver was arrested under the alias of Joseph Liss in October 1889 on charges of burglary, and served time in Sing Sing.

---

6 The words "The good heart of Israel son of David" translates to the Hebrew
  year (5)663 using Gematria counting rules.
7 Sing Sing Prison; transliteration of three Hebrew words.

APPENDIX B

Statistics Regarding Jewish, Italian, and Irish Criminals Incarcerated at Sing Sing

Admission of Jews to Sing Sing: 1880–1949

Decade	Number of Jews Admitted to Sing Sing	Percent of All Inmates Who Claimed Judaism as Their Religion Upon Admission	Jews as a % of New Yorkers as of Year Beginning Decade
1880s	214	2.6	6.7
1890s	439	5.7	7.8
1900s	793	10	11.6
1910s	1,761	16.1	19.1
1920s	1,752	14.9	26.5
1930s	1,537	10.3	25.5
1940s	865	7.5	27.1
Total	7,361		

Notes:
1. Based on Sing Sing admission records, New York State Archives, Albany.
2. NYC population figures taken from almanacs.
3. If the inmate was Jewish but claimed another religion, he would not have been counted.

Italian and Irish Representation of Sing Sing Inmate Populations compared with New York City Population

Year	% New Yorkers (City) Who Were Italian	% Sing Sing Inmates Who Were Italian	% New Yorkers (City) Who Were Irish	% Sing Sing Inmates Who Were Irish
1880		1		35
1900	6	11	21	26
1905		24		6
1910	11	22	14	2
1915		19		1
1920	14	17	10	2
1925		11		1
1930	15	21	9	2

Notes:
1. Sing Sing inmate ethnicity taken from federal and New York State censuses.
2. More than 90% of Sing Sing inmates were convicted in New York City.

Most Common Crimes Committed by Jewish Sing Sing Inmates: 1880–1949

Offense	% of Total Crimes Committed by Jewish Inmates	Cumulative % of Total Crimes Committed by Jewish Inmates
Grand Larceny	37	37
Burglary	19.5	56.5
Robbery	12.6	69.1
Conterfeiting/ Forgery	5.9	75
Assault	4.1	79.1
Stolen Property	4.1	83.2

Offense	% of Total Crimes Committed by Jewish Inmates	Cumulative % of Total Crimes Committed by Jewish Inmates
Homicide	3.7	86.9
Bigamy	1.8	88.7
Arson	1.6	90.3
Sex Offense	1.4	91.7
Other or N/A	1.4	93.1
Weapons Violation	1.2	94.3
Possession of Burglar's Instruments	1	95.3
Prostitution	0.8	96.1
Extortion/ Blackmail	0.8	96.9
Abandonment	0.6	97.5
Kidnapping/ Abduction	0.6	98.1
Fraud	0.5	98.6
Perjury	0.5	99.1
Drug Offense	0.4	99.5
Abortion	0.2	99.7
Bribery	0.2	99.9
Gambling	0.1	100
Embezzlement	0	100
Destruction of Property	0	100
Pornography	0	100
Total		100

Notes:
1. Crime obtained from Sing Sing admission records, New York State archives, Albany.
2. If the individual was convicted of multiple crimes, the more serious charge was selected.

Significant Differences in Crimes Committed by Jewish
Sing Sing Inmates on the Basis of Immigrant Status

Crime	% Instances Committed by "Native"	% Instances Committed by "Immigrant"
Abandonment	17.4	82.6
Abortion	29.4	70.6
Arson	17.6	82.4
Bigamy	27.9	72.1
Bribery	71.4	28.6
Robbery	74.4	25.6

Notes:
1. Nativity status obtained from Sing Sing admission records, New York State archives, Albany.

Immigrant Breakdown of Jewish Sing Sing Inmates:
Immigrants v. Native Born

Decade	Self-described as Immigrant (% of Jewish Inmates Admitted to Sing Sing During Decade	Self-described as Native Born (% of Jewish Inmates Admitted to Sing Sing During Decade
1880s	64.8	35.2
1890s	75.6	24.4
1900s	68.3	31.7
1910s	60.4	39.6
1920s	45.9	54.1
1930s	30.8	69.2
1940s	28.3	71.7

Age of Jewish Inmates Upon Admission to Sing Sing

Age	Percent	Cumulative Percent
<20	6.2	6.2
20–24	27.6	33.8
25–29	23.3	57.1
30–34	15.4	72.5
35–39	10.7	83.2
40–44	7.3	90.5
45–49	4.2	94.7
50–54	2.7	97.4
55–59	1.6	99
60+	1	100

Notes:
1. Age obtained from Sing Sing admission records, NY State Archives, Albany.

Jewish Criminal Recidivism (Returning to Sing Sing): 1880–1949

Number of Terms in Sing Sing	Total Admissions	Number of Distinct Individuals
1	5,106	5,106
2	1,438	719
3	501	167
4	244	61
5	40	8
6	24	4
7	7	1
Total	7,360	6,066

Notes:
1. Based on Sing Sing admission records, NY State Archives, Albany.
2. Does not account for "stretches" served in other NY DOCS correctional facilities.

APPENDIX C
Jewish Criminals Who Died in Sing Sing's Electric Chair

Name	Year of Execution
Adolph Koenig	1905
Harry "Gyp the Blood" Horowitz	1914
Jacob "Whitey Lewis" Seidenshner	1914
"Lefty" Louis Rosenberg	1914
Stanley Millstein	1916
Hyman Ostransky	1918
Jacob Cohen	1918
Julius Rothman	1922
Abraham Becker	1924
Joseph Diamond	1925
Morris Diamond	1925
George Appel	1928
Joseph Lefkowitz	1928
Israel Fischer	1929
Harry Dreitzer	1929
Isidore Helfant	1929
Harry Lipschitz	1931
Charles Markowitz	1932
Daniel Kriesberg	1934
Harold Seaman	1935
William Paskowitz	1935
Albert Fish	1936
Charles Kropowitz	1936

Name	Year of Execution
George Rosenberg	1936
Harry Eisenberg	1937
Arthur Friedman	1939
Sidney Markman	1940
Martin "Buggsie" Goldstein	1941
Harry "Pittsburgh Phil" Strauss	1941
Joseph Sonsky	1943
Emanuel "Mendy" Weiss	1944
Louis "Lepke" Buchalter	1944
Abraham Gold	1944
William Rosenberg	1949
Bernard Stein	1952
Julius Rosenberg	1952
Ethel Rosenberg	1952
Barry Jacobs	1954
Nathan Wissner	1955
Harry A. Stein	1955
Calman Cooper	1955
Total Number Jews Electrocuted at Sing Sing	41
Total Number Inmates Electrocuted at Sing Sing	614

APPENDIX D

The Interconnectedness of Jewish Criminals

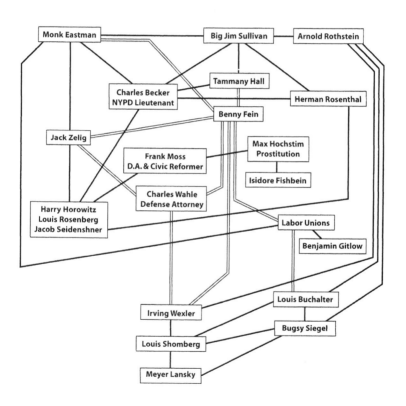

APPENDIX E

Jewish Chaplains at Sing-Sing

Name of Chaplain	Years of Service
Revs. H.P. & Dr. DeSola Mendez	1877
Rabbi Adolph Radin	1891-1898
Rabbi Israel Davidson	1900-1902
Rabbi S. Braverman	1907
Rev. J. Ludwig Stern	1911
Dr. Jacob Goldstein	1912-1914
Rev. Samuel Buchler	1914-1919
Rabbi Jacob Katz	1918-1950
Rabbi Jerimiah J. Berman	1950
Rabbi Irving Koslowe	1950-1999
Rabbi Charles Rudansky	2000-2002
Rabbi Chaim Epstein	Current

APPENDIX F

Addresses and Map of Jewish Criminals' Residences as Children and Young Adults

Monk Eastman
1881: East Seventy-fifth Street
1901: 101 East First Street (1)

Benny Fein
1887: 13 Forsyth Street (13)
1888: 239 Henry Street (9)
1889: 294 Cherry Street (15)
1904: 47 Norfolk Street (7)

Irving Wexler
1900: 101 Forsyth Street (5)
1905: Chrystie Street (4)

Harry Horowitz
1888: 419 Third Avenue

Louis Rosenberg
1891: 14 Suffolk Street (8)

Jacob Seidenshner
— : 75 Market Street (2)
1910: 201 East Second Street

Louis Buchalter
1897: 88 Essex Street (6)
1900–10: 217 Henry Street (14)

Benjamin Gitlow
1891: Cherry Street (17)

Louis Shomberg
1910: 114 or 149 Stanton Street (3)

*Benjamin "Bugsy" Siegel**
1910: 86 Columbia Street (10)
1920: 51 or 57 Cannon Street (11)

*Meyer Lansky**
1920: 6 Columbia Street (12)

Jacob Shapiro
1910 : 261 Monroe Street (16)

*Did not serve time at Sing Sing.

Numbers correspond with those in parentheses on facing page.

APPENDIX G

Prison Sentences Served by Major Characters in This Book

SING SING CORRECTIONAL FACILITY

Monk Eastman, 4/23/1904–6/19/1909
Benny Fein, 10/31/1908–1/29/1911
Benny Fein, 1/21/1914–6/1914
Harry Horowitz, 11/26/1912–4/13/1914
Louis Rosenberg, 11/26/1912–4/13/1914
Jacob Seidenshner, 11/26/1912–4/13/1914
Irving Wexler, 8/12/1915–2/1916
Louis Shomberg, 8/23/1915–3/1916
Louis Shomberg, 4/13/1917–12/5/1918
Louis Buchalter, 1/11/18–2/19/1918
Jacob Shapiro, 4/5/1918–8/7/1918
Benjamin Gitlow, 2/13/1920–6/15/1920
Louis Buchalter, 6/21/1920–3/16/1922
Benjamin Gitlow, Early 1921
Louis Shomberg, 7/1919–10/1922
Jacob Shapiro, 10/30/1922–12/2/1922
Louis Buchalter, 1/21/1944–3/2/1944 (electrocuted)
Jacob Shapiro, 5/9/1944–6/9/1947 (died in Sing Sing from natural causes)

NEW YORK STATE REFORMATORY AT ELMIRA

Irving Wexler, 10/1905–10/1906
Benny Fein, 6/2/1906–1/1908

Irving Wexler, 1/1907–4/1907
Mortimer Horowitz, 1911–? (Harry's brother)
Irving Wexler, 1912–?
Louis Shomberg, 5/8/1913–?
Nathan Seidenshner, 7/21/1914–12/1915
Jacob Shapiro, 10/16/1915–8/19/1917

FEDERAL PENITENTIARY AT LEAVENWORTH, KANSAS

Louis Buchalter, 1/2/1940
Irving Wexler, 7/1936–late 1940
Louis Buchalter, 4/19/1940–11/1942

NEW YORK (CITY) PENITENTIARY (BLACKWELL'S ISLAND)

Monk Eastman, 8/1898
Harry Horowitz, 1908
Monk Eastman, 5/1912
Jacob Shapiro, 7/11/1919–3/5/1920

NEW YORK HOUSE OF REFUGE

Benny Fein, 4/4/1900–5/7/1903
Harry Horowitz, 1906 (3 months)
Morris Seidenshner, 9/13/1907 (Jacob's brother)
Jacob Seidenshner, 8/18/1908

AUBURN CORRECTIONAL FACILITY

Irving Wexler, 2/1916–3/16/1917
Louis Shomberg, 3/1916–4/13/1917
Louis Buchalter, 2/19/1918–5/21/1918
Benjamin Gitlow, 1920

CLINTON CORRECTIONAL FACILITY

Monk Eastman, 7/17/1915–1917
Jacob Shapiro, 8/7/1918–2/6/1919
Louis Shomberg, 12/5/1918–7/1919
Benjamin Gitlow, 6/15/1920
Jacob Shapiro, 12/2/1922–6/30/1923

FEDERAL PENITENTIARY IN ATLANTA
Irving Wexler, 1935
Irving Wexler, 1/1943–1/1944

FEDERAL PENITENTIARY AT ALCATRAZ, SAN FRANCISCO
Irving Wexler, 6/1952

APPENDIX H

Overlapping Prison Sentences of Jewish Criminals

SING SING CORRECTIONAL FACILITY

Monk Eastman, 4/23/1904–6/19/1909
Benny Fein, 10/31/1908–1/29/1911
Benny Fein, 1/21/1914–6/1914
Harry Horowitz, 11/26/1912–4/13/1914
Louis Rosenberg, 11/26/1912–4/13/1914
Jacob Seidenshner, 11/26/1912–4/13/1914
Irving Wexler, 8/12/1915–2/1916
Louis Shomberg, 8/23/1915–3/1916
Louis Shomberg, 4/13/1917–12/5/1918
Louis Buchalter, 1/11/1918–2/19/1918
Jacob Shapiro, 4/5/1918–8/7/1918
Louis Buchalter, 6/21/1920–3/16/1922
Benjamin Gitlow, Early 1921
Louis Shomberg, 7/1919–10/1922
Jacob Shapiro, 10/30/1922–12/2/1922
Jacob Shapiro, 5/9/1944–6/9/1947 (died in Sing Sing from natural causes)
Louis Buchalter, 1/21/1944–3/2/1944 (electrocuted)

NEW YORK STATE REFORMATORY AT ELMIRA

Benny Fein, 6/2/1906–12/1908
Irving Wexler, 10/1905–10/1906
Irving Wexler, 1/1907–4/1907

AUBURN CORRECTIONAL FACILITY
Irving Wexler, 2/1916–3/16/1917
Louis Shomberg, 3/1916–4/13/1917

CLINTON CORRECTIONAL FACILITY
Jacob Shapiro, 8/7/1918–2/6/1919
Louis Shomberg, 12/5/1918–7/1919

FEDERAL PENITENTIARY AT LEAVENWORTH, KANSAS
Irving Wexler, 7/1936–late 1940
Louis Buchalter, 4/19/1940–11/1942

SOURCES BY CHAPTER

INTRODUCTION

Blumenthal, Ralph. *Miracle at Sing Sing: How One Man Transformed the Lives of America's Most Dangerous Prisoners.* New York: St. Martin's Press, 2004.

Diner, Hasia. *Lower East Side Memories: A Jewish Place in America.* Princeton: Princeton University Press, 2000.

Epstein, Lawrence J. *At the Edge of a Dream: The Story of Jewish Immigrants on New York's Lower East Side, 1880–1920.* San Francisco: Jossey-Bass, 2007.

Israelowitz, Oscar. *Lower East Side Tourbook: Seventh Edition.* Brooklyn, NY: Israelowitz Publishing, 2006.

Kozlovskii, P. G., E. P. Shlossberg, and E. L. Braver. *Vladenie Smorgon: A Guide to the Archival Collection of the Landlords of Smorgon Housed in the Central State Historical Archives of Belarus in Minsk, Nauka I Tekhnika, Minsk.* Salt Lake City, UT: LDS Family History Library, 1977.

Rischin, Moses. *The Promised City: New York's Jews, 1870–1914.* Cambridge, MA: Harvard University Press, 1977.

Wolfman, Ira. *Jewish New York: Notable Neighborhoods and Memorable Moments.* New York: Universe Publishing, 2003.

CHAPTER 1: ISAAC SPIER—PART I

Brooklyn Citizen. "Spear's Many Wives." July 27, 1897.

Brooklyn Daily Eagle. "Alleged Bigamist Held." August 5, 1897, p. 14.

Brooklyn Daily Eagle. "Spier's Two Wives." September 23, 1897, p. 2.

Brooklyn Daily Eagle. "Two Wives Claimed Him." July 27, 1897, p. 2.

Glass, Montague. *Potash and Perlmutter.* New York: Doubleday, 1911.

Harry First file, Robinson Locke Collection, Billy Rose Division, New York Public Library for the Performing Arts at Lincoln Center, New York, NY.

Herbert Edward Spier, marriage certificate # 12587, Manhattan, New York City Municipal Archives.

Ida Spear, 1900 U.S. Census, Westchester County, NY, enumeration district [ED] 139, Roll T623-1178; p. 3A.

Isaac Spier admission record to Sing-Sing, September 27, 1897, Record Group

B0143, Inmate admission registers, New York State Archives, Albany, NY.

Isaac Spier household, 1920 U.S. Census, Kings County, NY, enumeration district [ED] 673, Roll T625-1162; p. 2A.

Isaac Spier, 1900 U.S. Census, Westchester County, NY, enumeration district [ED] 107, Roll T623-1176; p. 11A.

Isaac Spier, marriage certificate # 5157, November 18, 1894, Kings County, NY, NYC Municipal Archives.

Kings County clerk's notebook, 1897, Kings County Courthouse, Brooklyn, NY.

Max Tarshis household, 1900 U.S. Census, Kings County, NY, enumeration district [ED] 92, Roll T623-1047; p. 7A.

New York Herald. "Two Say He is Their Husband." July 28, 1897.

New York Telephone Brooklyn Directories, 1941-52, California Genealogical Society, Oakland, CA.

New York Times. "Weather." August 6, 1895.

People of the State of New York vs. Isaac Spier alias Herbert Edward Spier, August 4, 1897, New York City Municipal Archives, New York, NY.

R.L. Polk 1933 Brooklyn Directory, Sutro Library, San Francisco, CA.

R.L. Polk 1935 Brooklyn Directory, Sutro Library, San Francisco, CA.

Sidney Spier, birth certificate # 29821, May 30, 1895, Kings County, NY, NYC Municipal Archives.

Variety. "Catches Her Husband." August 11, 1916, p. 7.

Variety. "Harry First 'Only Human.'" August 18, 1916, p. 5.

CHAPTER 2: SING SING'S BEGINNINGS AND THE EARLIEST JEWISH INMATES

Brooklyn Daily Eagle. "Alleged Fire Bugs Indicted." June 6, 1895, p. 4.

Brooklyn Daily Eagle. "Another Brooklyn Suspect." July 9, 1895, p. 4.

Brooklyn Daily Eagle. "Davis Replies to Backus." May 10, 1897, p. 14.

Brooklyn Daily Eagle. "Denies Having Confessed." June 1, 1895, p. 1.

Brooklyn Daily Eagle. "Firebugs' Secrets Laid Bare." December 19, 1896, p. 1.

Brooklyn Daily Eagle. "The Jewish Passover." April 16, 1875.

Brooklyn Daily Eagle. "Two of Them in this City." December 18, 1896, p. 3.

Heiman Kohnstam household, 1870 U.S. Census, Kings County Ward 21, New York, NY, p. 240.

Inflation Calculator, *http://www.westegg.com/inflation.*

Isaac Zeuker household, 1880 U.S. Census, Philadelphia County, PA, enumeration district [ED] 81, Roll T9-1169; p. 136.4000.

Isaac Zucker, 1910 U.S. Census, Ossining, Westchester County, NY, enumeration district [ED] 103, Roll T624-1089; p. 19B.

Isaac Zuker admission record to Sing-Sing, December 29, 1896, Record Group

[RG] B0143, Inmate admission registers, New York State Archives, Albany, NY.

Isaac Zuker admission record to Sing-Sing, February 11, 1897.

Lewis Gordon admission record to Sing-Sing, March 7, 1897.

Louis Rothman admission record to Sing-Sing, January 29, 1895.

Manifest, S.S. Ariel, arriving in New York, August 4, 1855, Mr. S. Kohnstamm, age 43; NARA roll M237-155, List number 745, Line 5, "Passenger Record." digital images, Ancestry.com (*http://www.ancestry.com*).

Materials from Karen Franklin, re: Solomon Kohnstamm case.

Max Grauer admission record to Sing-Sing, March 6, 1895.

Morris Schoenholtz admission record to Sing-Sing, October 18, 1895.

Morris Schoenholtz, marriage certificate # 41483, January 6, 1884, Manhattan, NY, NYC Municipal Archives.

New York Times. "Christmas in Sing Sing Prison." February 6, 1903, p. 12.

New York Times. "Gang Leaders Captured." June 5, 1895, p. 5.

New York Times. "Gordon Trial for Arson." December 3, 1895, p. 9.

New York Times. "Grauer Guilty of Arson." March 1, 1895, p. 14.

New York Times. "Grauer's Defense Today." February 27, 1895, p. 7.

New York Times. "Hebrew Festival in Sing-Sing Prison." September 8, 1877, p. 5.

New York Times. "Incendiary Kline Arrested." March 1, 1896, p. 3.

New York Times. "Knew All the Firebugs." February 22, 1895, p. 16.

New York Times. "The Kohnstamm Case—Forty-one Indictments Found—The Bail Reduced." June 12, 1863, p. 3.

New York Times. "The Kohnstamm Case—Motion to Arrest Judgement." May 29, 1864, p. 6.

New York Times. "The Kohnstamm Frauds, and Their Lesson." May 23, 1864, p. 4.

New York Times. "The Kohnstamm Frauds—Developments as the Extent and Magnitude of Prisoner." May 20, 1864, p. 2.

New York Times. "The Kohnstamm Frauds—Second Day of the Trial—Interesting Testimony." May 19, 1864 p. 2.

New York Times. "The Kohnstamm Frauds—The Testimony for the Defence." May 21, 1864, p. 3.

New York Times. "The Sentence of Kohnstamm." May 31, 1864.

New York Times. "Told of an Arson Plot." February 26, 1895, p. 16.

New York Times. "Zuker is Indicted Now." June 6, 1895, p. 9.

People of the State of New York vs. Isaac Zuker impleaded with Max Blum, New York Superior Court, December 17, 1896, Case # 3112, Special Collections, Sealy Library, John Jay College of Criminal Justice, New York, NY.

Rochel [Rachel] Zuker (John W. Bloomer household), 1910 Census, Manhattan

Ward 12, New York, NY, enumeration district [ED] 526, Roll T624-1021; p. 17B.

Trow's New York City Directory, 1875, Sutro Library, San Francisco.

Trow's New York City Directory, 1876, Sutro Library, San Francisco.

CHAPTER 3: EDWARD "MONK" EASTMAN

"20th Century Circumcision Statistics." *http://www.boystoo.com/history/ statistics.htm*.

"A Short History of Circumcision in the Physician's Own Words." *http:// www.noharmm.org/docswords.htm*.

"Funeral procession of 'Monk' Eastman." no. LC-USZ62-134669, Prints and Photographs Online, Library of Congress, *http://www.loc.gov/rr/ print/catalog.html*.

"Mara Bovsum: Monk Eastman— Gangster, Doughboy, Hero." *http://www. worldwar1.com/dbc/meastman.htm*.

"Monk Eastman Gang in Murder." *New York Tribune*. June 3, 1907, p.3, New York Public Library

"Monk Eastman." *http://en.wikipedia.com/wiki/monk_eastman*.

"New York Gangsters: Monk Eastman & Paul Kelley." *http://www. herbertasbury.com/billthebutcher/eastman.asp*.

"The Game of Faro." *http://www.beve.net/faro/rules.htm*.

"U.S. Circumcision Statistics." *http://www.cirp.org/library/statistics/USA*.

Asbury, Herbert. *Gangs of New York*. Garden City, NY: Garden City Publishing Company, 1928.

Civil War Pension Application, Mary Eastman (claimant), no. 717437, *http:// www.footnote.com*.

Edward Eastman admission record to Sing-Sing, no. 54863, April 22, 1904, Record Group B0143, Inmate admission registers, New York State Archives, Albany, NY.

Edward Eastman household, 1900 U.S. Census, Manhattan, NY, enumeration district [ED] 240, Roll T623-1092; p. 5B.

Edward Eastman, death certificate # 33332, December 26, 1920, Manhattan, NY, NYC Municipal Archives.

Frank Wouters and Ida Eastman, marriage certificate, #3076, June 22, 1898, Brooklyn, NY, New York City Municipal Archives.

George Parks household, 1880 U.S. Census, Manhattan, NY, enumeration district [ED] 610, Roll T9-896.

George Parks, death certificate, # 18881, June 6, 1896, Manhattan, NY, NYC Municipal Archives.

Mary Eastman, death certificate # 2430, November 22, 1903, Queens, NY, New York City Municipal Archives.

National Park Service, "Soldiers." database, *Civil War Soldiers & Sailors System* (http://www.itd.nps.gov/csww/ , entry for Samuel Eastman, Pvt., Co. E, 8 N.Y. State Militia, Union.

New York County, Coroner and Office of Chief Medical Examiner Records, 1823-1946, Edward Eastman, no. 5346, for Edward Eastman, December 27, 1929; New York City Municipal Archives.

New York Daily Tribune. "Kill a Man for $15." April 2, 1904.

New York Daily Tribune. "Raid on Eastman Gang." August 8, 1903.

New York Daily Tribune. "To Face Jersey Law: Extradition Ordered." August 4, 1903.

New York Times. "Dry Agent Sought in Eastman Murder." January 1, 1921, p. 3.

New York Times. "Eastman's Slayer Freed." June 24, 1923, p. 8.

New York Times. "Evil Day for Gang Rule." September 27, 1903, p. 12.

New York Times. "Lamar Prisoners Held." August 4, 1903, p. 3.

New York Times. "Leader Foley Settles Feud." October 2, 1902, p. 10.

New York Times. "Monk Eastman, Gangster, Murdered: Found in Union Square, Shot Five Times; His Partner in Bootlegging Suspected; A Liquor Peddler Sought." December 27, 1920, p. 1.

New York Times. "Said Brothers Shot Him." April 14, 1901, p. 2.

New York Times. "Trap Monk Eastman Fleeing In An Auto." May 18, 1915, p. 7

New York Tribune. "Board Paroles Monk Eastman." June 21, 1909, p. 4.

New York Tribune. "Convict Monk Eastman: Jury Within One of Return, Attempted Murder Verdict." April 15, 1904, p. 1.

New York Tribune. "Gang Kills Bartender: Two Others May Die." April 13, 1905, p. 3.

New York Tribune. "Monk Eastman Gang Busy." November 19, 1906, p. 1.

New York Tribune. "Stand By Eastman Gang: Monk is Discharged." September 17, 1903, p. 14.

New York Tribune. "Ten Years for Monk." April 20, 1904, p. 6.

New York Tribune. "Warring Gangs Terrorize the East Side." April 26, 1903, p. A7.

People of the State of New York vs. William Delaney alias Monk Eastman, Court of General Sessions, New York County, April 12, 1904, Case # 421, Special Collections, Sealy Library, John Jay College of Criminal Justice, New York, NY

Samuel Eastman household, 1870 U.S. Census, Manhattan, NY, Ward 13, District 3 (2nd Enum), Roll M593-1031.

Samuel Eastman, death certificate, # 29821, May 30, 1888, Manhattan, NY, NYC Municipal Archives.

Trow's New York City Directory, 1877, Sutro Library, San Francisco.

William Murray (Edward Eastman) admission to New York Penitentiary (Blackwell's Island), August 25, 1898, Record Group A0603-78, Registers of Commitments to Prisons, 1842-1908, New York State Archives, Albany, NY.

CHAPTER 4: "DOPEY" BENNY FEIN

"Index to Naturalization Petitions to the U.S. Circuit and District Courts for Maryland: 1797-1951." Jacob Feinschneider, July 22, 1884, FHL film # 1380476.

"World War I Draft Registration Cards, 1917-1918." digital images, Ancestry. com *(http://www.ancestry.com)*, Benjamin Feinschneider.

Baltimore City Directory, 1885, Sutro Library, San Francisco, CA.

Baltimore City Directory, 1886, Sutro Library, San Francisco, CA.

Benjamin Fein admission record to Sing Sing, 100903, April 1, 1942, Record Group B0143, Inmate admission registers, New York State Archives, Albany, NY.

Benjamin Fein admission record to Sing-Sing, 58571, October 31, 1908, Record Group B0143, Inmate admission registers, New York State Archives, Albany, NY.

Benjamin Fein admission record to Sing-Sing, 64128, January 24, 1914, Record Group B0143, Inmate admission registers, New York State Archives, Albany, NY.

Benjamin Fein household, 1905 New York State Census, New York County, ED: 5, Block: 6, AD: 8, FHL film: 1930255.

Benjamin Fein household, 1920 U.S. Census, Kings County, NY, enumeration district [ED] 340, Roll T625-1153; p. 15B.

Benjamin Fein household, 1930 U.S. Census, Brooklyn, Kings County, NY, enumeration district [ED] 747, Roll 1529; p. 16A.

Benjamin Fein household, New York State Census, 1925, Kings County, ED: 11, Block: 2, AD: 6, Page 34, Manhattan, FHL film: 526417.

Benjamin Fein, death certificate, # 15036, Kings County, New York, July 23, 1962, New York City Department of Health.

Benjamin Feinschneider, marriage certificate # 9899, June 28, 1917, Kings County, NY, NYC Municipal Archives.

Brooklyn City Directory, 1904-5, Sutro Library, San Francisco, CA.

Bureau of Social Morals: Stories 168, 260, 282, 443, 700, 719, Kehillah Records, Judah Magnes Collection, Central Archives for the History of the Jewish People, Jerusalem, Israel.

Email correspondence and interview with Geoff Fein.

Jacob Fein household, 1905 New York State Census, Kings County, ED: 18,

. AD: 7, FHL film: 1930252.

Manhattan City Directory, 1887-8, Sutro Library, San Francisco, CA.

Manhattan City Directory, 1888-9, Sutro Library, San Francisco, CA.

Manhattan City Directory, 1890-1, Sutro Library, San Francisco, CA.

Manhattan City Directory, 1899-1900, Sutro Library, San Francisco, CA.

Manhattan City Directory, 1901-2, Sutro Library, San Francisco, CA.

Manhattan City Directory, 1904-5, Sutro Library, San Francisco, CA.

New York House of Refuge, no. 28018 (August 14, 1900), Record Group A2088, Inmate Admission Registers, New York House of Refuge, 1882-1932, New York State Archives, Albany, NY.

New York Times. "'Dopey Benny' in Sing Sing." January 25, 1914, p. 21.

New York Times. "'Dopey' Benny at Large." May 30, 1915, p. 8.

New York Times. "2 Texas Merchants Held with Thieves." March 13, 1941, p. 44.

New York Times. "Held in Acid Throwing." July 30, 1931, p. 22.

New York Times. "Police Upset Alibis of Four Gangsters." January 12, 1914, p. 18.

New York Times. "Two Gang Leaders Convicted in Thefts." October 25, 1941, p. 34.

Paul A. Fein, obituary, Miami Herald, July 2, 2002.

People of the State of New York vs. Benjamin Fein, Court of General Sessions, January 19, 1914, Case # 1817, Special Collections, Sealy Library, John Jay College of Criminal Justice, New York, NY.

Reformatory at Elmira, no. 14780, June 2, 1906, Record Group B0131, Admission Registers, Elmira Reformatory, 1877-1950, New York State Archives, Albany, NY.

CHAPTER 5: "GYP," "LEFTY," AND "WHITE": THE BECKER/ROSENTHAL AFFAIR

"Baldy Jack Rose is Dead Here at 72." October 9, 1947, p. 52.

Cohen, Stanley. *The Execution of Officer Becker: The Murder of a Gambler, The Trial of a Cop, and the Birth of Organized Crime.* New York: Carroll & Graf Publishers, 2006.

Dash, Mike. *Satan's Circus: Murder, Vice, Police Corruption, and New York's Trial of the Century.* New York: Crown Publishers, 2007.

Frank Moss, The American Metropolis from Knickerbocker Days to the Present Time, New York City Life in All Its Various Phases, Collier, New York, 1897, New York Public Library

Harry Horowitz admission record to Sing-Sing, no. 62828 (November 26, 1912), Record Group B0143, Inmate admission registers, New York State Archives, Albany, NY.

Harry Horowitz, 1910 U.S. Census, Blackwell's Island, New York County, NY, population schedule, enumeration district [ED] T624-1038.

Harry Horowitz, birth certificate # 11380, April 21, 1888, Manhattan, NYC Municipal Archives.

Harry Seidenshner household, 1910 U.S. Census, Manhattan, NY, enumeration district [ED] 880, Roll T624-1031; p. 3B.

Index to the Testimony and Proceedings before the Lexow Committee Investigating the New York Police Department, 1899, New York Public Library.

Jacob Herwitz household, 1900 U.S. Census, Manhattan, NY, population schedule, enumeration district [ED] 909, Roll T623-1121; p. 17B.

Jacob Rosenberg household, 1910 U.S. Census, Bronx, NY, population schedule, enumeration district [ED] 1628, Roll T624-1003; p. 2B.

Jacob Seidenshner admission record to Sing-Sing, no. 62825 (November 26, 1912), Record Group B0143, Inmate admission registers, New York State Archives, Albany, NY.

Joseph Seidenshner household, 1920 U.S. Census, Manhattan, NY, enumeration district [ED] 162, Roll T625-1187; p. 9B.

Klein, Henry H. *Sacrificed: The Story of Police Lieutenant Charles Becker.* New York: Isaac Goldman Co., 1927.

Listings for surname Zajdensznir (and surnames which sound the same [Soundex]) in Jewish Records Indexing: *http://www.jewishgen.org/ jri-pl/.*

Logan, Andy. *Against the Evidence: The Becker-Rosenthal Affair.* New York: McCall Publishing Company, 1970.

Louis Rosenberg admission record to Sing-Sing, no. 62824 (November 26, 1912), Record Group B0143, Inmate admission registers, New York State Archives, Albany, NY.

Louis Rosenberg, birth certificate, # 15839, May 9, 1891, Manhattan, NYC Municipal Archives.

Louis Seidenshner, 1910 U.S. Census, Leavenworth, KS, enumeration district [ED] 91, Roll T624-444; p. 8B.

Louis Seidenshner, marriage certificate # 29533, November 10, 1912, Manhattan, NY, NYC Municipal Archives.

Manifest, *S.S. Pennsylvania*, October 25, 1901, p. 0372, entries for Chaje, Josef, Jacob, Leibel, Jorasl, Nochem, and Tante Seidenschmir, Statue of Liberty-Ellis Island Foundation (*http://www.ellisisland.org*).

Mazet Committee Report (Report of the Special Committee of the Assembly Appointed to Investigate the Public Offices and Departments of the City of New York and the Counties Therein Included), 1900, New York Public Library.

Morris Seidenstein (Seidenshner) case file, New York House of Refuge, no. 30865 (September 13, 1907), Record Group A2064, New York House of Refuge: Inmate Case Histories, 1824-1935, New York State Archives, Albany, NY.

Nathan Seidenshner case file, New York House of Refuge, no. 31226 (April 13, 1908), Record Group A2064, New York House of Refuge: Inmate Case Histories, 1824-1935, New York State Archives, Albany, NY.

Nathan Seidenstein/Shneider (Seidenshner) admission record to New York State Reformatory at Elmira, no. 23166 (July 21, 1914), Record Group B0131, Admission Registers, Elmira Reformatory, 1877-1950, New York State Archives, Albany, NY.

New York Times. "Becker Accuser Dies; Hid From Underworld." August 1, 1936, p. 30.

New York Times. "Becker Unnerved Goes to Chair; His Bonds Slip." July 31, 1915, p. 1.

New York Times. "Crane Presses His Charge." October 17, 1896, p. 9.

New York Times. "Gambler Who Defied Police is Shot Dead." July 16, 1912, p. 1.

New York Times. "Girl's Flat May Harbor Gunmen." August 24, 1912, p. 1.

New York Times. "Gyp's Brother Moves On." December 8, 1912, p. C6.

New York Times. "Luban Gets 12 Years for Mail Box Fraud." December 5, 1920, p. 19.

New York Times. "One Horowitz Jailed." July 28, 1912, p. S5.

New York Times. "Statement by Cirofici at Sing-Sing Two Hours Before Execution." April 14, 1914, p. 1.

New York Times. "Vallon Found in Pittsburgh." July 28, 1915, p. 2.

People of the State of New York v. Charles Becker, New York Supreme Court, October 7, 1912, Case # 3198, Special Collections, Sealy Library, John Jay College of Criminal Justice, New York, NY.

People of the State of New York v. Charles Becker, New York Supreme Court, May 11, 1914, Case 3232, Special Collections, Sealy Library, John Jay College of Criminal Justice, New York, NY.

People of the State of New York v. Jacob Seidenshner, Frank Cirofici, Louis Rosenberg, and Harry Horowitz, New York Supreme Court, November 8, 1912, Case # 3200, Special Collections, Sealy Library, John Jay College of Criminal Justice, New York, NY

Root, Jonathan. *One Night in July.* New York: Coward McCann, Inc., 1961.

Root, Jonathan. *The Life and Bad Times of Charlie Becker.* London: Secker & Warburg, 1962.

Trow's New York City Directory, 1889, Sutro Library, San Francisco.

Trow's New York City Directory, 1904, Sutro Library, San Francisco.

Trow's New York City Directory, 1907, Sutro Library, San Francisco.

Wikipedia, entry for Lenox Avenue Gang, *www.wikipedia.com.*

CHAPTER 6: ISIDORE FISHBEIN—PROSTITUTION

Adler, Polly. *A House is Not a Home.* New York: Popular Library, 1953.

Bristow, Edward. *Prostitution & Prejudice: The Jewish Fight Against White Slavery, 1870–1939.* New York: Schocken Books, 1983.

Gilfoyle, Timothy. *The City of Eros: New York Prostitution and the Commercialization of Sex, 1790–1920.* New York: W.W. Norton & Company, 1992.

Isidor Fishbein admission record to Sing-Sing, 64100, January 16, 1914, Record Group B0143, Inmate admission registers, New York State Archives, Albany, NY.

People of the State of New York v. Isidore Fishbein and Hazel Jackson, Court of General Sessions, January 5, 1914, Case # 1807, Special Collections, Sealy Library, John Jay College of Criminal Justice, New York, NY.

Rosen, Ruth. *The Lost Sisterhood: Prostitution in America, 1900–1913.*

Vincent, Isabel. *Bodies and Souls: The Trafficking of Jewish Prostitutes in the Americas.* New York: William Morrow, 2005.

CHAPTER 7: ISRAEL DOBRENIEWSKI: ABANDONMENT AND BIGAMY

Bernard, Jacqueline. "The Children You Gave Us: A History of 150 Years of Service to Children." Jewish Childcare Association of New York, 1973.

Bogen, Hyman. *The Luckiest Orphans: A History of the Hebrew Orphan Asylum of New York.* Chicago: University of Illinois Press, 1992.

Freeze, ChaeRan. *Jewish Marriage and Divorce in Imperial Russia.* Waltham, MA: Brandeis University Press, 2001.

Gilfoyle, Timothy J. "The Hearts of Nineteenth Century Men: Bigamy and Working Class. Marriage in New York City, 1800–1890." *Prospects* 19 (1994): 135–160.

Igra, Anna R. "Other Men's Wives and Children: Anti-Desertion Reform in New York, 1900–1935." Ph.D. thesis at Rutgers University, New Brunswick, NY, 1996; available at http://www.proquest.com/products_umi/dissertations/disexpress.shtml.

Israel Dobrenefsky admission record to Sing-Sing, 63406, May 13, 1913, Record Group B0143, Inmate admission registers, New York State Archives, Albany, NY.

Israel Dobrenefsky admission record to Sing-Sing, 69463, September 4, 1918, Record Group B0143, Inmate admission registers, New York State Archives, Albany, NY.

Materials from Joan Adler & Bobbie Furst, relatives of Israel Dobrenefsky.

Metzker, Isaac. *A Bintel Brief: Sixty Years of Letters from the Lower East Side to the Jewish Daily Forward, Letters to the Jewish Daily Forward*. New York: Schocken Books, 1990.

CHAPTER 8: BENJAMIN GITLOW: ANARCHY

"Gitlow's Defense is a 'Red' Speech: Ex-Assemblyman Calls No Witness, but Receives Court's Permission to Make Statement." February 5, 1920, p. 3.

Benjamin Gitlow admission record to Sing Sing, 70900, February 13, 1920, Record Group B0143, Inmate admission registers, New York State Archives, Albany, NY.

Epstein, Melech. "The Jew and Communism: The Story of Early Communist Victories and Ultimate Defeats in the Jewish Community, U.S.A., 1919–1941." Trade Union Sponsoring Committee, 1959.

Gitlow, Benjamin, 1891–1965, Benjamin Gitlow Papers, (UNCC Mss 108), J. Murrey Atkins Library, University of North Carolina at Charlotte.

Gitlow, Benjamin, 1891–1965, Benjamin Gitlow Papers, Hoover Institution Archives, Stanford University, Stanford, CA.

Gitlow, Benjamin. *I Confess*. New York: E. P. Dutton & Company, 1940.

Louis Gitlow household, 1920 U.S. Census, Kings County, NY, enumeration district [ED] 310, Roll T625-1152; p. 4B.

New York Times. "2 Rabbis Denounce Red Label on Wise." September 14, 1953, p. 2.

New York Times. "Blacklisting Laid to 4 Big Networks: Civil Liberties Union Says Two Stations Also Used Political Grounds to Bar Performers." April 9, 1952, p. 33.

New York Times. "Celler Asks House Inquiry to Hear Reply to Charges Linking 2 Rabbis to Communists." September 23, 1953, p. 9.

New York Times. "Communists Name Gitlow for Mayor: Radicals Nominate a City Ticket Headed by Ex-Assemblyman Convicted of Anarchy." August 27, 1921, p. 4.

New York Times. "Gitlow, 'Red' Candidate for Mayor, Moved to a Prison Far from City Campaign." September 4, 1921, p. 1.

New York Times. "Jewish Unit Vows Communist 'Purge': League Forms Here to Ferret Out 'All Communist Activity in Jewish Life.'" March 15, 1948, p. 7.

New York Times. "On Television: How Stalin Plans to Take Over America— Ben Gitlow." February 6, 1952, p. 37.

New York Times. "Theatre Group Plans to Fight Communism." October 10, 1950, p. 39.

People of the State of New York v. James J. Larkin, New York Supreme Court,

April 16, 1920, Case # 3260, Special Collections, Sealy Library, John Jay College of Criminal Justice, New York, NY.

Personal knowledge of son, Benjamin Gitlow Jr.

U.S. Supreme Court, Case 268 U.S. 652 (1925), *Gitlow v. People of State of New York*, http://caselaw.lp.findlaw.com/scripts/getcase.pl?court=us&vol=268&invol=652.

CHAPTER 9: ISAAC SPIER—PART II

Brooklyn Daily Eagle. "Say His Cash is Short: Joseph Spier is Accused of Larceny by Employers." 1916.

Case File: *People of State of New York v. Joseph Spier*, NYC Municipal Archives, New York, NY

New York Times. "Two Are Arrested on Extortion Charge." June 28, 1925, p. 23.

New York Times. "Two Held in Income Tax Fraud." June 29, 1925, p. 2.

CHAPTER 10: LOUIS "LEPKE" BUCHALTER

"Yellow (Police) Sheet." Murder Inc. files, Mayor O'Dwyer Papers, New York City Municipal Archives.

Barnett Buch(h)alter, death certificate, # 33009, November 4, 1910, Manhattan, NY, NYC Municipal Archives.

Barnett Buchalter household, 1910 U.S. Census, Manhattan Ward 7, New York, NY, enumeration district [ED] 82, Roll T624-1008; p. 16A.

Burton B. Turkus Papers, Lloyd Sealy Library, John Jay College of Criminal Justice, New York, NY.

Charles Kauvar household, 1920 U.S. Census, Denver, CO, enumeration district [ED] 216, Roll T625-161; p. 3B.

Dewey, Thomas E. *Twenty Against the Underworld.* Garden City, NY: Doubleday & Company, 1974.

Kavieff, Paul R. *The Life and Times of Lepke Buchalter: America's Most Ruthless Labor Racketeer.* Fort Lee, NJ: Barricade Books, 2006.

Louis Buchalter admission record to Sing Sing, no. 102894, January 21, 1944, Record Group B0143, Inmate admission registers, New York State Archives, Albany, NY.

Louis Buchalter admission record to Sing Sing, no. 68820, January 12, 1918, Record Group B0143, Inmate admission registers, New York State Archives, Albany, NY.

Louis Buchalter FBI file, obtained via FOIA request, Federal Bureau of Investigation, Washington, DC.

Louis Buchalter File, [RG] B0145, Case files of inmates sentenced to electrocution, New York State Archives, Albany, NY.

Louis Buchalter, marriage certificate # 19699, March 20, 1931, Manhattan, NY, NYC Municipal Archives.

Manhattan City Directory, 1897–8, Sutro Library, San Francisco, CA.

Manhattan City Directory, 1898–9, Sutro Library, San Francisco, CA.

Manhattan City Directory, 1899–1900, Sutro Library, San Francisco, CA.

Manhattan City Directory, 1906–7, Sutro Library, San Francisco, CA.

Manhattan City Directory, 1907–8, Sutro Library, San Francisco, CA.

Manhattan City Directory, 1909–10, Sutro Library, San Francisco, CA.

Manifest, *S.S. Berengaria*, arriving in New York, September 3, 1935, Louis Buchalter, age 38; "Passenger Record." digital images, Ancestry.com (*http://www.ancestry.com*).

Manifest, *S.S. Paris*, arriving in New York, January 13, 1931, Louis Buchalter, age 33; "Passenger Record." digital images, Ancestry.com (*http://www.ancestry.com*).

Manifest, *S.S. Paris*, arriving in New York, September 17, 1931, Louis Buchalter, age 35; "Passenger Record." digital images, Ancestry.com (*http://www.ancestry.com*).

Manifest, *S.S. Rex*, arriving in New York, November 9, 1933, Louis Buchalter, age 37; "Passenger Record." digital images, Ancestry.com (*http://www.ancestry.com*).

New York Times. "Fur Racket Chiefs Flee U.S. Trial; $3,000 Bail of Buchalter and Shapiro is Forfeited and Warrants Issued." July 7, 1937, p. 17.

New York Times. "Gang Leader Slain at Court House Door as Police Guard Him; Gunman Shoots 'Kid Dropper' as He Enters Taxi with Detectives— Chauffeur Wounded." August 29, 1923, p. 1.

New York Times. "Lepke Half Brother Dies in Suicide Pact; Ends Life with Wife by Gas in Bronx Apartment." December 27, 1939, p. 13.

New York Times. "Racketeer Gone; Bail is Forfeited; Jacob (Gurrah Shapiro Fails to Appear and Court Orders Warrants Issued." June 22, 1937, p. 17.

New York Times. "Two Convicted as Fur Racket Terrorists After Federal Jury Deliberates 33 Hours." November 8, 1936, p. 1.

Rose Buchalter household, 1920 U.S. Census, Brooklyn Assembly District 4, New York, NY, enumeration district [ED] 197, Roll T625-1149; p. 14A.

Wetzel, Donald. *Pacifist*. Sag Harbor, NY: Permanent Press, 1986.

Chapter 11: Irving "Waxey Gordon" Wexler

"Beer Baron Max Hassel." *http://www.berkshistory.org/articles/hassel.html*.

"Egan's Rats." *http://en.wikipedia.org/wiki/Egan's_Rats*.

"Egan's Rats." *http://www.crimelibrary.com/gangsters_outlaws/family_epics/louis/3.html*.

Asbury, Herbert. *The Great Illusion: An Informal History of Prohibition*. Garden City, NY: Doubleday & Company, 1950.

Beile Wechsler, death certificate, #8966, April 8, 1898, Manhattan, NY, NYC Municipal Archives.

Benjamin Lustig (a.k.a. Isadore Wechsler) admission record to New York State Reformatory at Elmira, no. 13984, October 7, 1905, Record Group B0131, Admission Registers, Elmira Reformatory, 1877–1950, New York State Archives, Albany, NY.

Berkshire Eagle. "Waxey Gordon May Get Break for Lack of a Fingerprint." Pittsfield, MA, November 14, 1951.

Block, Alan. "The Snowman Cometh: Coke in Progressive New York." *Criminology* 17, no. 1 (May 1979), pp. 75–99.

Block, Alan. *East Side, West Side: Organizing Crime in New York City, 1930–1950*. New Brunswick, NJ: Transaction Publishers, 1983.

Chicago Daily Tribune. "Seize Gordon as Kingpin in Drug Traffic." August 3, 1951, p. 1.

Chicago Daily Tribune. "Senators Learn of Surplus War Goods Rackets." September 22, 1944, p. 19.

Dewey, Thomas E. *Twenty Against the Underworld*. Garden City, NY: Doubleday & Company, 1974.

DOCS Today. "Elmira." October, 1998.

Harry Brown (a.k.a. Waxey Gordon) admission record to Sing Sing, no. 66389, August 12, 1915, Record Group B0143, Inmate admission registers, New York State Archives, Albany, NY.

Irving Wexler admission record to Sing Sing, December 13, 1951, Record Group B0143, Inmate admission registers, New York State Archives, Albany, NY.

Irving Wexler, "Notorious Offender Series" file, Record Group (RG) 19, National Archives and Records Administration, College Park, MD.

Irving Wexler, death certificate, #52-064942, June 24, 1952, CA Department of Health Services, Sacramento, CA.

Isidore Wechsler, marriage certificate #30170, December 9, 1913, Manhattan, NY, NYC Municipal Archives.

Isidore Wechsler, marriage certificate #31053, December 17, 1913, Manhattan, NY, NYC Municipal Archives.

Isidore Wechsler, marriage license #31725, December 9, 1913, Manhattan, NY, NYC Clerk's Office.

Joplin Globe. "23 Are Indicted for Distributing Heroin in Nation." Joplin, MO, March 8, 1952.

Lipsius, Morris (Kayo). "I Put the Finger on Waxey Gordon." *Saturday Evening Post*. February 23, 1952.

Louis Wexler household, 1900 U.S. Census, Manhattan, New York, NY, enumeration district [ED] 114, Roll T623-1085; p. 14B.

Louis Wexler household, 1905 U.S. Census, Manhattan Assembly District 8, New York, NY, election district [ED] 7, FHL microfilm 1432883.

May, Allan. "Waxey Gordon's Half Century of Crime." *http://crimemagazine. com/waxey.htm.*

Nathan Wexler, 1910 U.S. Census, (New York House of Refuge) Manhattan Ward 12, New York, NY, enumeration district [ED] 296, Roll T624-1013, p. 5B.

New York Times. "'Waxey' Gordon Sued on Income Payments." December 2, 1939, p. 12.

New York Times. "13 Seized in Offices Along Broadway as Bootleg Chiefs." September 24, 1925, p. 1.

New York Times. "4 Gordon Accusers Murdered to Date." July 4, 1933, p. 30.

New York Times. "Black Market Laid to Waxey Gordon." October 9, 1942.

New York Times. "Contempt Charged in Gordon Inquiry." September 16, 1933, p. 30.

New York Times. "Coroner Frees Gunman: Lacked Evidence on Which to Hold Them for Killing Straus." January 16, 1914, p. 10.

New York Times. "Dives to Make an Arrest: Detective Finds Wexler in Swimming and Goes in After Him." July 19, 1915, p. 7.

New York Times. "Drug Ringleader Murdered in Auto as Rum Raid Informer." September 26, 1925, p. 1.

New York Times. "Fence Charge Laid to Waxey Gordon." November 5, 1947, p. 30.

New York Times. "Gang Shots Linked to War Over Beer." May 26, 1933, p. 17.

New York Times. "Gangsters Up Today: Strauss Murder Suspects before Coroner—Sweeney on Trial." January 15, 1914, p. 5.

New York Times. "Gordon as Golfer Insured for $30,000." November 24, 1933, p. 4.

New York Times. "Gordon in Tears at Son's Funeral." December 9, 1933, p. 34.

New York Times. "Gordon Refused $600,000 for Plant." November 29, 1933.

New York Times. "Gordon's 'Millions' Told to High Court." January 3, 1936, p. 42.

New York Times. "Gordon's Son Dies in an Auto Crash." December 7, 1933, p. 46.

New York Times. "Grand Jury Indicts 15 as 'Rum Ring." October 31, 1925, p. 19.

New York Times. "Liquor Gang Killed Husband, She Says: Mrs. Fuhrmann

Charges Dry Agent Was Not a Suicide by Was Slain." February 7, 1926, p. 3.

New York Times. "Police Upset Alibis of Four Gangsters." January 12, 1914, p. 18.

New York Times. "Returns to Face Buckner: Back from Europe, Wexler Denies Leading Big Liquor Ring." October 21, 1925, p. 25.

New York Times. "Waxey Gordon Dies in Alcatraz at 63." June 25, 1952, p. 1.

New York Times. "Waxey Gordon Gets New Term in Prison." January 5, 1943, p. 21.

New York Times. "Waxey Gordon in Prison." December 15, 1951, p. 21.

New York Times. "Waxey Gordon, Picked Up as Vagrant, Is Told by Police to Stay Out of New York." November 18, 1941, p. 27.

New York Times. "Waxey Gordon's Term is Up." October 21, 1940, p. 15.

New York Times. "Wexler Goes to Prison: Former Beer Baron Begins Term of Sugar-Rationing Fraud." January 15, 1943, p. 10.

Oakland Tribune. "Gordon, Last of Bootleg Kings?" December 23, 1933.

Soundex Index to Petitions for Naturalization filed in Federal, State, and Local Courts located in New York City, 1792–1906, Louis Wechsler, New York, NY, USA: National Archives and Records Administration, Northeast Region.

Story about Jew Murphy, Waxie Gordon and Jack Pipes, Bureau of Social Morals, Kehillah Records, Judah Magnes Collection, Central Archives for the History of the Jewish People, Jerusalem, Israel.

Taggert, Ed. Bootlegger: Max Hassel, The Millionaire Newsboy. iUniverse Incorporated, 2003.

U.S. Supreme Court, Petition for Writ of Certiorari, Irving Wexler v. United States of America, October Term, 1935.

CHAPTER 12: LOUIS SHOMBERG: BEHIND THE SCENES

"Virgil Peterson Testimony to Kefauver Committee, U.S. Senate Special Committee to Investigate Organized Crime in Interstate Commerce, July 7, 1950." http://www.onewal.com/kef/kefp2.html.

"World War I Draft Registration Cards, 1917–1918." digital images, Ancestry. com (http://www.ancestry.com), Louis Shomberg, registration done at Sing Sing Prison, Ossining, NY.

Benjamin Siegel, FBI file, obtained via FOIA request, Federal Bureau of Investigation, Washington, DC.

Block, Alan. East Side, Westside: Organizing Crime in New York, 1930–1950. New Brunswick, NJ: Transaction Publishers, 1999.

Elya Yershombek (Louis Shomberg) birth registration, December 21, 1895, St. Georges in the East, London, Office of National Statistics, U.K.

Esther Shomberg, marriage certificate # 31451, November 14, 1929, Manhattan, NYC Municipal Archives.

Esther Shomberg, marriage certificate # 8922, April 17, 1916, Manhattan, NYC Municipal Archives.

Henry Goldberg (Louis Shomberg) admission record to Sing Sing, no. 66414 (August 23, 1915), Record Group B0143, Inmate admission registers, New York State Archives, Albany, NY.

Henry Goldberg admission record to New York State Reformatory at Elmira, no. 23022 (May 8, 1913), Record Group B0131, Admission Registers, Elmira Reformatory, 1877-1950, New York State Archives, Albany, NY.

Henry Goldberg, FBI file, obtained via FOIA request, Federal Bureau of Investigation, Washington, DC.

Jacob Shapiro, FBI file, obtained via FOIA request, Federal Bureau of Investigation, Washington, DC.

Jewish Records Indexing (JRI), Poland, *http://www.jewishgen.org.*

Joseph Martin column, *New York Daily News*, June 24, 1953.

Konigsberg, Eric. *Blood Relation.* New York: HarperCollins Publishers, 2005, p. 150.

Louis Shomberg household, 1930 U.S. Census, Manhattan, NY, enumeration district [ED] 424, Roll T626-1154; p. 26B.

Louis Shomberg Petition for Naturalization (1952), petition no. 617157, Southern District of New York; Records of the District Courts of the United States, Record Group 21, National Archives—Northeast Region, New York City.

Louis Shomberg, A(lien)-file, no. A04 199 623 (includes E-file E-094712), obtained via FOIA request from National Records Center, Lee Summit, MO.

Louis Shomberg, divorce certificate # 3965, May 9, 1940, Miami, Office of Vital Statistics, Tallahassee, FL.

Louis Shomberg, marriage certificate # 2505, May 17, 1926, Bronx, NYC Municipal Archives.

Louis Shomberg, no. 266-28-4441, Social Security Death Index, *http://ssdi. genealogy.rootsweb.com/.*

Manifest, *S.S. Baltic*, November, 1914, stamped p. 317, line 30, Abraham Shomberg, age 57, *http://www.ellisisland.org.*

Manifest, *S.S. Morro Castle*, arriving in Los Angeles, February, 1931, Mae Shomberg, age 25; "Passenger Record." digital images, Ancestry.com (*http://www.ancestry.com*).

Manifest, *S.S. Virginia*, arriving in Los Angeles, February, 1936, Louis Shomberg, age 41; "Passenger Record." digital images, Ancestry.com (*http://www.ancestry.com*).

Meyer Lansky, FBI file, obtained via FOIA request, Federal Bureau of Investigation, Washington, DC.

Mortimer, Lee. "New York Confidential" Walter Winchell Column (Lee Mortimer substituting for Walter Winchell), *New York Daily Mirror*, August 13, 1953.

New York Herald Tribune. "N.Y. Police Veto Help for Coast in Crime War." November 16, 1937.

New York Times. "13 Men, 5 Companies Accused of Fraud." July 16, 1964, p. 8

New York Times. "Deportation Hearing Ends." June 26, 1953, p. 32.

New York Times. "Deportation is Fought." July 7, 1953, p. 28.

New York Times. "Gangsters Admit Killing." August 11, 1915, p. 10.

New York Times. "Racketeer and a Red Facing Deportation." June 24, 1953, p. 14.

New York Times. "Shomberg Deportation Hearing." June 25, 1953, p. 20.

New York Times. "U.S. Gang Network is Barred in Inquiry." September 4, 1939, p. 20.

Pegler, Westbrook. "Probe on Gambling." *New York Journal American*, June 7, 1950.

People v. Henry Goldberg, Court of General Sessions, City and County of New York, August 5, 1915, Case # 2195, Special Collections, Sealy Library, John Jay College of Criminal Justice, New York, NY.

Personal knowledge of great-niece, Joanne Shomberg. Shomberg had personal interactions with Louis Shomberg and heard stories growing up as a child.

Sidney Zion column, *Soho Weekly News*, March 20, 1975, p. 3.

Thompson, Craig, and Allen Raymond. *Gang Rule in New York: The Story of a Lawless Era*. New York: Dial Press, 1940.

Trow's New York City Directory, 1909–1910, Sutro Library, San Francisco, CA.

U.S. Federal Court, Southern District of New York, *United States v. Morton Binstock, et al.*, 1967, Case no. 64 Cr. 655; location no. 31540, ordered from National Records Center, Lee Summit, MO via NARA's Northeast Region New York Office.

U.S. Supreme Court, Case 03-445 (2003), *Jose Luis Perdomo-Padilla v. John Ashcroft*, *http://www.usdoj.gov/osg/briefs/2003/0responses/2003-0445. resp.pdf.*

U.S. Supreme Court, Case 348 U.S. 540 (1955), *Shomberg v. United States*, *http://caselaw.lp.findlaw.com/scripts/printer_friendly.pl?page=us/348/540.html.*

Wall Street Journal. "Belmont Oil Case Jury Convicts Two of Fraud." February

1, 1967, p. 26.

Wall Street Journal. "Figure in Belmont Oil Stock Fraud Sentenced to Jail Term of 30 Days." March 9, 1967, p. 2.

Zion, Sidney. *Markers.* New York: Dell Publishing, 1990.

CHAPTER 13: ISAAC SPIER—PART III

Abraham Spier household of Abraham Spier, 1891 United Kingdom Census, RG12, Piece 1736, Folio 26, Page 46, GSU roll 6096846, *http:// www.1901censusonline.com.*

Abraham Spier household, 1901 United Kingdom Census, *http:www.1901censusonline.com.*

Abraham Spier, death certificate, September quarter, 1893, Volume 5b, Page 557, *http://www.findmypast.com.*

Abraham Spiers household, 1881 U.K. Census, RG11, Piece 1080, Folio 11, Page 16, GSU roll 1341254, *http://www.ancestry.com.*

Berrol, Selma. *East Side/East End, Eastern European Jews in London and New York, 1870–1920.* Westport, CT: Preager Publishers, 1994.

Bishop, John George. *Peep Into the Past: Brighton in the Olden Time.* Brighton, England: J. G. Bishop, 1892.

Brighton and Lewis Urban Study Centre. *Back Street Brighton.* Brighton, England: Queenspark Books, 1989.

Brighton and Lewis Urban Study Centre. *Backyard Brighton.* Brighton, England: Queenspark Books, 1988.

Correspondence from Chief Rabbi in London, Part of the Susser Archives, *http://www.thorngent.eclipse.co.uk/susser/chiefrabbi.htm.*

Dobkin, Monty. *More Tales of Manchester Jewry.* Manchester, England: Neil Richardson (Publisher), 1994, p. 22.

Fishman, William J. *East End 1888.* Philadelphia: Temple University Press, 1988.

Gartner, Lloyd P. *The Jewish Immigrant in England, 1870–1914.* London: George Allen and Unwin, Ltd., 1960.

Household of Abraham Spier, 1891 United Kingdom Census, RG13, Piece 3767, Folio 156, p. 37.

Jewish Chronicle. "Hasty Internments." April 4, 1890, p. 7.

Jewish Chronicle. "In the Provinces: Manchester." January 22, 1909, p. 25.

Jewish Chronicle. "Shechita Board: Wanted, Secretary." May 24, 1907, p. 2.

Jewish Chronicle. "Situations Vacant." December 28, 1900, p. 4.

Jewish Chronicle. "The Provinces: Manchester." April 8, 1892, p. 4.

Jewish Yearbook, 1885, Brighton and Hove Local Studies Library.

Julia Spier, marriage certificate, Sheffield, June quarter, 1898, Volume 9c, Page 1077, *http://www.findmypast.com.*

Manchester Evening Chronicle. "Nerves and Insanity: Jewish Minister's Suicide in City Residence." July 4, 1910, Manchester Public Library.

Manchester Guardian. "Jews and Meat—The Rule in England." July 12, 1907, p. 10.

Manchester Guardian. "Kosher Meat—Curious Jewish Libel Case." July 11, 1907, p. 3.

Manchester Jewish Telegraph. "Abraham's Journey." November 19, 1999.

Melville, Lewis. *Brighton: Its History, Its Follies, and Its Fashions.* London: Chapman and Hall, 1909.

Minutes of Manchester Board of Shechita, GB/NNAF/C179386, Manchester Archives and Local Studies Library, Manchester, England.

Musgrave, Clifford. *Life in Brighton.* Hamden, CT: Archon Books, 1970.

Public Notice by E. Trotzkey, July 28, 1907, Manchester Jewish Museum.

Rebecca Spier, marriage certificate, September quarter, 1893, Volume 5b, Page 557, *http://www.findmypast.com.*

Rose, Millicent. *The East End of London.* London: Cresset Press, 1951.

Roth, Cecil. *The Rise of Provincial Jewry.* Sheffield, 1950.

Susser, Bernard. *The Jews of South-West England: The Rise and Decline of Their Medieval and Modern Communities.* Exeter, England: University of Exeter Press, 1993.

CHAPTER 14: MY TOUR OF THE PRISON

Number 1500. *Life in Sing Sing.* Indianapolis, IN: Bobbs-Merrill Company, 1904.

The Lulav and the Etrog, *http://www.mazornet.com/jewishcl/Holidays/sukkot/sukkot-lulav.htm.*

APPENDIX A: VERY SHORT STORIES

"Adkamut—Translated from the Aramaic and Source of the hymn: O Love of God." *http://www.edhaor.org/Akdamut.html.*

"Akdamut and Ketuvah." *http://www.ou.org/chagim/shavuot/akdamot.htm.*

Bernard Balkman admission record to Sing Sing, no. 81005 (July 7, 1928), Record Group B0143, Inmate admission registers, New York State Archives, Albany, NY.

Harry Dreitzer admission record to Sing Sing, no. 80805 (April 2, 1928), Record Group B0143, Inmate admission registers, New York State Archives, Albany, NY.

Harry Pincus admission record to Sing Sing, no. 88943 (April 5, 1934), Record Group B0143, Inmate admission registers, New York State Archives, Albany, NY.

Hyman Brecker admission record to Sing Sing, no. 81006 (July 7, 1928), Record

Group B0143, Inmate admission registers, New York State Archives, Albany, NY.

Isidore Helfant admission record to Sing Sing, no. 80804 (April 2, 1928), Record Group B0143, Inmate admission registers, New York State Archives, Albany, NY.

Israel Fischer admission record to Sing Sing, no. 80803 (April 2, 1928), Record Group B0143, Inmate admission registers, New York State Archives, Albany, NY.

Jerry Feller admission record to Sing Sing, no. 115816 (June 15, 1954), Record Group B0143, Inmate admission registers, New York State Archives, Albany, NY.

Joseph Liss admission record to Sing Sing, October 12, 1889, Record Group B0143, Inmate admission registers, New York State Archives, Albany, NY.

"Kingston Yellow Jackets vs. Sing Sing Black Sheep." Mutual Welfare League football game program, October 22, 1963, Papers of Lewis Lawes, Lloyd Sealy Library, John Jay College of Criminal Justice, New York, NY.

Murray Schuster admission record to Sing Sing, no. 115862 (June 22, 1954), Record Group B0143, Inmate admission registers, New York State Archives, Albany, NY.

New York Times. "Boloney Bandits Seized." April 5, 1938, p. 9.

New York Times. "'Pants Gang' Gets $300 in Brooklyn Hold-ups." March 15, 1928, p. 17.

New York Times. "'Pants Gang' Pair Get Long Terms." June 6, 1928, p. 3.

New York Times. "7 'Baloney Bandits' Receive Long Terms." May 5, 1938, p. 3.

New York Times. "Seven Coinmakers in Secret Service Net." December 9, 1901, p. 14.

New York Times. "Six Plead Guilty in Bombing Plot: Alleged Weathermen to be Sentenced on May 7." March 19, 1971, p. 34.

New York Times. "Slayer of 2 Detectives Wins Rights Suit." July 29, 1972, p. 53.

New York Times. "Threats to Kill an Informer: Member of Alleged Gang of Counterfeiters Who Betrayed Associates Asks for Protection." October 10, 1895, p. 9.

New York Times. "3 of 'Pants Gang' Sentenced to Die; Court Gives Maximum Prison Term to Fourth Member, Who Testified for State." April 3, 1928, p. 31.

New York Times. "Thug Gets 30 to 60 Years: Convicted of Robbing Night Club Dancer in Her Hotel Room." December 21, 1937, p. 20.

New York Times. "Youths Rob Store, Then Get Lost in It." March 18, 1954, p. 38.

Poem from Rabbi Israel Davidson file, Jewish Theological Seminary of America, New York, NY.

Van Onselen, Charles. *The Fox & the Flies: The World of Joseph Silver, Racketeer & Psychopath*. London: Jonathan Cape, 2007.

APPENDIX E: JEWISH CHAPLAINS AT SING SING

New York Times. "Aaron Halle Executed." August 5, 1902, p. 2.

New York Times. "Birthday Dinner to Dr. Radin." August 7, 1898, p. 6.

New York Times. "Buchler Convicted of Stealing $200." May 5, 1932, p. 7.

New York Times. "Rabbi Irving Koslowe, 80; Gave the Rosenbergs Last Rites." December 7, 2000, p. B15.

New York Times. "Rabbi Jacob Katz of Sing Sing Dead: Prison Chaplain for 32 Years, Longest in State's History—Led Bronx Congregation." March 26, 1950, p. 92.

New York Times. "Rabbi J. J. Berman, Chaplain, Is Dead." January 6, 1955, p. 27.

New York Times. "Rabbi Opposes Executions: Sing Sing Chaplain Advocates Movement to Abolish Capital Punishment." April 18, 1914, p. 4.

New York Times. "To Relieve the Unfortunate." February 6, 1893, p. 9.

Society for Aid of Jewish Prisoners annual reports, Dorot Division, New York Public Library.

OTHER RELATED BOOKS

Christianson, Scott. *Condemned: Inside the Sing Sing Death House*. New York: New York University Press, 2000.

Conover, Ted. *Newjack: Guarding Sing Sing*. New York: Vintage Books, 2001.

Downey, Patrick. *Gangster City: The History of the New York Underworld, 1900–1935*. Ft. Lee, NJ: Barricade Books, 2004.

English, T. J. *Paddy Whacked: The Untold Story of the Irish American Gangster*. New York: HarperCollins, 2005.

Fried, Albert. *The Rise and Fall of the Jewish Gangster in America*. New York: Columbia University Press, 1993.

Gilfoyle, Timothy J. *A Pickpocket's Tale: The Underworld of Nineteenth-Century New York*. New York: W. W. Norton & Company, 2006.

Katcher, Leo. *The Big Bankroll: The Life and Times of Arnold Rothstein*. New York: Da Capo Press, 1994.

Morris, James McGrath. *The Rose Man of Sing Sing: A True Tale of Life, Murder, and Redemption in the Age of Yellow Journalism*. New York: Fordham University Press, 2003.

Pietrusza, David. *Rothstein*. New York: Carroll & Graf Publishers, 2003.

Rockaway, Robert A. *But He Was Good to His Mother: The Lives and Crimes of Jewish Gangsters*. Jerusalem: Gefen Publishing House, 1993.

Turkus, Burton B. *Murder, Inc.: The Story of the Syndicate*. New York: Da Capo Press, 2003.

Weissman Joselit, Jenna. *Our Gang: Jewish Crime and the New York Jewish Community, 1900–1940*. Bloomington, IN: Indiana University Press, 1983.

RELATED VIDEOS

Bugsy. Tri-Star, 1991.

"The History of the Mafia." Godfathers Collection, History Channel, A&E Television Networks, 2003.

Lansky. HBO Home Video, 1999.

"Lawbreakers: Death Row Diaries." History Channel, A&E Television Networks, 2002.

"Louis Lepke." Biography Channel, A&E Television Networks, 2002.

Mobsters. Universal Studios, 2003.

"The Rise and Fall of the Jewish Mobster." American Justice, A&E Television Networks, 1996.

Rogue's Gallery: Bugsy Siegel. Andrew Solt Productions, 1997.

INDEX

A COP'S TALE: NYPD THE VIOLENT YEARS
Jim O'Neil and Mel Fazzino

A Cop's Tale focuses on New York City's most violent and corrupt years, the 1960s to early 1980s. Jim O'Neil–a former NYPD cop –delivers a rare look at the brand of law enforcement that ended Frank Lucas's grip on the Harlem drug trade, his cracking open of the Black Liberation Army case, and his experience as the first cop on the scene at the "Dog Day Afternoon" bank robbery. A gritty, heart-stopping account of a bygone era, *A Cop's Tale* depicts the willingness of one of New York's finest to get as down-and-dirty as the criminals he faced while protecting the citizens of the city he loved.

$24.95 – Hardcover – 978-1-56980-372-1
$16.95 – Paperback – 978-1-56980-509-1

BLACK GANGSTERS OF CHICAGO
Ron Chepesiuk

Chicago's African American gangsters were every bit as powerful and intriguing as the city's fabled white mobsters. In this fascinating narrative history, author Ron Chepesiuk profiles the key players in the nation's largest black organized crime population and traces the murderous evolution of the gangs and rackets that define Chicago's violent underworld.

$24.95 – Hardcover – 978-1-56980-331-8
$16.95 – Paperback – 978-1-56980-505-3

BLOOD AND VOLUME: INSIDE NEW YORK'S ISRAELI MAFIA
Dave Copeland

Ron Gonen, together with pals Johnny Attias and Ron Efraim, ran a multimillion-dollar drug distribution and contract murder syndicate in 1980s New York. But when the FBI caught up, Gonen had to choose between doing the right thing and ending up dead.

$22.00 – Hardcover – 978-1-56980-327-1
$16.95 – Paperback – 978-1-56980-145-1

BRONX D.A. TRUE STORIES FROM THE DOMESTIC VIOLENCE AND SEX CRIMES UNIT
Sarena Straus

If you dealt with violence all day, how long would it be before you burned out? Sarena Straus was a prosecutor in the Bronx District Attorney's office, working in an area of the Bronx with the highest crime and poverty rates in America. This book chronicles her experience during her three-year stint with the Domestic Violence and Sex Crimes Unit, combating crimes and women and children and details how and why she finally had to give up the job.

$22.00 – Hardcover – 978-1-56980-305-9

CIGAR CITY MAFIA: A COMPLETE HISTORY OF THE TAMPA UNDERWORLD
Scott M. Deitche

Prohibition-era "Little Havana" housed Tampa's cigar industry, and with it, bootleggers, arsonists, and mobsters–plus a network of corrupt police officers worse than the criminals themselves. Scott M. Deitche documents the rise of the infamous Trafficante family, ruthless competitors in a "violent, shifting place, where loyalties and power quickly changed."

$16.95 – Paperback – 978-1-56980-287-8

CONFESSIONS OF A SECOND STORY MAN: JUNIOR KRIPPLE-BAUER AND THE K&A GANG
Allen M. Hornblum

From the 1950s through the 1970s, the rag-tag crew known as the K&A gang robbed wealthy suburban neighborhoods with assembly-line skills. Hornblum tells the strange-but-true story thru interviews, police records and historical research, including the transformation of the K&A Gang from a group of blue collar thieves to their work in conjunction with numerous organized crime families helping to make Philadelphia the meth capital of the nation.

$16.95 — Paperback — 978-1-56980-313-4

DOCK BOSS
Eddie McGrath and the West Side Waterfront
Neil G. Clark

At a time when New York City's booming waterfront industry was ruled by lawless criminals, one gangster towered above the rest and secretly controlled the docks for over thirty years. *Dock Boss: Eddie McGrath and the West Side Waterfront* explores the rise of Eddie McGrath from a Depression Era thug to the preeminent racketeer on Manhattan's lucrative waterfront. McGrath's life takes readers on a journey through the tail-end of Prohibition, the sordid years of violent gang rule on the bustling waterfront, and finally the decline of the dock mobsters following a period of longshoremen rebellion in the 1950s. This is the real-life story of the bloodshed that long haunted the ports of New York City.

$17.95 — Paperback — 978-1-56980-813-9

DOCTORS OF DEATH
TEN TRUE CRIME STORIES OF DOCTORS WHO KILL
Wensley Clarkson

These mystifying and spine-tingling stories are just what the doctor ordered and they are all true. *Doctors of Death* presents ten hair-raising real life accounts of killing and mayhem in medical training ultimately causing others to die. With a sharp eye for the sort of detail that only true cases can have, they are woven together with some of the most horrifying killings that ever occurred.

$17.95 — Paperback — 978-1-56980-806-1

FRANK NITTI: THE TRUE STORY OF CHICAGO'S NOTORIOUS "ENFORCER"
Ronald D. Humble

Frank "The Enforcer" Nitti is arguably the most glamorized gangster in history. Though he has been widely mentioned in fictional works, this is the first book to document Nitti's real-life criminal career alongside his pop culture persona, with special chapters devoted to the many television shows, movies and songs featuring Nitti.

$24.95 — Hardcover — 978-1-56980-342-4

GAMING THE GAME: THE STORY BEHIND THE NBA BETTING SCANDAL AND THE GAMBLER WHO MADE IT HAPPEN
Sean Patrick Griffin

In June 2007, the FBI informed the NBA that one of its referees, Tim Donaghy, was the subject of a probe into illegal gambling. With Donaghy betting on games he officiated, a trail unraveled that led to the involvement of Donaghy's childhood friend and professional gambler Jimmy Battista. Researched with dozens of interviews, betting records, court documents and with access to witness statements and confidential law enforcement files, this book is a "must-read" for any NBA fan.

$16.95 – Paperback – 978-1-56980-475-9

GANGSTER CITY: THE HISTORY OF THE NEW YORK UNDERWORLD 1900-1935
Patrick Downey

This is an illustrated treasure trove of information about New York City's gangsters from 1900 through the 1930s. Told in depth are the exploits of Jewish, Italian and Chinese gangsters during New York City's golden age of crime. No other book delivers such extensive detail on the lives, crimes and dramatic endings of this ruthless cast of characters, including Jack "Legs" Diamond and the sadistic Dutch Schultz.

$16.95 – Paperback – 978-1-56980-361-5

GANGSTERS OF HARLEM: THE GRITTY UNDERWORLD OF NEW YORK'S MOST FAMOUS NEIGHBORHOOD
Ron Chepesiuk

Author Ron Chepesiuk creates the first comprehensive, accurate portrait of Harlem gangs from their inception, detailing the stories of the influential famed gangsters who dominated organized crime in Harlem from the early 1900s through the present. In this riveting documentation, Chepesiuk tells this little known story through in-depth profiles of the major gangs and motley gangsters including "Nicky" Barnes, Bumpy Johnson and Frank Lucas.

$16.95 – Paperback – 978-1-56980-365

GANGSTERS OF MIAMI: TRUE TALES OF MOBSTERS, GAMBLERS, HIT MEN, CON MEN AND GANG BANGERS FROM THE MAGIC CITY
Ron Chepesiuk

Miami has been the home for a colorful variety of gangsters from its early days to the modern period. These include the notorious smugglers of the Prohibition era, famous mobsters like Al Capone and Meyer Lansky who helped make Miami a gambling Mecca, the Cuban Mafia which arrived after Cuba fell to Castro, the Colombian cartels during the cocaine explosion, the Russian mafia after the fall of the Soviet Union, and the street gangs that plagued Miami after the advent of crack cocaine.

$17.95 – Paperback – 978-1-56980-500-8

I'LL DO MY OWN DAMN KILLIN': BENNY BINION, HERBERT NOBLE AND THE TEXAS GAMBLING WAR
Gary W. Sleeper

People know of the notorious Benny Binion for opening the Horseshoe and becoming the most successful casino owner in Las Vegas. But before he became the patron saint of World Series Poker, Binion led the Texas underground in a vicious, nefarious gambling war that lasted over fifteen years. Author Gary Sleeper presents the previously unseen details of Benny Binion's life leading up to his infamous Las Vegas days, when he became the owner of the most successful casino in the world.

$16.95 – Paperback – 978-1-56980-321-9

IL DOTTORE: THE DOUBLE LIFE OF A MAFIA DOCTOR
Ron Felber

The inspiration for Fox TV's drama series, "Mob Doctor," IL DOTTORE is the riveting true story of a Jewish kid from the Bronx who became a Mafia insider and physician to top NY Mafia dons such as John Gotti, Carlo Gambino, Paul Castellano, and Joe Bonanno. Eventually, he had to make a choice between loyalty to the mob and remaining true to his Hippocratic Oath, all under the watchful eye of New York's top federal prosecutor, Rudolph Giuliani.

$16.95 – Paperback – 978-1-56980-491-9

JAILING THE JOHNSTON GANG: BRINGING SERIAL MURDERERS TO JUSTICE
Bruce E. Mowday

This is the inside story of the dedicated law enforcement team that brought to justice serial murderers Norman, David and Bruce A. Johnston Sr. For more than a decade the Johnston Gang terrorized communities throughout the East Coast of the U.S. by stealing millions of dollars worth of property. But in 1978, fearing that younger members of the gang were going to rat them out, the brothers killed four teenagers and nearly killed Bruce Sr.'s own son.

$16.95 – Paperback – 978-1-56980-442-1

LUCKY LUCIANO: THE MAN WHO ORGANIZED CRIME IN AMERICA
Hickman Powell

He was called the Father of Organized Crime. Born in Sicily and reared in poverty he arrived with his family on New York's Lower East Side in the early 20th century. He grew up among Irish Jewish and Italian youths dedicated to crime, some of them going on to become world class thugs. This book is written by a top investigative reporter who followed Luciano's trial from its inception to the jury verdict. He not only interviewed Luciano but also the assorted prostitutes and pimps who testified against him.

Lucky Luciano was responsible for the infamous Atlantic City gathering of the nation's top mobsters that included Al Capone, Meyer Lansky and Frank Costello and where they were persuaded to run crime as a business.

$16.95 – Paperback – 978-1-56980-900-6

MILWAUKEE MAFIA: MOBSTERS IN THE HEARTLAND
Gavin Schmitt

Milwaukee's Sicilian underworld is something few people speak about in polite company, and even fewer people speak with any authority. Everyone in Milwaukee has a friend of a friend who knows something, but they only have one piece of a giant puzzle. The secret society known as the Mafia has done an excellent job keeping its murders, members and mishaps out of books. Until now.

$16.95 – Paperbackr – 978-0-9623032-6-5

MURDER OF A MAFIA DAUGHTER THE LIFE AND TRAGIC DEATH OF SUSAN BERMAN
Cathy Scott

Susan Berman grew up in Las Vegas luxury as the daughter of Davie Berman, casino mogul and notorious mafia leader. After her father died she learned about his mob connections. Susan then dedicated her life to learning about Vegas and its underworld chiefs. When Kathie Durst - the wife of her good friend, Robert Durst, mysteriously disappeared Durst was a prime suspect but the case was never solved. After the Kathie Durst case was reopened, the DA wanted to question Susan about what she knew regarding a phone call Kathie supposedly made to her medical school dean saying she was sick and wouldn't be at school. Soon after the Kathie Durst case was reopened, Susan Berman was found dead, shot in the back of head. No forced entry, no robbery, nothing missing from her home.

$17.95 – Paperback – 978-0-934878-49-4

SHALLOW GRAVE
THE UNSOLVED CRIME THAT SHOOK
THE MIDWEST'
Gavin Schmitt **NEW**

An upright citizen kidnapped in public and dumped in a shallow grave. A police chief's wife arrested for murder. A mobster kidnapped and threatened by the FBI. And an ongoing corruption probe looking at everyone from the lowest bookie all the way up to judges and prosecutors. What is going on in small town America? Follow the exploits of the police, FBI and Bobby Kennedy himself as they try to put together the pieces and catch the bad guys… if they can.

$17.95 – Paperback – 978-1-56980-808-5

STOLEN MASTERPIECE TRACKER:
INSIDE THE BILLION DOLLAR
WORLD OF STOLEN MASTERPIECES
Thomas McShane with Dary Matera

Legendary undercover FBI agent Thomas McShane is one of the world's foremost authorities on the billion-dollar art theft business. For thirty-six years, McShane matched wits with some of the most devious criminal masterminds of the 20th and 21st centuries. Here he presents a unique memoir that gives readers a thrilling ride through the underworld of stolen art and historical artifacts. Written with veteran true crime author Dary Matera, this captivating account is as engaging as it is informative.

$17.95 – Paperback – 978-1-56980-519-0

TERRORIST COP: THE NYPD
JEWISH COP WHO TRAVELED
THE WORLD TO STOP TERRORISTS
Mordecai Z. Dzikansky with
Robert Slater

Terrorist Cop is a colorful, haunting and highly graphic tale of retired New York City Detective First Grade Morty Dzikansky. Dzikansky first patrolled Brooklyn streets with a yarmulke on his head. A rise through the ranks would eventually bring him to Israel, monitoring suicide bombings post 9/11. It was part of Commissioner Ray Kelly's plan to protect New York from further terrorist attacks, but it led to Morty becoming a victim of post traumatic stress disorder.

$24.95 – Hardcover – 978-1-56980-445-2

THE JEWS OF SING SING
Ron Arons

Sing-Sing prison opened in 1828 and since then, more than 7000 Jews have served time in the famous correctional facility. The Jews of Sing-Sing is the first book to fully expose the scope of Jewish criminality over the past 150 years. Besides famous gangsters like Lepke Buchalter, thousands of Jews committed all types of crimes—from incest and arson to selling air rights over Manhattan—and found themselves doing time in Sing-Sing.

$22.95 – Hardcover – 978-1-56980-333-2

THE LIFE AND TIMES OF LEPKE
BUCHALTER: AMERICA'S MOST
RUTHLESS RACKETEER
Paul R. Kavieff

This is the first biography of the only organized crime boss to be executed in the United States. At the height of his power, Louis "Lepke" Buchalter had a stronghold on the garment, banking and flour tracking industries. As the overseer of the killing-on-assignment machine known as "Murder Inc.," his penchant for murder was notorious. This impeccably researched book traces the story from childhood, through the incredibly sophisticated rackets, to his ultimate conviction and execution. All the names, dates and brutal murders are described here, in a unique history of labor unrest in turn-of-the 20th century New York. In the end, it was an obscure murder that led to his conviction and execution.

$16.95 – Paperback – 978-1-56980-517-6

THE MAFIA AND THE MACHINE: THE STORY OF THE KANSAS CITY MOB
Frank R. Hayde

The story of the American Mafia is not complete without a chapter on Kansas City. "The City of Fountains" has appeared in the **The Godfather**, **Casino**, and **The Sopranos**, but many Midwesterners are not aware that Kansas City has affected the fortunes of the entire underworld. In **The Mafia and the Machine**, author Frank Hayde ties in every major name in organized crime—Luciano, Bugsy, Lansky —as well as the city's corrupt police force.

$16.95 – Paperback – 978-1-56980-443-8

THE PURPLE GANG: ORGANIZED CRIME IN DETROIT 1910-1946
Paul R. Kaveiff

In Prohibition era Detroit, a group of young men grew in power and profile to become one of the nation's most notorious gangs of organized crime. **The Purple Gang**, as they came to be called, quickly rose to power and wealth leaving law enforcement powerless against the high-profile methods of the gang. During the chaos of the Prohibition era, the fearless "Purples" rose to the highest ranks of organized crime and then shattered

it all with bloodthirsty greediness and murderous betrayal.

$16.95 – Paperback – 978-1-56980-494-0

THE RISE AND FALL OF THE CLEVELAND MAFIA
Rick Porrello

This is the fascinating chronicle of a once mighty crime family's birth, rise to power, and eventual collapse. The Cleveland crime family comprised of the notorious Porrello brothers, was third in power after New York City and Chicago, had influence with mega-mobsters like Meyer Lansky, and had a hand in the development of Las Vegas. At center stage of this story is the Sugar War, a series of Prohibition gang battles over control of corn sugar, a lucrative bootleg ingredient.

$16.95 – Paperback – 978-1-56980-277-9

THE SILENT DON: THE CRIMINAL UNDERWORLD OF SANTO TRAFFICANTE JR.
Scott M. Deitche

For thirty years he was Tampa's reigning Mob boss, running a criminal empire stretching from the Gulf Coast of the U.S. into the Caribbean and eventually, the island paradise of Cuba. After the fall of Batista and the rise of Castro, Santo Trafficante, Jr. became embroiled in the shadowy matrix of covert CIA operations, drug trafficking, plots to kill Castro and ultimately, the JFK assassination. Trafficante's unique understanding of the network of corrupt politicians, heads of state, non-traditional ethnic crime groups, and the Mafia enabled him to become one of the pivotal figures in the American Mafia's powerful heyday.

$16.95 – Paperback – 978-1-56980-355-4

BARRICADE BOOKS TRUE CRIME

THE VIOLENT YEARS: PROHIBITION AND THE DETROIT MOBS
Paul R. Kavieff

In **The Violent Years**, author Paul Kavieff has once again masterfully fused the historical details of crime in Detroit with the true flavor of the Prohibition era. For those found with new prosperity after World War I ended, it became a status symbol in Detroit to have one's own personal bootlegger and to hobnob with known gangsters. Numerous gangs scrambled to grab a piece of the profit to be made selling illegal liquor which resulted in gruesome gang warfare among the many European ethnic groups that were involved.

$16.95 — Paperback — 978-1-56980-496-4

THIEF! THE GUTSY, TRUE STORY OF AN EX-CON ARTIST
William Slick Hanner with Cherie Rohn

William "Slick" Hanner delivers action-packed drama just as he lived it: as an outsider with inside access to the Mafia.

Here's the gutsy, true story of how a 1930s Chicago kid with street smarts and a yearning for excitement catapults into a crime-infested world. Cherie Rohn details all of the hilarious, aberrant, exhilarating details of Hanner's adventures in this sharp, insightful biography about secrets of the Mafia.

$22.00 — Hardcover — 978-1-56980-317-2

For more information, contact:
Carole Stuart at 201-266-5278 or
Email: cstuart@barricadebooks.com

Order through your National Book Network rep or directly from:
National Book Network
15200 NBN Way
Blue Ridge Summit, PA 17214
Phone: Customer Service:
1-800-462-6420
Email: Custserv@nbnbooks.com
Fax: 1-800-338-4550